Messerschmitt Me 328
Development & Politics

MESSERSCHMITT ME 328

DEVELOPMENT & POLITICS

Dan Sharp

TEMPEST BOOKS

DAN SHARP is the author of more than a dozen books about aircraft and aviation, specialising in archival research on German Second World War aircraft development.
He graduated with a Bachelor of Arts degree in history from the University of Liverpool before starting a career in publishing. Born in Lincoln, he now lives in Nottinghamshire.

Published in Great Britain by Tempest Books
an imprint of Mortons Books Ltd.
Media Centre
Morton Way
Horncastle LN9 6JR
www.mortonsbooks.co.uk

ISBN 978-1-911704-20-1

Typeset by Jayne Clements (jayne@hinoki.co.uk), Hinoki Design and Typesetting

Original cover artwork by Piotr Forkasiewicz

Profile artworks by Zoltán Csombó

Acknowledgements
Thanks to Stephen Walton, Steve Coates, Peter Ocker, David Schwartz, Michael Baumgartl, Christoph Bergs, Richard Carrick, Eddie Creek, Zoltán Csombó, Gerrit Faust, Ian Fisher, Carlos Alberto Henriques, Scott Lowther, Clare Mulley, Steve O'Hara, Haruki Ohmori, Ronnie Olsthoorn, Matthias Röschner and Calum Douglas.

For Jamie McGinnes

CONTENTS

INTRODUCTION 9

CHAPTER 1 12
Origins: 1928 to February 1942

CHAPTER 2 34
Light Fighter and Multirole: March 1942 to August 1942

CHAPTER 3 52
Flying Artillery to Vulkan: September to December 1942

CHAPTER 4 76
JSF to the 'Stop' Order: December 1942 to September 1943

CHAPTER 5 130
'Self-sacrifice' Aircraft: September 1943 to November 1944

SUMMARY 152

APPENDIX I 155
Horace 'Rex' King on the Me 328 B

APPENDIX II 158
German Version of the Suicide Weapon

COLOUR PROFILES 167

ENDNOTES 180

BIBLIOGRAPHY 184

INDEX 185

INTRODUCTION

Stoney-faced in front of her American interrogators in November 1945, famous German test pilot Hanna Reitsch explained an extraordinary plan to sacrifice fanatical young pilots by drugging them and having them crash small wooden gliders laden with explosives into high-value Allied targets such as warships or headquarters. The glider in question was referred to as the Messerschmitt Me 328.

Up to 1945 the Allies had had little to no intelligence on this type, just the occasional mention in captured reports or garbled second-hand accounts.[1] Most other advanced or experimental aircraft that reached prototype stage had been spotted during aerial reconnaissance and given a code name based on the airfield where they were first sighted plus their estimated wingspan in feet. Messerschmitt's Me 264 four-engine bomber, for example, was initially known as 'Lechfeld 127', Heinkel's He 162 was dubbed 'Schwechat 25', Arado's Ar 234 was 'Rechlin 46' and Dornier's Do 335 was 'Lowenthal 47'.

The Me 328, however, was never identified—despite prototypes being constructed and test-flown over the course of several years. It was a 'secret project' that actually remained secret, at least until the closing stages of the war. It was not until February 11, 1945, that somewhat reliable information was received. USSAF[2] Air Intelligence Summary No. 66 of February 11, 1945, stated: "From ground sources in Holland has come a report describing in general terms a Messerschmitt jet-propelled aircraft bearing the designation Me 328. The information originated with a Dutchman formerly employed along with German engineers at the Jacobs-Schweyer plant in Darmstadt from January to August 1943, where he had seen a fuselage of the aircraft he described.

"The Me 328 is stated to be a single-seater plane of all-wood construction, powered by two jet units. The cockpit is said to have been hermetically sealed for high-altitude flight,[3] the landing gear is reported to consist of two skids placed in tandem. A catapult is said to have been used for take-off. Speeds of from 520 to 740mph are supposed to have been attained. This is almost certainly an exaggeration, since the only jet unit known to have been sufficiently developed by the Germans to produce anything like these figures is the Jumo 004 used on the Me 262—and it is incapable of producing the thrust necessary for such speeds.

"Taking into account the dates of the informant's sojourn in Darmstadt, it is quite likely that he had seen components of one of several Messerschmitt jet-propelled prototypes. A number of such planes were undoubtedly completed and tested prior to commencement of series production of the Me 163 and 262, and the Me 328 referred to may have been one of these experimental models."

As time wore on and the war ended, further information was received in dribs and drabs—a reasonably thorough if not entirely accurate outline being presented by Horace

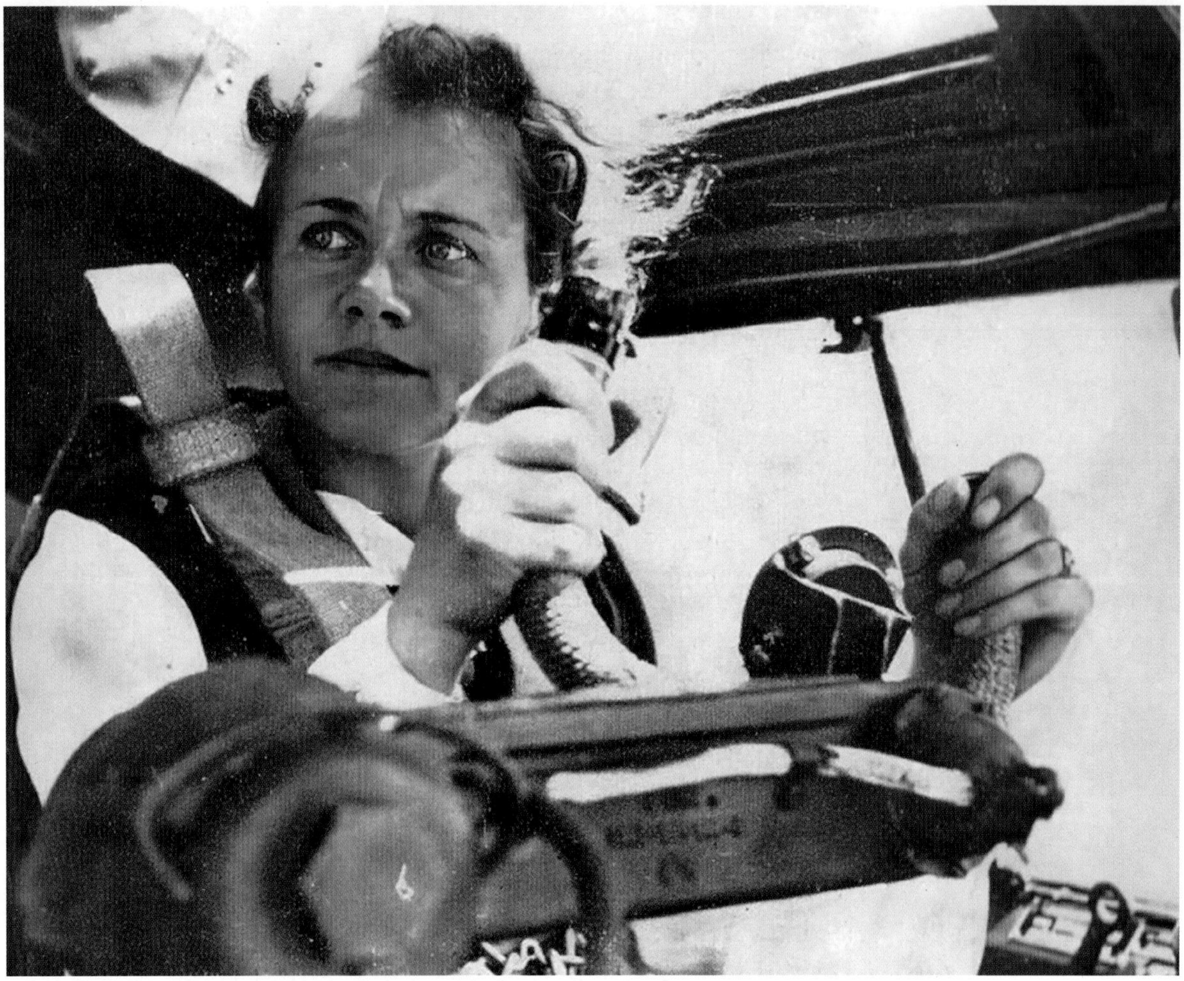

Famous test pilot and Nazi true believer Hanna Reitsch.

'Rex' King in British intelligence A.I.2.(g) Report No. 2356 of August 29, 1945 (see Appendix I). Interviewed on September 7, 1945, the former head of Messerschmitt's Project Office, Woldemar Voigt, provided his own Me 328 description. He said it was a "small single-seat anti-invasion bomber. Two Argus 014 engines (V1-jet engines) of 300kg [thrust] each.

"Technical features: Wing area of 7.5m^2 and 9.2m^2 for the prototypes and the production machine respectively. Gross weight 7.1 tons with a 1,000kg bomb; weight empty for landing 1.7 tons.

"The Me 328 was designed for assisted take-off only by means of a catapult or by a special towing method. We devised the following method and had it tested by the DFS (Ainring): (The problem was to make possible an extreme wing loading for take-off (the weight empty was no problem for the Me 328)): the towing and the towed plane were interconnected by a rather short tow attached near the c.g. of the two planes respectively; the tug began to climb with a speed inferior to the safe flying speed of the towed plane, the latter being carried by the tow hanging almost vertically below the tug. Take-offs and landings were exercised and seemed to cause no difficulties and trouble to the pilot. The tests were exercised by a He 111 carrying a Ju 87. A droppable undercarriage was used for the take-off, the landing being executed on a central skid.

"Performance (calculated): Max. speed about 700km/h (435mph) at ground level; range with a 1,000kg bomb 520km (320 miles). The flight testing of the prototype without engines gave good results. The pilots blamed the low towing speed of the Me 110 and the bad field of view from the 328 at high angles of attack. Special devices were necessary to shorten the landing run on wet lawn.

"With engines no satisfactory results were obtained until the development was stopped: the engine itself did not work satisfactorily and did not give the expected thrust: the noise of the engine was hardly bearable without a sound-proof cabin; the vibrations of the engines were detrimental to the strength of the airframe; there was no unanimity between the RLM [Reichsluftfahrtministerium—the German Air Ministry] and our firm as to the economy of the take-off methods.

"The Me 328 was not ordered in series; the development was stopped when the turbojet engines proved to be

Messerschmitt Project Office chief Woldemar Voigt.

reliable and the Me 262 was given higher priority. The Me 328 was the only model designed and constructed during the war by Messerschmitt which was not ordered in series."

Voigt's statement offers an oddly selective and incomplete description of the Me 328, though whether his interrogators would have realised that is unclear. Exactly what was meant by his 'anti-invasion bomber' term is similarly unclear; the type is a powered aircraft with only "the prototype" being a glider; he focuses heavily on the towed take-off aspect of its design and twice says that no series production model was ever ordered.

Was Voigt even describing the same Me 328 as the one that Reitsch would assert, two months later, had been intended for use as a piloted glide-bomb? He mentions three organisations in connection with the type: Messerschmitt itself, the DFS (Deutsche Forschungsanstalt für Segelflug—an organisation specialising in the manufacture of wooden gliders) and the RLM. But the Allies already had reliable evidence from the Dutchman employed by Jacobs-Schweyer Flugzeugbau (JSF) at Darmstadt that examples of the Me 328 had been worked on there, with two skids in tandem rather than a single central skid. Voigt fails to mention this entirely. And he fails to mention a great deal more besides, such as the fact that he was personally present at a meeting in June 1944 where the Me 328 was handed over to Gothaer Waggonfabrik (GWF) for mass production as a suicide weapon on behalf of Reitsch and other supporters of the 'manned glide bomb' concept.

The otherwise incredibly detailed Air Technical Intelligence Review Report No. F-IR-6-RE Survey of Messerschmitt Factory and Functions, Oberammergau, Germany,[4] which was based on interrogations of dozens of senior company staff includes mention of such obscure prototypes as the Me 161 and Me 109 H, as well as detailed descriptions of unbuilt types such as the P 1111 and P 1112, as well as the Enzian flak rocket, makes almost no mention of the Me 328.[5]

It wasn't just the Allies who failed to get the full picture either. Economy with the truth appears to have been a hallmark of the Me 328 programme throughout its existence. Surviving documents on this enigmatic machine are fewer and further between than they are for many other wartime prototype aircraft—with certain key events in its timeline having been so thoroughly erased that they are only known through forgotten non-subject-specific summaries, second-hand accounts and postwar interview reports where the interviewee, perhaps, felt at liberty to offer details which might otherwise have remained under wraps.

Unusually for a German wartime aircraft development, it seems that no one was proud to have worked on the Me 328 and many of the documents associated with it were destroyed—probably before the war ended.[6]

It is difficult to conclude that the Me 328 was anything other than an aircraft most people were happy to forget. If ever there was an aircraft that came with a stigma attached, it was this one.

It could perhaps be said that a certain reluctance to be associated with the type was an understandable consequence of its convoluted development, being passed from manufacturer to manufacturer without ever becoming a priority project. But as with most, if not all, of its products Messerschmitt apparently retained design authority over the Me 328 until the end.

It might equally be said that the type was an unmitigated failure, that the most fundamental building block of its design—extremely high wing loading—was a relic of Messerschmitt's philosophy circa 1941 when the tiny record-breaking Me 209 was still being developed as a fighter. And the lightweight Argus pulsejets initially relied upon to allow such a high wing loading never achieved the output optimistically projected for them by their manufacturer. The harmful vibrations they generated could not be overcome either, rendering the powered Me 328 a fatally flawed product right up to its cancellation.

Nobody likes to be associated with abject failure, just as nobody involved was keen to admit their part in enabling the Nazi fanaticism of Reitsch and the other 'self-sacrifice' supporters.

Back in the mid-to-late 1930s, however, the pulsejet seemed like one of Germany's most promising new technologies—particularly when it came to military applications…

1

ORIGINS: 1928 TO FEBRUARY 1942

Munich-based engineer Paul Schmidt began to study intermittent explosions of petrol-air mixture as a means of generating thrust for aircraft propulsion in 1928.[1] He came up with a 'thrust generator' design and applied for a patent to cover it at the end of the following year.

Granted in April 1930, it outlined a tube where air came in at one end through a valve and was mixed with petrol before being ignited, the valve automatically closing. With the valve closed, the expanding hot gases produced by the explosion would be directed towards the open end of the tube, generating propulsive thrust. When the pressure of the gases had dissipated sufficiently, the valve would open automatically, allowing more air into the tube and allowing the cycle to repeat.

This type of system went by a multitude of different names before, during and after the Second World War but would today be best known as a pulsejet.

Schmidt tended to refer to his invention a Schmidt-tube or 'Schmidtrohr'—even though he later came to acknowledge that the process had actually been discovered in 1906 by Russian engineer Vladimir V. Karavodin.[2] After four more years of work, including unsuccessful efforts to build a functioning prototype, on August 14, 1934 he approached the German Air Ministry with designs for three potential pulsejet-powered vehicles: an interceptor, a bomber and a flying bomb.[3]

The interceptor, described by Schmidt as an 'Abwehrflugzeug' or 'defence aircraft', was a single-seat low-wing monoplane of conventional layout except for the installation of four pulsejets clustered together in the rear fuselage, exhausting below the tail fin. It is unclear from the surviving drawing exactly where the inlet for these motors would be positioned—the chin at the front of the aircraft seemingly being the most likely location.

The interceptor's wingspan of 6.4m,[4] with a wing area of 6.8sqm, made it extremely small and there would be no wheeled undercarriage—take=off instead being accomplished with the use of a jettisonable wheeled dolly and landing via a retractable skid. Armament would be two fixed forward-firing heavy machine guns in the nose with 600 rounds each or a single cannon. Maximum climbing speed was expected to be 100 metres per second, or 360km/h.

The bomber was of a broadly similar design but substantially bigger. No precise dimensions were given but based on the interceptor's design and scale, the bomber had a wingspan of 19-21m, putting it between the Do 17 at 18m and the He 111 at 23m. This time a total of six pulsejets were grouped together in the rear fuselage but again there was little indication of exactly where their associated air inlet would be located. The undercarriage

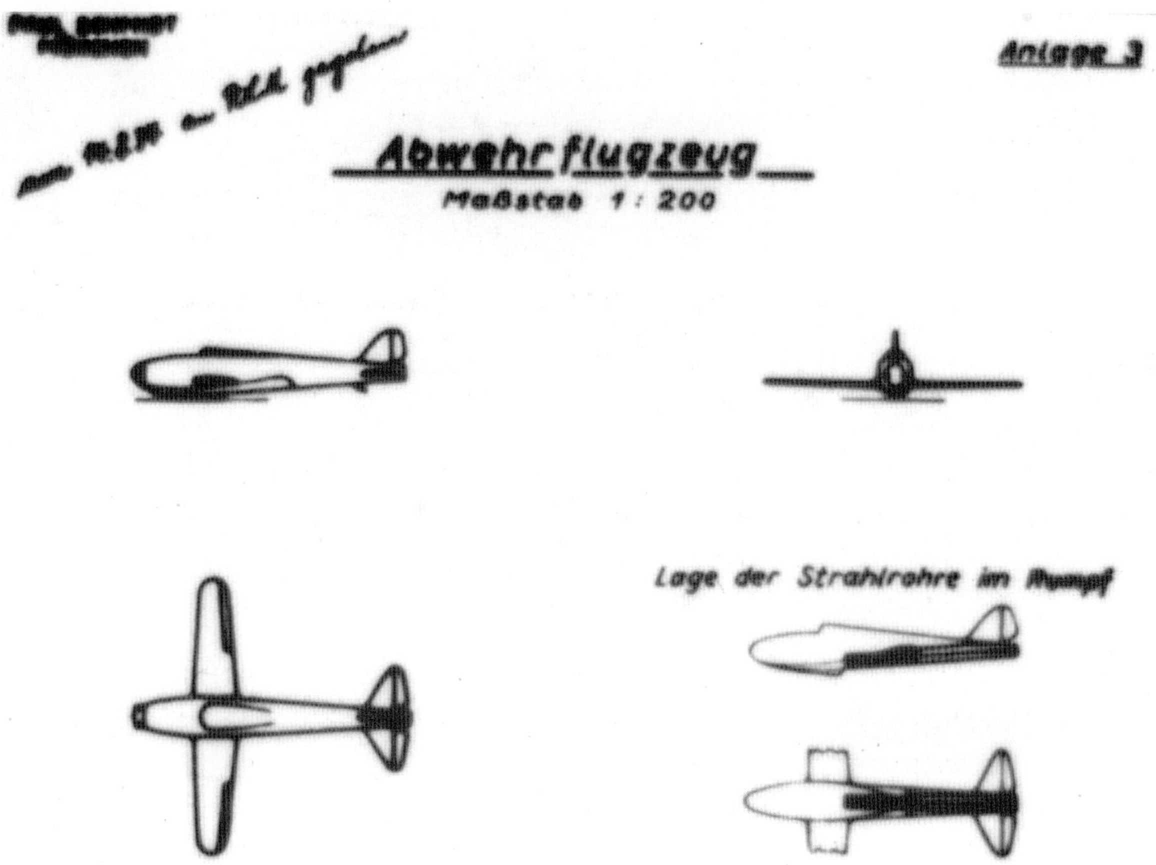

The first of three concepts submitted to the German Air Ministry by Paul Schmidt on August 14, 1934, was for an interceptor powered by four pulsejets clustered together in the rear fuselage. It was designed to land on a retractable skid.

was of typical tail-dragger layout and four machine guns would be available for defence. It had a crew of just three and bomb load was three tons.

Lastly there was Schmidt's flying bomb, labelled as a 'Flugtorpedo' in the report he presented to the Air Ministry. This had a slender, tapering, cigar-shaped fuselage with just a single pulsejet in the rear. Attached to the bomb's forward section were two stubby wings with an overall span of 1.3m and a strong dihedral. At the extreme rear were three identical and equally spaced triangular fins, arranged rather like the fletching of an arrow. The whole contraption was to weigh 500kg and would be launched almost vertically from a ramp.

Once it had taken off, it was expected to achieve a maximum speed of 800km/h at 2,000m altitude—much faster than any aircraft of the period was able to achieve and extremely difficult to shoot down, particularly when also taking into account its diminutive size.

Exactly what the Air Ministry thought of these concepts is unknown but Schmidt's work on pulsejets continued and he was evidently able, eventually, to produce sufficient thrust for aircraft propulsion, albeit only under laboratory conditions.[5]

THE ARGUS REYNST-POT

Just over two years after Schmidt's pulsejet presentation to the Air Ministry, in the autumn of 1936, the Berlin-based Argus Motoren company began to consider the design and manufacture of small motorised remote-controlled target aircraft for the German military—drones. This was evidently a private-funded venture, rather than being based on any particular requirement or contract with the Air Ministry.[6]

Alexander Lippisch at the DFS was signed up to provide the airframeon April 7, 1937, and the C. Lorenz company was contracted to develop the guidance system 19 days later.

The initial result of this work was a small remote-controlled aircraft dubbed 'Flakzielgerät 43' (FZG 43),[7] which was powered by a 3hp petrol engine. A follow-up of similar design, but with an 8hp engine intended for close reconnaissance, was then worked on.

On August 21, 1939, a representative of the Air Ministry's Technical Office engines department LC 3, Helmut Schelp, approached Argus to begin work on a primitive take-off aid for aircraft based on an innovative foreign design. In a report produced for the Allies after the war,[8]

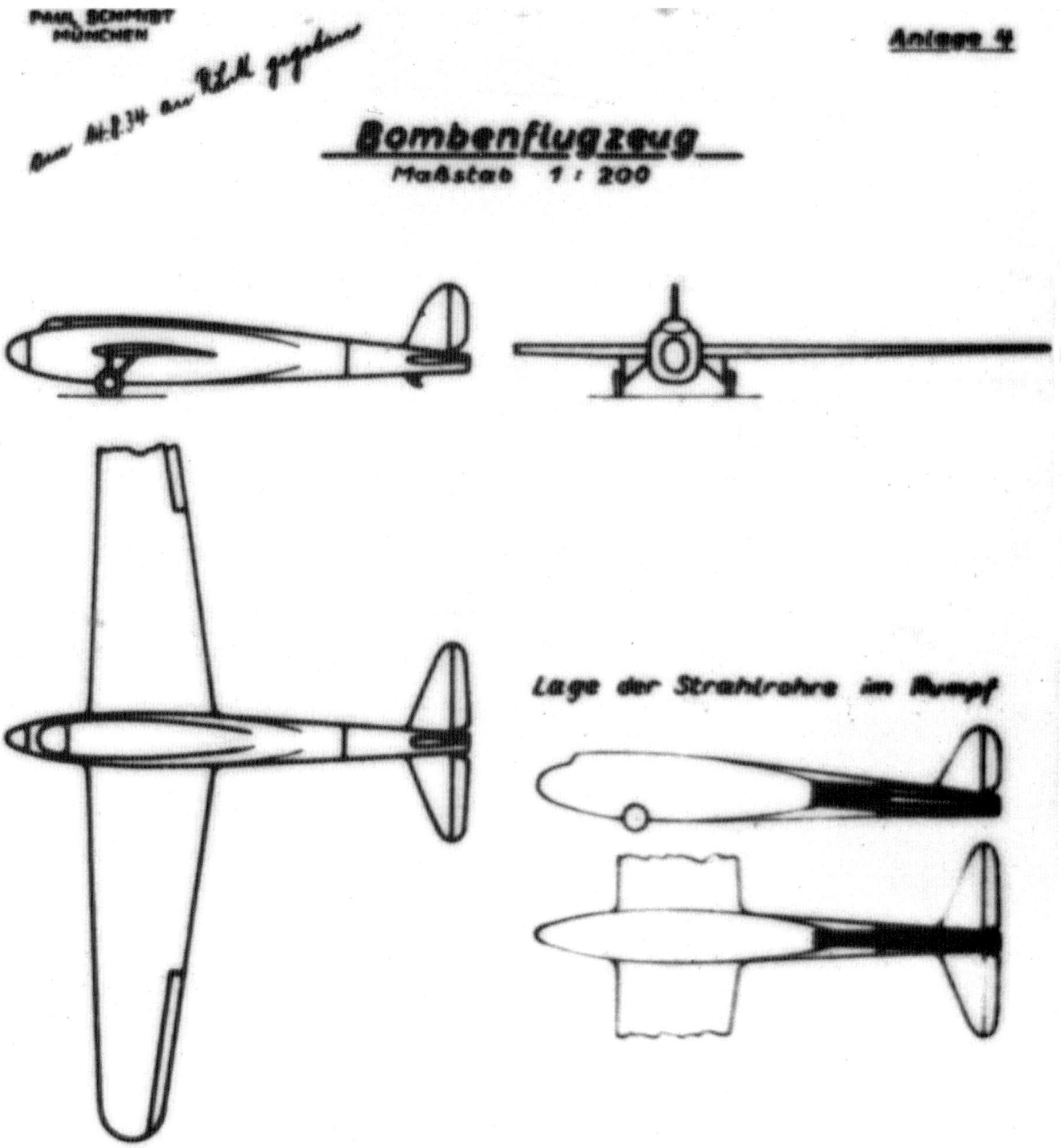

The pulsejet-powered bomber designed by Schmidt in 1934. It had no fewer than six engines—all in the rear fuselage.

Argus engineer Günther Diedrich wrote: "After the first engines of the resonator-combustion type, there did not follow any continuous line of development until P. Schmidt of Munich started his work in about 1930, or until the proposal at the same time of [Francois] Reynst of Holland [actually Switzerland].

"The engine of Reynst could also be classified as an explosion resonator. The pot-shaped engine operated with self-ignition. Intake air and exhaust gases passed through the same opening. The Reynst plant was brought to the machine laboratory of the Technical High School of Dresden to function as a steam generator.

"The first experimental work of the author, who had been engaged in jet engine development at the aero engine factory of Argus, began in November 1939, motivated by a suggestion from the Air Ministry. He was to develop a device on the style of the Reynst-pot, which was to be employed as an aid for take-off. The technique which Reynst had previously developed was not known at that time by the Argus firm, so that it was a completely new field for us.

"The author was to make thrust measurements of the exhaust gas nozzle and to experiment with mixtures. Within a month a model of an explosion-resonator operating with compressed air was built and was demonstrated. [It was a] ... 600mm engine which was spoken of as a resonator-burner. The exhaust tube had a diameter of 20mm; the exhaust frequency was close to 200 cycles per second.

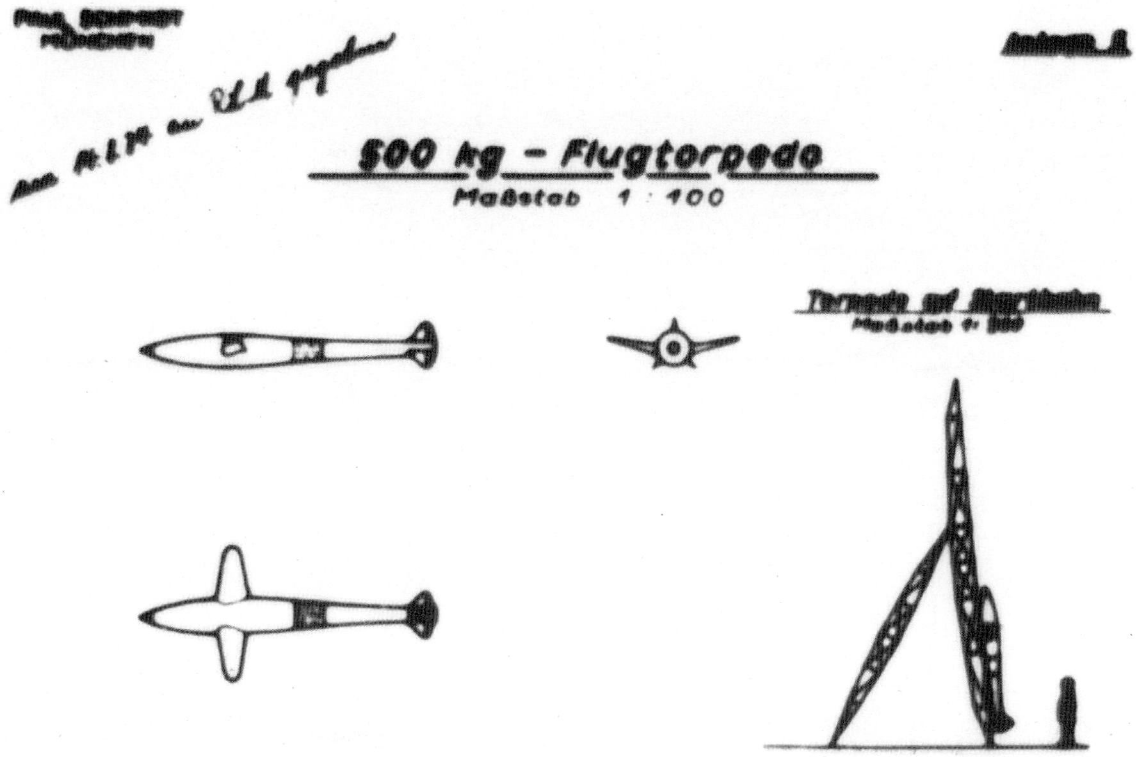

Schmidt's flying torpedo design — including a near-vertical launch ramp.

"The air flow was arranged so that a small amount of air opposite to the inflow direction caused the formation of ring vortices, which caused a high flow resistance (aerodynamic choking through the Borda annular orifice and vortex flow). Special attention was directed to the steady internal mixture formation through high-pressure fuel atomisation, which allowed the attainment of a satisfactory resonator engine with automatic ignition."

The Second World War began just 11 days after Diedrich got started on his Reynst-pot development. Shortly thereafter his colleague Fritz Gosslau, coordinator of the FZG 43 project, came up with a new concept for an unpiloted vehicle: a flying bomb intended for long-range missions. His initial report on this, dated November 8, was presented to the Air Ministry the following day under the code name 'Fernfeuer'. According to an Argus report on this project, "the technical design of the long-range bomb in 1939 was more complicated than that of the 'V 1' [the famous pulsejet-powered flying bomb of 1944]. This was due to two factors: 1. Tactical. The front line in 1939 required a relatively long flight distance, which could only be managed with a petrol engine driving a propeller (a penetration depth of 1,000km was required!). 2. Political. Air warfare in 1939 only permitted attacks on military targets. The accuracy required here could only be achieved using electronic navigation".[9] C. Lorenz was retained to handle the guidance system of Fernfeuer while Arado was contracted to design the airframe.

On November 13, 1939, Diedrich commenced practical tests of a propulsive tube he had developed from the Reynst-pot. Ten days after that, Gosslau went back to the Air Ministry with an updated version of his Fernfeuer proposal which now included drawings of the piston engine-powered airframe designed by Arado. Another week later, on November 30, Schelp and his colleague Waldmann visited the Argus plant to meet with Gosslau and Diedrich and watch a practical demonstration of the latter's tube in action.

The post-meeting summary stated: "At the instigation of the Air Ministry LC 3, Argus began initial attempts to develop a continuously operating air jet engine. A first preliminary test run led surprisingly quickly to initial success. On November 30 the Ministry officials were shown the first test model in operation with a measured vibration number of 210 Hertz and an air flow of 20kg/h. It was determined that this was the first deflagration jet engine demonstrated to the Ministry that worked properly.

"Since the approach promises success, Argus will receive a contract for further development. The work will initially focus on clarifying fundamental questions. The next practical test rig should be built about three to four times as large in order to exclude coincidences and to allow perfect measurements.

"Argus suggests giving the further experimental models

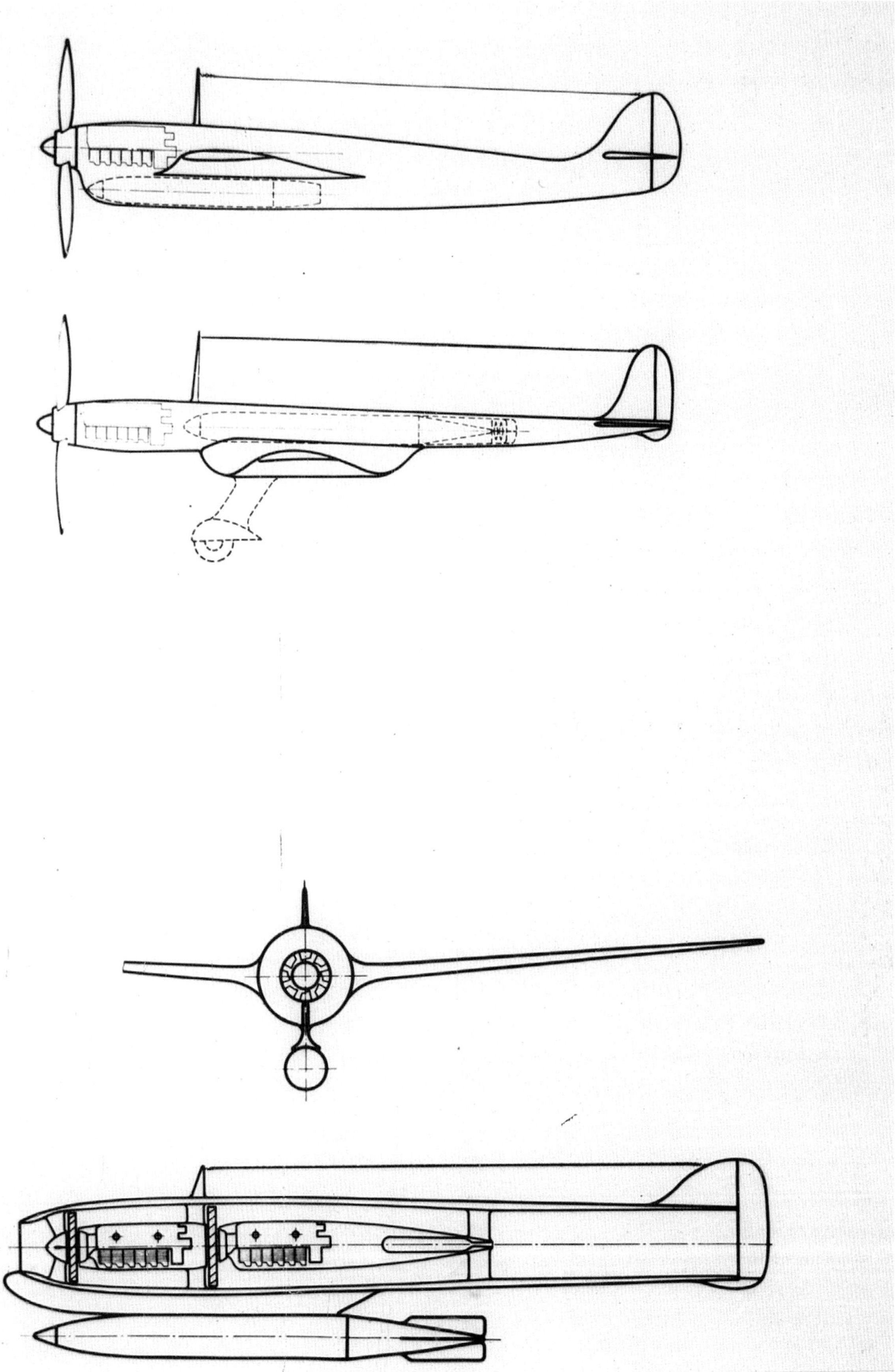

Drone designs from an Argus report dated November 22, 1939, contemporary with Diedrich's commencement of work on the Reynst-pot. From top—Lufttorpedo I, Lufttorpedo II and Lufttorpedo III. The latter was to be powered by a motorjet comprising two As 410s. The airframes are said to have been developed under contract by Arado.

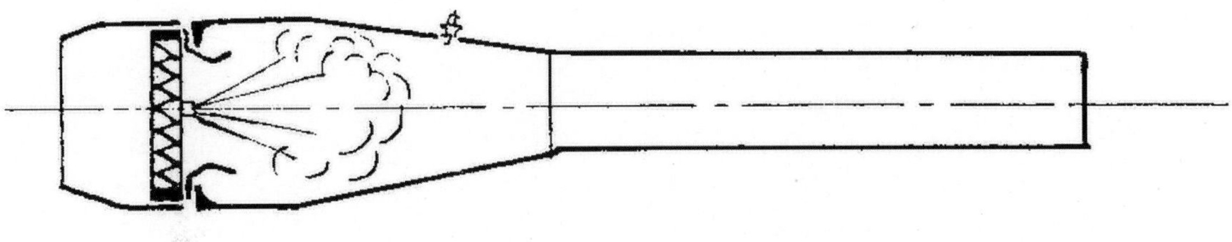

Diagram from Diedrich's report showing a much-simplified view of how the Argus pulsejet worked—with the spring flap-valve grid or 'shutters' just aft of the inlet. With the valves open, fuel was injected into the airstream via pipes on the back of the grid before the valves snapped shut and the swirling fuel/air mix was ignited.

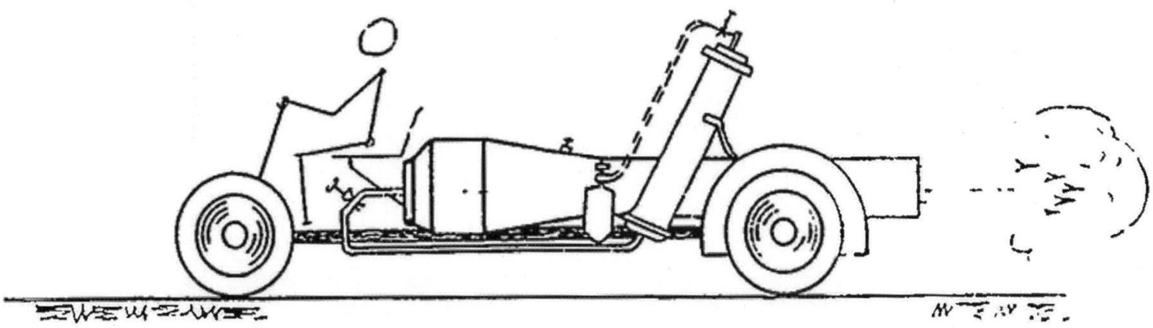

Diedrich's diagram showing the pulsejet powered car he made and reportedly road-tested up to 100km/h in early 1941.

an aerodynamic external shape from the outset". Gosslau further suggested that using Diedrich's surprisingly successful tube—effectively an independently developed pulsejet—to power Fernfeuer would result in a weight reduction of around 500kg.[10] The successful demonstration and this suggestion evidently convinced Schelp and Waldmann that Argus's Reynst-pot derived pulsejet was no longer simply a would-be take-off aid but a potentially valuable propulsion system in its own right.

Flight testing of the Argus pulsejet suspended below a Gotha Go 145 trainer began on April 30, 1941.

'BORROWING' FROM SCHMIDT

The Air Ministry consequently decided that the previously separate efforts of Schmidt and Argus on pulsejet technology should be combined, or at least that their knowledge should be shared.

In his report to the Allies,[11] Diedrich recalled: "In the early part of 1940 … the Air Ministry strove for cooperation between the firms of Schmidt and Argus and paved the way for mutual visits and exchange of experiences. Schmidt then made a single visit to the Argus firm in February 1940.

"After taking into account the knowledge of the existing developmental state of the Schmidt Explosion Resonator, it appeared to be expedient that both developments should at first proceed separately, since both partners had still not arrived at a fully developed type."

This exchange of data seems to have been significantly more beneficial to Argus than it was to Schmidt however. Diedrich continued: "Contact with Schmidt in February 1940 had shown that [they] had developed the flap-valve considerably farther than the Argus firm, whose first goal was the flow valve without flaps. A design of the conical form with a simple flat valve construction proved to be very advantageous for the ensuing engine development, as only a spring-flap type was necessary and only a simple assemblage was required."

In other words, Argus simply took Schmidt's ingenious spring flap-valve grid—or 'shutters'—and applied it to their own tube. Diedrich went on: "In [the remainder of] 1940 the main development work was concentrated on the mixture formation. The author held fast to his idea embodied in the first burner type of steady internal high pressure mixture formation, and in January 1941 he succeeded through the invention of the nozzle cover in solving the mixture formation problem perfectly in an easy manner, using rotating fuel nozzles."

Schmidt's shutters and Diedrich's fuel/air mixture system proved to be an extremely fortunate combination.[12] Diedrich swiftly built a working prototype pulsejet tube and installed it in a four-wheel car chassis, which was ready for road testing by the end of January 1941.

According to his report: "The author undertook the first road experiments with a reaction-car to compare the thrusts obtained in acceleration tests against those measured on the test stand. This first resonator-car, on account of its experimental construction and because of the limited working length of the test track, could not be driven faster than about 100km/h (62.2mph)."

With this data in hand, Diedrich was next able to test his prototype engine in flight. He wrote: "During April 1941, the first flight investigations took place with a resonator-engine of 300mm exhaust tube diameter. It was done at first purely to test its functioning in flight. For this purpose the tube was placed under the fuselage of a biplane, [arranged] so that the aircraft had enough ground clearance during take-off." Flight testing of Diedrich's pulsejet, slung beneath a Gotha Go 145 biplane trainer, commenced on April 30, 1941.

"At the end of 1941 the Argus aero-resonator was, with regard to thrust stand advancements, completely developed to a mature type. Starting and regulation processes were also cleared up, so that special development projects could be set up when the exact employment purpose of this engine was decided."

Regarding the official name chosen for the engine, Diedrich later added: "The resonator engine built by the Schmidt firm after 1940 proved itself both in the Braunschweig wind tunnel and on the test stand to be neither superior nor able to compete with the Argus design. Thus it is often found in history that because of the type of competition described here, the inventor is surpassed. In the name selected by the Air Ministry, the 'Argus-Schmidt-Tube', both the pioneering work of Schmidt and the forceful development of the Argus firm were duly recognised."

The device Diedrich had created, utilising Schmidt's spring-flap valve grid, would eventually receive the designation As 014, though this name seldom appears in documents relating to the Me 328. And it was no ordinary engine. Several modern-day reproductions have been built and filmed in operation. The sound has to be heard to be believed; a suitable audio analogy might be a swarm of angry flying insects, each bigger than your fist, trapped inside an enormous low-resonating container; or perhaps an old-fashioned television set tuned to static, with the volume cranked up so high that the speaker is overwhelmed and the sound distorts to a deep and deafening drone.

In every case, on startup the engine belches out a great cloud of flames from its exhaust which then settles into a swirling, pulsating jet of bright orange fire several feet long which persists for the duration of its run. The metal engine casing begins to glow orange and then red after only a brief time.

Diedrich may have thought that the worrying sensory overload of ear-splitting sound, extreme radiant heat and uncontained flames that his engines produced was purely a short-term cosmetic concern and that ongoing development would result in something less clearly dangerous. More likely, he simply thought it was a price worth paying given the engine's advantages in terms of thrust produced versus weight and cost.

MESSERSCHMITT P 79

The Messerschmitt company had been given Air Ministry approval to work on a jet fighter design in October 1938,[13] resulting in the P 65—which would eventually receive the official designation Me 262. It had been agreed almost from the outset that the P 65 would be powered by BMW turbojets, with both the P 3302 and P 3304 being specified at various times. However, by the beginning of 1941 it was clear that BMW's turbojet programme was in trouble. The company sent Messerschmitt a note on January 7, 1941, stating that no engines would be available for the foreseeable future[14]—leaving the Me 262 without a power plant.

A new BMW delivery schedule was issued in the first week of February, promising a pair of usable P 3302 prototypes during March,[15] but these failed to materialise. Then a glimmer of hope appeared on the horizon, Messerschmitt's Project Office evidently receiving details of Schmidt's—rather than Argus's—ongoing pulsejet work.

Schmidt was expecting to achieve 500kg of thrust with the production model SR500 tube, which would weigh just 80kg. BMW's turbojets were expected to achieve around 600kg thrust but with an anticipated weight of 600kg per unit.[16] The SR500's reportedly outstanding power-to-weight ratio, not to mention its simplicity and inexpensive construction, must have seemed almost too good to be true but nonetheless in May 1941 the Project Office, led by Voigt, seized upon it as the answer to their propulsion problems.

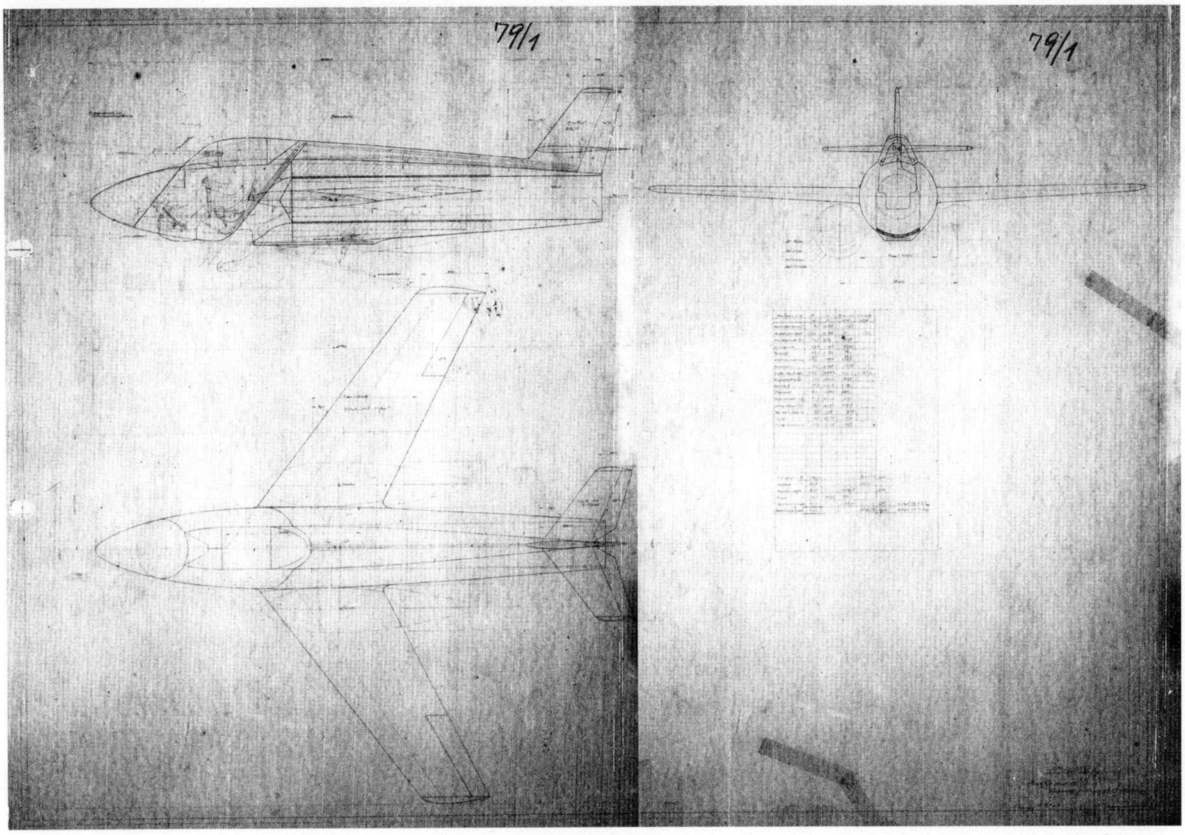

The first Messerschmitt P 79 design had a single Schmidt pulsejet mounted centrally within its fuselage—with the fuel tank wrapped around it. The drawing also shows a mid-wing layout, central landing skid and a bomb under each wing root.

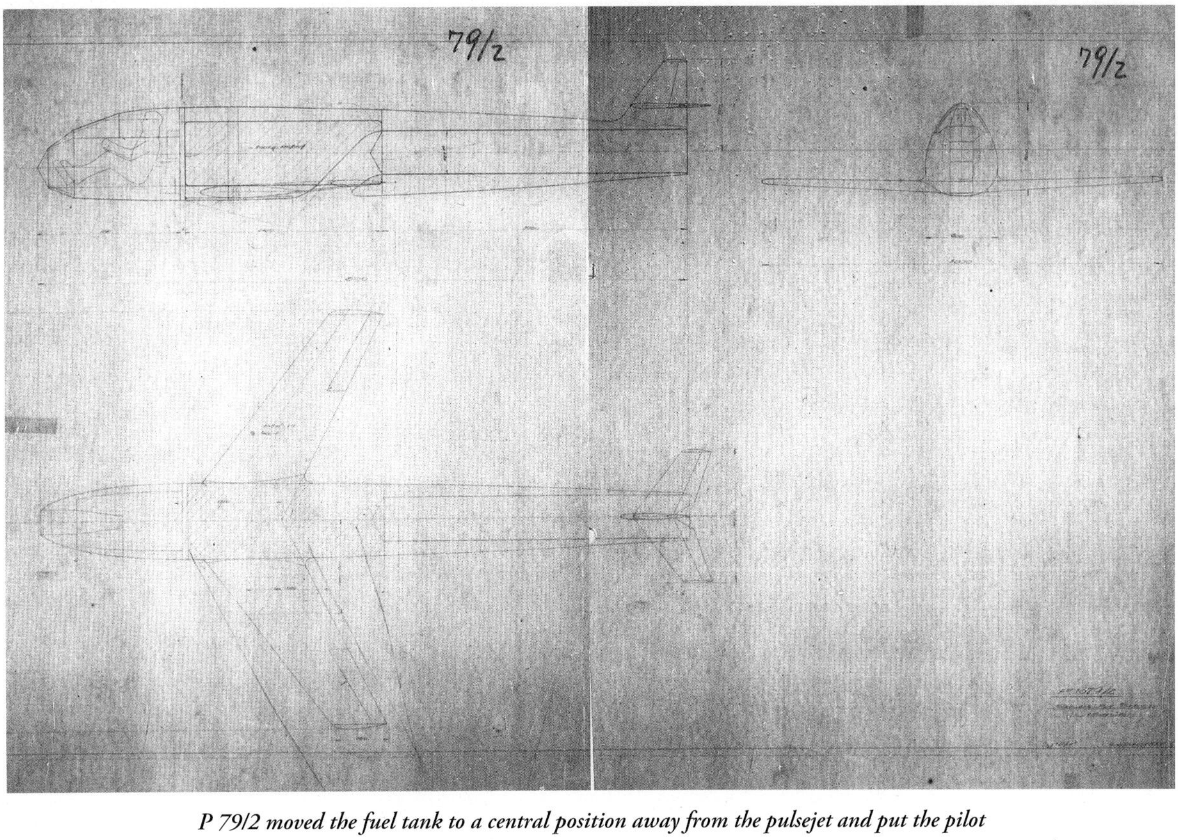

P 79/2 moved the fuel tank to a central position away from the pulsejet and put the pilot up front in a fully glazed nose, resulting in an oddly distended layout.

They initially began working out what performance might be achieved by fitting the Me 262 with pulsejets[17] but soon began to consider an entirely new aircraft instead, under the designation P 79. Rather than allowing themselves to be constrained by the conventions of airframe design up to that point, the Project Office engineers considered a wide variety of different configurations with the goal of finding the ideal vehicle for the new propulsion system.

This exploratory work took place between May and August 1941 and was summed up in a report entitled Flugzeuge mit Strahlrohren—aircraft with pulsejets.[18] This pointed out that the lightweight SR500 allowed for an aircraft with small wings and consequently low drag. It stated: "The reduction in wing area alone results in an increase in speed of approx. 7% when using a pulsejet compared to the turbojet of the same power. Taking into account the reduction in the size of the tail unit, the reduction in the airframe weight (wings, landing gear, etc.) and the associated further reduction in size, a speed increase of 10% or more is possible." A cautionary note was added, however, concerning pulsejet fuel consumption which was said to be twice as high as it was for turbojets.

When formulating an airframe suitable for pulsejet propulsion, the designers were required to assume a heavy load—up to 2,000kg, particularly of bombs—from the outset. Climbing performance was considered less important for the purpose of this study than outright straight-line speed and swept wings were to be used in every case. A further study concentrating on climbing performance over horizontal speed was promised, but it is unknown whether this was ever delivered.

Messerschmitt had been told that "the largest pulsejet currently under development generates 500kg of thrust (it is not yet possible to say whether an increase in the size of the engine is possible)" so the Project Office report stated that "with the intention of keeping the airframe as small as possible, the following [P 79] designs were intended for 500kg engines".

Finally, the designers had been asked to assume five possible roles for the pulsejet-powered aircraft: "fighter—high speed, good climbing performance, range of up to 800km; reconnaissance aircraft—good climbing performance and maximum altitude, sufficient range at high altitude; interceptor—outstanding climbing performance with short flight times; bomber—sufficient top speed with enclosed bombs to outrun today's fighters; parasite aircraft (as a bomber or fighter)—compact size.

With all this in mind, Messerschmitt's designers came up with at least 21 different configurations for pulsejet-powered aircraft labelled P 79/1 to P 79/17 (handwritten at the top of each drawing—the drawings themselves use the alternative project numbering style of P 1079). The additional four layouts resulted from P 79/10 and P 79/13 each being presented in three iterations: P 79/10a, 10b, 10c, 13a, 13b and 13c. Only 11 of the 21 have survived to the present day—the other ten are currently unknown.

ELEVEN (SURVIVING) P 79S

Messerschmitt's P 79/1 was essentially an aircraft wrapped around a pulsejet tube but retained a superficially conventional external form. The engine filled most of the central and rear fuselage, with a fuel tank wrapped around it, and exhausted beneath the swept tail fin. The tailplanes and wings were also swept, with the official design drawing depicting a large bomb beneath the wing root on either side. Air entered the engine through a slot intake on the aircraft's underside, just aft of the cockpit. The cockpit itself had an unremarkable-looking canopy positioned atop the fuselage, with a raised spine containing the control linkages extending back to the tailfin. Within the cockpit, the pilot had a bombsight positioned in front of him, just below his eyeline, so he could see above it during flight or lean in to look through it as required.

The aircraft's nose contained a second fuel tank and the landing gear consisted of a rather flimsy and insubstantial-looking skid retracting into the lower fuselage.

A brief set of notes appended to the drawing pointed out that the fuel tank encircling the pulsejet was a "fire hazard", that total fuel capacity was 1,200 litres and that the engine intake form was "unfavourable". There was no room to accommodate more engines or engines of different sizes, the bombs could not be enclosed in this configuration and the engine was also supporting the tailplane.

P 79/2 was a far more unusual-looking design. Its slender fuselage was 8.1m long and this time the pulsejet filled only the rear section, with the centre accommodating the single large fuel tank. The pilot sat in front of the tank within a glazed nose and neither ejection seat nor bombsight were depicted—there were no bombs under the swept wings either. Their span—legible in this drawing—was just 5m and they were positioned well to the front of the aircraft, attached to the underside of the fuel tank section just aft of the cockpit. The undercarriage was still a skid and the engine intake remained a slot set aft of the wings.

The drawing notes this time highlighted the clear separation of cockpit, fuel tank and engine sections and the fuel tank capacity of 1,200. The criticism of the intake as "unfavourable" was repeated.

P 79/3 was said to be a "further development" of P

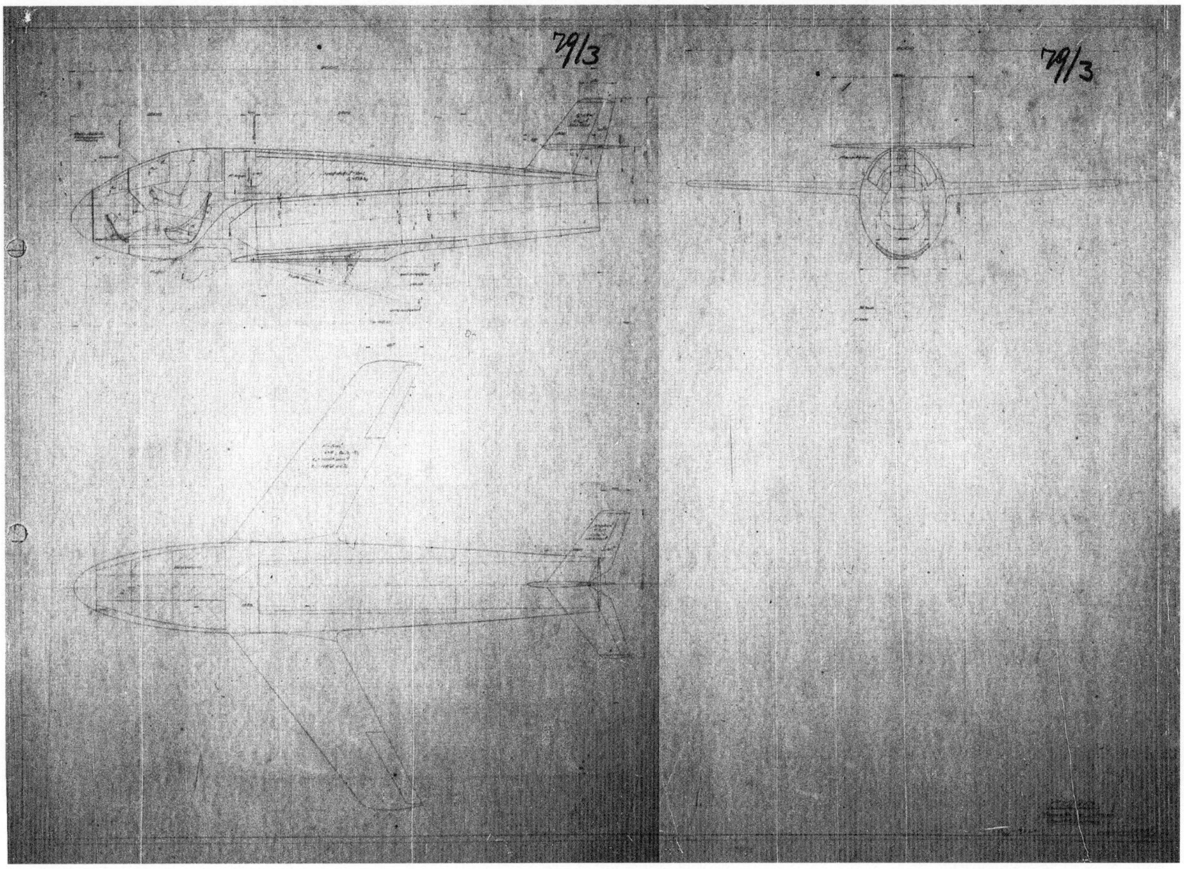

Said to be a development of P 79/1, P 79/3 revised the pulsejet position, intake shape and cockpit design.

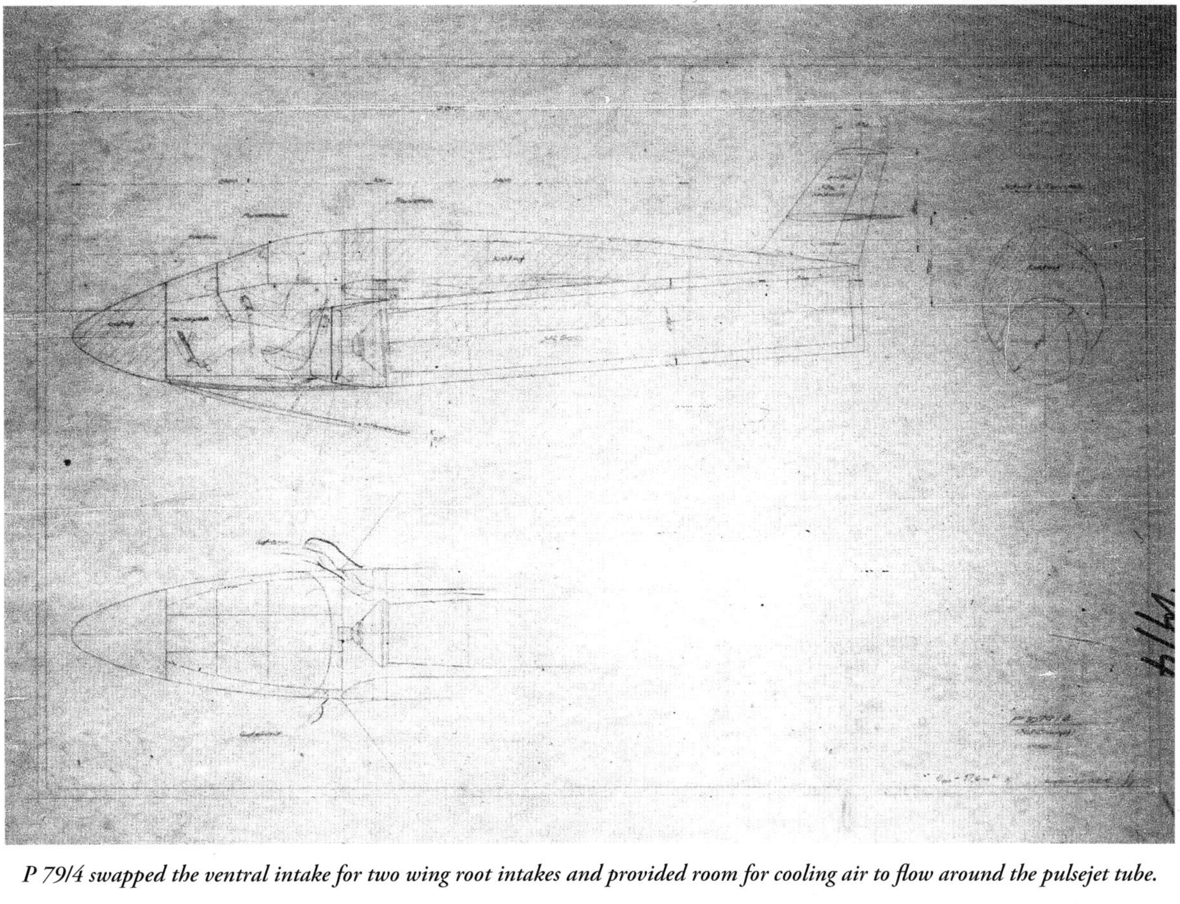

P 79/4 swapped the ventral intake for two wing root intakes and provided room for cooling air to flow around the pulsejet tube.

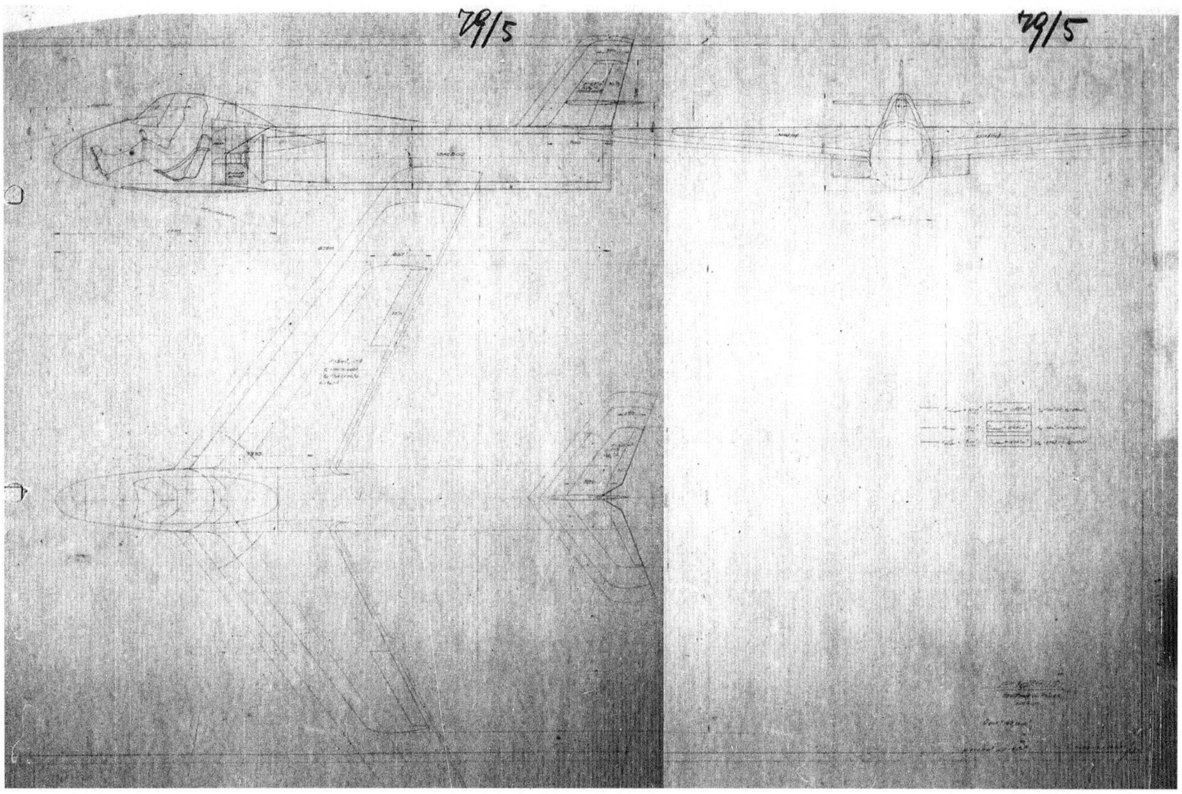

A key difficulty of earlier iterations was solved in the P 79/5—the fuel tanks were separated from the hot pulsejet by relocating them to the wings. This allowed for an economically slender fuselage but necessitated very large wings.

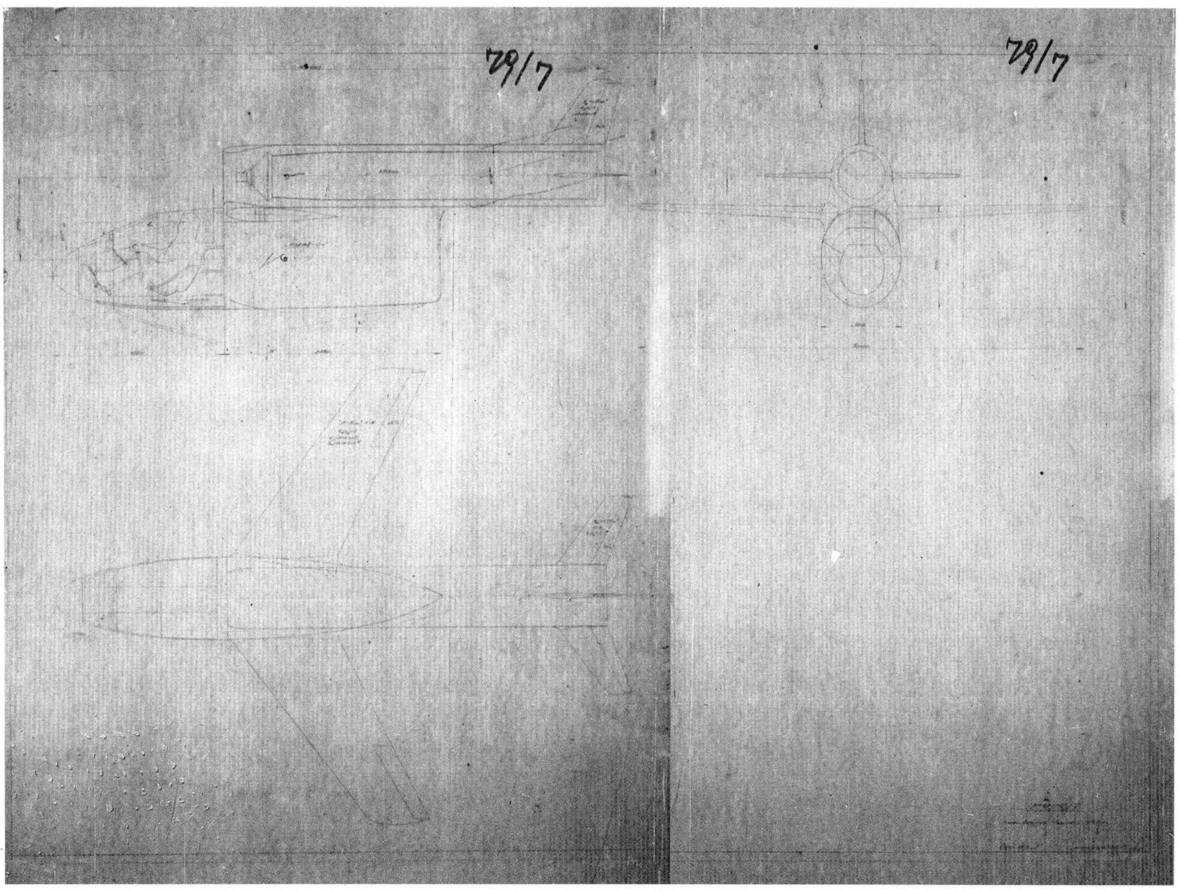

The wing tanks of P 79/5 were simply not viable, yet the pulsejet needed to be separated from the fuel and also needed a simplified intake—resulting in P 79/7's unusual tapering rear fuselage and dorsal pulsejet.

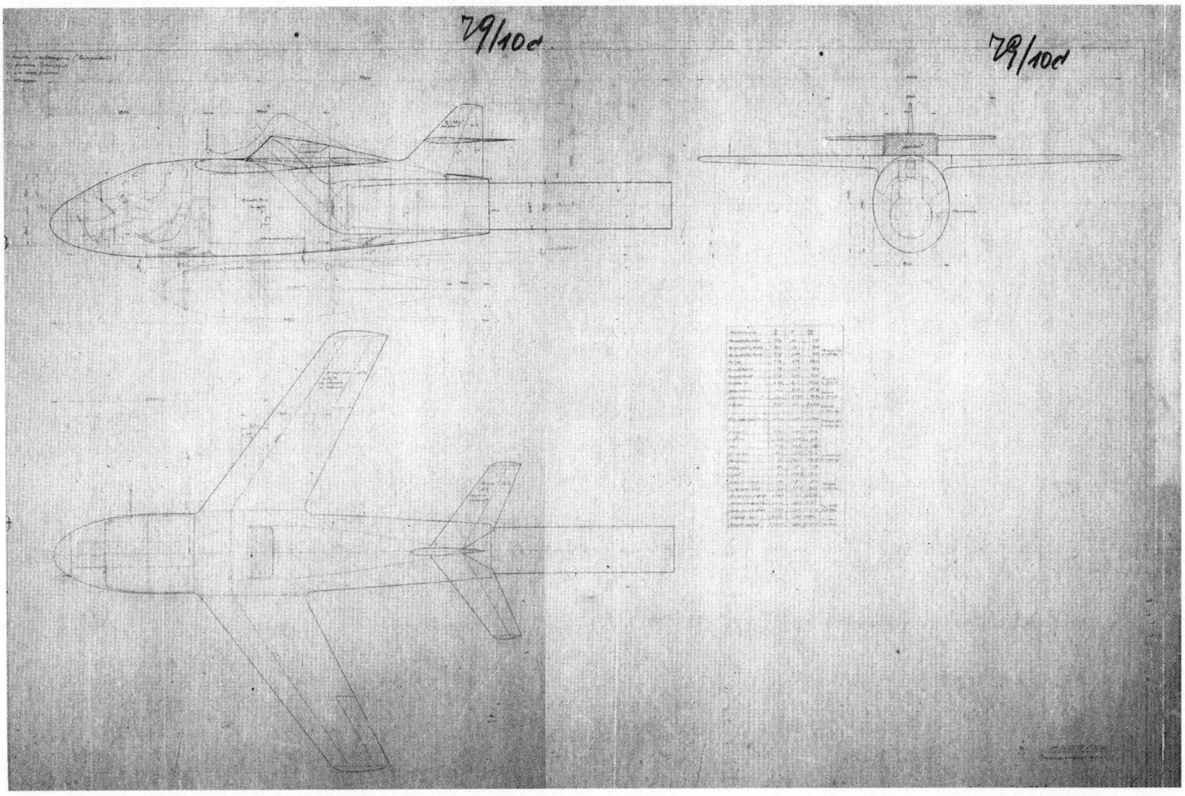

P 79/10c—the last of the first tranche of P 79 designs—kept the pulsejet away from the rest of the aircraft by having most of it protruding from its rear end. The dorsal intake was, however, regarded as a retrograde step.

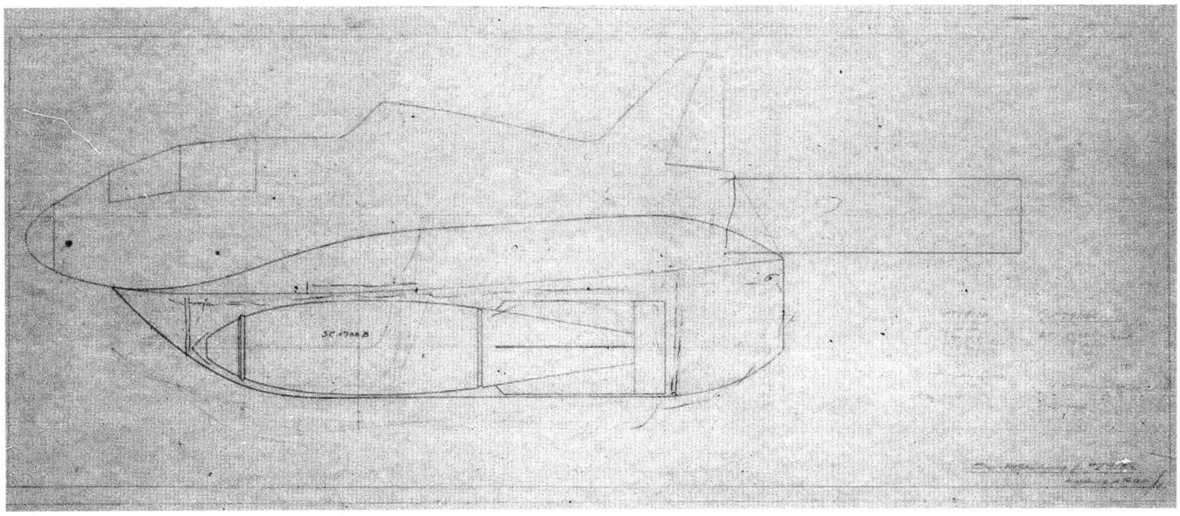

A key aspect of the P 79 series was the need to carry a heavy bomb load. This diagram shows the P 79/10c fitted with an aerodynamic fairing over its underslung bomb.

79/1. A key innovation was to angle the pulsejet downwards at the forward end, putting its inlet closer to an enlarged intake slot on the aircraft's underside. In addition, the cockpit canopy was now glass panes set into the fuselage, rather than being raised above it. This had the dual benefits of creating an aerodynamically cleaner airframe without the P 79/1's raised spine and providing increased internal volume for fuel. The landing skid, swept wings and swept tail surfaces were all carried over from the earlier designs. On the design drawing, very faintly, a bomb was visible suspended directly below the fuselage in the forward view only.

The noted benefits of the P 79/3 were "slightly improved air intake" and "improved visibility" but the design returned to the unsafe engine-enveloping fuel tank and also had an "unfavourable centre of gravity".

P 79/4 appears to be yet another iteration on the P 79/1-3 theme. The nose fuel tank has been reinstated—to restore the centre of gravity, according to the notes—and the pulsejet has been both moved to the bottom of the fuselage and suspended within a capacious engine bay. This was presumably intended to provide a buffer of cooling air between the sides of the pulsejet and the fuel tank above it. The air would come from the same wing root intakes intended to feed the pulsejet itself. The skid undercarriage was also repositioned to sit beneath the cockpit, perhaps to mitigate the impact of landing on the pilot more directly.

P 79/5 effectively rebooted the design sequence by moving the fuel tanks into the wings. This resulted in just about the smallest possible airframe, with even more of the fuselage consisting of little other than the pulsejet itself, suspended within its engine bay. This was fed by boxy underwing intakes reminiscent of the radiators on an inline piston engine aircraft. The cockpit at the front of the aircraft was extremely compact—the design illustration failing to show the instrument panel that had been present for earlier iterations—but visibility would have been excellent. Although the drawing is not entirely clear on the positioning of the skid, it would appear to be below the cockpit again.

Shifting the fuel into the wings also meant that several capacity options were now available: if 330 litres was enough, then wings with an area of 5sqm could be fitted. Wings of 8sqm would accommodate 640 litres and 10sqm would provide space for 920 litres.

P 79/6 is not known to have survived.

P 79/7 was another reboot—this time with the engine housed in a nacelle above the fuselage, forming a tail boom. The cockpit was similar to that of P 79/3 but with the pilot in a slightly more reclined position and with the skid below, as seen on the later iterations. Behind the pilot, the truncated rear fuselage housing the fuel tank tapered away to a point below the pulsejet nacelle. Unlike every known earlier design, P 79/7's wings were set high rather than being in the mid-wing position. This might make the design appear top-heavy but Messerschmitt was expecting the pulsejet to be incredibly light, so most of the aircraft's mass would still be low down in the cockpit and rear fuselage. The notes referring to this design point out that the air intake is "significantly improved".

P 79/8, 9, 10a and 10b are also lost, but the evolutionary line between P 79/7 and P 79/10c is clear: they have nearly identical cockpit/skid structures and wing positions.

P 79/10c attempted to retain something of P 79/7's intake position while shifting the pulsejet itself into the rear fuselage. But rather than using the engine nacelle to form the tail as before, the fuselage was cut short, with the fin and rudder mounted on top, aft of the intake, and more than half of the engine's length was allowed to protrude unclad from the rear of the aircraft. Now the designers once again turned their attention to bomb attachment. The primary design drawing shows a single large bomb—seemingly an SC 1000 or larger—suspended directly below the fuselage, its length almost matching that of the aircraft itself. A supplemental drawing shows the same airframe but with an extravagant aerodynamic fairing covering the bomb. The notes on this design referred to the dorsal intake position as "undesirable" and the aerodynamic fairing as "unfavourable, especially with two bombs". Fuel capacity was said to be 800 litres.

Designs P 79/1 to P 79/10c certainly existed as early as May 22, 1941, since P 79/4, 5, 6, 7, 8, 9 and 10c appear together on a graph bearing that date. P 79/11, 12, 13a and 14 do not seem to have survived into the modern era but these too certainly existed as they all appear together on a second graph dated June 10, 1941. This graph gives details of the Schmidt pulsejets expected to power each one and suggests that whatever their design looked like, P 79/11 and P 79/12 were intended to be flexible. The former could have either a single SR500, an SR800 or an SR1000, while the latter could accommodate an SR500 or an SR800. The P 79/13a would have two SR400 tubes and the P 79/14 would have one SR800. A comparison was made between the four designs based on them having a total of 800kg thrust each.

MORE ENGINES, OR LARGER

A third graph dated June 18, 1941, compared the P 79/13b, 15, 16 and 17—grouping these together because they were each equipped with pulsejets intended to produce 1,000kg thrust.

P 79/13b was a landmark design. For the first time in the sequence, it featured two SR500 pulsejet engines rather than one (the only other twin-engine design, P 79/13a, having had two SR400s as mentioned above). The cockpit was largely the same as it had been for P 79/7 and P 79/10c but with a hump housing the wing structure behind the pilot's head, tapering rearwards onto a low, flat, wedge-shaped fuselage. The thick end of the wedge, behind the cockpit, housed a 900-litre capacity fuel tank, while further towards the tail was an equipment bay. This is the first time such a feature appears in the known design sequence, since previously the equipment had been housed directly behind the pilot's seat. Equally unusually, the equipment bay had its own small landing skid, supplementing the one further forward below the cockpit. On either side of the fuselage was a bulky cylindrical engine

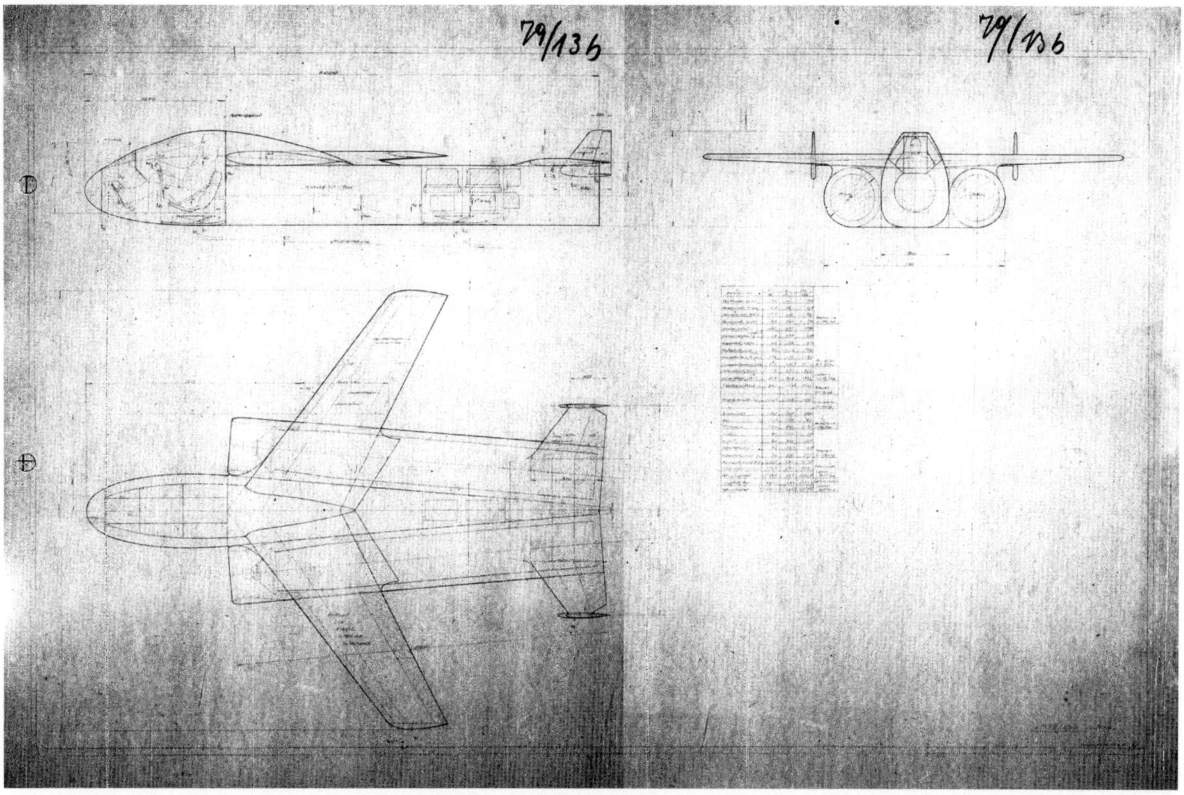

The three P 79/13 designs /13a, /13b and /13c each had two pulsejets rather than one — the only three designs in the P 79 series to have this feature — though only the /13b design has survived. Two engines gave better performance than one and the under-wing engine position meant easy access for maintenance and unobstructed intakes.

Designs P 79/15, /16 and /17 were all variations on a theme. P 79/15 had its pulsejet centrally mounted in a flat asymmetrical fuselage — providing space for extra fuel or a second crewman.

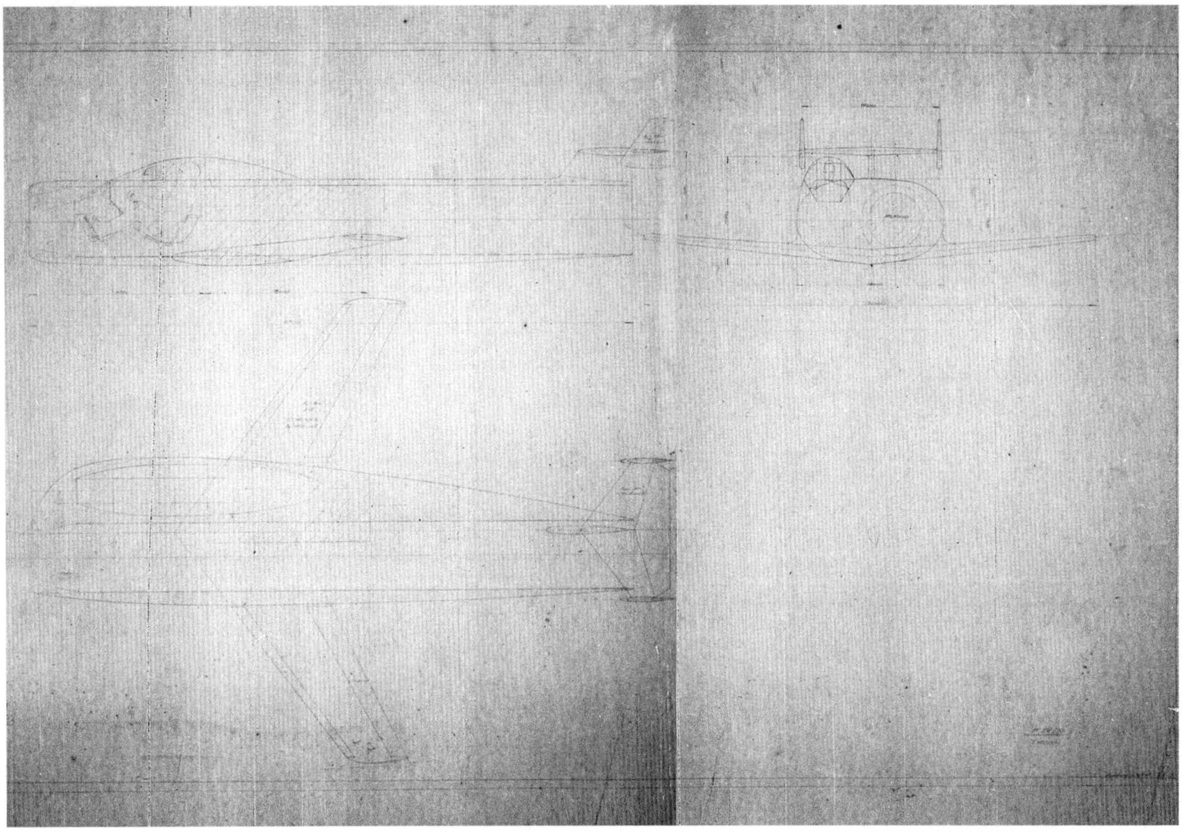

P 79/16 was largely the same as P 79/15 but with the port side fuselage deleted—the aircraft now largely consisting of a winged pulsejet nacelle with the cockpit and fuel tank tacked on the side.

nacelle and attached to each of these at the rear was a tailplane and vertical fin/rudder.

The designers clearly felt that they were onto something with the P 79/13b. The notes, while not universally positive, reflect this optimism: "use of two engines; air entry significantly improved; unfavourable arrangement of radio equipment; clear and cheap construction; easy interchangeability of the engines; uncertainty in stability; good possibility to accommodate the bombs, even with two; relatively simple solution for the dive brake (always fin centre section); better flight performance than single engine designs".

P 79/14 is lost and the remaining three designs in the known sequence, P 79/15, 16 and 17 seemingly belong together as iterations on a common theme, predicated upon the availability of a much larger pulsejet of unknown type.

P 79/15 had this large pulsejet mounted centrally within its very broad, flat, fuselage—the big circular intake positioned right at the front in the centre. The pilot sat on one side, making the design one of only two asymmetrical P 79s, and much of the remaining fuselage capacity was used to house additional fuel; presumably such an enormous pulsejet would be extremely thirsty. The wings were set low, on the underside of the aircraft, and the tail consisted of three triangular surfaces attached to the tail end of the fuselage. No attempt to depict landing gear appears to have been made.

In the notes, the intake arrangement was described as "perfect" and the fuel capacity was given as "1,540 litres or, when using the entire left fuselage compartment, 2,375 litres". If it wasn't full of fuel, the left side compartment gave the "possibility of two-man crew" but if there wasn't a second cockpit there was "poor visibility with one man crew". Finally, there was a "possibility to accommodate the bombs as in design P 79/13b".

P 79/16 was the other asymmetrical design and mostly consisted of P 79/15 but with the left side entirely omitted. This left a fuel capacity of just 770 litres and the tail surfaces were rearranged so that the plane with twin fin plates attached sat atop a narrow support at the end of the fuselage.

P 79/17—perhaps the most viable-looking design from the entire sequence—was accurately described in the notes as "modification of design P 79/16 (rotation around the longitudinal axis by 90 degrees)". So where previously the cockpit had sat to one side of the large pulsejet's nacelle, it now perched neatly on top of it. The remainder of the fuselage was slightly reshaped to form a hump over the pulsejet housing and a regular set of tail surfaces was

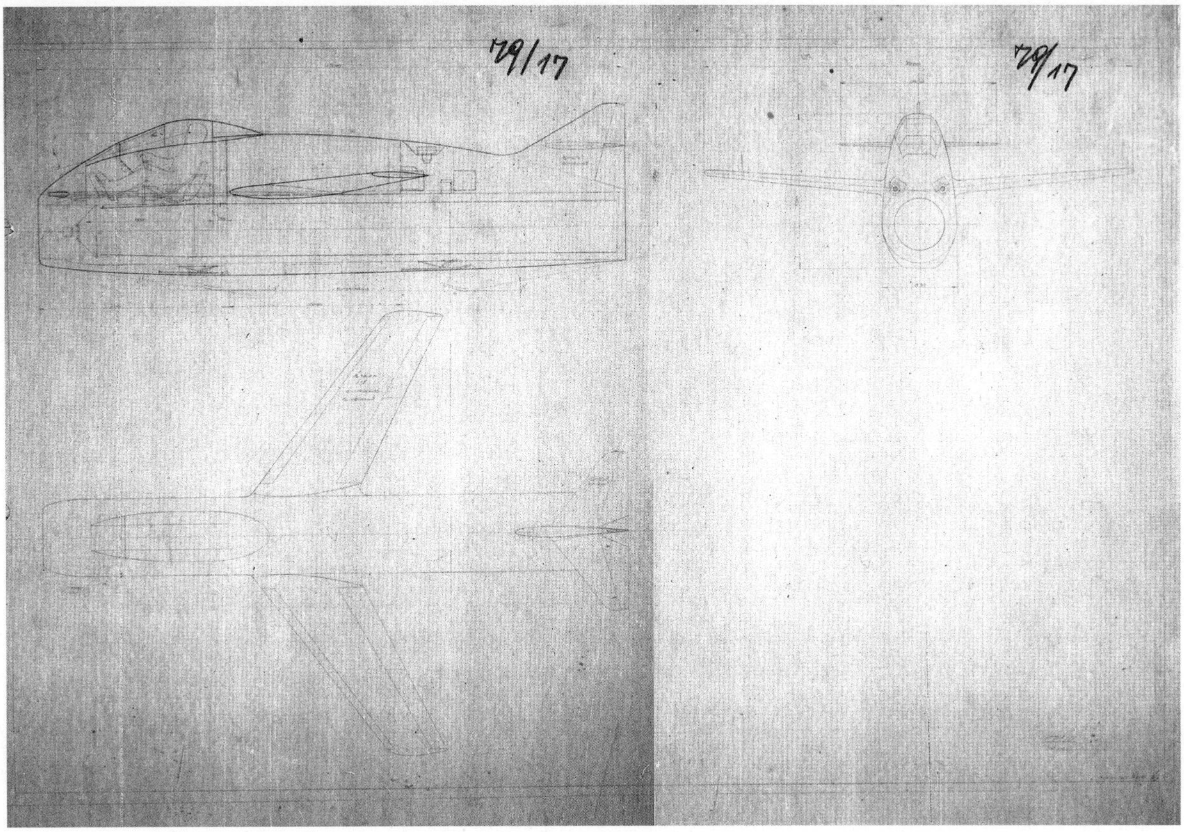

The P 79/16 fuselage rotated through 90 degrees resulted in the P 79/17—the last known design in the series and also, perhaps, the most realistically configured for a single internally-housed engine. Messerschmitt's designers were unable to work out how it might be made to carry bombs, however.

affixed to the rear end. The single 800 litre fuel tank filled the space between the cockpit up front and the tail section equipment bay. Rather than some enormous bomb being appended to the design, there was a machine gun or cannon installed on either side of the pilot. The wings were mid-set and the landing gear consisted of the double skid arrangement last seen on P 79/13b.

The notes go on to cite a number of advantages to P 79/17: "improved visibility; improved stability around the transverse axis; possibility of installing fixed weapons in the nose of the fuselage" but the big disadvantage as far as the original design criteria were concerned was "no possibility of arranging and accommodating the bombs sensibly".

P 79 CONSTRUCTION DESCRIPTION

Appended to the earlier reports, drawings, notes and graphs relating to the P 79 designs were a number of additional graphs dating from late July 1941, referring simply to the 'P 79' as a single design or to the P 79/13 alone. Among other documents there was a speed comparison graph which plotted the performance of the P 79/13 against that of the Bf 109 F dated August 1, 1941,[19] a comparison of weights between the P 79, Me 262 and Bf 109 F dated July 28, 1941,[20] a comparison between the P 79 and Bf 109 D, dated July 31, 1941,[21] and a full albeit unillustrated build description of the 'P 79' dated August 1, 1941, and signed by Messerschmitt engineer Rudolf Seitz.[22]

It appears that P 79/13, the only twin-engine variant of the series, had been chosen as the primary P 79 design. The build description however, while it somewhat described the P 79/13b as illustrated, deviated in various details and it would appear that the aircraft being outlined was a further development beyond that design—a P 79/13c.[23]

Under 'purpose of use', the build description stated that "the aircraft is designed as a short-range jet bomber. The most important thing is that the aircraft with the largest bomb load still achieves flight and climb speeds which ensure that it can safely escape enemy fighters. The take-off takes place by detaching from the exterior of a carrier aircraft (Me 323, Do 17). By replacing the bomb kit with a weapon system, the aircraft can be used as a fighter and interceptor. Because of its small dimensions, it can also be accommodated inside a host aircraft as a parasite aircraft (fighter or bomber)".

The P 79 was described as a "cantilevered, two-engine high-wing aircraft in all-metal construction with retractable landing skids and an enclosed cockpit". It was to be stressed for fighter operations and "during construction, the greatest attention is paid to cheapness and simplicity with a view to the aircraft entering service as soon as possible".

The fuselage was to consist of the cockpit, fuselage mid-section containing the fuel tank, and fuselage end-section which functioned as a tail boom. The description says: "As an immediate solution, a normal cockpit with primitive equipment is planned, which can later be exchanged for a fully equipped pressurised cabin without any significant changes to the rest of the aircraft. Flat front windows are made of bulletproof glass. The cockpit can be quickly separated and jettisoned from the rest of the aircraft in an emergency.

"The middle part of the fuselage has a rectangular cross section and is covered with flat metal sheets. The fuselage side walls are shielded against radiant heat in areas of higher temperatures. The end of the steel fuselage acts as a partition between the engines located on the sides and carries the tail unit on top."

The radio system was positioned between the cockpit and the fuel tank while the skid struts and control rods were to be housed "in the gussets between the fuselage and the engine". There would be three skids—two up front and one to the rear, all of which lay flush against the underside of the fuselage when retracted.

Inside the cockpit, the pilot got standard fighter-type controls with the engine monitoring gauges, skid extension and trim controls on his left and with radio, bomb release, other electronic controls and oxygen system on his right. Armour plates, 55kg of them in total compared to 42kg on the Bf 109 F, protected him against incoming fire from the front and sides. The canopy was a folding Plexiglas design with "inserted bulletproof glass".

A notable change from the P 79/13b design was the tail unit—which evidently comprised a more conventional single fin and rudder arrangement on the P 79/13c, with the swept tailplane being attached to the fin. The swept wings would be "attached to the fuselage from above and secured by four main fittings". Split flaps would be used for landing and full span leading-edge slats would be provided. A dive brake was to be installed "to enable proper bomb aiming during a dive" but its location was not given.

It seems as though, rather than bulky nacelles, the 500kg thrust engines would be attached directly to the sides of the aircraft using brackets, though they would still be "arranged converging towards the rear on both sides of the fuselage". Ditching the nacelles "enables the engine to be removed quickly and changed. It is also possible to install engines of a different size without making any significant changes to the airframe". Evidently the engines could be started in flight using on-board equipment.

Even though the nacelles were gone, Messerschmitt still believed that additional cooling was necessary and as such "the engines are cooled by a cooling jacket placed around the actual thrust tubes, through which part of the inlet air is passed".

Rather than incorporating a separate fuel tank within the fuselage behind the cockpit, that section of fuselage would be tightly riveted and would become one big fuel tank. In addition, the description notes, "by extending this part of the fuselage forward, it is possible to provide sufficient fuel for greater range. An additional fuel tank can be accommodated under the fuselage in the bomb fairing". The pulsejets would be supplied by four pumps, each capable of providing 1,000 litres per hour.

Electrical power would come from a 2,000W windmill-type generator and the radio antenna would be housed inside the leading edge of the fin. An intercom system linking the P 79's pilot to the crew of the host aircraft would also be provided.

The tiny aircraft—with a wing area of just 7sqm compared to the Bf 109's 16.02sqm—was expected to carry two 1,000-1,800kg bombs (a maximum bomb load of 3,600kg) "which are housed under the fuselage in a detachable fairing. Instead of two bombs, one bomb and an additional fuel tank can be accommodated in such a fairing. A toggle switch is used to operate the bomb drop".

Wing loading without the bombs was 387kg/sqm, or 502kg/sqm with bombs. The Bf 109 F's wing loading, for comparison, was 170kg/sqm. High wing loading is only possible when the aircraft can fly sufficiently fast to avoid a stall, and generally results in reduced manoeuvrability and a high landing speed. Messerschmitt appears to have considered that the ability to outrun enemy interceptors was more important than turning performance—and therefore opted to retain an extremely high wing loading for the P 79.

RIVALRY WITH LIPPISCH

Glider designer Alexander Lippisch, formerly of the DFS, had transferred to Messerschmitt with some of his team on January 2, 1939, where he continued to work on a government project to fit a tailless glider with a rocket motor, known as Projekt X. Though a famous and well-respected professional, indeed, a hero to some, Lippisch certainly appears to have had a special talent for rubbing certain people up the wrong way. He felt he had been forced out

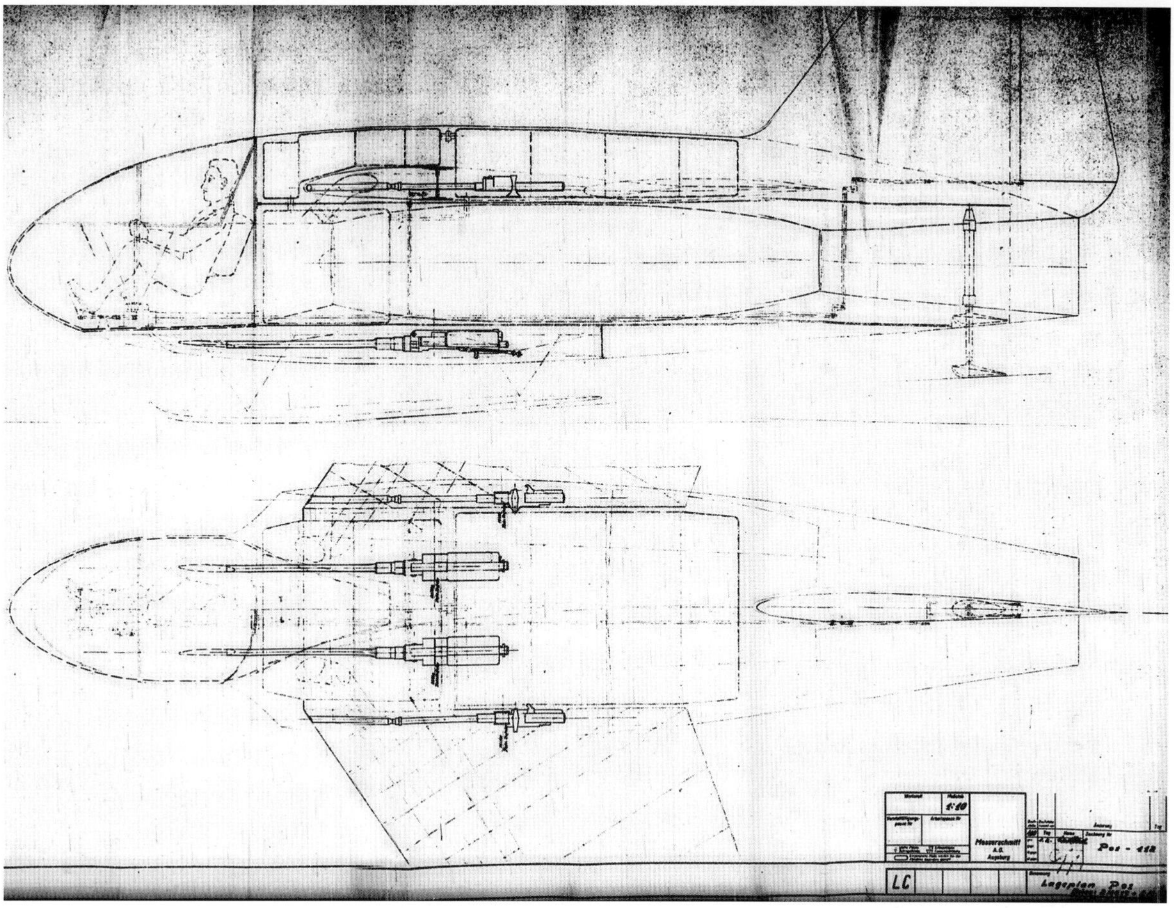

Messerschmitt P 01-112, dated February 1, 1940. A product of Abteilung L, the P 01-112 was effectively a twin-jet competitor for the main Project Office's P 65—the Me 262. Some of its features—such as the cockpit, swept wings and landing skid would be staples of the Project Office's P 79 series more than a year later.

of the DFS by its leader Walter Georgii, his fellow glider designer Hans Jacobs and his former brother-in-law, also a DFS manager, Fritz Stamer. At Messerschmitt, Lippisch was not put to work in the main Project Office, then led by Robert Lusser. Instead, he was allowed to run his own separate design and projects department known as Abteilung L. According to Lippisch's autobiography, Erinnerungen: "We were a sort of secret department, because we were supposed to build and test the rocket-powered experimental aircraft, the aerodynamics of which we had already worked on at the DFS. Of course, the rocket propulsion was strictly secret, so that the whole department had to be housed in a special part of the building with appropriate security at the doors. Since no other room was available at that time, we moved into a large screening room on the top floor of the main building".[24]

Abteilung L received special treatment too, at least initially. According to Lippisch's book: "In the morning a waitress with a large tray would be admitted to our secret room. We would then have the Bavarian-style quite-rich breakfast. This went very well until the commercial director, Mr Kokothaki, accidentally rode in the same elevator as the waitress, with the large tray full of treats for Abteilung L. This resulted in a somewhat excited discussion and my gentlemen then had to eat their breakfast in the canteen."

It wasn't long before a rivalry began to grow between the Project Office under Voigt, Lusser's replacement following his departure shortly after Lippisch's arrival, and Abteilung L. The latter tended to produce tailless alternatives to the Project Office's designs, the twin-jet P 01-112, for example, being a direct if somewhat fanciful competitor for the Me 262. But it also provided support for the Project Office as required on upgrades for in-production types and its main work concerned Projekt X, which was gradually coalescing into the Me 163 rocket-propelled interceptor.

By early August 1941, just as Voigt's team were rounding out their work on P 79, the installation of the first Me 163 prototype's rocket motor began along with preparations for its first powered test flight. This took place on August 13 with test pilot Heini Dittmar at the controls and was reportedly a resounding success. Lippisch at this point intended the Me 163 as a purely experimental prototype to test the concept of a rocket-propelled fighter;

his plan for an in-service interceptor was a larger design designated P 05, the official description of which was published on August 27.[25]

Meanwhile, the head of procurement for the Luftwaffe, Ernst Udet, had evidently witnessed a powered test flight of the Me 163 over the Peenemünde and during a subsequent meeting with Air Ministry Technical Office representative Max Pendele, Technical Office specialist Hans-Martin Antz and Dittmar present, announced a number of decisions[26]—though whether these had been made in response to requests from Lippisch or whether had come up with them himself is unclear. The former seems more likely.

Udet said that Abteilung L should be moved to Obertraubling (most likely to the site of Messerschmitt's Regensburg factory); that "machines designed by Lippisch should be named in such a way that the name Lippisch is expressed", in other words that the 'Me' of 'Me 163' should be replaced by an 'Li' for Lippisch;[27] that construction of the first "machines", presumably production model Me 163s, should be accelerated so they could be put into service in 1942; that "the personnel required by Lippisch for this purpose are provided" and that a description of the aircraft should be handed over to Hermann Göring.

This evidently prompted Willy Messerschmitt to hold a meeting with Lippisch on August 28, during which the two reached "a complete agreement" that Abteilung L would not, in fact, be moved to Obertraubling and would remain in Augsburg. During a meeting on August 29 between the head of the Technical Office Gottfried Reidenbach, Antz and Messerschmitt directors Theo Croneiss and Fritz Hentzen—with neither Lippisch nor Willy Messerschmitt present—Udet's various decisions were discussed and "Mr Antz announced that the Voigt Project Office had now also submitted projects to the Technical Office that were strongly based on the designs of the Lippisch project office. He had received draft P 1079/13c, dated August 11, 1941, [from Voigt] and remarked that although it was not a tailless machine, it was a machine with a strong [wing] sweepback and jet propulsion. Mr Antz further noted that when the project was handed over, Mr Voigt said that this would make further development and construction of the Me 163 and the interceptor [presumably the P 05] superfluous.

"In this regard, Director Hentzen noted that Prof. Messerschmitt considered the strong sweepback of fast aircraft to be necessary based on studies by Prof. [Albert] Betz and had therefore given appropriate instructions for the project planning. Brigade Leader Croneiss said that Prof. Messerschmitt... expressly emphasised that he had prohibited the Voigt Project Office from planning and developing tailless aircraft, as this was and should remain the exclusive area of work of the Lippisch project office."[28]

Based on the testimony supplied by Antz, it would appear that the P 79/13c, here referred to as the P 1079/13c, had been fully fleshed out by August 11. Furthermore, Voigt apparently regarded the design as so promising that it would render the risky[29] Me 163 and P 05-based interceptor unnecessary. It is hard to see Voigt's motive in passing this along to Antz as anything other than an attempt to upstage Abteilung L. At this point Voigt perhaps thought of the pulsejet as his 'silver bullet' in the struggle between the two project offices—its purported light weight, impressive anticipated performance and incredibly cheap construction made it a potential game-changer for the air war, at least until the Allies captured one and copied it.

P 79 PROTOTYPE PLANNING

Little is known of the work that took place on the P 79/P 1079 during the four months between August 11 and December 17, 1941, since no documents on it are known to survive from that period. However, on December 17 a meeting was held at Adlershof in Berlin between Ministry representatives and Messerschmitt's Seitz and Hermann Behrbohm to discuss the P 1079.[30]

Seitz and Behrbohm presented some data on the intended prototype design: wing area was 7.5sqm, wingspan was 6.4m and fully loaded weight was 2,200kg. Two pulsejets providing 150kg thrust each would initially be fitted, later to be swapped for two 250kg thrust models then two 400kg units or possibly four of the 250kg units. Straight line speed with two 250kg units was calculated to be around 700km/h.

Discussion about different load cases followed, along with some consideration being given to ailerons, landing flaps, the air brake, the rudder, the landing skid and the forces generated when the aircraft was being towed by its host aircraft.

For taxiing and take-off, a "probably four-wheeled" dolly, would be provided. Finally, there was some discussion about the aircraft's use as a bomber and essentially "details are not yet known about the use as a bomber".

On December 21, a chart was produced comparing seven designs—five different P 1079s, the Bf 109 F and the Bf 109 D.[31] Three of the P 1079s had a wing area of just 5sqm and differed only in the thrust of their engines. One had two 150kg pulsejets, one a pair of 250kg pulsejets and the third a pair of 400kg pulsejets. These were expected to have top speeds (without bombs and with

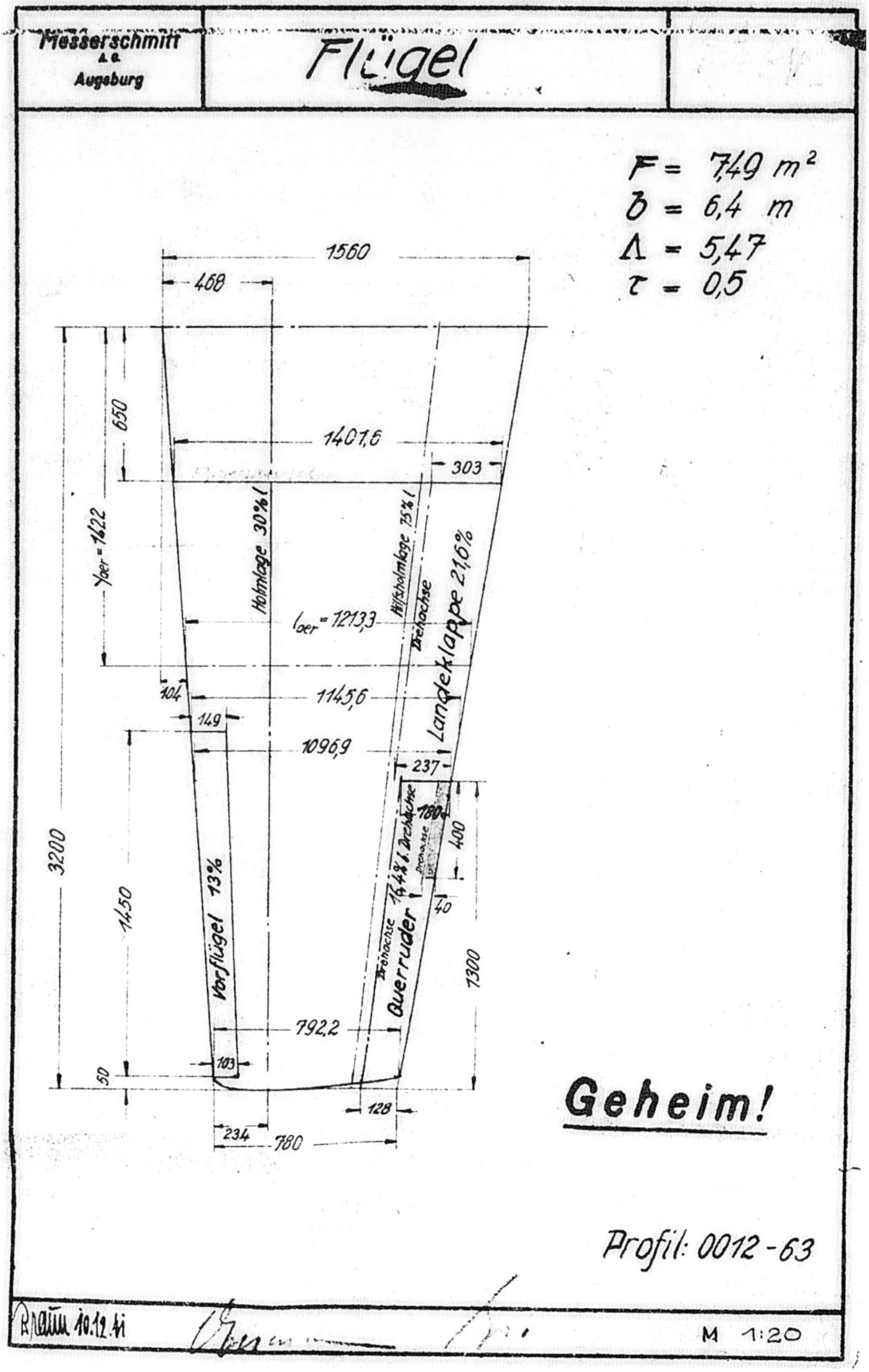

This may be the earliest known drawing of a straight wing associated with the P 79 series—all the original designs having had swept wings. Dated December 10, 1941, its form and dimensions match those of wings appearing on Me 328 designs three and a half months later.

half fuel) of 630km/h, 835km/h and 1,060km/h respectively at sea level, dropping a little to 590km/h, 820km/h and 1,055km/h at an altitude of 4,000m. Evidently the 2x150kg design was incapable of carrying any substantial bomb load but the other two could carry 1,400kg of bombs. The result of doing so was a drop in top speed to 530km/h for the 2x250kg design and 725km/h for the 2x400kg design.

The other two P 1079s were different versions of the first prototype: the 7.5sqm wing area P 1079 V1. One version had two 150kg pulsejets while the other was to be equipped with two 250kg pulsejets. Top speeds at ground level were 585km/h and 765km/h, the bigger wing having robbed the aircraft of 45km/h and 70km/h respectively.

Comparative values for the Bf 109 D weren't given but the Bf 109 F powered by a DB 601 E, with a wing area of 16.1sqm, was said to be capable of 526km/h at ground level and 614km/h at 4km altitude. This meant that even powered by the weakest projected pulsejets, the P 1079 still ought to be significantly faster than the Luftwaffe's latest standard fighter.

It is noteworthy that all pulsejets mentioned on the chart were Argus, rather than Schmidt, models.

The Air Ministry prototypes production schedule of February 1, 1942, listed three P 1079s—V1, V2 and V3. The first was scheduled for completion in June 1942, the second in August and the third in October.[32] An appended note read: "Project completed. In construction." By February 3, 1942, discussions were taking place at Messerschmitt about the delivery of equipment for the three aircraft.[33]

A week later, on February 10, Voigt signed off on a specification document for the "Me 328 (P 79)" prototypes.[34] This is the earliest known use of Me 328 as the official Air Ministry designation for what had been the P 79/P 1079, the Ministry having presumably now given Messerschmitt a contract to produce the trio of prototypes.

In its "guidelines for construction", the document also made it clear that the Me 328's role was that of a parasite fighter and "in view of the task ... low construction weight is required. The design must be suitable for mass production ... A later conversion to a pressurized cabin is to be expected. A fuselage extension for the purpose of increasing the size of the fuel tank in front of or behind the cockpit must be possible.

"The engine installation should be designed in such a way that it is possible to easily replace them with larger engines as well as to arrange several engines under, and in certain circumstances above, the wing".

The fuselage would be made from steel in three sections, the tailplanes would be lifted directly from the Bf 109 F production line and the fin would be made out of wood. Two fuel tanks would need to contain a minimum of 200 litres each. Maximum take-off weight was just 1,000kg.

In terms of equipment, the Me 328 V1 would have a coupling at the front for fixed towing and a "carrying tow coupling" at or above the centre of gravity for 'parasite' launch tests. A radio system was "desirable" and the fuel pump would be powered by a Seppeler GW.1 propeller generator and two batteries. Under the "not required" section were "weapons capability, bomb attachment point, armour, ejection seat".

Instrumentation in the cockpit included an airspeed indicator, an altimeter, variometer, clock, fuel gauge and possibly also a fuel pressure gauge. Engine monitoring gauges were "not required (information from Argus)".

DFS BROUGHT ON BOARD

Voigt's February 10, 1942, specification document is the earliest evidence of the DFS's involvement with the Me 328. It sets out a division of labour in building the prototypes between Messerschmitt and the DFS at Ainring. The former would manufacture the fully equipped and fitted out fuselage along with the skid and take-off dolly and the ready-made Bf 109 F tailplanes. The latter would manufacture and supply the wooden wings, including all flaps, ailerons and slots, the engine attachment points on those wings and the wooden tail fin. A deadline of April 10, 1942, had been given for delivery of the first set of wings complete with engine fittings and fin.

Testing of the Me 328 was divided into two parts—preliminary testing and flight testing. The preliminary work was to investigate "the most favourable engine arrangement with regard to cooling and drag when mounted under the wings (preliminary tests at Argus and the DFS, using information supply by Messerschmitt AG)" and to test the Seppeler generator at speeds greater than 500km/h.

Flight testing would be split between Messerschmitt and the DFS. Messerschmitt would test the aircraft's flight characteristics "take-off using normal tow, on dolly, tow machine probably a Bf 110" while the DFS would "test the applicability of the various towing procedures (general towing, towed take-off, towed landing, reattaching in flight, refuelling in flight etc.), towing machine He 111 H-6".

Finally, the specification gave some 'organisational guidelines': "The novelty of the task (parasite aircraft in fixed or towed mode), the novelty of the engines used and the partial outsourcing of the design and construction of the airframe to subcontractors require extremely close cooperation between all parties in view of the deadlines set. To ensure that everything runs smoothly, Mr Seitz from the Project Office is employed as a type supervisor."

It is perhaps an indication of the general situation at Messerschmitt during early 1942 that this plan fell apart almost immediately. The following day, the Me 328 production schedule was handed to Willy Messerschmitt by company inter-departmental liaison officer Kaiser, "and it was pointed out that the timely construction of the skid with dolly, the towing device, equipment and the in-fuselage engine systems (fuel tank and operating system) has not yet been secured. It fails essentially due to the lack of work capacity available within the individual processing groups.

"I therefore once again suggested that we might consider outsourcing the fuselage design and construction to the DFS, especially since, according to a recent announcement from the DFS, the V1 would be expected to be completed at the end of April. For the well-known reasons (avoiding duplication of work), Prof. Messerschmitt forbade any discussion of this proposal and demanded that [work allocated to] all other construction groups (i.e. apart from the fuselage) that we could not meet the schedule on time should be assigned to the DFS".[35]

This terse response from the company chairman evidently led to a meeting the following day, February 12, between Kaiser, Seitz and an assortment of Messerschmitt construction office representatives.

The stated purpose of this was "to clarify the start of work [on the Me 328], the dates and the allocation of work for the still unplanned construction groups, skid with dolly, towing device, equipment and the engine system in the fuselage (fuel and operating system)". Willy Messerschmitt having already opened the door to the offloading of additional work to the DFS, this is exactly what happened.[36]

The construction documents for the nose-mounted towing attachment point would be handed over to the DFS within a week. The skid and "a simple starter car" for the Me 328 V1 would still be built at Messerschmitt, final delivery being scheduled for March 20, but "the final launch vehicle for the aircraft with bomb and skid will be awarded to the DFS for design and production with the deadline for the V2 parts from the DFS being May 1, 1942". The Seppeler generator would go directly to the DFS so they could design and build its wing attachment point. The question of who should construct the fuel tank system could not be clarified because the head of Messerschmitt's propulsion group, Werner Beese, was unavailable.

But even this wasn't enough. The Messerschmitt company was buckling under the weight of all the tasks it was expected to complete. Five days after Kaiser's meeting, Reidenbach at the Ministry's Technical Office wrote to Willy Messerschmitt, saying that "the DFS has announced, following a discussion with the Messerschmitt company, that all constructive and structural work on the three prototype P 1079 aircraft will now be carried out at the DFS in Ainring.

"I agree to this, but ask you to have the work in progress at Ainring supervised by the gentlemen in your Project Office. In view of the final purposes and types of use of the P 1079, which still need to be clarified, I think it is right to design these three experimental aircraft as simply as possible, i.e. in tubular steel and wooden construction. This also makes it possible to produce this aircraft using the production and operating resources available at DFS and to relieve the burden on your factory's prototype construction department. Furthermore, I will try to speed up the work in Ainring by temporarily providing a few designers who have experience in this construction method".[37]

Willy Messerschmitt wrote a short letter back to Reidenbach on February 24 to clarify the situation: "We have agreed with the DFS that they will design and build as many parts of the above-mentioned aircraft [Me 328] as possible, under the supervision of a gentleman from our Project Office. We only design and build the fuselage and the landing skid. These parts were already too advanced [in construction], so switching to DFS Ainring would have led to an unnecessary delay."[38]

These brief discussions concerning a lack of capacity to build the Me 328 at Messerschmitt were very much a sideshow to the storm enveloping the company at this time. Its two main factories—Augsburg and Regensburg—had been embroiled in an increasingly bitter dispute about who would have to build the Bf 109's intended successor, the Me 309, during the autumn and early winter of 1941-42, neither eager to begin the establishment of a whole new production line.

Worse still, work on the firm's Bf 110 replacement, the Me 210, had been going badly wrong since the autumn of 1941. The type had been ordered into full series production before its developmental difficulties had been resolved and pilots were discovering that the early examples retained potentially lethal flaws. These included unpredictable stall behaviour, unexplained engine fires and a tendency to flip onto its back while taxying. With questions now being asked at the highest levels of government about Messerschmitt's apparent inability to fix the Me 210, the company was pouring its resources into the twin-engine type, to the detriment of its other projects including the Me 309, Me 262—and Me 328.

2

LIGHT FIGHTER AND MULTIROLE: MARCH 1942 TO AUGUST 1942

THE ME 210 programme may have been teetering on the brink of total collapse throughout March 1942—and threatening to drag the rest of the Messerschmitt company down with it—but the Project Office was still able to continue mapping out the Me 328's future development path.

A new report was issued on March 31, 1942, entitled Flugzeuge mit Strahlrohren—the exact same title given to the August 1, 1941, report which had outlined the early work carried out on P 79/P 1079.[1] Rather than focusing on the Me 328 as a single fixed airframe, ready for production as a fighter, a bomber or a fighter-bomber, this emphasised the type's fluid design and adaptability to different roles through radical changes in its layout.

The preface noted that "pulsejets, which have been in development for around two years, are used for the first time on the Me 328 aircraft" and gave six reasons why building a pulsejet-powered aircraft was a good idea: significantly better performance than piston engine aircraft; quick and easy to manufacture; low engine weight allowing for a small aircraft and reduced cost in materials; the engines' development potential for higher thrust; the opportunity to build it in large numbers before the enemy could copy it; and the immediate usability of the engine in its existing form.

The report went on: "In order to take the lowest possible risk with regard to flight characteristics, the shape and arrangement of the wing and tail unit were adopted from known aircraft; in order to avoid any problems in terms of cooling, the engines were arranged on the wing and the construction of the airframe was kept as simple as possible.

Regarding the "technical aspects" of the project, "because of their extremely low weight (an engine with 150kg thrust weighs 47kg), the pulsejets allow the development of relatively small aircraft with extremely high performance. The higher specific fuel consumption of the pulsejets is largely offset by the low weight of the airframe.

"From flight speeds of 750km/h upwards, aircraft with piston engines become less economical than aircraft with pulsejets if they are designed for the same landing speed."

Somewhat buried amid all this positivity, however, came the first sign from Voigt's team that pulsejets might not actually be the miracle solution to an incredibly cheap high-performance aircraft that they might initially have appeared to be: "TL engines (turbojet engines) are clearly superior to pulsejets and at all speeds."

After this rather incongruous bullet point, which failed to elaborate on exactly why turbojets were so superior, the praise for pulsejets continued unabated: "In addition to the performance side, the pulsejet also has the advantage of being extremely low cost: a piston engine, for example for the Me 109, is estimated to take around 8,000 construction hours, propeller and adjustment system not included; irrespective of the performance difference, pulsejets require less than 100 working hours to make.

"The construction hours required for turbojets cannot yet be precisely estimated, but will not be significantly lower than for piston engines. The number of hours required to build a single-engine aircraft (without equipment) is reduced to around a third when using pulsejets, an advantage that will have a decisive influence on the aircraft industry, especially during the war. Further advantages of the pulsejet include: low sensitivity to battle damage, easy maintenance and easy handling".

MULTIROLE ME 328

The report suggested four roles for the Me 328: fighter, bomber, parasite fighter and reconnaissance platform but "due to its high performance, the aircraft is particularly suitable as a fighter. Version I [Ausführung I] has a wing area of 7.5sqm and a fixed armament of 2 x MG 151; two pulsejets with 300kg thrust each are provided for propulsion, which will initially be replaced by four pulsejets of 150kg thrust each on the first prototypes. Take-off initially takes place on a jettisonable trolley and landing takes place on a skid. A wheeled undercarriage can be retrofitted later.

"Version II has an optional bigger wing with 12sqm area and has increased armament (additionally 2 x MK 105, 1 x MG 151 to the rear), four pulsejets with 300kg thrust each are provided. The range of both versions can be significantly increased by increasing the size of the fuel tank using a fuselage extension".

Either version could be used as a bomber if required. Version I would need booster rockets to take off but Version II, with 1,200kg total thrust from its quartet of engines, wouldn't.

When it came to using the Me 328 as a parasite fighter—attached to, towed by, or carried within a host bomber—Version I "meets the requirements ... due to its small dimensions (about half the size of the Me 109) and its low weight. For such an operation, the aircraft is fitted with a towing device to connect it to the parent aircraft (Fw 200, He 177, Me 264). By reattaching and refuelling in flight (in principle already clarified through tests), multiple uses are possible during a mission.

"The [anticipated] final form of the [parasite fighter] airframe is to have an even smaller wing area; a decision will only be made once the test results with the 7.5sqm wing area are available. The weight of the parasite fighter with enough fuel for half an hour at full throttle is around 1,650kg.

"As a parasite bomber, the aircraft can be towed for long distances to be brought within 150-200km of the target; it can then carry out independent attacks with the heaviest bombs (e.g. SD 1400) and then be brought home by the parent aircraft. In addition, the aircraft can be taken on merchant ships and submarines and, due to its low weight, can be launched from on board without much effort. The landing takes place on the skid in the water, after which the aircraft is taken back on board."

As far as reconnaissance was concerned, Version II could "be easily converted into an armed, high-speed reconnaissance aircraft".

Structurally, "the Me 328 airframe is constructed as simply as possible (fuselage with a circular cross-section, continuous wings, engine suspended under the wing, etc.). The fuselage structure is chosen in such a way that it is possible at any time to insert a cylindrical fuselage spacer without any other significant changes and thus approximately double the fuel tank capacity. The installation of armoured fuel tanks is possible at any time. The engine is arranged in such a way that it can be replaced with a more powerful one with virtually no modification. It is also possible to arrange several engines next to or on top of each other. The aircraft can also be optionally equipped with wings of different sizes".

PROTOTYPES ON ORDER

An update on the status of the Me 328's practical development was also included in the report—divided into 'airframe' and 'engine'. Under airframe, it stated "the Technical Office originally commissioned Messerschmitt AG to build three prototypes corresponding to the fighter Version I, with the design and construction of the wing and fin being awarded to DFS Ainring. The number of prototype machines was later increased to ten, all of which were to be built using a simple design by DFS Ainring. These prototypes are intended to test the aircraft's general characteristics, the towing process, re-attachment and refuelling in flight, the influence of extremely high wing loading, swept wings, fixed and dropped weapons.

"At Messerschmitt AG, the construction of the fuselage (sheet steel) including the internals is essentially completed, and a design attempt for the fuselage is already under construction. At DFS the wing is already under construction, the fin and [another] fuselage (steel tube/wood) are still under construction; the tail plane is taken over from the Me 109."

The first prototype was expected to be ready for flight testing by May 1, 1942. In addition, "attempts are being made to improve both the sheet steel construction used at Messerschmitt AG and the fuselage construction chosen

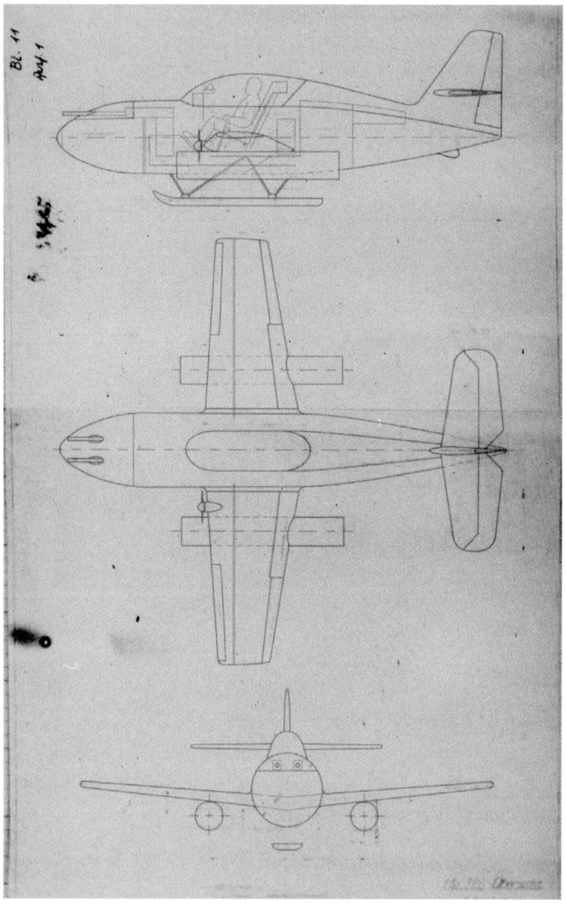

Me 328 Jäger Ausführung I from the report of March 31, 1942. This is the classic low-wing, twin-pulsejet, skid-landing Me 328 V1 type design, albeit fitted with a pair of MG 151/20s.

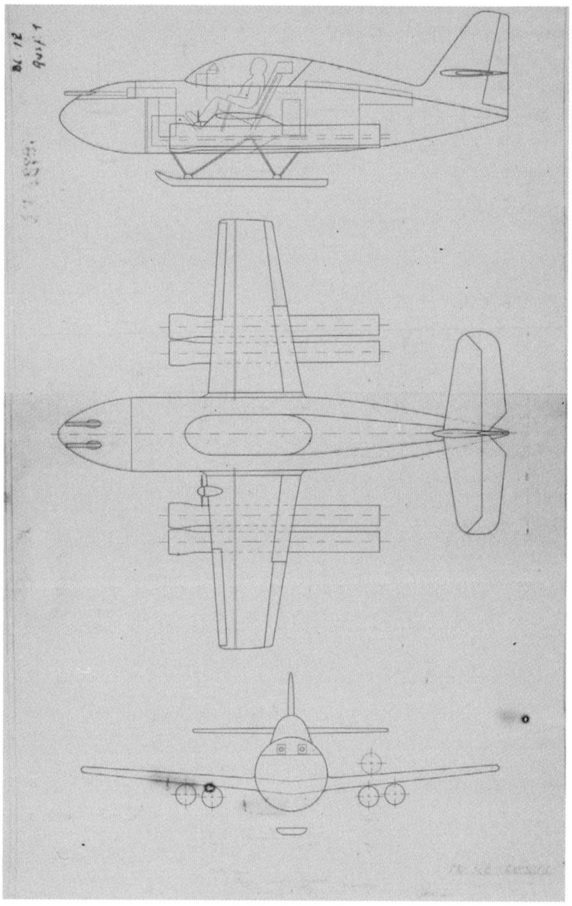

Me 328 Jäger Ausführung I with four pulsejets rather than just two. The forward view appears to suggest that an arrangement with six pulsejets—an additional one above each wing—was also considered.

by DFS so that a larger series of parts can be based directly on to the prototypes."

Under engine, the report stated: "Engines with 150kg thrust available immediately, service life (due to valve springs) proven to be two hours; engines are continually undergoing flight testing. Engines with 300kg thrust are being developed and will be available in a few months.

"The testing has so far taken place smoothly and without any setbacks; of course, it is still to be expected that difficulties will arise during testing on a broader basis, which could limit the use of the engines, postpone it or possibly prohibit it. On the other hand, in our opinion, the mere fact that real mass production of aircraft and engines is possible for the first time on this new basis makes it necessary to advance development with a view to [their] early use."

TEN ME 328S

A data sheet rounded out the written part of the report, providing dimensions and other details of six variants: Fighter Version I, Bomber Version I, Fighter Version I with extended fuselage, Fighter Version II, Bomber Version II and reconnaissance. All variants were single-seaters and all were to be powered by Argus-made pulsejets. The first three had a total thrust of 660kg each. The last three had a total thrust of 1,320kg each. None of the designs quite corresponded to those outlined earlier on in the text.

Fighter Version I had a wingspan of 6.4m and wing area of 7.5sqm. It was 6.83m long and stood 2.1m high. Armament was two MG 151/20s with 200 rounds each. Fuel capacity was 740 litres and top speed was given as 755km/h at sea level or 745km/h at 4km altitude.

Bomber Version I also had a wingspan of 6.4m and the same wing area and length. It was 2.5m high—presumably to accommodate the bomb underneath—and had both the same internal armament and fuel capacity. Top speed while carrying 500kg of bombs was 680km/h at sea level or 665km/h at 4km altitude.

Fighter Version I with Extended Fuselage was 8.63m long, boosting its fuel capacity to 1,520 litres but was otherwise the same as Fighter Version I.

Fighter Version II had a wingspan of 8.5m and wing

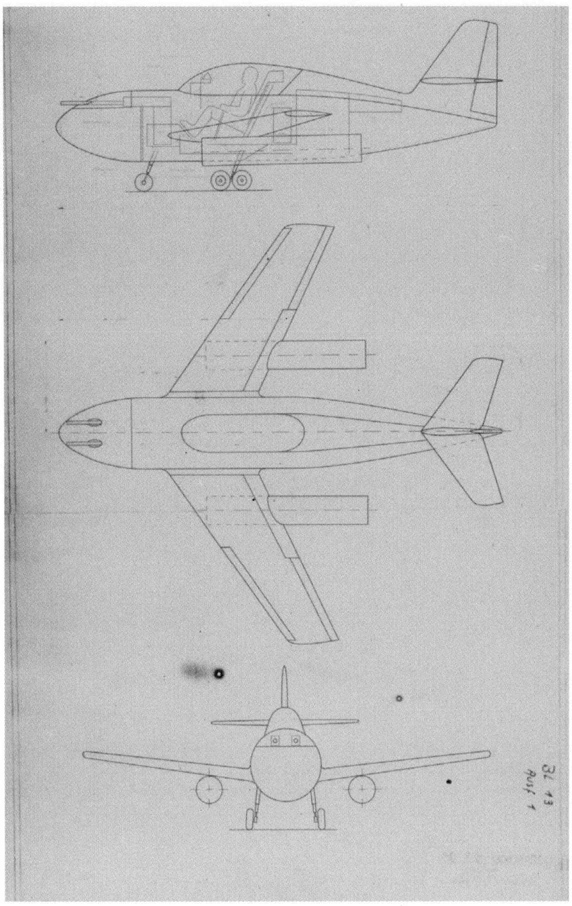

A third variant of Jäger Ausführung I but now with swept wings and tailplanes as well as a highly unusual six-wheeled undercarriage.

area of 12sqm. It was 8.63m long and 2.1m high. Armament was three MG 151/20s with 200 rounds each, plus two MK 105 cannon with 50 rounds each. Fuel capacity was 1,520 litres and top speed was given as 920km/h at sea level or 915km/h at 4km.

Bomber Version II had mostly the same dimensions and fuel capacity as Fighter Version II but was 2.5m high—again, probably to account for the 1,000kg of bombs attached to the fuselage underside. It was armed with just the standard two MG 151/20s and top speed at sea level was 800km/h and 790km/h at 4km.

The reconnaissance type had exactly the same dimensions as Fighter Version II but only the pair of MG 151/20s for armament. Internal fuel load was reduced to 1,140kg to allow room for the camera bay. Its performance, however, was unsurprisingly the best of the bunch at 928km/h sea level and 922km/h at 4km.

The report was 15 pages long and the last six pages each featured a three-view drawing of an Me 328 variant. But only two of these can reasonably be said to depict any of the six variants just outlined—and the drawings as they appear in the only known surviving copy of the document are badly faded. Inexplicably, all six have "Ausf. 1" written on them and the title of each within the drawing itself is given simply as "Me 328—Übersicht" or 'overview'. Most of the remainder of the text detail is too far gone to make out.

It is clear from looking at the designs that much additional work was carried out on the basic twin-engine P 79/13 template of eight months earlier, though little to none of that interim work is known to have survived in any detail. Every Me 328 design has a nose compartment for weaponry and/or fuel, a little more reminiscent of P 79/1 and /4 than P 79/13. This was presumably for centre of gravity reasons. In addition, all powered Me 328 designs feature freely suspended pulsejets that are clearly separated from the fuselage and positioned to point directly forwards. Finally, the curved fuselage appears to have the most in common with P 79/17 of all the P 79 designs. In short, the somewhat fanciful concept designs of August 1941 had been distilled, refined and methodically reworked into a much simpler and more practical aircraft series by March 1942.

Page 11 shows Fighter Version I—looking very much as the 'classic' twin-engine 'Me 328 A', essentially the Me 328 V1 or Me 328 V02, is commonly understood to look today, except for the long barrels of its MG 151/20s protruding from the tip of its nose. Its wings are straight, its tailplane is labelled "Me 109" (perhaps the only annotation in any of the drawings that can actually be read) and it has a lone Seppeler generator attached to its port wing root.

Page 12 depicts Fighter Version I but with four pulsejets, two under each wing. In fact, the front view faintly shows another pulsejet, positioned on top of the port wing directly above the inboard underwing engine. None of the text within the report mentions a four- or even six-engine short-fuselage Me 328, making it a unique variant. And the pulsejet units themselves are much longer than those shown in the drawing of Fighter Version I, with a wider inlet tapering slightly into a slender tube. None of the other five drawings show this pulsejet type.

Page 13 features another unique iteration of Fighter Version I. The propulsion system is back to just two pulsejets—but now suspended beneath swept-back wings. The Bf 109 tailplane is gone, replaced with a swept unit, and perhaps most unusually of all a six-wheeled undercarriage is fitted. Rather than a nosewheel and mainwheels, the Page 13 design has four struts, two on either side, with a single small wheel attached to each strut at the front and two identically sized wheels attached to each strut at the back. No indication is given of how these wheels were supposed to retract, if they were supposed to retract.

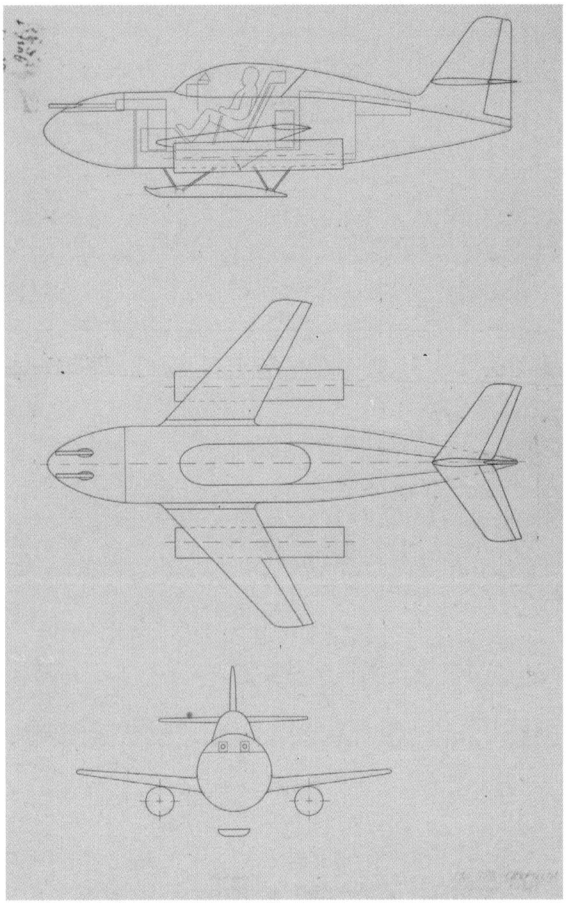

Extremely small swept wings were shown on the fourth and final version of the Jäger Ausführung I design depicted in the March 31, 1942 report. This time the standard landing skid was shown.

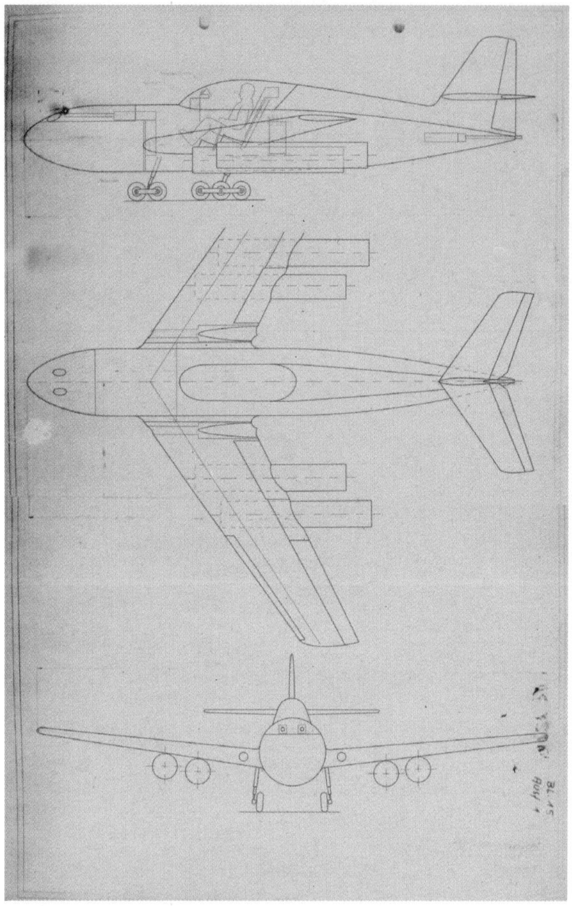

Me 328 Jäger Ausführung II had long swept wings and a stretched fuselage, MK 105 cannon in its wing roots, two MG 151/20s in its nose and a third in its tail pointing rearwards — not to mention a ten-wheeled undercarriage.

Perhaps they were to be jettisoned on take-off—but if so, no supplemental skid is depicted.

Page 14 goes back to the Fighter Version I design again, including the skid this time, but now fitted with incredibly short swept wings and narrower swept tailplanes than those shown on Page 13. Another unique design, this perhaps represents the ideal parasite fighter—with wings too short for independent takeoff on the ground but just long enough to effect operations and reattachment to the host aircraft.

Page 15 shows Fighter Version II—perhaps the most optimistic expression of the Me 328's development potential ever committed to paper. The extended fuselage is immediately apparent, as are the long swept wings with a total of four pulsejets attached. The supplemental MK 105 cannon are installed in the wing roots and, visible in the side view, the third MG 151/20 is housed in the tail, pointing rearwards. The two fixed forward-firing MG 151/20s are now accommodated within a nose so long that their barrels no longer protrude. The potentially non-retractable wheeled undercarriage is again part of the design but with two wheels on each front strut and three on each rear strut for a total of ten wheels.

Page 16 shows Fighter Version II without the supplemental armament, which could make it a depiction of the reconnaissance type, but there is no indication in the admittedly faded surviving drawing of any camera equipment being installed.

Meanwhile, on April 8, 1942, the DFS began conducting a lengthy series of wind tunnel tests on an Me 328 model that would be reconfigured over time to reflect a wide range of different potential fuselage and wing lengths, engine positions, aerodynamic aids and more.[2] The stated goal of these tests was to "find the most favourable position and arrangement of the engines ... in addition measurements were taken with a bomb form and with external fuel tanks attached to the wingtips. The tailplane effectiveness was examined at three different height positions".

THE ME 210 DISASTER

Just six days before the publication of the new Flugzeuge mit Strahlrohren report, on March 25, 1942, Willy Messerschmitt had used the factory public address system at

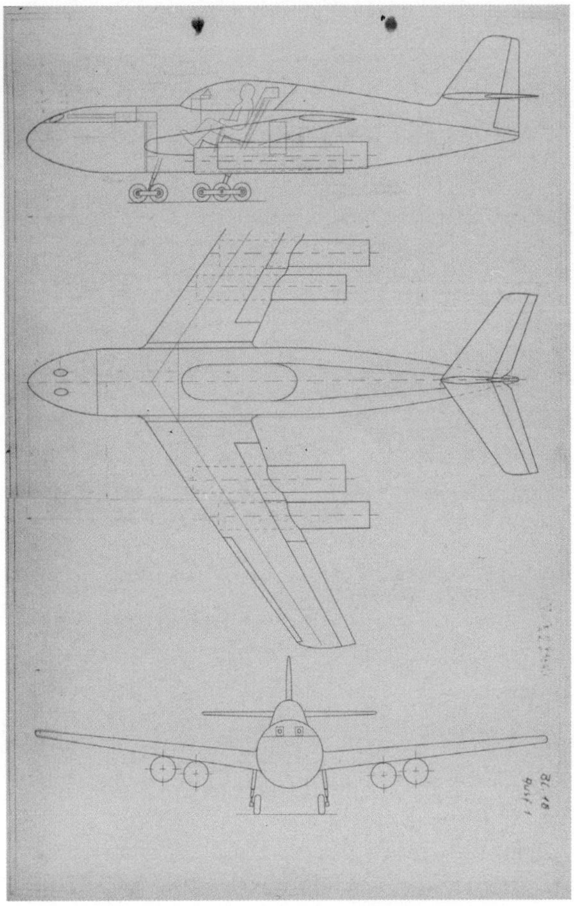

A second, lighter, version of Me 328 Jäger Ausführung II, minus the wing root and rearward-facing weapons.

Augsburg to reassure his workers that rumours he had "fallen out of favour" with Göring thanks to the Me 210 situation were entirely false.[3] However, a fortnight after the report's publication, on April 14, during the Air Ministry management meeting,[4] Luftwaffe chief engineer Generalstabsingenieur Roluf Lucht suggested that the best way to avert the Me 210 crisis would be to "take the management [away] from [Willy] Messerschmitt". Head of Luftwaffe procurement Generalluftzeugmeister Erhard Milch, who had taken over from Udet following the latter's suicide on November 17, 1941, replied: "You don't have to worry… in the worst case, I will confiscate the plant and assign Messerschmitt to a general manager. Nowadays that is easily possible."

He then arranged a meeting with the chairman of the Messerschmitt company's supervisory board, Friedrich Seiler, to discuss it.

On April 19, Göring ordered the cancellation of the Me 210.[5] At around the same time, Lucht travelled to Augsburg and personally informed Willy Messerschmitt that he was being removed from the chairmanship of his own company.[6]

As a notorious micromanager, Messerschmitt had been at the heart of all decision-making at his company—whether it concerned design, development, construction, production or even staffing—and Milch's decision to have him removed led to chaos and paralysis within Germany's main source of fighter aircraft. The cancellation of the Me 210 was also financially disastrous for Messerschmitt as a company, apparently pushing it towards bankruptcy.[7] And on April 30 Messerschmitt's board of directors unanimously decided that "Professor Willy Messerschmitt will carry out his duties as senior design engineer of the company for the duration of the war". Croneiss became chief executive and operations director for the Augsburg works, while Seiler became chairman of the board.[8]

The Ministry meeting on May 5 then heard from Luftwaffe test centres chief Edgar Petersen that a design change conceived and implemented by Willy Messerschmitt prior to his censure—extending the Me 210's fuselage—had actually resulted in a dramatic improvement.[9] Milch conceded that he had "received a letter in which I was told that the flight characteristics of the aircraft were absolutely perfect, despite the high speed".

Milch then reported to Göring on May 9 that "the flight characteristics of the Me 210 were correct due to the lengthened fuselage and modification of the tail unit and the installation of slots".[10] Luftwaffe Chief of Staff Hans Jeschonnek said his staff would immediately test the modified Me 210 and Göring then "postponed the order to dismantle the Me 210 until the test results were received". Despite everything, Messerschmitt had solved the problem and the Me 210, following a redesignation to Me 410, would now go on to enter front line service.

ONE LAST ME 328 DESIGNER

While all eyes may have been on the Me 210 and the fate of Willy Messerschmitt, yet another production programme being run by his company had been struggling and this would have a direct impact on the Me 328.

Croneiss had been summoned to appear before the Air Ministry managers meeting on May 19, 1942, to discuss the Me 323 powered transport glider.[11]

He opened his speech to the assembled Ministry men by saying that he could not guarantee the scheduled delivery of the first five Me 323s in July 1942 because testing had not been fully completed and because the company's Regensburg facility had a shortage of alloys.

He said that repeated requests for more materials had been sent to the Ministry and "in order to ensure timely series production, I shut down the Me 328 and 329 design office in Augsburg from yesterday and reallocated the designers to the 323, with one exception, to Leipheim. There are 10 designers."

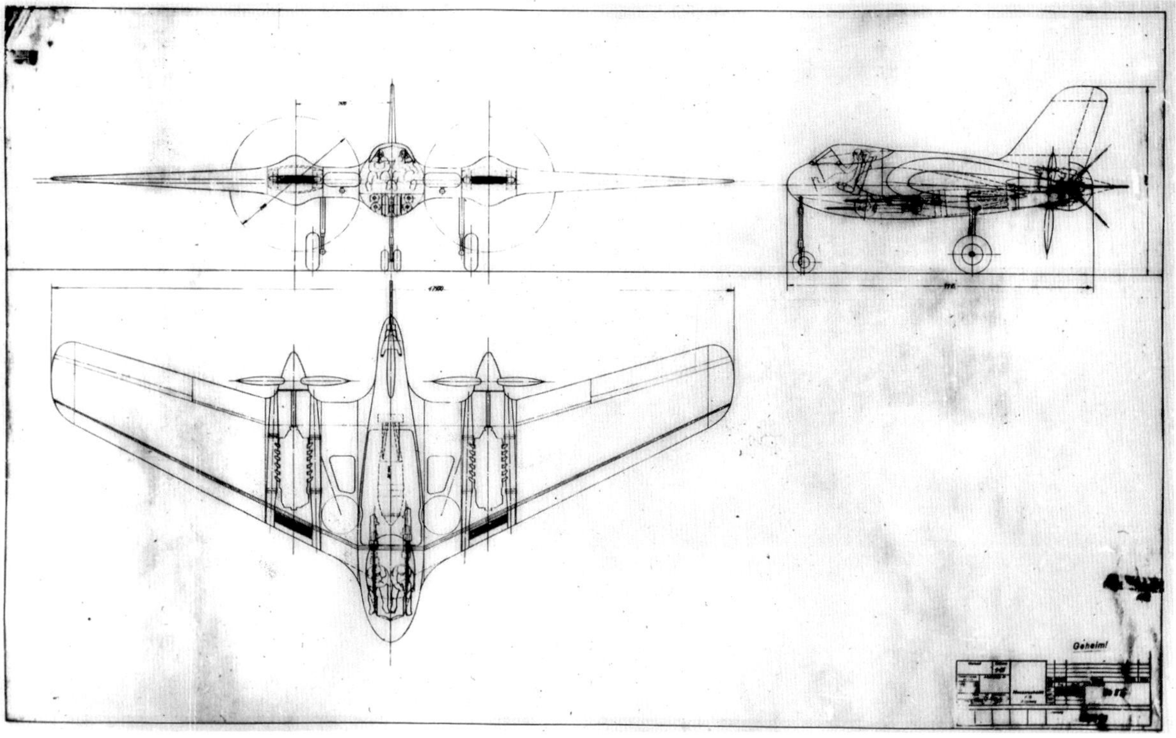

The Messerschmitt Me 329 fighter-bomber, an Abteilung L competitor for the Me 210 which, alongside the Me 328, had its design team stripped away in May 1942 to support the ailing Me 323 programme.

Milch asked what the Me 328 and 329 were, and Croneiss described the Me 328 as a parasite aircraft and the Me 329 as a development of the Me 210 which "has incredibly thick wings, so that there are now concerns that it will be too slow and that as a result we will have to abandon this programme altogether".[12]

Precisely who the sole designer left to work on both the Me 328 and Me 329 was is unclear, but it seems likely that it was Rudolf Seitz. Less than a month after Croneiss's decision to strip designers from the Me 328 to prop up the Me 323, on June 15, Seitz produced a new report which reiterated much that had appeared previously in Flugzeuge mit Strahlrohren on March 31.

The Me 328's potential roles were now cited as bomber first, then light fighter, parasite fighter, long-range fighter and reconnaissance aircraft. Describing the bomber variant, Seitz wrote: "The type is specially designed for heavy bombing daytime attacks (e.g. [using] SD 1400) on heavily defended targets (these are made possible by the increased speed of about 700 to 950km/h, which is significantly higher than the performance of current fighters with piston engines)."

Of the fighter variant, he wrote: "The aircraft type is able to use its high performance in unchanged form [i.e. unchanged from the bomber] as a fighter. Due to the twin-engine version, the large range (with large fuel tanks the range has been calculated as 1,400km) can be fully utilised even when flown over the sea. For use as a parasite fighter a towing device (rigid towing) for connection to the host aircraft Fw 200, He 177, Me 264 is provided. The reattachment during flight is has been shown to work by preliminary tests. The weight of the parasite fighter with fuel for half an hour's flight at full throttle is about 1,650kg."

As usual, very little ink was expended on describing the reconnaissance variant: "Employment as an extremely high-speed reconnaissance aircraft is possible with suitable equipment."

Under 'features', Seitz went back over the "high performance" to be expected from pulsejets and how cheap they were to make. He stated that sufficient wing area had been provided for a normal (non-towed) take-off in the light fighter role, after which the wheeled undercarriage would be jettisoned, followed by a skid landing. When used as a long-range fighter or bomber, launch would require a Madelung catapult or a towed take-off behind a Bf 110, He 111, or similar piston engine aircraft. The Me 328's fuel tank would normally hold 1,000 litres but the fuselage extension could feasibly double this.

Fixed armament was still planned—two MG 151s—and the ideal bomb load would be a single SD 1400. The original plan to allow the inclusion of a pressure cabin at some point had now been dropped entirely "for reasons of simplification and time saving".

The DFS flight-tested a pair of Argus pulsejets beneath the wings of a DFS 230 glider. Even at this early stage, concerns were expressed about the radiant heat and strong vibrations produced by the engines.

A table was included which compared an Me 328 powered by two 400kg thrust pulsejets against a DB 605-powered Bf 109 G and a DB 601 F-powered Me 210, showing that the Me 328 was expected to wipe the floor with both of them performance-wise: 885km/h top speed at 6,000m altitude compared to 660km/h for the 109 and 587km/h for the 210, for example.

Under 'development status', Seitz claimed that 150kg thrust pulsejets had "completed continuous running [tests] with two hours at full throttle without problems" and "flight testing of the engines up to 550km/h at 6,000m altitude has been carried out". The engine with 400kg thrust was still "in development".

Regarding airframes, three prototypes with sheet steel fuselages were apparently under construction at Messerschmitt, to be provided with wings and tailfins by the DFS and "the design documentation is arranged so that a larger production series can be based directly on the prototypes". The first of these was expected to be ready to fly at the beginning of July 1942. In addition, the DFS was still expected to produce ten further prototypes, two of which were currently under construction. These too were expected to be airworthy by early July.

DFS 230 WITH PULSEJETS

Few records have survived regarding Argus's pulsejet-testing regime, though numerous test vehicles are thought to have been employed—including a Bf 109 with the engine being attached beneath its fuselage.[13] Exactly when the DFS installed a pair of the company's pulsejets beneath the wings of a DFS 230 glider for testing is similarly unclear. However, Messerschmitt test pilot Karl Baur made two flights in it at Ainring on July 3, 1942.[14]

His terse post-flight report stated: "An Argus tube at a distance of approx. 40cm below wing, shielded from the wooden surface by a light metal sheet. Monitoring devices in the cockpit: a control valve with a pressure gauge to regulate the injection pressure; a switch for start ignition; a lever for quick or emergency release.

"Result: The aircraft was towed at a speed of 140km/h behind an He 45 to 600m. At this altitude the speed was increased to 180km/h and the engines were started one after the other as follows: the injection pressure was set to 0.8-1 atmospheres and the ignition was switched on. The power levers were then pushed all the way forward and the engines began to work. The noise of both engines corresponds in volume to two running engines in the Bf 110. The airframe is subjected to fairly hard vibrations.

"After just a few minutes of operation, both pipes are glowing red; the heat can be felt in the cabin—apparently due to radiation. With 100% power the aircraft can be flown horizontally at 110km/h. This corresponds to a thrust of approx. 90kg per device. The target performance is 150kg. The power jump using the power levers is far too large and, since there is no thrust monitoring device, the engines cannot be regulated for practical operation. The performance can be adjusted a little more precisely by changing the injection pressure using the control valve.

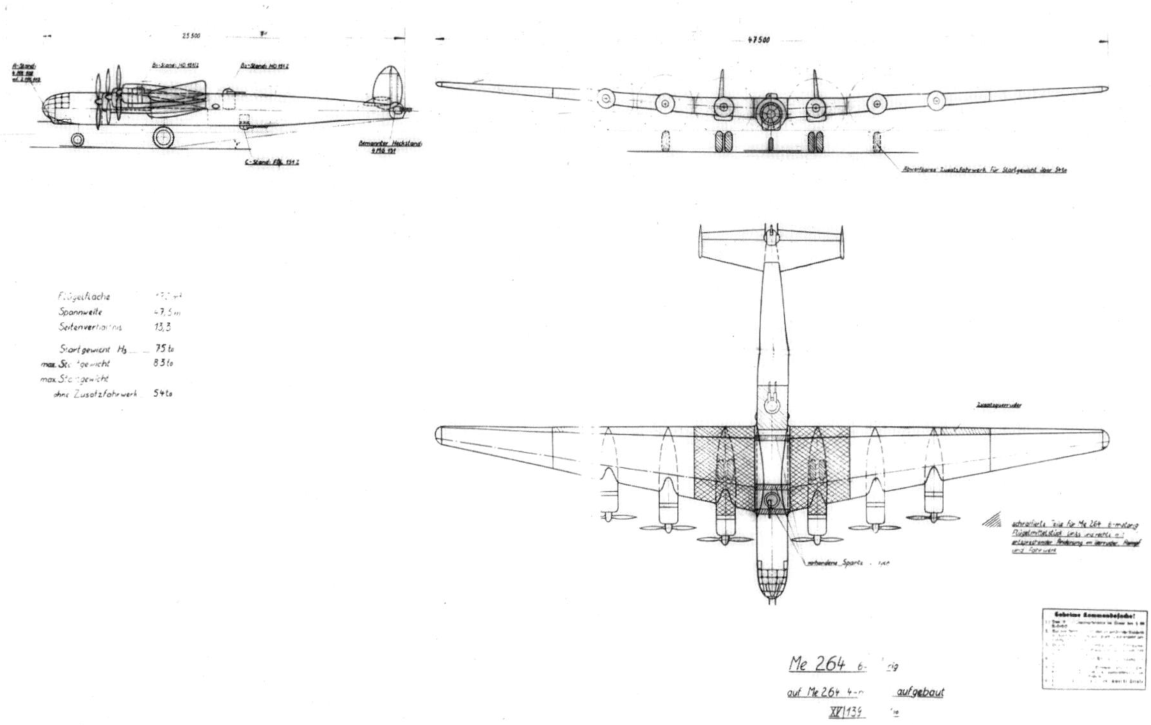

The six-engine Messerschmitt 'Me 264 6-motorig', known at one point as the Me 364—a conversion of the standard Me 264 to an extreme long-range variant. This design was considered the only viable way of launching direct bombing raids on the American east coast as of May 1942. It also had the potential, it was thought, to carry parasite aircraft such as the Me 328.

If the power lever is throttled too much, the engines stop and have to be started again. To do this, the aircraft must be dived to at least 150km/h. In general, the engines still seem unfinished. The landing was carried out as a glider landing after the engines were stopped by pulling back the power levers."

This was hardly a glowing endorsement of the pulse-jets' performance. They had delivered only 60% of the promised thrust, which in itself was far short of what Argus claimed they would ultimately be capable of, and it had proven difficult to regulate them with any degree of precision. They had also caused the airframe, and presumably the pilot too, to suffer strong vibrations—though the noise appears to have been bearable, assuming the noise produced by an ordinary Bf 110 with its engines on was bearable.

AMERIKABOMBER

The Me 210 and Me 323 weren't the only Messerschmitt production programmes in peril as Milch strove to get Willy Messerschmitt ejected from the leadership of his own company. The firm had been invested in the design and development of large long-range aircraft since the late 1930s, particularly with the Me 261, and had secured a production contract for 30 examples of its successor, the Me 264, in April 1941 at the second-tier 'SS' urgency level.[15] It was to be built, on Hitler's orders, as an 'Amerikabomber' for attacking the American east coast.

However, Jeschonnek wrote to Milch's office on April 25, 1942, following the Me 210's cancellation, to say that "after Generalfeldmarschall Milch reported to the Reichsmarschall [Göring] in one of the latest meetings[16] that the Me 264 in its current state of development is out of the question for use as an Amerikabomber with a significant bomb load, it is thus established that what the Me 264 was intended to do by the Führer and the Supreme Commander in Chief cannot be fulfilled.

"GL [the Air Ministry] is asked to inform us how and under what technical conditions the urgent command requirement for the provision of a bomber aircraft that can drop a significant bomb load at night in the area of the American east coast, at least, can be technically solved, and which projects currently under development have a chance of successfully meeting this basic requirement. The rapid realisation of the above Führer requirement is essential and tactical limitations, i.e. restrictions in the bomb load, armament and performance, would be accepted for the time being if the possibility of an Amerikabomber can be technically proven at all ... It has been determined that GL/C-E 2 has already placed the order to deliver the 30 Me 264s as long-range reconnaissance aircraft. This seems to indicate that GL/C-E [the Technical Office] has no interest in developing the Me 264 as a long-range bomber with about twice the performance of the He 177. This lack of interest is not shared by the Luftwaffe command staff".[17]

This message, implying that the Ministry was defying a direct order from Adolf Hitler, seems to have spurred the Technical Office into immediate action. By May 9, Flugbaumeister Walter Friebel, head of the Technical Office's C-E 2 (Aircraft) department, had prepared a detailed analysis of the options available for fulfilling the Amerikabomber role—ready to present it to Jeschonnek personally at a meeting planned for May 12.

After outlining a number of approaches, he wrote: "The task of completing the America mission in direct flight was continued, especially when the war with America broke out. The Messerschmitt company proposed an initially theoretical solution in the autumn of 1941, with six engines of the DB 603 class and 70-80t all-up weight with a range of 15,000km carrying a payload of approximately five tons ... as an additional task for this company this was unthinkable. This was also clear to the company themselves. They therefore looked for a more realistic way of achieving this case and around the beginning of 1942 consideration was given to converting the Me 264 to a six-engine design in a simple way, using the components Me 264 as much as possible to achieve the same thing as with an elaborate new project.

"Today it can be said that this work seems promising and that in this way it is certainly possible to cover direct flight to America with BMW 801 engines. However, the practical implementation of the work depends on the question of Messerschmitt's development capacity, which has not yet been resolved. This further development is also one of the reasons why GL considers the completion of the Me 264 to be expedient, since in this way, at least soon, invaluable experience can be gained for the six-engine further development. This proposal by Messerschmitt is currently as the only one that safely covers direct flight to America."

He said that such a specialised aircraft had "a few special properties": getting it off the ground would require jettisonable extra landing gear wheels; tactical use would be limited by a lack of manoeuvrability; dive-bombing was not possible; naval warfare would be difficult since it wouldn't be able to launch torpedoes. But it would be possible to use remote controlled weapons and "development work is ongoing to enable such large aircraft to attack by means of small aircraft carried on board. [Work on] experimental aircraft of this type is in progress and the basic tests are being carried out. Reconnecting the parasite aircraft to the host has already been carried out in some cases, and in other cases they should still take place [later] this year. The parasite aircraft are single-seaters, very small (6sqm wing area compared to, for example, 14sqm with Me 109), very fast (jet engines) and are designed for missions lasting half an hour to an hour.

"They are particularly suitable for attacking ship targets with one to two bombs weighing a total of 1,000kg. Work on solving the task of locating the host aircraft by the parasite aircraft is also in progress. The parasite aircraft can be used both for bombing and to repel enemy fighters. For example, a Ju 390 can take two parasite aircraft. The arrangement when used as a parasite bomber is planned so that the parasite aircraft can be reloaded with bombs during the flight.

"In summary, according to GL's proposal, the following work is ongoing in the field of long-distance aircraft: 1) The Me 264 is being pushed forward as the fastest possible solution for an American mission. 2) The refuelling procedure required for this will probably still be clarified in the course of 1942. 3) With emphasis on ranges of up to approx. 10,000km, with larger loads, better equipment and more versatile usability (transporters, parasite aircraft), the Ju 390 is in development. 4) Investigations with the aim of a direct flight to America are being accelerated (Me 264 six-engine). 5) Use of the Ju 290 up to distances of 8,000km is being investigated, whereby possibly simultaneous use of the type as a refuelling aircraft for Me 264 comes into question."

One of the roles proposed for the Me 328 right at the outset—included in the August 1, 1941, report—was that of parasite fighter. The company had evidently outlined this role to the Technical Office but had not linked it to the extremely slender Me 264, thereby leading to the inference that parasite Me 328s would operate from the capacious holds of Ju 390s.

However, Messerschmitt had other plans.

ME 328 AS A PARASITE

Four days after Baur's flights in the pulsejet-powered DFS 230, on July 7, 1942, the Project Office issued a new report on the Me 328—this time focusing solely on its adaptation and operation as a parasite fighter.[18]

The report began by stating that "if you want to increase the flight performance of the above model [Me 328], the improvement in engine performance must go hand in hand with a significant improvement in the aerodynamic quality of the aircraft, namely those parts that are known to be the first to be [Mach] critical.

"The main cause of increasing drag at higher Mach numbers is the suddenly sharp increase in wing drag; with the help of a swept-back wing, a delay in the increase in drag into the range of even larger Mach numbers can be expected. However, as recent DVL measurements have shown, the sweepback angle has a much smaller influence on the Mach shift in the above sense than was previously assumed.

"The following conclusions can be drawn from the above process: in order to reduce the Mach influence in a certain speed range, the sweepback would have to be increased significantly (estimated at 50 degrees), on the other hand, landing aircraft with such large sweep angles is very difficult (due to stalling); or you would have to move the wing backwards, around a fixed point... in order to increase the sweep and thus increase the Mach number, which would only be possible with great effort. The landing could then take place at a significantly lower sweepback angle, if possible zero degrees.

"Another possibility would be to rotate the wing around a point on the root profile, but since the wing moves backwards, the tail unit would also have to be extended backwards at the same time. However, these two possibilities were not considered in detail for the time being. Such wing rotations are very difficult to carry out structurally and statically, and the fuselage-wing transition (fillet) can hardly be cleanly arranged, even though it has a decisive influence on aerodynamics and flight characteristics."

In other words, Messerschmitt had actually considered variable geometry wings as early as 1942—the wings sweeping back for high-speed flight then sweeping forwards to create more lift at lower speeds and for landing. But this had unsurprisingly been ruled out due to structural complexity.

However, there was another possibility: "for take-off and landing, a wing unit that is located within another is extended in the direction of the wingspan; and for high-speed flight [this is retracted, leaving] only a small, unswept wing area".

If the Me 328 was used as a parasite aircraft, in association with a much larger multi-engine 'host' aircraft, there were three possibilities for attachment: towing, rigid attachment and internal carriage. In the first case, the parasite would remain outside the host, taking off from home base as an unpowered glider at the end of a tow line behind the bomber. In the second, it would be externally clamped to the host—either suspended below or positioned atop it. In the third, the host would feature a fuselage of sufficient girth to accommodate the parasite internally.

According to the report: "If you look at the above order of arrangements as a development process [i.e. towing as the first developmental step, attachment as the second and internal carriage as the fully mature system], which would not be without justification, you can see that in the expected final state, the accommodation of the parasite aircraft in the fuselage of the host aircraft, there is a need for the wings to be foldable or partially retractable."

There were "a number of reasons for this arrangement, despite the apparently great effort on the airframe side (host and parasite aircraft). This doesn't just concern the reloading of bombs and ammunition, the maintenance of the parasite aircraft, the repair of minor damage caused by enemy action etc. It is seen from the point of view that the host aircraft itself can no longer carry out the bombing due to excessive enemy defences, but it can fly in the vicinity of the operating area, possibly at high altitude, and the actual bombing attack is then flown by the very small parasite aircraft, which is also extremely fast. Thought: this is a development that we should approach very quickly.

"The accommodation of the parasite aircraft in the fuselage of the host aircraft requires, as already mentioned, foldable or partially retractable wings, but the folding wing has, among other things, the fundamental disadvantage that when the parasite aircraft is detached from the host, the former has to be lowered slightly [out of the host's fuselage], then the wings have to be brought into flight position and locked, only then can the separation from the host aircraft take place. The parasite aircraft with a partially retractable wing, on the other hand, is released from its suspension point like a bomb, which completes the entire process.

"For all of these reasons, as well as due to the previous performance considerations at high Mach numbers, the design of the parasite aircraft with a partially retractable wing was considered from the point of view that such a design of the wings only makes sense if they are relatively easy and extremely cheap to manufacture. The current shortage of raw materials and labour has been largely taken into account.

"A study was therefore carried out into unit weights of aircraft with a partially retractable wing at various different spans, wing sizes, etc. assuming that the wing is made from wood and that the wing thickness is around 9%."

However, while the calculations assumed ordinary wood, the report stated that the preferred construction material was a sort of chipboard (forms made from compressed wood chips and resin) known as Homogenholz, which was produced in Germany at that time using a commercial machine devised by German inventor Max Himmelheber and patented in 1932.

There were said to be six advantages of employing partially retractable wings and three disadvantages. The

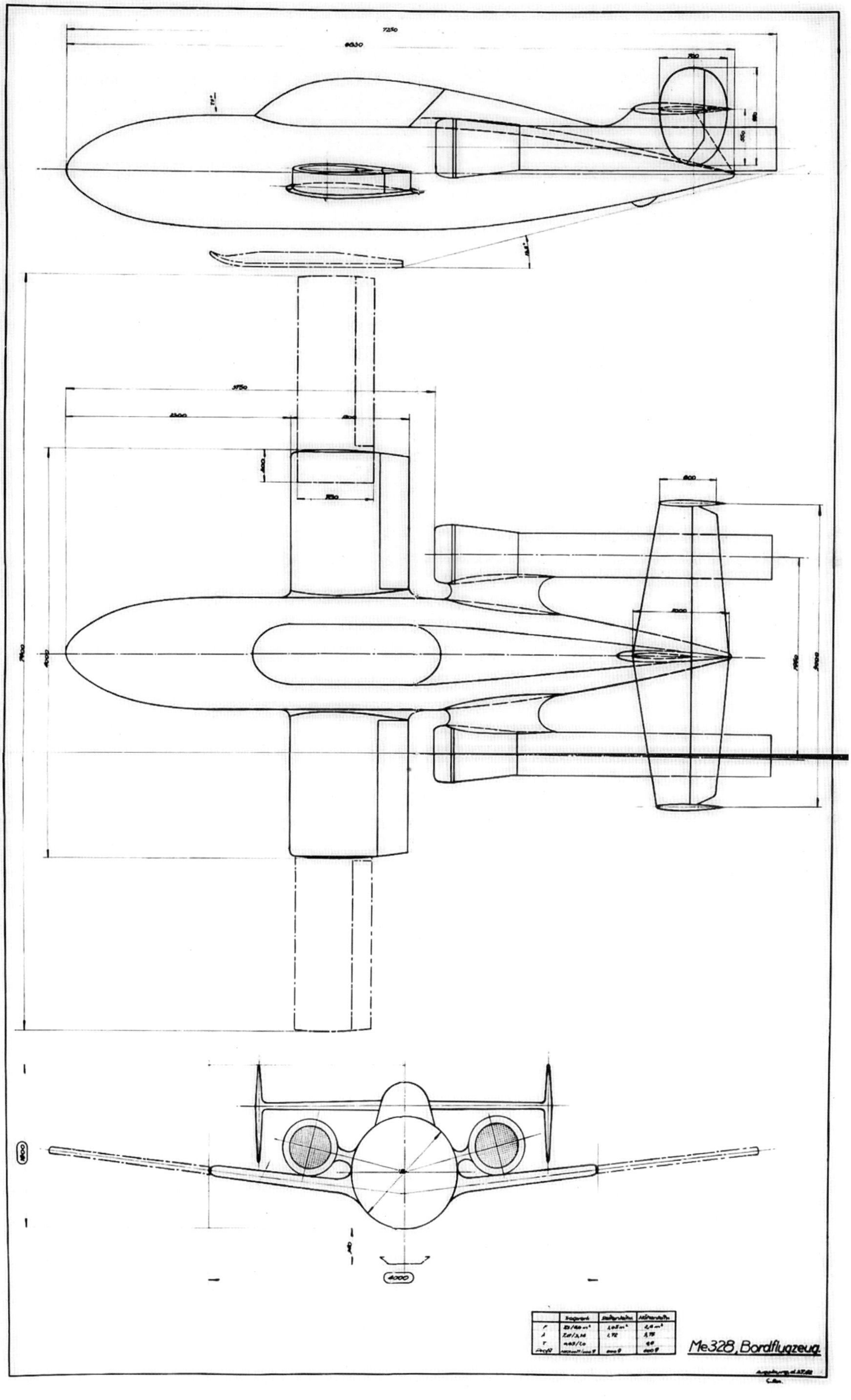

The compact Me 328 Bordflugzeug with twin-tail—rather than a tall tailfin—and extendable wings, dated July 3, 1942.

first advantage was the supposed ease with which the parasite could be taken back on board and then released from the airborne host. The second was the extendable wing itself, "which is only used for interception, extended gliding, external landing, etc." In other words, it was envisioned that the wing would remain retracted during normal operational flight. Evidently, if the aircraft would be required to take off independently, "a special wing profile (curved, fixed or double slots, special flaps, etc.) that is particularly suitable for these cases can be provided".

The third advantage was low drag from the tiny wings in their retracted position and the fourth was "an increase in speed compared to aircraft of normal design under otherwise identical conditions", again thanks to the small wing. Fifth, "the entire wing, both rigid and extendable, can be made either from wood (planing and milling) or better and cheaper from Homogenholz (casting or pressing) with easily portable lightweight wing units". This led to the sixth and final advantage: "Enormous savings in metal (duraluminium), working hours and therefore manpower."

The disadvantages were the time it would take to develop and test the extendable part of the wing, the difficulty of landing the aircraft without the host—since the landing speed would be very high, and finally the difficulty of providing control surfaces that would be similarly effective whether the wings were extended or retracted.

THE HOST AIRCRAFT

Perhaps the biggest disadvantage of building the Me 328 as a parasite that could be carried internally was the need to design and build a host aircraft big enough to carry it. It wouldn't fit within a standard Me 264, nor even the six-engine variant envisioned—since that would simply have longer wings and a longer fuselage.

So, for the purpose of carrying parasite aircraft, the report stated that "the Me 364 with a corresponding fuselage was considered as the host aircraft and a rough draft of it was added to indicate the [necessary] structure and size".

Messerschmitt's contemporary Me 364 description[19] states that "the six-engine long-range bomber Me 364 was developed from the four-engine Me 264 with a new wing profile, using the existing four-engine components under construction. By inserting new wing spacers, each with an engine, the wing area was increased from 125sqm to 170sqm. The required fuselage extension was achieved by inserting a cylindrical intermediate piece approximately 3.10m long into the Me 264 fuselage.

"The following components are adopted from the Me 264: the wing with ailerons and flaps and all installations and attachments except for the landing gear, which is removed and the unoccupied space is used to accommodate fuel; the fuselage with the cockpit and bomb bay with all installations and equipment except for the nosewheel landing gear, which has been reinforced for the higher flying weight. The aft end of the Me 264 fuselage is attached to the cylindrical fuselage insert. The weapon installation is omitted in this part. The crew rest area has been changed. Of the tail surfaces, only the tailplane has been enlarged by inserting intermediate pieces. The fin is adopted without any changes.

"The following components have to be redesigned for the Me 364: an intermediate wing section to the left and right of the fuselage with landing flaps, new main landing gear and additional engine systems; the reinforced nosewheel; a cylindrical fuselage extension intermediate piece in which the entire rear defensive armament is installed, as well as an intermediate piece for the control system; the cockpit—with a change from gauges, controls and electronics for four engines to a system for six."

Evidently three drawings, now lost, had been appended to the Me 328-as-a-parasite report originally, showing three different versions (labelled A, B and C) of the Me 364 reconfigured as a host aircraft. Version A apparently showed "the accommodation of a parasite aircraft in an ellipse-like fuselage cross section formed from two curved arcs, which is arranged so that the parasite aircraft can be positioned with the payload both under the wings and under the fuselage, with the bombs that are ready for reloading being conveniently stacked on top of each other in a framework in the space to the right and left of the tip of the fuselage, as shown". Some concern was raised about ground clearance for this design if the original undercarriage was to be retained.

For Version B, "an attempt was made to hang two parasite aircraft one above the other in a correspondingly larger fuselage". This version needed a new, taller, undercarriage. And in Version C, the Me 364's wings were shifted from a shoulder-mounted position to the mid-fuselage and the undercarriage was made non-retractable. The wing repositioning meant both parasite aircraft carried internally had to be shifted to make room for the wing spar.

The two Me 328 sketches appended to the report did survive, however. The first showed Messerschmitt's recommended arrangement: broadly similar to earlier designs but with stubby rectangular wings, from which even stubbier sections could be extended, its engines shifted to the rear fuselage sides and a twin-fin tail fitted to reduce height. Length was 6.83m excluding the pulsejets, or 7.25m with them, and wingspan was 4m or 7.4m in extended configuration. Wing area was 4.8sqm/7.5sqm respectively.

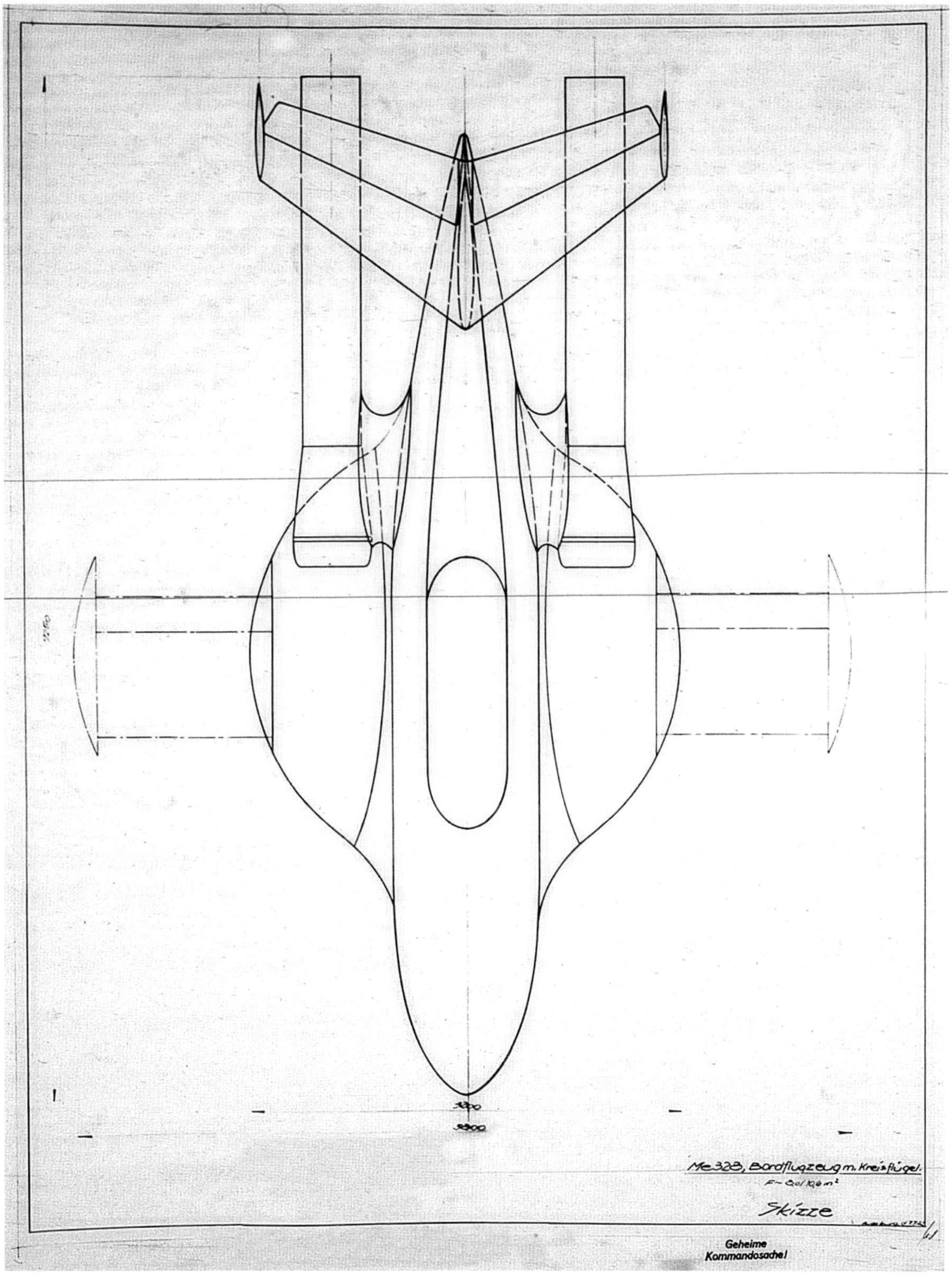

The "even more advanced development" Me 328 Bordflugzeug mit Kreisflügel, dated July 7, 1942. It appears that no side or forward views were presented in the original report.

The second sketch was briefly mentioned right at the end of the report: "For the sake of completeness, it should be mentioned that for a later, even more advanced development, a parasite aircraft with a circular wing (i.e. thin profile and sweep angle effect) [in German, "ein Bordflugzeug mit Kreisflügel"] and extendable additional wing surface (for take-off, landing, interception, extended gliding, etc. as before) with altitude-equivalent ailerons etc., was designed for speeds at particularly high Mach numbers. A sketch design is included."

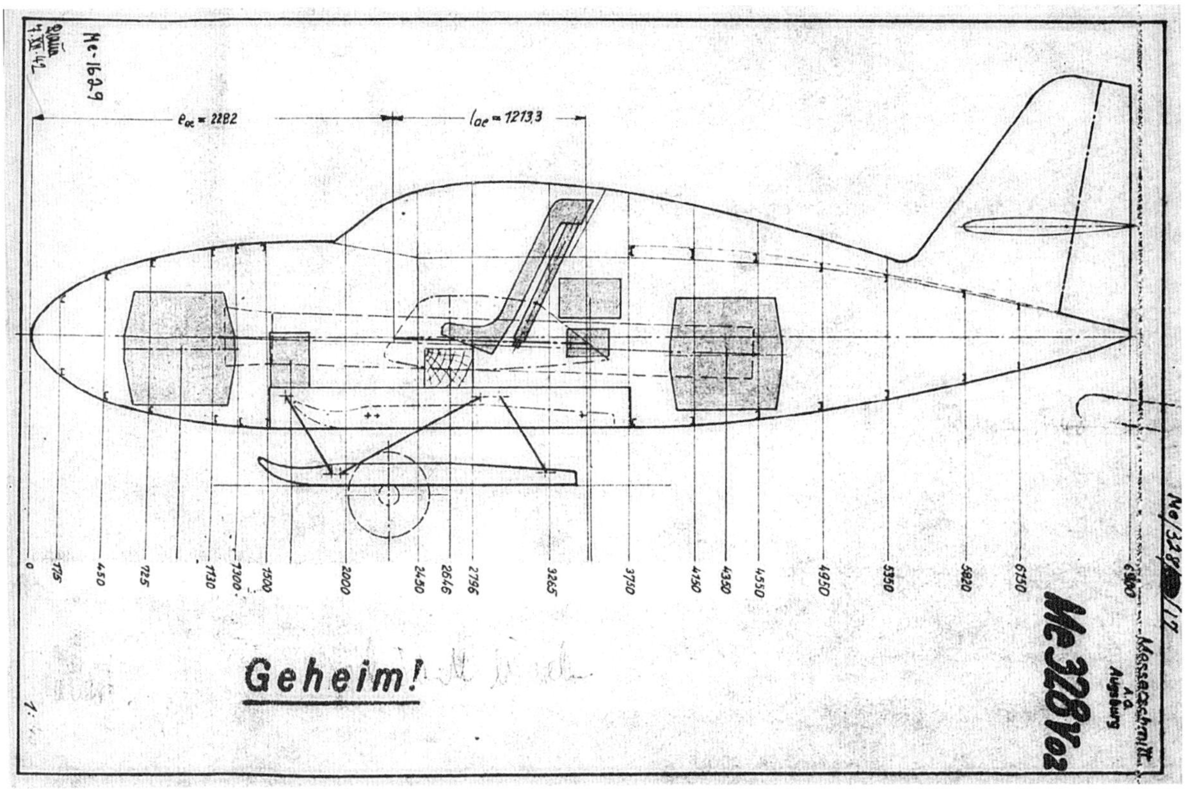

Even as the Bordflugzeug report was being published and the DFS was preparing to flight-test the Me 328 V1 prototype, Messerschmitt continued to work on the steel-skinned Me 328 V02—the only example actually built by the company. This diagram is dated July 7, 1942.

This drawing showed possibly the oddest Me 328 design ever committed to paper. Only a top view was presented, with a fuselage and engine attachment arrangement very similar—if not identical—to that of the recommended design. But where that aircraft had sharply angled rectangular wings, this one had extremely deep yet smoothly curved half-moon type wings. This gave it a wingspan, in retracted configuration, of just 3.2m—increasing to 5.8m if the rectangular extensions were deployed. Length, from the tip of the nose to the pulsejet exhausts, was 7.25m. The twin-fin tail was retained but this time the tailplanes were swept.

In summary, the report stated: "If you can't decide on a dedicated parasite aircraft yet, so be it. However, the design of the Me 328 with partially retractable wing should still be seriously considered, since then only the first mentioned advantage [the ease of use with a host aircraft] will be eliminated and all the others will still rightly continue to exist, also with a view to later developments."

ME 328 V1 FIRST FLIGHT

While the Project Office had been working on somewhat far-fetched schemes for a future Me 328, the DFS at Ainring was close to completing the first prototype—the Me 328 V1—by July 1942. No contemporary record of this aircraft's first flight is known to exist but DFS test pilot Erich Klöckner, in a piece written for a book of recollections compiled by well-connected Luftwaffe test pilot Wolfgang Späte during the early 1990s,[20] claimed that its first towed flight was on August 1, 1942.

He wrote: "In mid-1942 I was commissioned to help design a pilot's seat in the DFS test workshops in Ainring. A very secret flying machine was under construction there, which was presented to me with the name 'P 1079'. If necessary, I was supposed to say what was needed and to suggest changes. I didn't even know at the time that the bird would later be called Me 328. It was about to enter the final phase of its development—I was to fly it.

"At that time, no one could or wanted to tell me what task this bird was supposed to fulfil. At my insistence, Felix Kracht, the head of the Institute for Aircraft Construction, finally informed me shortly before the completion of this 'plywood bomber'.

"The Me 328 was planned as a so-called disposable aircraft. It was cheap, so its production costs were low. It could be discarded after use. It had an almost cylindrical fuselage 6.8m long with a wingspan of 6.4m and a 7.5sqm wing area. The ailerons were only 10cm deep and the 'ship' had to be going relatively fast before they could take effect

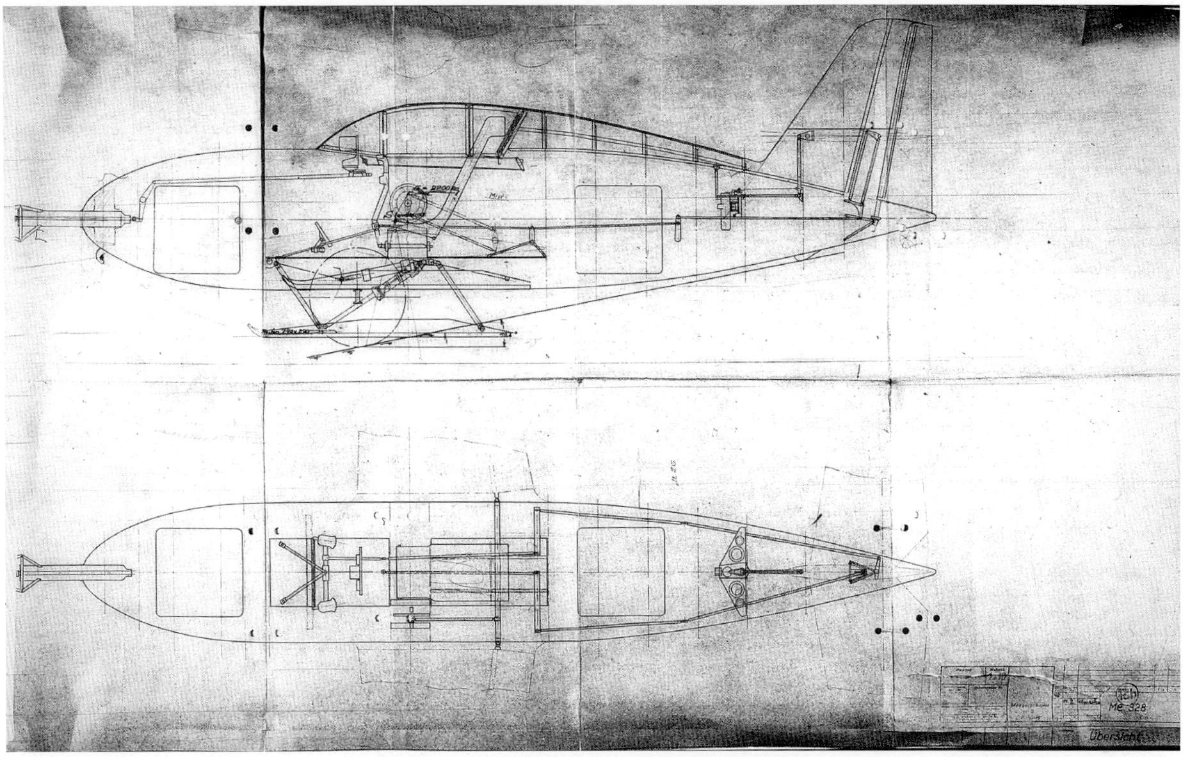

Me 328 drawing showing the control linkages. The canopy type depicted was only ever used on the non-flying Me 328 V02.

... This Me 328 V1 was launched on a two-wheeled chassis, which was jettisoned after take-off. The landing had to take place on a spring-loaded skid.

"The prototype was ready to fly at the end of July. I flew to Hörsching with Kurt Oppitz in an He 111, which was intended to tow the still engineless airframe, to make preparations for the first take-off. The engines were not yet ready for use. So the initial testing would take place after a towed take-off with a subsequent engineless flight as a glider. [By now] I was as familiar with the pilot's seat as if I had flown in it for a long time. The weather was very hot at the end of July 1942.

"Three days had already passed waiting. Either it was too gusty (thermals) or there was a thunderstorm or the wind was constantly changing. I had insisted on optimal weather conditions, including sufficient air temperature. The engines of the He 111 had to be at full power so that I could take off... On August 1, 1942, we waited until the evening for the summer heat to cool down. For almost an hour and a half I sat strapped into the machine, the cockpit canopy was wide open.

"Suddenly I feel pressure in my stomach. Unbuckle the parachute! Get out of the cockpit! Get off the wing! And 'he reaches the farm by the skin of his teeth'."[21] To put it another way, Klöckner abruptly discovered that he needed to use the bathroom and barely made it there in time.

He goes on: "I came back and everyone was laughing—Professor Georgii, Caroli, [who was] the head of testing at Messerschmitt, Kracht and the many 'experts' who never seem to miss such an event. There were 20 people standing around. I went to Oppitz at the towing machine and went over the final arrangements again. He was supposed to stay on the ground with the He 111 until there was just enough time for him to pull up over the picket fence on the eastern edge of the airfield. My biggest concern was that the climb after take-off might not be enough to get me up through the propeller wash.

"While I was getting back in, Professor Georgii came up to me again, shook my hand and wished me a good flight. My respect for my top boss dictated that I not let on that this in no way helped to improve my peace of mind. But now it could start. Some evening coolness had set in and the He 111 was already in starting position with its engines running. The rope was hooked up. I locked the canopy. Now I was alone with myself and my guardian angel.

"Five seconds of closing my eyes and I was focused. I raised my arm. The signal was passed on to Oppitz via the starting flag. Our tow train started to roll at 7.50pm. As the speed increased, I found myself right behind the He 111. It had long been airborne while I was still rolling and rolling [on the ground]. I finally felt the responsiveness of the controls. Oppitz was already close to the edge of the airfield where he had to pull up. Then I pulled hard on the stick; the Me 328 made a jump and I was not only free [of the ground], but also through the propeller wash in one go.

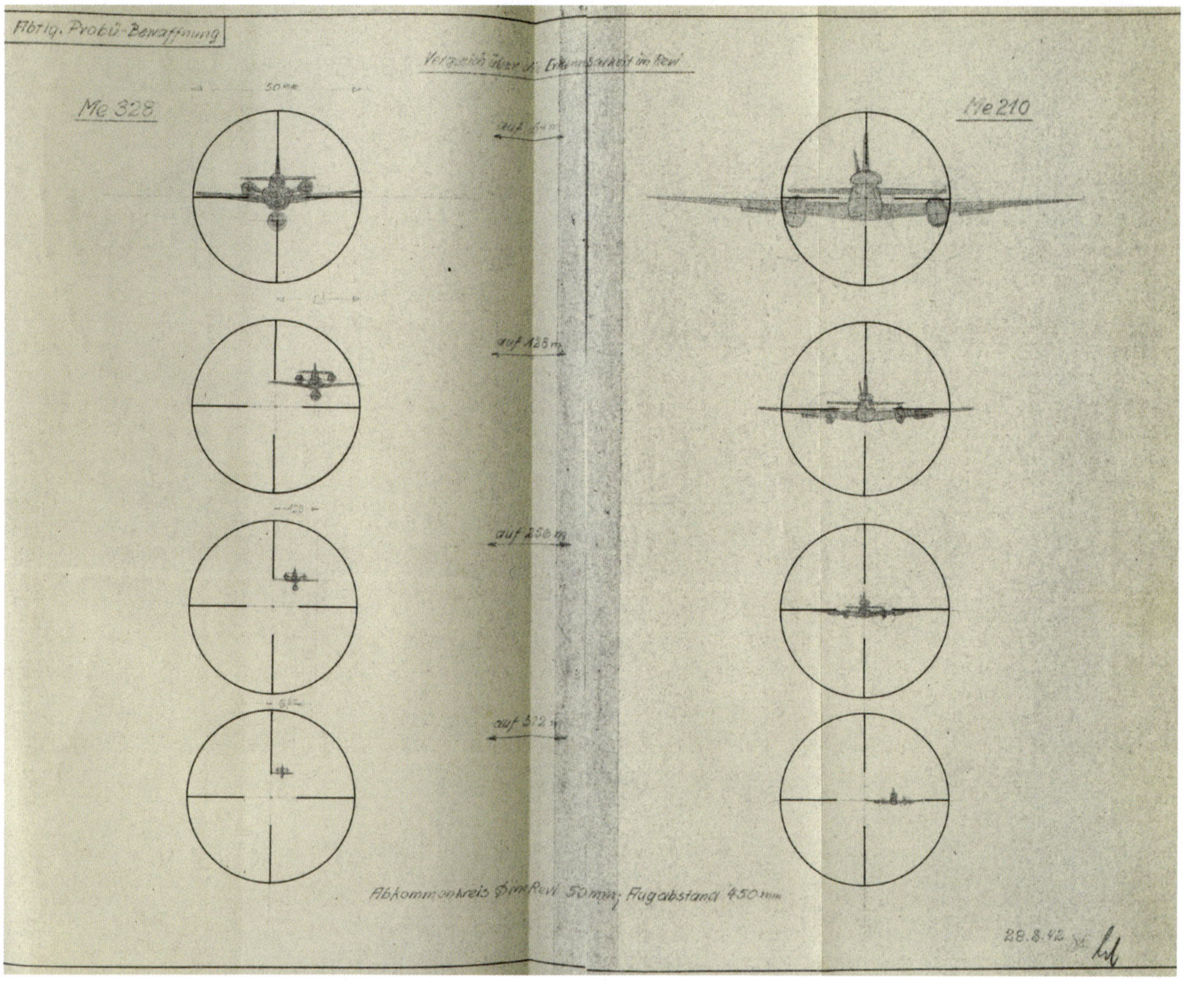

Diagram showing how difficult the Me 328 would be to hit, compared to the much larger Me 210, dated August 28, 1942.

"As an experienced glider pilot, I had jettisoned the landing gear at the moment of take-off. And I flew above the prop wash in a normal long tow as if it were the hundredth time [I had done it]. During the take-off roll, the He 111 had been difficult to see because the high nose of the [Me 328's] fuselage took away a lot of visibility. With a wing loading of 150kg/sqm, the Me 328 was easy to tow at a speed of 250-260km/h. At this speed she had full rudder effectiveness.

"From take-off to release, the flight went exactly according to the flight plan. At an altitude of 3,000m, near the airfield, I released. Kracht had already told me that the aircraft might be sensitive around the longitudinal axis due to the small wingspan. That's how it was. At around 380-400km/h a tiny aileron deflection was enough to start a roll. According to our gliding flight programme, we only had 2,000m of altitude in which to collect data. With a sink rate of around 7m/s, there were only about four minutes available for this. I could only make short notes on my kneeboard, nothing more. A slight pressure [on the stick] was enough and 500km/h was displayed on the airspeed indicator. I converted the excess speed back into altitude—like in a glider, only with a hell of a lot more speed and rate of descent.

"What was striking was the large intercept radius. Landing preparations had to begin at an altitude of 1,000m. I had to arrive at certain altitudes over predetermined terrain points in order to turn at last into the final approach at 200km/h and aim for the grass part of the airfield. I was about 1m high above the hedge at the edge of the field and then let the 'ship' touch down as the speed decreased. If I ever wanted something bad to happen to someone, I would let them land in an aircraft with unsprung, extra-wide skids at a touchdown speed of 170km/h on a dry, rock-hard, bumpy grass track. I screamed out loud as it compressed my spine. It was 8.15pm when the earth had me again. A minute later, Kurt Oppitz also touched down with the towing machine. I no longer had any objections against handshakes.

"In the period that followed, I carried out a total of 24 flights without an engine with this and the next prototype, some of them using the Mistel configuration."

Shortly after his first flight with the Me 328, mostly likely within a month of it, Klöckner was given a closely-related mission. He wrote: "Apparently because I had... tested the airframe of the Me 328, I was subsequently given the task of flight-testing the engine intended for it. It was the so-called 'Argus tube' with 150kg thrust, which was primarily intended to power unmanned aircraft and glide bombs. It was a pulsejet, externally not much more than a tube with a valve and flaps at the front. That's why it was also known as the 'stove pipe'. Ram air[22] was admitted through the flaps, while fuel was intermittently injected into the combustion chamber behind it and burned. The flap system allowed the burned gases to escape rearwards as thrust. The opening and closing of the flaps occurred at a frequency of around 50Hz.

"So the flight testing of these Argus tubes at the DFS became one of my tasks. The first engines were mounted on a DFS 230. They could only be started on the ground (i.e. when stationary) if compressed air was blown into the flaps... to replace the missing ram air. In the beginning the pipes often went out, especially when airspeed fell below a certain level.

"In practice, I was towed to an altitude of 1,000m in a DFS 230 with two Argus tubes attached under the wing. When the throttle lever was in the 'start' position, fuel was injected into the combustion chamber and the ignition was switched on at the same time. As a rule, there was then a dull bang and a noticeable jerk forward.

"After the first few long flights with engine thrust, I noticed severe joint pain, especially in my right wrist. This phenomenon was soon clarified. The oscillation frequency of the pulsejet was, as mentioned at the beginning, 50Hz. Resonant vibrations arose in the tubular steel fuselage, which were transmitted to my wrist via the control stick. I had to stop flying... because the joint pain was simply unbearable and there was no feeling or strength in my right hand, which I needed for steering and especially for landing.

"In the period that followed, other DFS pilots also flew this Argus tube test. I remember a case in which the rear entrance door suddenly tore off and flew away due to the aforementioned resonance vibrations on the hinges."

3

FLYING ARTILLERY TO VULKAN: SEPTEMBER TO DECEMBER 1942

Having pushed the Me 328 as the Project Office's much more compelling alternative to Abteilung L's Me 163, Woldemar Voigt appears to have become personally invested in its success.

He produced the most detailed report on it yet[1] on September 1, 1942, with an introduction written in the first person, which made some extremely questionable claims about the aircraft and demanded—practically begged—that it be given full government support with the highest possible priority over other projects as a 'special campaign'.

Voigt's model for this proposed 'special campaign' was Unternehmen Warschau or 'Operation Warsaw'—the urgent production programme initiated in the autumn of 1940 to build a fleet of enormous transport gliders for the invasion of Britain. Messerschmitt's part of this was codenamed Warschau-Süd or 'Warsaw-South'. From a standing start in November 1940, the company had to design and then build the Me 321 in record time. For this purpose, a dedicated design bureau was established at Leipheim and with a programme of round-the-clock working the first example was ready to fly in February 1941—just 14 weeks after the instruction to proceed with construction.

The September 1 report, entitled 'Me 328. Special Promotion for Development and Production', began: "In my opinion, the development and testing of the Me 328 airframe and engine has now progressed to such an extent that it can be viewed as proven that a fast bomber of decisive importance to the war can be made ready for the front line in an unusually short time with very little risk.

"I therefore propose, after appropriate review of my points of view set out below, as well as after consultation with the engine development company [Argus] and the relevant authorities, to declare the Me 328 as the main aircraft in a special campaign and to start final testing, final development and series production, leaving aside other tasks and preparations."

He gave a number of "facts [which] underline the importance of the Me 328 fast bomber"; firstly, "the Führer stated to Prof. Messerschmitt in 1941: 'If we had 200 bombers which could carry out targeted bombings in England during the day, England would already be finished'." And "for the same reason, the State Secretary ordered the Me 329 fast bomber from our company 'more urgently than SS'."[2]

This appears to be a reference to the ongoing rivalry between Voigt's Project Office and Lippisch's Abteilung L—with the Me 329 perhaps being cited as an example of a less promising design that had nevertheless been given priority. Considering that, four months earlier, Milch had asked Croneiss what the Me 329 actually was, and Croneiss had replied that it was a possible Me 210 replacement that wasn't looking too promising, it seems unlikely that Milch had been quite as desperate to see it put into production as Voigt may have thought.

Now however, Voigt was apparently so confident of the Me 328's potential that he even felt able to chastise the Ministry's handling of his project thus far: "The preparatory work for a special campaign must start now. The previous treatment of the Me 328 with lower priority, which was completely useless in every respect (including for engine development), has already resulted in a delay of at least half a year. The testing process has shown that without a fundamental change in the working procedure [i.e. a higher priority rating], results cannot be expected in the foreseeable future.

"It would be a catastrophe of a magnitude that is difficult to imagine if the British, either through their own work or through espionage, were to get ahead of us by putting fast bombers into service, so that the German fighter defence would be powerless against targeted daytime attacks."

He recommended six immediate actions: completion of the sheet steel Me 328 V02 prototype at Augsburg using "special measures"; formation of a dedicated group to thoroughly test both airframe and engines; finalisation of the design in either its current form or a larger longer-range version; the launch of a Warschau-Süd style production campaign; construction of a series production model; and finally "faster engine development (increase in thrust, reduction in fuel consumption, improved altitude performance) must be enforced at Argus with extreme pressure".

DESIGN AND PERFORMANCE

Voigt's report then offered a table comparing the Me 328's performance against both the DB 605-powered Bf 109 G and the DB 601 F-powered Me 210. Assuming a pair of 300kg thrust pulsejets, the 328 was expected to reach 800km/h at sea level or 910km/h with 400kg pulsejets. The 109 G could manage only 535km/h and the 210 just 482km/h. At an altitude of 6km however, the difference was a little less marked with the Me 328's speed dropping to 775km/h or 865km/h, while the 109 G's rose to 666km/h and the 210's to 587km/h.

In his accompanying notes, Voigt offered reassurances that a 500kg bomb-carrying 328 would be 175km/h or 275km/h faster than a 109 G with the same load. Even carrying double that payload—1,000kg, which the 109 G couldn't manage—the 328 would still be 105km/h or 205km/h faster.

Under a heading of 'tactical performance' he wrote: "The most important tactical performance characteristic is the fact that the Me 328, when flying low, i.e. below the effective reach of the aircraft search devices [presumably radar rather than searchlights], with a high bomb load, reaches a cruising speed that is well above the maximum speed of enemy fighters. It is also important to point out that it is always possible to subsequently increase the speed by adding more powerful engines without any other significant modifications to the aircraft, up to the limits imposed by compressibility (further increase is possible after the introduction of the swept wing). Range can be maintained by increasing the size of the fuel tank."

Evidently "the flight characteristics [of the Me 328] were tested up to a speed of 450km/h by a pilot assigned to the Luftwaffe test centres and found to be OK. The rudder forces are small, the rudder effects are very large, stability around all axes and rolling behaviour in straight flight and while turning is good according to the flight results so far. Difficulties due to the unusually small dimensions have not yet arisen; only a reduction in the rudder effect is desired.

"In the course of a complete flight test, complaints are ... still to be expected, but based on the tests so far it can be said with certainty that in the flight weights and speed ranges examined there are no flight characteristics problems that could endanger the use of the fast jet bomber."

In his recollection, Klöckner had noted that at higher speeds, due to its short wingspan, the Me 328 became increasingly sensitive along its longitudinal axis and Voigt did address this point: "The rolling behaviour, which appears to be harmless in its current state, should not change significantly; only an approximately 60% increase in the speed of all movements ... is expected. The dynamic stability, which cannot be fully verified mathematically, can cause great difficulties; in my opinion, it is actually the only risk that could possibly lead to the Me 328 being abandoned as a jet bomber, as there is no guarantee that any difficulties that may arise will be remedied.

"It is therefore urgent to ensure that flights with the highest weight can be carried out as quickly as possible so that a decision can be made in good time about whether it can be used as a bomber or as a fighter. The flight characteristics with attached pulsejets still need to be tested. Setbacks are possible in relation to rolling, but it can be predicted with great certainty that these difficulties can be eliminated by suitable fairing or by relocating the engine to the [tail] end of the fuselage. In this area too, rapid testing is necessary.

"The operational landing wing load is 40% higher than

The Me 328 V1 jettisoning its undercarriage wheels during a towed take-off. The photograph is one of a sequence featured in Voigt's September 1, 1942 report.

Me 328 V1 in flight as viewed from the ground.

Skid extended, the Me 328 V1 approaches the airfield to land.

Touchdown on the grass. The Me 328 V1 was the only prototype to feature that distinctive three-frame canopy.

the value flown so far. Since experimental landings without flap deflection and with a low angle of attack were carried out with very good results, difficulties are not likely. The airframe currently being tested [Me 328 V1 in glider configuration] corresponds in its external dimensions to the aircraft with an enlarged [fuel] tank."

THE TAKE-OFF

Addressing 'starting aids', Voigt was forced to admit that "for use as a bomber, the aircraft is fundamentally dependent on the use of starting aids (catapult start, towing, etc.). This limitation is initially a disadvantage compared to the Me 109 fighter-bomber". He then offered some spurious information about jet engines, albeit from the standpoint of 1942 when jet engines were still an emerging technology: "The thrust performance of all jet engines known to date is poor at take-off compared to the performance of propeller engines. The launch of a bomb-loaded jet aircraft without any aids would require an engine that could not be used in high-speed flight until we can technically and economically reach speeds of the order of magnitude of the speed of sound".

He next explained the reasoning behind giving the Me 328 an unnervingly high wing loading: "Jet engines and especially pulsejets, in conjunction with the bomb load, result in such a large difference between take-off weight and landing weight that it is uneconomical for performance and [fuel] consumption reasons to set the wing area based on the take-off condition."

In other words, the wing size required for the fuel- and bomb-laden Me 328 (max. take-off weight up to 1,400kg including two 500kg bombs) to perform a normal take-off would be far larger than the aircraft would need in order to land safely, once its fuel had been burned off and its bombs dropped. So why not give it wings that were only suitable for the lightweight landing condition from the outset and get it into the air using other means?

Voigt said that using a catapult would "be cheaper than the rocket devices [RATO] currently used on larger bombers". This launch system would be essential "since [by] using such launch methods it is possible to build aircraft that are equivalent or superior to enemy jet fighters in terms of speed and climb performance".

The catapult in question had apparently already been designed and built by the Forschungsanstalt Graf Zeppelin, with 20 examples available and more under construction: "The catapult is designed for the launch of the He 111; for our smaller weights and higher take-off speeds, the introduction of an additional pulley (reverse pulley) is necessary. The parts for this test setup are finished and [have been] delivered to FGZ. The testing depends on the availability of an Me 328 or Me 163.

"The towed take-off, for which the Me 328 was originally designed, was basically tested at the DFS. There were no difficulties and they are even less likely to arise for the Me 328 than for the tested aircraft (Habicht glider). The use of the catapult would be preferable as it requires far fewer personnel and also allows for a faster turnaround (with He 111, the time required per take-off is eight minutes). On the other hand, the towed start offers the possibility of completing part of the approach (sea approach towards England) while being towed, in order to increase range."

The Me 328's design also allowed some flexibility with regard to its pulsejets: "Since the engines are completely suspended on the exterior, changing the engine to another version is possible at any time and without any significant work effort. For training purposes, the aircraft is best equipped with 2 x 150kg thrust [pulsejets]. To further increase performance (approx. 760km/h with a 1,000kg bomb), four pulsejets with 300kg thrust each can be installed. The range naturally decreases accordingly; if necessary, the reduction can be fully or partially offset by increasing the size of the [fuel] tank."

The SC 500 RS rocket-propelled bomb—shown here attached to a Bf 110—was developed by the German Air Ministry "specially for the Me 328" in its 'flying artillery' role.

AIRBORNE 'STALIN'S ORGAN'

Essential to Voigt's offering was the use of the SC 500 RS rocket-propelled bomb, "the development of which was undertaken by the Air Ministry specifically for the Me 328" because it promised "very special advantages". According to the report: "The bomb [SC 500 RS] is launched at a distance of approx. 1,000m [from the target] at low altitude with an inclination of 20° and, due to its final speed of over 400m/sec, has a penetrating power which is comparable to that of heavy ship guns. A very decisive advantage of this bomb is that it detonates on the target

Another SC 500 RS rocket bomb, this time carried by an Me 410 A-1, as pictured in a report produced by the Luftwaffe's Rechlin test centre.

This low quality but unique image shows the terrific exhaust blast produced during an SC 500 RS being ground-launched from an Me 210 during tests at Rechlin.

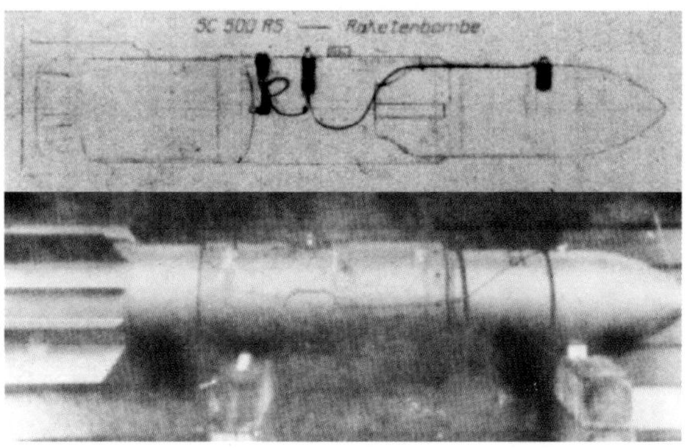

Another low quality Rechlin image, this time showing the internal layout of an SC 500 RS—which was literally an SC 500 bomb inserted into the front of a metal tube with a solid rocket motor inserted to the rear.

immediately before the attacking aircraft flies over it. It is expected that the defence of a ship, for example, is significantly disrupted in the critical seconds." In other words, the impact of the bomb would cause the defenders to duck for cover—discouraging any return fire against the low-flying Me 328.

Development of the SC 500 RS for the Me 328 seems to have happened quickly, though exactly when the concept originated, and whether it really was developed from scratch for the Me 328, is unclear. Either way, Voigt's comment implies a programme being undertaken with the full knowledge and support of the Air Ministry's Technical Office.

According to a report from the Rechlin test centre written two years after the fact,[3] a 'programme for the development and testing of rocket launches from aircraft' had been proposed on March 20, 1942, which was "intended to prove that for the first time extremely heavy projectile weapons (similar to the heaviest artillery) could also be used from the air".

The report stated that "the SC 500 RS is an SC 250 bomb equipped with a rocket engine and a tail unit. It is manufactured by the Rheinmetall-Borsig company. The maximum diameter is 42cm, the length is about 2.6m. The middle piece between the rocket chamber and the bomb part is used to accommodate the normal bomb attachment point, the fuse release and the rocket ignition. The large remaining space can alternatively be filled with approx. 80kg of Fp 60/40 explosives or any control devices at the expense of the RS projectile's acceleration.

"A 12-fin tail unit made of an electron casting, which covers the rocket nozzles, gives the projectile sufficient stability. The weight of the SC 500 RS is approx. 570kg with a propellant charge of 65kg propellant powder (diglycol) and an explosive charge of 130kg Fp 60/40. The propellant charge burns within two seconds at normal temperature and accelerates the projectile to approx. 210m/sec using 12 propellant nozzles. An overpressure nozzle closed by a spring valve prevents an excessive buildup of pressure in the combustion chamber".

Given that the SC 500 RS was an SC 250 bomb wedged into an oversize metal cylinder with a basic solid-fuel rocket motor inserted into the rear, and a cavity in between for the very basic electrical systems needed, it does seem possible that it was put together in a hurry.

Certainly, Rheinmetall-Borsig was conducting tests with it in prototype form over the Lebasee (Lebsko Lake) in Pomerania by April 28, 1942.[4] The 1944 Rechlin report noted that "due to a lack of smaller German tail-stabilised rocket bombs, all preliminary tests on the ground and in the air were carried out with captured and partly converted Russian RS bombs". Presumably this is a reference to RS-82/RS-132 type rocket-powered projectiles of the sort fired from Katyusha artillery units—which would mean that the intent was to turn the Me 328 into a flying 'Stalinorgel' or 'Stalin's organ'—the German nickname for the Katyusha.

The Rechlin report also noted that "although the

underside of the fuselage is completely exposed to the blast jet for about 0.2 seconds when the SC 500 RS is launched for both aircraft types [test rounds being fired from a Bf 110 and an Me 410], no fire damage has occurred so far and is probably not to be expected due to the short firing time combined with the high airflow speed".

Voigt went on to say that a new sight for launching the SC 500 RS had been developed by Steinheil, based in Munich, "which is currently being tested" but "as an alternative solution, the normal Revi with a swivelling base plate (as used with the Ju 87) is possible. The BZA should also be installed". The Bomb Ziel Automat (BZA) was an analogue bombsight computer which controlled a mark on the pilot's sight. It was able to establish the aircraft's dive angle and altitude for itself but the pilot had to manually enter airspeed, wind speed and other variables. Using this data, the computer moved the mark and when it lined up with the target the pilot released the bombs.

Evidently "the GL/C-E 6 office[5] expects particularly good results from the Me 328, as all sighting issues are greatly simplified due to the high trajectory speed and the resulting slightly curved bomb trajectory. This is of course especially true when using the RS bomb."

If the SC 500 RS and a dedicated sight for launching it were developed specifically for the Me 328, this could almost be regarded as an example of the 'weapon system' concept—where an airframe and its systems are developed to suit one another from the beginning—some seven years before that term was first used in reference to the Convair F-102 Delta Dagger.

NO GUNS

The two MG 151s previously planned had been deleted from the design since "a defensive weapon is unnecessary because the aircraft cannot currently be attacked due to its high speed. Attacking enemy aircraft is not the bomber's job. Equipping [it] with the [previously] planned armament is only necessary when there are enemy aircraft with such performance that the Me 328 is no longer adequately protected by its speed alone, even with more powerful engines". Ditching the MG 151s also saved around 240kg in weight and the Me 328's "speed and climb performance after the bomb is dropped is increased so that it is still slightly above that of the equivalent jet fighter". It also reduced complexity, meaning "a very considerable reduction in the design and manufacturing effort, thus making it possible to bring the jet bomber to the front at earlier dates and in larger quantities".

That said, apparently "a weapons upgrade kit for subsequent attachment to the jet bomber is also [being] investigated". This would allow the aircraft to be used as a fighter and Voigt thought that "the Me 328 will become important for reconnaissance operations (armed reconnaissance missions); [but] the investigations are not yet completed".

The aircraft would have two fuel tanks—the rear tank being used up first, followed by the front tank "which contains the fuel for the return flight". The front and sides of the latter would be made from steel armour so that "the pilot is... excellently protected against fire from the front (i.e. against ground defence from the target)". There would be no back armour for the pilot.

Voigt expected that, in addition to this armour, the Me 328 would be protected by its "unusually small size" and "as an indication of this, it is stated that, for example, the wing area is not even half as large as that of the Me 109 and only 20% of that of the Me 210". Furthermore, "due to the small size of the Me 328, detection by visual observation may be more difficult than with normal aircraft. The disadvantage is the noise, which is probably greater than with gasoline engines, as well as the fairly large exhaust flame, which cannot be eliminated using flame dampeners etc. Since the aircraft has no significant metallic surfaces with the exception of the fuel tanks and the engines, it can be assumed that the electrical search devices [i.e. radar] will only find it very late."

SAFE PULSEJETS

Despite the undeniably worrying experiences of the DFS team while flight-testing prototype units from Argus (see Chapter 3), Voigt somehow felt able to claim that the pulsejets underpinning the Me 328's viability as a combat aircraft were not only completely safe but actually safer than piston engines due to their inherent simplicity.

Under the heading of 'operational safety', he wrote: "It is very likely that the operational safety of the Me 328 with pulsejets will be considerably better than that of normal aircraft; this point must be particularly emphasized, as one is initially inclined to assume the opposite in view of the new and untested engines. The engine basically only consists of the following four parts: pipe body, valve box, nozzles and spark plug; the possibility of error is of course significantly reduced compared to the complicated Otto engine.

"The pipe body is currently executed in a safe manner. It can probably be considered completely operationally safe because it is subject to little stress and because the test samples worked perfectly even with tubular bodies made of sheet metal (with a reduced service life). The valve boxes are generally replaced after every flight to replace

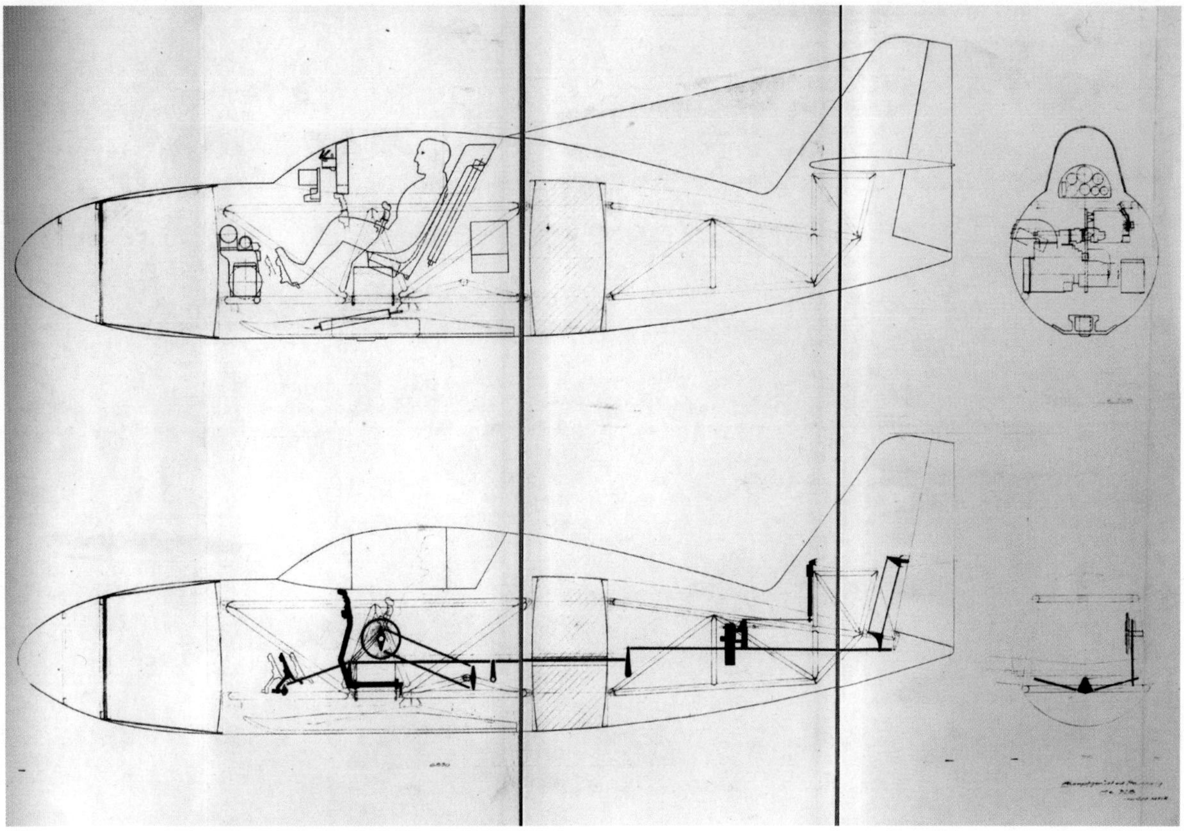

The low-wing Me 328 prototype's cockpit and skid layout. In the original design, the landing skid tucked up inside the aircraft—so that in flight it was flush against the underside.

the valve springs. It has been proven that the service life of the valves is longer than the flight duration of the Me 328 and that, after the failure of individual valve springs, the engine can be operated for a longer period of time with little reduced performance. The nozzles currently used by Argus are nonadjustable and contain no moving parts. The risk of failure should therefore be completely avoided by filtering the fuel. Otherwise, [even] if a single nozzle is blocked, the engine remains operational, albeit with reduced performance. The ignition system is only required to start the engine. A failure of this system during operation only leads to a malfunction if it becomes necessary to restart a stopped engine in flight.

"The injection pump with its energy supply (prop generator, or as an alternative solution, on-board unit) is not considered in this context, as it is to be seen as a component belonging to the airframe and there is at risk of failure at any time. The pulsejet falling out of sync and stopping without mechanical damage has so far only been observed when fuel is oversaturated; difficulties cannot arise because the engine starts up again by itself immediately in flight... The following major sources of trouble are eliminated in the engine alone: the entire engine with pistons, bearings, valves, lubricant and coolant system, charger, mixture and boost pressure regulators, ignition system, etc., as well as the propeller with adjustment system and automatic adjustment system, as well as the coolant and lubricant system with hoses, radiators and automatic control elements.

"It can also be assumed that, due to its small size and robust simplicity, as well as the very low level of equipment, failures will only occur to a limited extent. In particular, it should be noted that no hydraulics are installed and that the pneumatic system only covers the landing gear extension (landing gear retraction in flight is not necessary). Engine maintenance in front-line operations is limited exclusively to regularly replacing the valve boxes after each flight and monitoring the pipe for burning. The valve boxes are reused after the springs have been replaced. There is no need to maintain other components."

While much of what Voigt wrote was technically true, he takes no account of—and makes absolutely no mention of—the vibration issue. Presumably this was not widely known at the time, though he must have been aware of it himself, and he was gambling on a technical solution being found which would negate its deleterious effects before they became common knowledge.

In summarising the engines' development, he wrote: "Although the engines are fundamentally new and not well-tested, they have repeatedly demonstrated sufficient

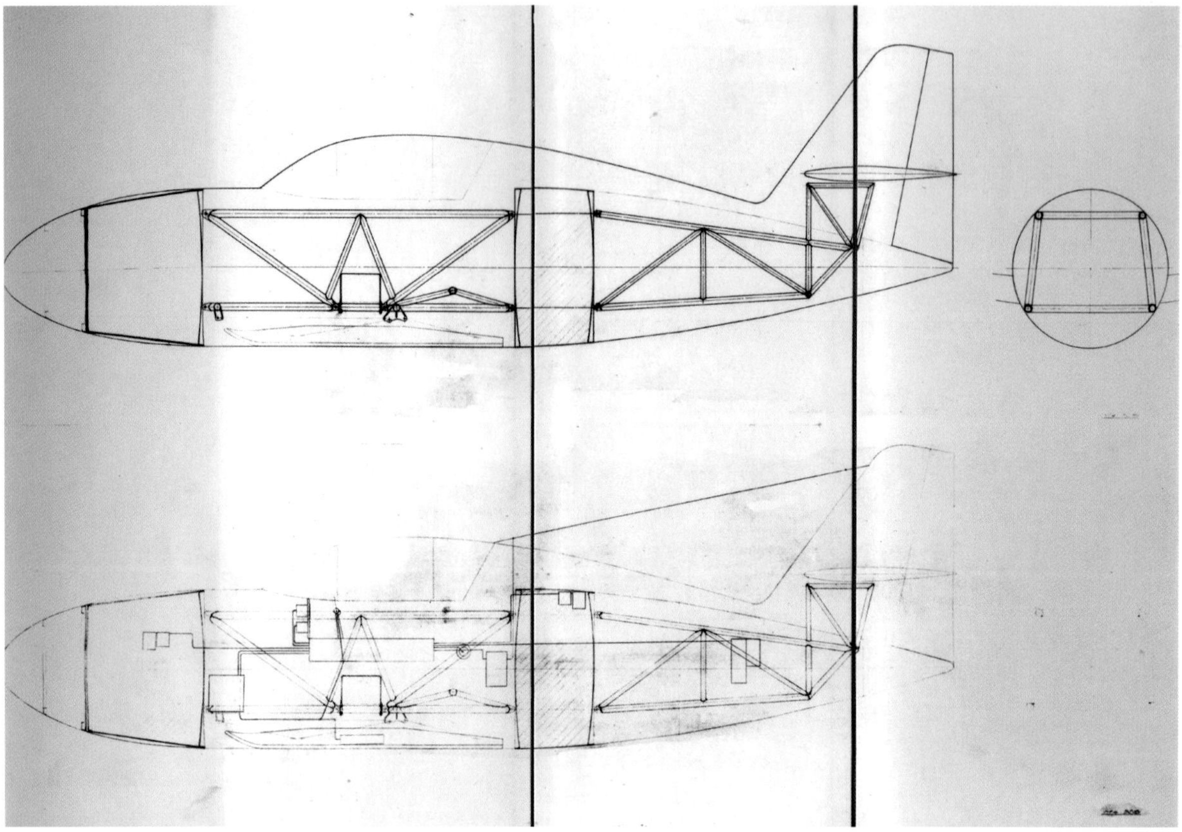

Structural layout of the low-wing Me 328 type, showing its steel tube skeleton.

operating time for the flight duration of the Me 328. A failure of one or more valves (up to approx. 20% of all valves!) does not lead to the failure of the engine, but only to a moderate reduction in performance, so in contrast to piston engines, an engine malfunction does not force the flight to be aborted immediately. Added to this is the very high level of safety provided by the multi-engine design."

Indeed, "Dr Goslau from Argus states: during bench testing, an operating time of two hours is normally achieved until the first valve fails. The engine then continues to run for a longer period of time (as mentioned: another two hours?), with the performance slowly decreasing due to the failure of additional valves. Since the [Me 328's] longest flight duration with an enlarged [fuel] tank is 1¼ hours, the operating time achieved can be described as absolutely sufficient for the intended use, especially taking into account the safety provided by the multi-engine arrangement and the favourable behaviour of the engines after the first valve breaks occur. It is not known how many tests have been carried out to confirm the operating time".

Unlike the vibration issue, Voigt was forced to address the pulsejet's poor performance at high altitudes: "The performance above 7km altitude has not yet been achieved, but it is not required for bomber operations. At even higher altitudes, which would also be of interest for fighter use, difficulties are quite likely (reduction of the ignition speed at low air density and possibly Mach number influences in the valves or poor opening of the valves due to the low external pressure)."

And something that must have been common knowledge, and which therefore had to be addressed, was the pulsejets' incredible thirst. As with other aspects of the project, he worked hard to find a way of turning this negative into a positive: "The fuel consumption per km of bomb transport performance when used with an SC 1000 is about twice as high as that of the Me 210. This price, which is paid for a significantly higher approach speed and a 300-400km/h higher escape speed, is fairly equivalent to the value for the Me 109 G when used with an SC 250. This comparison with the Me 109 (which is only approved for 250kg bombs!) shows that this effort is now considered appropriate for significantly lower speeds."

THE WARSCHAU-SÜD MODEL

Having heavily promoted the Me 328's anticipated effectiveness as a flying naval gun and the remarkable simplicity and absolute safety of its design, Voigt next turned to the enormous savings that could be realised if only it could be rushed into mass production, Me 321-style.

The report stated: "The Me 328 model offers rare possibilities for production in large quantities, both in terms of production in accordance with the Warschau-Süd special campaign and in terms of normal mass production. The advantages in this regard are so crucial that they alone justify the implementation of the special campaign proposed.

"The cost of building materials is initially illustrated by the empty weights: Me 328 = approx. 1,250kg, Me 109 G = approx. 2,250kg, Me 210 = approx. 7,000kg. Despite the significantly increased bomb load [capability], the weight is not much more than half that of the Me 109 (the comparison with the Me 309 would be even more favourable).

"The use of lightweight alloy is almost completely avoided in the construction of this aircraft. For production as part of a special campaign, the use of lightweight alloy for the fuel tanks and for individual skin panels (nose) is planned in order to avoid the transition to less proven and less easy to implement construction methods. For normal large-scale production, sheet steel is intended for these components. The rest of the airframe is made of wood and tubular steel.

"A very special saving of the highest quality materials is also made with the engine. The effort required to manufacture the engines is only a very small fraction of the effort required to manufacture a piston engine today."

Evidently the Me 328's twin pulsejets weighed a total of 250kg, where as the DB 605 of an Me 109 G was 1,240kg and the two DB 601 Fs of an Me 210 weighed around 2,500kg together. The cost of an Argus pulsejet was given as RM 100-400 for a 150kg thrust unit, which "would result in a total engine price of RM 400-1,600 for the installation of 4 x 150kg!" The total cost of an Me 328 with two units was around RM 2,000 compared to the total cost of a DB 605-powered Me 109 G at RM 43,000 or a twin DB 601 F-powered Me 210 at RM 76,000.

"The jet pipes are currently made from Sicromal.[6] However, accepting a moderate reduction in service life, production can probably be switched exclusively to fuel-efficient steel. Difficulties in this regard, especially with fast aircraft, are not expected based on Argus's experience with test engines made from deep-drawn[7] sheet metal.

"The structure of the aircraft was designed from the outset with special consideration of mass production and has recently been largely converted to a more straightforward structure based on the experience gained in building the V1 and V02. The middle part of the fuselage consists of a simple tubular steel frame, which is covered with cylindrical curved plywood panels. The tail end is aft of the landing gear and is also cheap thanks to its small size... The fin is of the same design as the wing, the tailplane is adopted unchanged from the Me 109, with the exception of the reinforcements required by the higher speed. When attaching the engines to the fuselage, sheet metal covering may be necessary for the rudder."

Compared to the Me 321, Voigt argued, the risk of the proposed 'special campaign' would be minimal: "The Me 321 was an aircraft of a size for which we had no experience whatsoever in terms of flight and operating characteristics (towing and construction weight). The decision to carry out the special campaign to produce 200 [Me 321] aircraft was made at a time when only a preliminary project for the aircraft, a preliminary weight calculation... and a rudder power estimate were available. On the other hand, the Me 328 is an aircraft whose size does not differ significantly from the one we know (wing area = 7.5sqm compared to 10sqm for the Me 209); In addition, the airframe has already flown with good results... so we already have an overview of the flight characteristics and they can be finally assessed shortly. There is therefore hardly any risk from the airframe today and any issues can be completely eliminated after a few weeks of intensive testing."

Voigt claimed that construction of the Me 328's components could "be accommodated by any company (Regensburg, Jacobs, Hirth etc.) without the need for special knowledge and experience, as is the case with the large welded parts of the Me 321. The manufacturing process, including the transportation of materials, semi-finished parts and completed assemblies within and between the manufacturing plants, is of course made easier by the [aircraft's] small dimensions. The additional effort for installing and operating the engines should not be significantly greater than what had to be accepted for setting up, operating and dropping the [RATO] rocket devices on the Me 321."

He outlined the timetable achieved with the Me 321 "being the most urgent" project within the company: "From the first suggestion by Prof Messerschmitt to delivery of the first machine—4.5 months, to delivery of the 55th machine—8 months, to delivery of the 100th machine—~13 months. Therefore, provided there is sufficient working capacity, it can be assumed with complete certainty that it is technically possible to bring out several hundred [Me 328] machines by May 1943, i.e. by spring 1943. Since all preliminary considerations for the task, preliminary designs and project work were carried out during the development and construction period of the Me 321, used [here] as a basis, the schedule estimate certainly contains reserves."

Now it was time to address "a very big disadvantage"

Rear-side views of the Me 328 V1 in its original glider configuration in tail-down pre-launch position with take-off wheel set attached.

Rear and side views of the Me 328 V1 glider in tail-high landing position, minus the take-off wheels.

when it came to the 'special campaign': "Since secrecy in Germany is extremely poor (this can already be proven for the Me 328!) it is to be expected that the enemy will know about the work on the pulsejets and the Me 328 very early on. If the pace of development here is insufficient, it can be seen that the fast jet bomber with its war-decisive capabilities will be used against us.

"This danger is greatly increased by the fact that perhaps this year pulsejets will be used as aircraft auxiliary engines for tasks that are not of the same importance to the war against England and will be lost there. This fact forces us to complete and implement the development that has now started as quickly as possible in order to avert a serious danger. In addition, real secrecy must be ensured under all circumstances through consultation with the Technical Office and premature deployment for tasks that are not crucial to the war and in insufficient numbers must be prevented."

FREEING CAPACITY

Right at the end of his report, Voigt presented the thorniest issue when it came to establishing his Me 328 'special campaign'—production capacity, or the lack of it. Nevertheless, he was adamant that the required manpower and materials had to come from… somewhere: "The expected technical possibilities, and the danger of the enemy using the jet bomber, force this capacity to be freed under all circumstances, even if this makes it impossible to carry out any other tasks.

"An absolute prerequisite for successful implementation is the use of a first-class prototype builder in the construction office or possibly processing in a special group (like Me 321) under excellent leadership. The Technical Office must of course be required to provide staff… it is to be expected that the required capacity will have to be made available by cancelling orders.

"The need for designers should not be very great. Since an average of 20 people were involved in the development of the Me 321, the construction of the Me 328 according to the same guidelines can certainly be completed with 10 designers. Development in a series production-ready form will probably not require much more time, but requires significantly greater design capacity.

"In my opinion, the following tasks can be postponed compared to the Me 328 special campaign: Me 323 with Ju 88 engine; Me 109 armed-reconnaissance (will be replaced by Me 328); Me 329 (work for the later future and capacity-wise much heavier than Me 328); Me 210 further development as a replacement for the follow-up with DB 603 [i.e. Me 410 replacement]; Me 264 (possibly further trimming or resetting of the works).

"Manufacturing capacity: The production should be easier to accommodate than the [initial] construction. According to our current knowledge, the following positions are possible: Mtt. GmbH Regensburg; Jacobs-Schweyer, Schempp-Hirth, Graf Hagenburg. [Prisoner

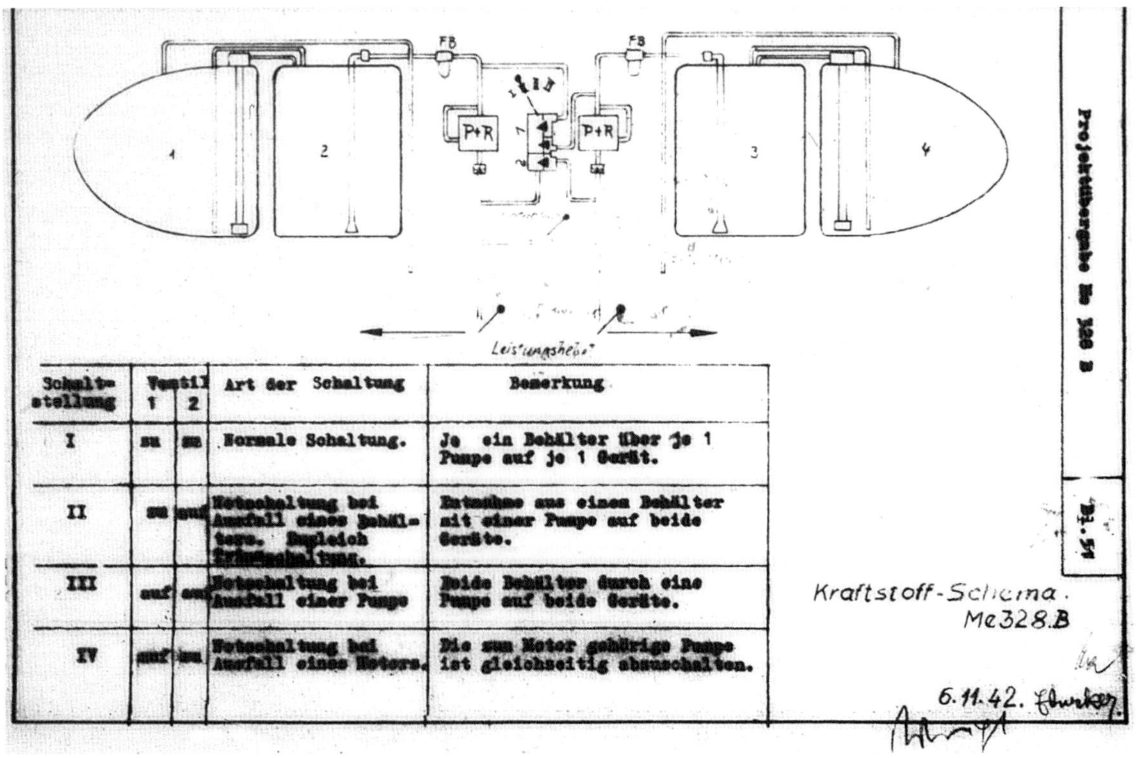

Me 328 B fuel system diagram dated November 6, 1942. This appears to be the earliest known use of the 'Me 328 B' designation.

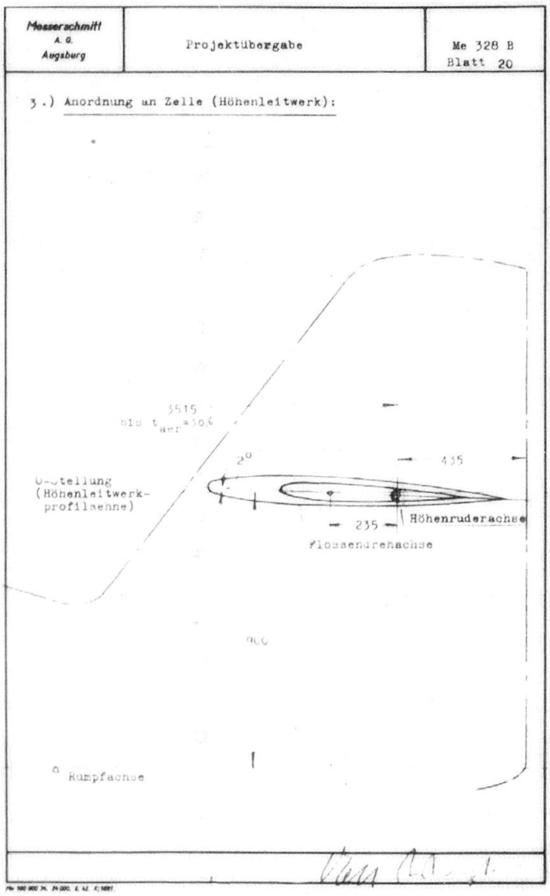

The detail design of Messerschmitt's intended series production model Me 328 B came together during November and December 1942. This drawing shows the tailplane position.

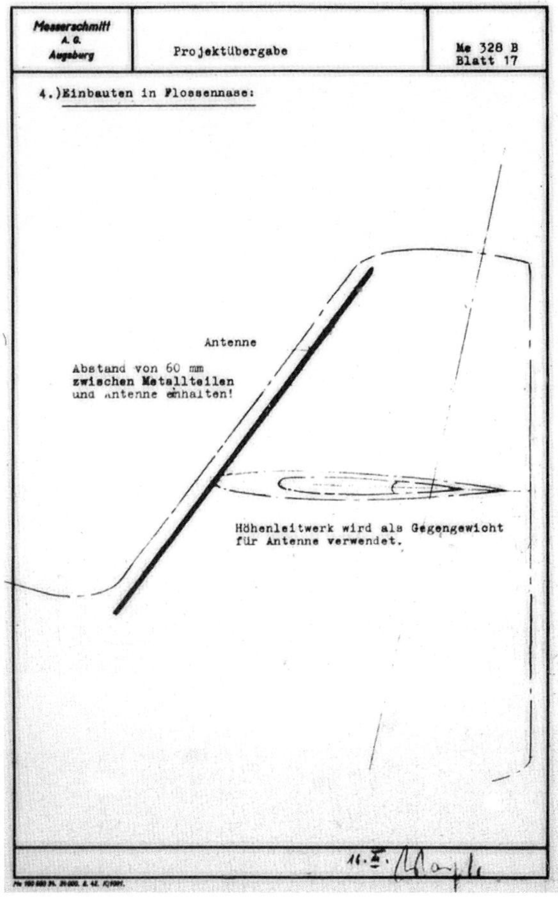

Antenna in the leading edge of the Me 328 B's fin. The drawing is dated November 16, 1942.

of war] Russians will certainly also be able to be used for the processing."

At the very end of his report, Voigt added a section entitled 'tactical risk': "Considering the risk of failure in development also includes clarifying the question of whether, after the technical problem has been completely solved, the possibility and necessity of frontline deployment still exists with certainty. The great efforts that were made to carry out the Warschau-Süd operation with complete technical success were initially quite fruitless as the intended deployment against Britain was not carried out.

"The Me 328 is not expected to fail due to the lack of tactical operational necessity. The need for targeted bombing attacks against strongly defended targets in the area of the front, or up to 300km behind it, will be present at all times—both in operations against England, as well as in trench or fortress warfare and in mobile warfare. Likewise, an aircraft will always be needed that can attack warship and merchant ships at sea and in harbour with a certain chance of success, even with the strongest defences. Using it as a fighter aircraft with appropriate armament will always be worthwhile."

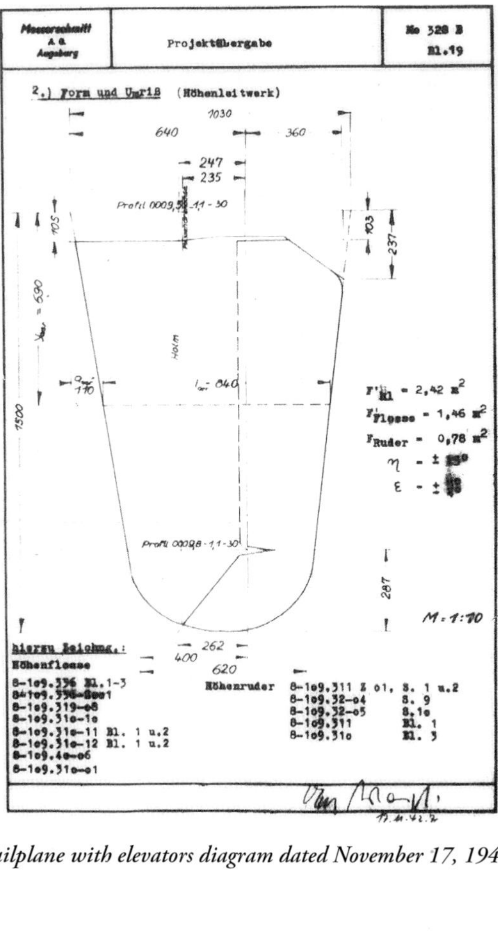

Tailplane with elevators diagram dated November 17, 1942.

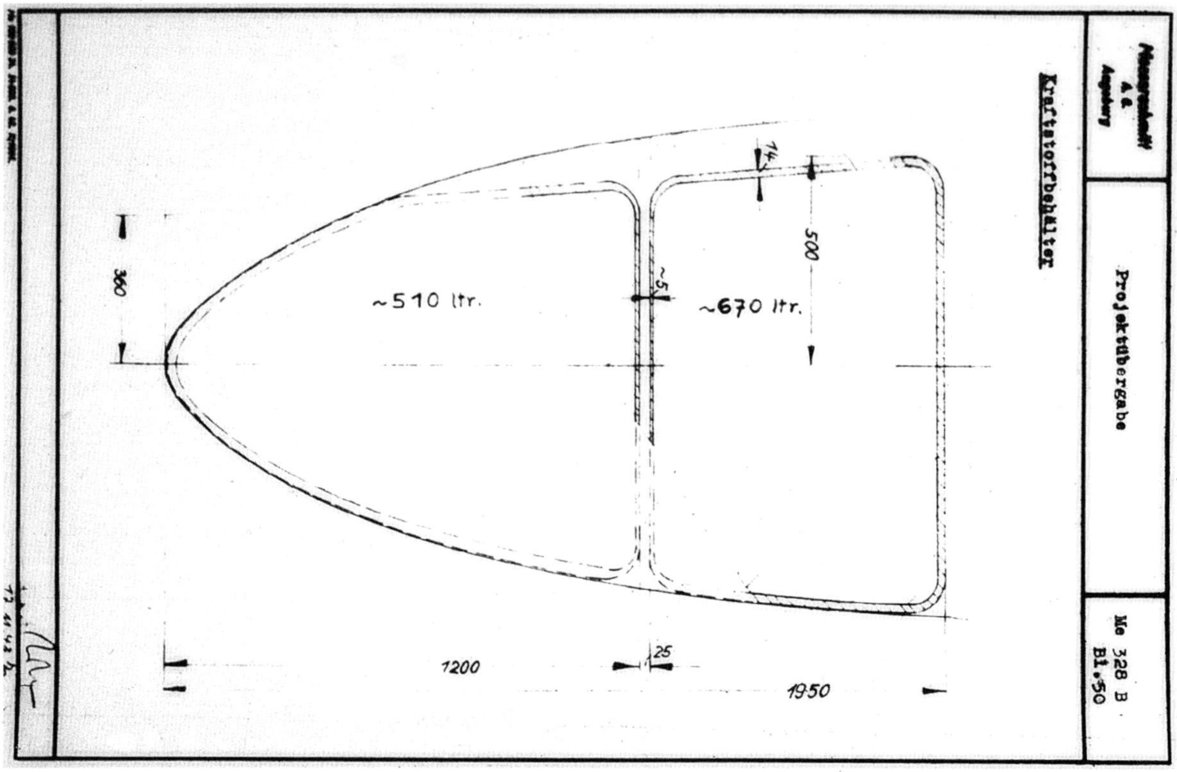

Both the nose and tail of the Me 328 B, despite its small wings and hefty bomb load, were to be filled with fuel—the nose containing a total of 1,180 litres.

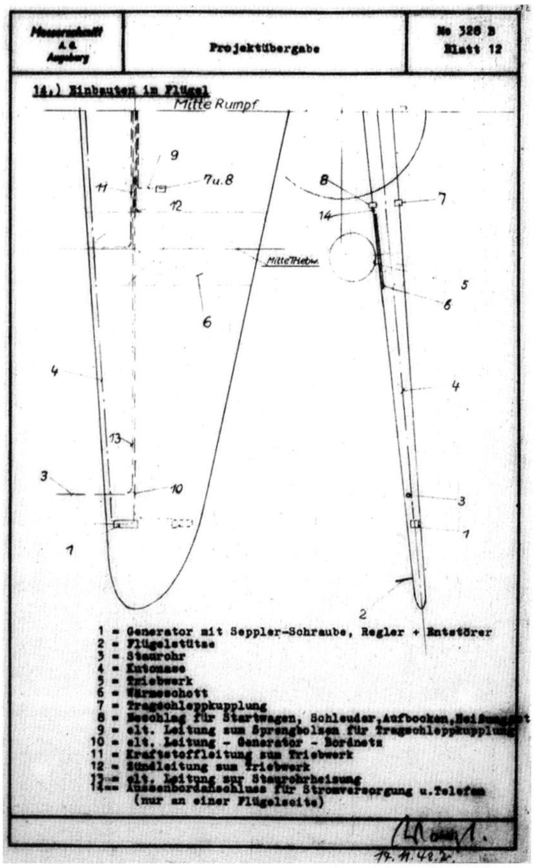

This diagram shows the high wing position intended for the Me 328 B—a key point of structural differentiation between the B-type and the original low-wing Me 328 prototypes.

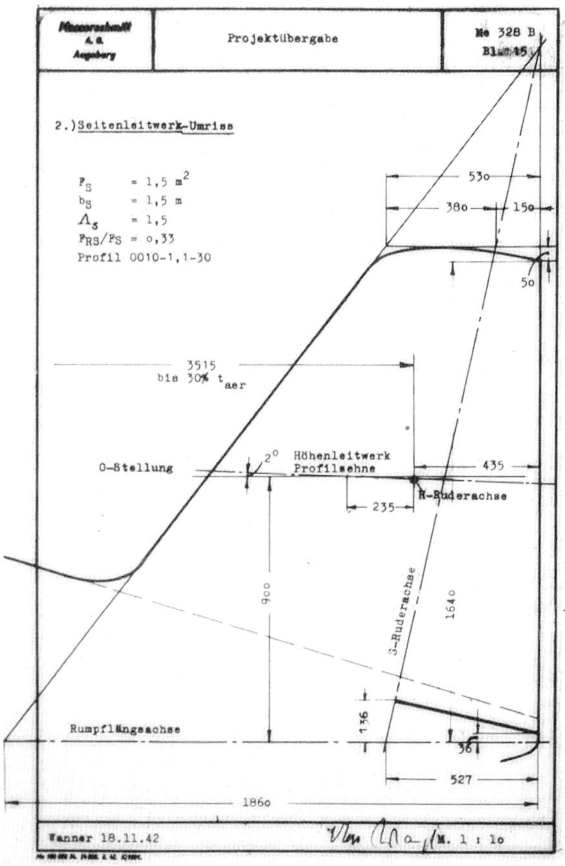

Me 328 B tailfin and rudder outline, dated November 18, 1942.

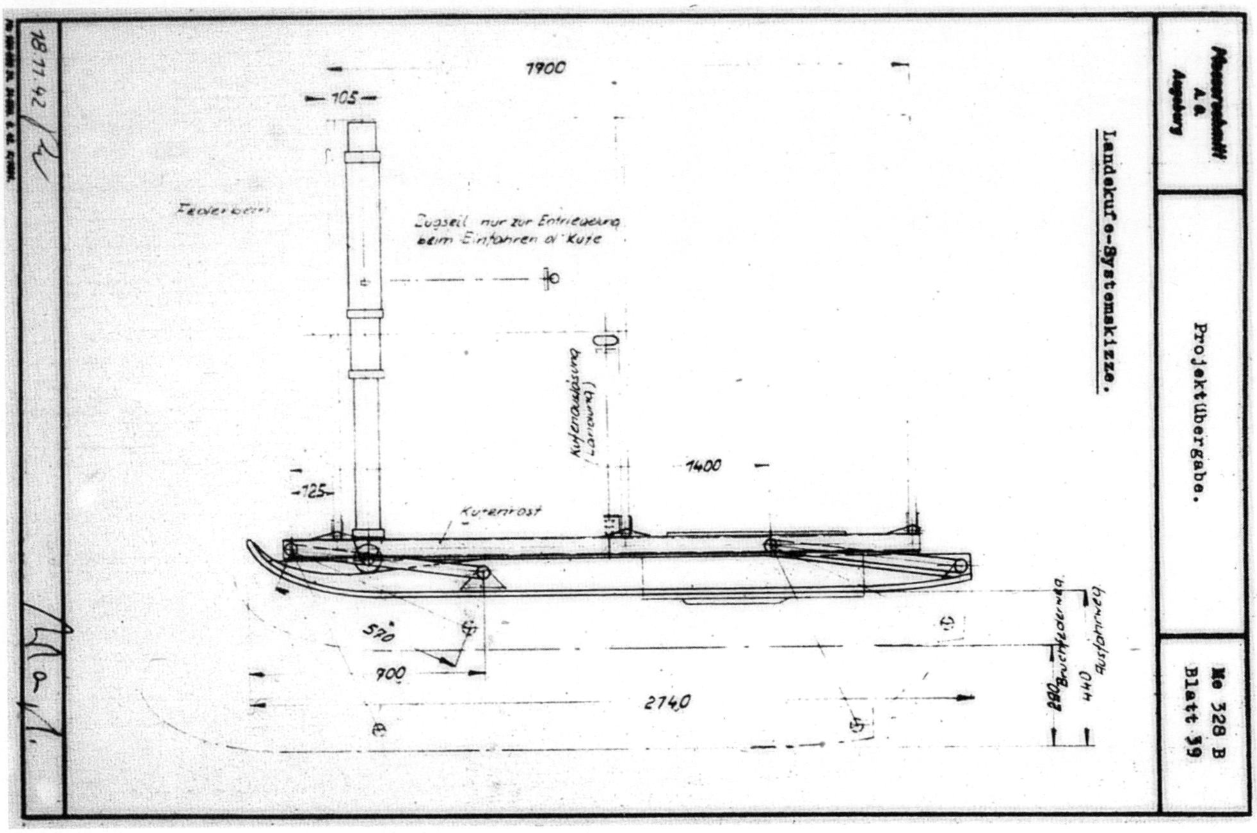

Landing skid design for the Me 328 B from November 18, 1942.

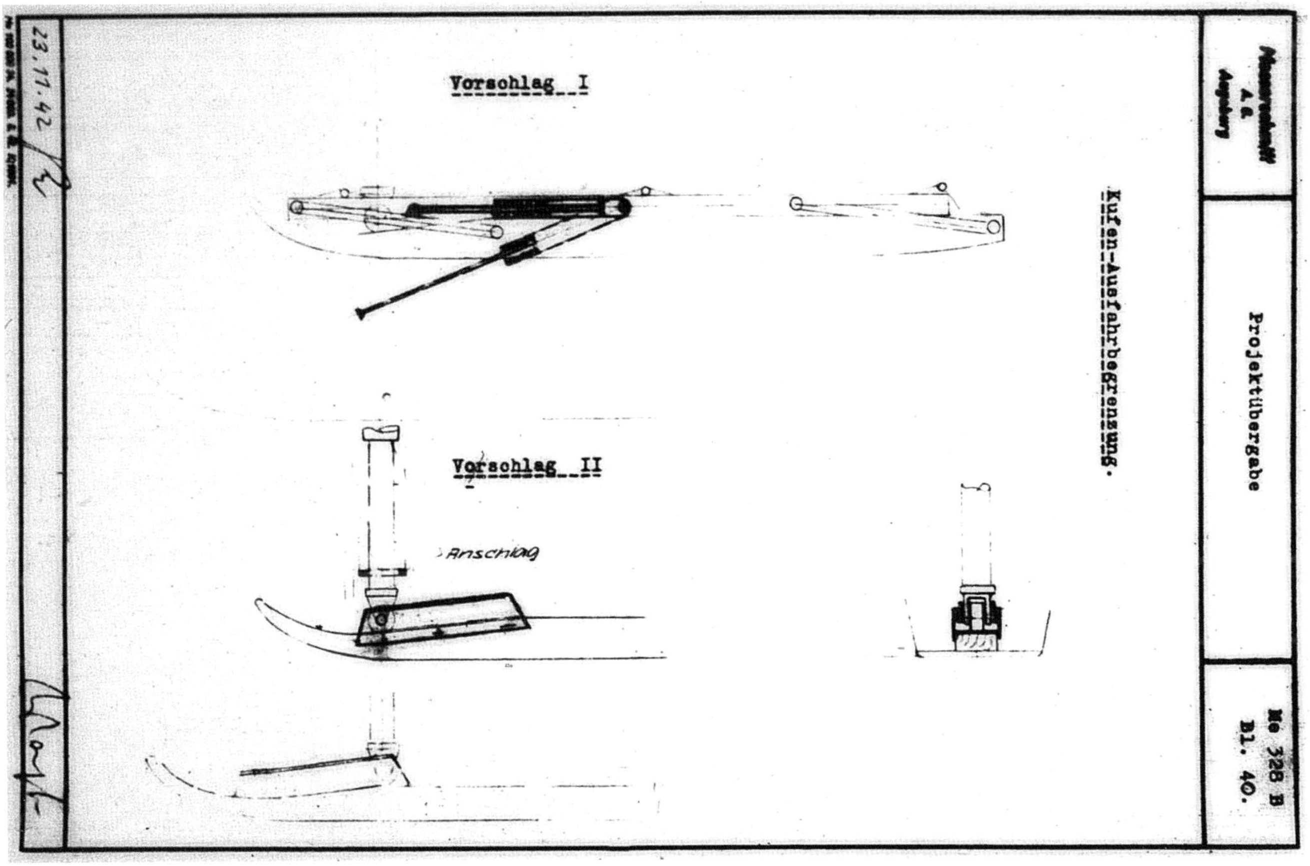

Designs for the Me 328 B's skid extension limiter.

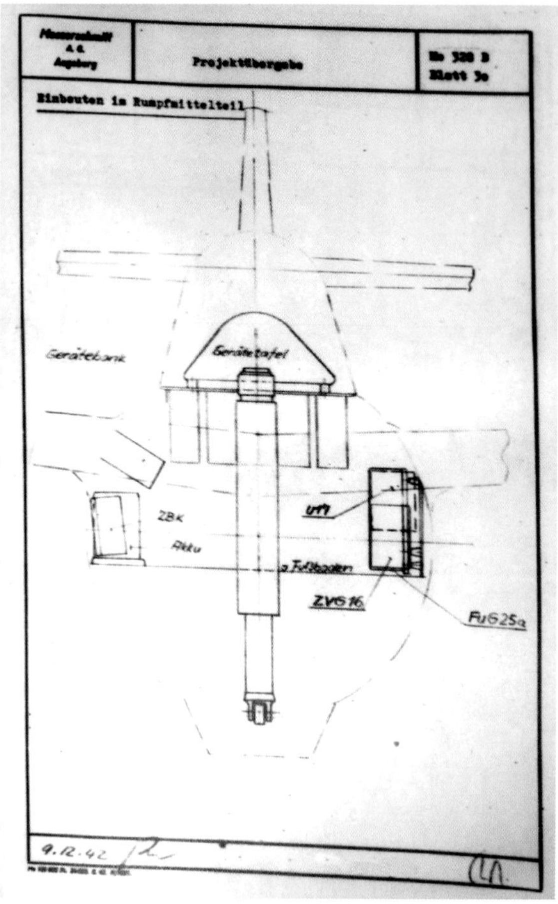

Slightly warped image showing equipment installations in the centre section of the Me 328 b—including the pilot's instrument panels. Again, note the high wing position.

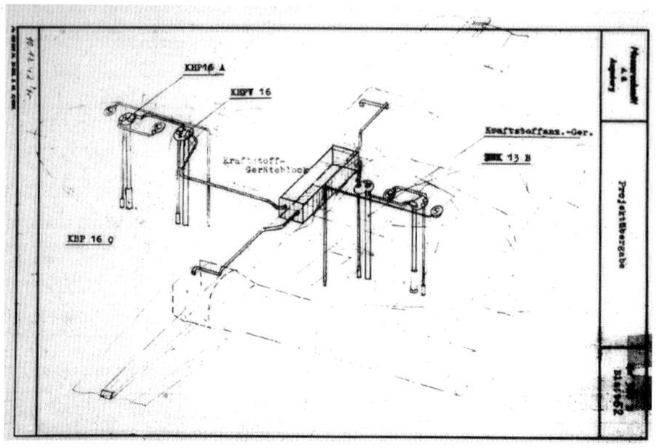

Me 328 B fuel control system in a diagram dated December 10, 1942.

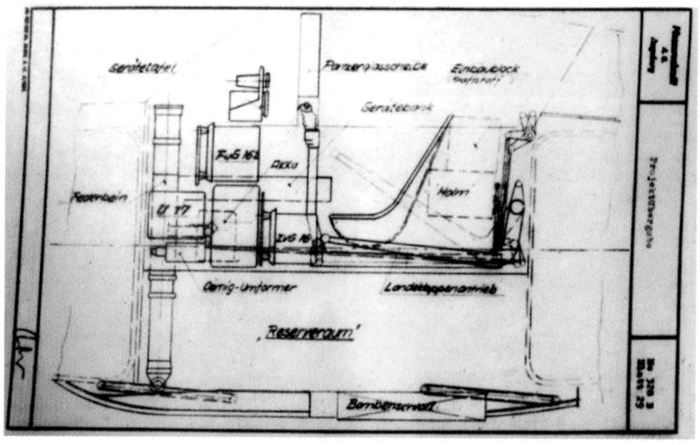

Layout of the Me 328 B's cockpit—including seat, instrument panels, equipment and bulletproof glass plate.

ME 328 BUZZ BOMB

Two weeks after the publication of his mammoth Me 328 'special campaign' report—its contents presumably still very much on his mind—Voigt came up with another use for the aircraft. Why not fit it with a basic guidance system and turn it into an unpiloted flying bomb?

Willy Messerschmitt outlined the idea to Theo Croneiss in a memo on September 15, 1942: "For a long time I've been thinking about how we can bombard London continuously with cannon, artillery pieces and the like from the Channel coast. In a discussion today, Mr Voigt made the suggestion to install the simple remote control [system] of the remote-controlled gliding bombs in the 328 and to catapult these aircraft, equipped with explosives, to the Channel coast without a crew and to take them to England via the guidance beam route. Installation is incredibly easy, as the aircraft can be made entirely out of wood using the most primitive design and the Schmidt engines are also surprisingly cheap.

"Even if it is not expedient to use such devices against the enemy after the first tests with the engine and the 328 have been completed, it is still important to prepare for such a thing, since [this] use is only possible when there are a few thousand aircraft available, so as not to alert the enemy prematurely (of course, this method can also be used at a correspondingly greater distance—perhaps with less accuracy)."[8]

This would appear to have been a case of 'great minds think alike' since Milch had given the order to proceed with full-scale development of the V-1 flying bomb (aka Fi 103, aka FZG 76)—essentially the same system Voigt had described—a little under three months earlier on June 19, 1942.[9] There is no evidence that Voigt or anyone else at Messerschmitt was aware of the V-1 at this time, though it is possible that such information could have found its way to the company via contacts at the Air Ministry or via Argus.

ME 328 V1 DESTROYED

Within two months of Klöckner's first flight in the Me 328 V1 (see Chapter 2), but after he had been rendered unable to fly it by vibrations from the pulsejet-powered DFS 230, the aircraft was fitted with a pair of underwing Argus pulsejets and test-flown in that configuration. Exactly who made this flight, and how many powered flights there were with the Me 328 V1 in total, is unknown[10] but anecdotally

Me 328 V1 fitted with both wing root-mounted Seppeler generator and underwing pulsejets. The photo comes from a DFS report dated December 17, 1942—by which time the V1 had already crashed and been destroyed during pulsejet flight-testing.

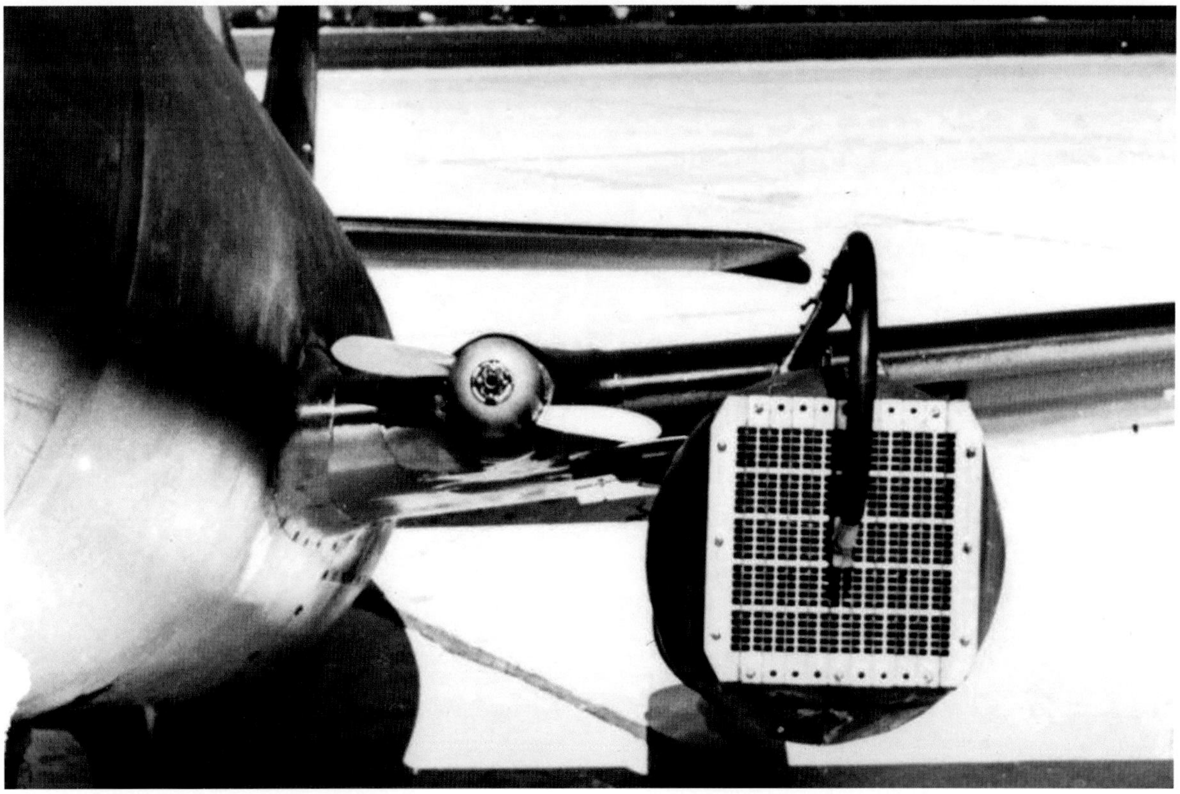

Generator and engine close-up from the December 17, 1942, DFS report. Early project documents suggest that the Me 328 V1 was intended to have only one Seppeler generator, in the port wing. The caption from the original report reads: "View from the front. The [fuel] pump is installed in the wing between the engine and fuselage, driven by a Seppeler propeller." There is no known surviving photo showing the starboard wing and whether it was actually fitted with a second generator in the end is unclear.

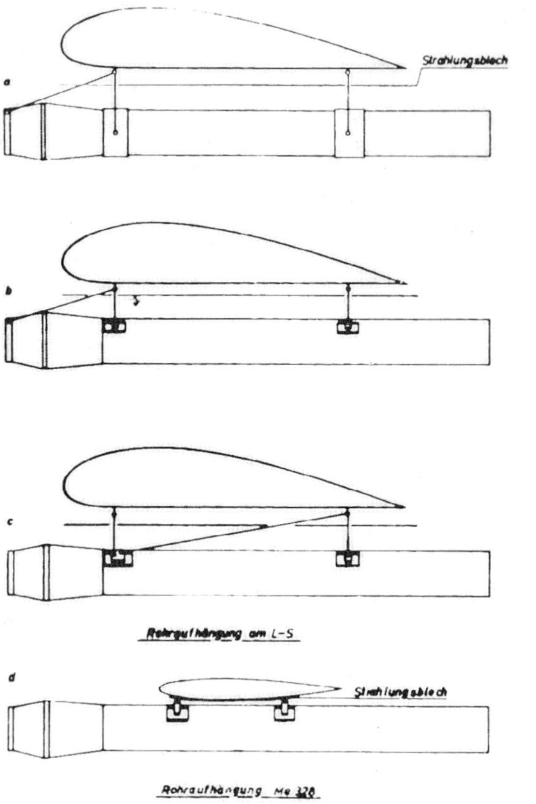

Diagram from the DFS report showing the different pulsejet attachment arrangements used for the DFS 230 aka 'L-S' compared to that used for the Me 328.

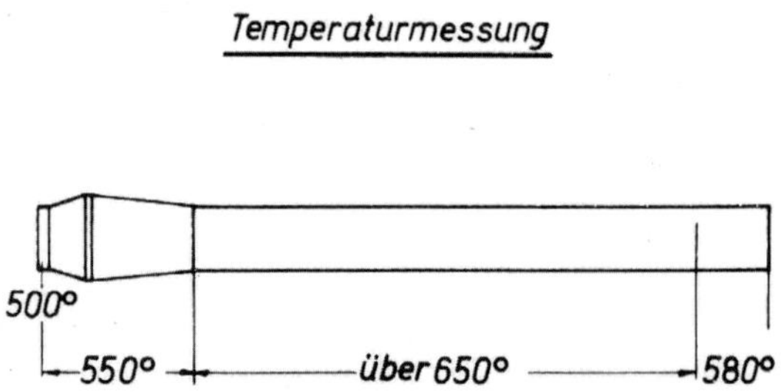

DFS diagram showing the temperatures reached by Argus's prototype pulsejets during testing.

it appears that the pilot who took over from Klöckner as the 'lead' on the Me 328 was Rudolf 'Gretchen' Ziegler.

The DFS's situation report for the period up to September 30, 1942,[11] stated that: "The [Me 328] V1 and V2 have been completed. The flight testing of the V1 was carried out gradually, initially with the lowest flight weight and without engine installations and attachments, then the flight weight was slowly increased to around 1,500kg corresponding to a wing loading of 200kg/sqm. Engine testing then began. On the 30th flight, the V1 was completely destroyed because a control line for the elevators resonated with the engines and broke."

Again, it is unknown who was at the controls of the aircraft but an independent report[12] by an engineer of the Wilhelm Schmidding company, who happened to be at Hörsching gathering data for the company's own pulsejet experiments a few months later, noted: "The Argus tubes generate such vibrations on the fighter that in the V1 model there was a permanent break in the altitude control line and the machine was no longer manoeuvrable, so the pilot had to bail out."

Nearly three years later on July 1, 1945, shortly after the war, the head of the DFS's Air Construction Institute, Felix Kracht, was interviewed by Allied intelligence officers about his work. Discussing the Me 328, he said: "Both propelling units... were to be suspended one from each side of the fuselage, underneath the wings. The DFS had objections to the method of suspending of the engines and against the construction of the fuselage. However, in compliance with the wish of Messerschmitt, this method was accepted.

"Construction work was started in the beginning of 1942 and the first model was flown in August 1942. Altogether three planes were produced. The first one was wrecked through the vibrations of the engines, while the other two were destroyed in Hörsching on May 5, 1945."[13]

Again it appears likely, though not certain, that the pilot who bailed out of the Me 328 V1 when its controls failed was Ziegler. It seems that with the Me 328 V1 destroyed, flight-testing continued with the now completed Me 328 V2—though without engines fitted. Another throwaway line from the DFS summary of September 30 is also worthy of note here: "The construction of a V4 fuselage began, in which the pilot's seat was moved to the nose." There is no known drawing or blueprint depicting an Me 328 with its cockpit set right at the front of the aircraft, though as noted in Chapter 1, several P 1079 designs had this feature.

Willy Messerschmitt wrote a memo to Voigt's office on October 12, 1942, which clearly indicated that the Me 328 in its existing form would need significant changes while being prepared for series production. He wrote: "When the Me 328 series is revised, it must be clarified in a joint discussion with me whether it is not possible to integrate the modified pulsejets organically into the airframe so that their additional drag is reduced to a minimum."[14] Again, no evidence is known to exist suggesting that an Me 328 was ever designed with its engines built into its airframe.

An Air Ministry production schedule issued at the beginning of November 1942[15] shows three Me 328 airframes under construction at Messerschmitt: V6, V7 and V02. The entries for the first two were annotated "all work stopped" but the note beside the third, the V02, stated: "Currently in final assembly. General testing planned." Presumably the DFS had been working on the V1 to V5 prototypes, with the first two completed and the fourth being rearranged with a nose cockpit. The V6-V7 at Messerschmitt had been cancelled but the V02—evidently the same as the original V1 but with a fuselage made from welded sheet steel[16]—was nearing completion.

BAUR'S FLIGHT TEST

Klöckner had evidently made his first unpowered flight in the Me 328 V2 on October 31, from 2.30pm to 2.58pm, and then made further flights in it on November 2, 3 and 4. The following day, November 5, 1942, Messerschmitt company test pilot Karl Baur made what appears to have been his only flight in an Me 328, specifically the V2, at Hörsching from 3.30pm to 3.50pm. In his report,[17] written four days later, he noted that "due to bad weather conditions, only one flight (towed flight) at 3,000m followed by a glide flight was possible".

The aircraft's take-off weight was an extremely light 1,020kg with the centre of gravity set at 27%. No engines were fitted but the aircraft had a "new canopy with flat windows".

Baur's experience was similar to Klöckner's. He wrote: "Take-off with flap position 20-degrees. When taxiing, the tow plane (an He 111) cannot be seen at first due to the [aircraft's] nose-high attitude. Only after about 200m of rolling distance can the tail be lifted off. The take-off speed is approximately 180km/h, the taxiing distance is approx. 800m on a concrete track. At this high speed, it is not easy to keep the 328 behind the tow plane on the current two-wheel chassis with a smaller track width. Take-offs on uneven turf are likely to be difficult and are even considered impossible by pilot Ziegler, who has made most of the flights so far.

"The towing flight does not cause any difficulties at a towing speed of at least 260km/h. The angle of attack in tow is about three degrees with 20% flap deflection. When the flaps are retracted, the angle of attack is greater than five degrees. The fuselage snout again obscures the view of the tow plane. With higher wing loading, the conditions become even more unfavourable, so that the limit will soon be reached in terms of increasing weight in towing flight.

"During gliding, the stall behaviour could only be observed briefly. The aircraft does not tend to tip over dangerously when stalling with the flaps retracted and extended, as the inner wing always loses airflow prematurely. The right inner wing is disturbed by the installation of the fuel pump, which causes a larger area on the

The Messerschmitt Me 328 V2 low-wing prototype prior to the installation of its pulsejets and its nose-mounted Seppeler generators. The flat-windowed canopy described by Baur, however, has been fitted.

right side to be disturbed when stalled and as a result a damped movement around the longitudinal axis occurs when stalled.

"With the flaps retracted, the right inner wing already shows a fault area behind the pump at 210km/h. At 200km/h a third of the right and left wings have already lost airflow and at 190km/h the aircraft finally stalls with a slight right turn around the longitudinal axis.

"The pitot tube attached to the fin is occluded and the speed indicator suddenly drops to less than 100km/h. A quick recalculation shows that the expected speed values are not achieved. It is suggested to resolve the problem on the inner wing by relocating the fuel pump and adding a small fillet.

"When turning, the early loss of airflow over the inner wing is unpleasantly noticeable... In horizontal flight, the main problem is the forward visibility, which in my opinion does not allow bombs to be dropped [accurately] in horizontal flight and only allows shooting. The lines of sight available are much smaller than with the 110. Even if visibility is brought to the level of the 110 by changing the fuselage nose, that is still not enough for the use of the 328. In addition, the Argus engines obscure the view and thereby create a blind spot of 45 degrees to the side.

"For these reasons, the fuselage must be fundamentally changed and the pilot's seat must be moved to the nose of the fuselage. This has various advantages: 1) The visibility question is 100% solved. 2) The fuel tanks can be placed around the centre of gravity. 3) The engines can, or must be attached to the fuselage so that they exhaust behind the tailplane.

"This brings two main advantages: a) The pressure wave behind the engines can no longer damage the airframe (in the DFS 230 even steel pipes broke as a result and the break in the 328 V1 could also be attributed to this). b) The engines can be relocated at the height of the fuselage axis and therefore do not bring about any change in stability, as is to be expected from the experience with the 262 due to the engines being located low down below the wing.

"The rudder effect of is good. However, this should not be a reason to make the ailerons smaller again, for example. The rudder forces are very small up to the speeds of 500km/h, the forces are well coordinated. The sliding rolling moments are very large. It is recommended to change the anhedral shape to minus half a degree on a test machine.

"Landing is not easy due to the high speed and rate of descent and is roughly equivalent to landing the 109 with the engine stopped. After touchdown, the aircraft slides approx. 400m on dry grass and up to 900m on wet grass! As long as braking or something similar is not possible, this remains the case.

"Landing is often made more difficult because the windows fog up. Better ventilation of the cabin must therefore be provided. In view of the high landing speed, rollover protection must [also] be provided.

"The canopy with flat windows has proven itself. Since curved panes are almost never free of distortion, it is recommended to always use flat panes in the new cabin. The pilot's seat in the 328 V2 is uncomfortable because it is too narrow at shoulder height and [the aircraft] can only be flown with a back parachute. In all cases, a seat parachute must be provided.

"There is a limit to the wing loading for testing in normal aircraft towing of approx. 200kg/sqm. For this reason, the questions that arise during towing and skid starting must be clarified as quickly as possible. In addition, the question of engines is still largely unresolved." Klöckner then evidently recorded two more Me 328 V2 flights on November 10.

SPÄTE PUTS THE KNIFE IN

At this point—mid-November 1942—it must have been reasonably clear to all parties that the Me 328 had some serious problems. The pulsejets, particularly the vibrations they generated and their resulting impact on the airframe needed to be addressed but there seems to have been a real difference of opinion on how best to go about it. Some favoured redesigned attachment points under or above the wings while others believed that attaching the engines to the rear fuselage would make the biggest difference. Ongoing wind tunnel tests at Messerschmitt and elsewhere aimed to address this issue.

And every pilot who had flown the aircraft to date had identified the lack of visibility over the long up-raised nose during the take-off run as a hazard. Baur had suggested moving the cockpit into the nose and the DFS had indeed been working on a variant, the Me 328 V4, with that configuration. However, Voigt's Project Office seems to have been opposed to alteration and as a result, the options for a different mode of take-off were reassessed.

Apparently six more Me 328/He 111 towed take-offs took place at Hörsching from November 24-30 and on November 25, 1942, the Project Office produced a new data sheet[18] for the Me 328 B. Drawings illustrating the design and features of this new variant—Voigt's 'flying artillery' bomber—had been steadily accumulating since at least the beginning of November. And they showed a design which appeared to increasingly diverge from that of the Me 328 V1/V02/V2 template as time wore on.

The latter now became the 'Me 328 A', where all previous designs no matter how different had been simply labelled 'Me 328'.

The sheet described the Me 328 B as 7.05m long and 2.85m high with a wingspan of 7m and a wing area of 8.5sqm; it was to be powered by two 400kg thrust Argus pulsejets. These specifications made the type significantly different in every way from the various designs outlined by the Project Office at the end of March 1942, eight months earlier, and somewhat different from the design outlined towards the end of June, five months earlier.

Inspector of Fighters Adolf Galland ordered Wolfgang Späte, then serving with Me 163 test unit Erprobungskommando 16, to visit Hörsching in late November to assess the Me 328 V2. He reportedly set off on November 24 and went by way of Augsburg—so by the time he got there he found that the weather conditions were too poor to allow a take-off in the prototype. In his Ekdo. 16 Work Report 13 he noted that "a weather situation with a cloud height of 3,000m, which is absolutely necessary for flights with the Me 328, is not expected before mid-December. A preliminary report is therefore presented below, based on information from the Messerschmitt company's chief pilot Baur and Dipl.-Ing. Ziegler".[19]

The report itself painted a fairly bleak picture of the Me 328's prospects: "The current development of the Me 328 does not appear to be so advanced that it can be clearly seen whether it will actually meet the requirements and have the performance and characteristics that have been calculated for it.

"The result of the flight tests to date can be summarised as follows: the aircraft with a wing loading of 150kg/sqm can take off like a glider when towed behind an He 111 and can be maintained at a speed of 260km/h when towing. Take-offs with high wing loads can only be carried out using a tow or catapult start, which is currently being prepared. With the landing gear currently in use, the towing start is very difficult because you cannot see the He 111 from the Me 328 during the first hundred metres of taxiing.

"In free flight (after releasing) the Me 328 descends at around 7m/sec or 4m/sec when using Argus tubes, each with a thrust of 150kg. The He 111 [when] used as the towing machine cannot reach an altitude of significantly more than 3,000m. Since landing preparations have to be made after descending to an altitude of 1,000m, only about four to eight minutes are available for testing purposes—between 3,000m and 1,000m altitude. The top speed in a dive has so far only been 500km/h. Gliding usually takes place at 200-300km/h. The aircraft should have satisfactory flight characteristics, i.e. well-balanced rudder pressures and rudder effects.

"Despite sufficient elevator effect, at 150kg/sqm wing loading the turning radius is already disproportionately large, as is the interception radius... Visibility is severely impaired by the front part of the fuselage, so much so that during slow flight [coming in to land] obstacles in the flight path cannot be seen when close to the ground. Finding the target [during operations] may also be hampered by the poor visibility, but at least it would still be somewhat possible.

"To land, you must flare at 200km/h (always assuming 150kg/sqm wing loading). Landing on the skid requires about 500m slide distance on dry grass and 1,000m on wet grass. No landing has been attempted in snow. Without braking equipment (brakes on the skid or brake rockets), a normal airfield would not be sufficient for landing in snowy conditions.

"The Argus tubes used so far were measured on the test stand with a maximum thrust of 150kg each. The flight tests at the Argus company had initially shown that with increasing speed there was not a decrease in performance—as originally assumed—but rather an increase in performance. The measurement of the 150kg pipes on the Me 328 or on a DFS 230 used as a test vehicle at Hörsching have recently shown just the opposite. According to the experiences there, the pipes appear to be dependent not only on altitude but also on speed, i.e. as the speed increases, the performance of the pipes drops significantly. If this statement is correct, the entire Me 328 programme would be called into question for the time being, even if the 300kg tubes planned for the final version turned out to be dependent on the speed.

"In order to be usable at the front, the following conditions would have to be met [by the Me 328]: 1) The aircraft must be able to take off properly while being towed and using a starting aid. It must be possible to do this with the maximum wing loading intended for frontline operations. 2) The flight characteristics would have to be satisfactory even with a higher wing load than the maximum tested so far of 180kg/sqm; the landing speed of the upgraded machines with Argus tubes and a minimum fuel reserve must remain within tolerable limits. 3) The Argus tubes intended for the operational machines must not show the drop in performance with an increase in speed that has been observed with the tubes previously used. If this cannot be avoided there must be such a power reserve that the calculated top speeds remain secure."

Writing about his trip to Hörsching some 40 years later,[20] Späte recalled: "This mission might have been a 'mission to heaven' for me—the Me 328 was still so unfinished at the time that I would have had a good chance of breaking my neck with it. But the weather gods seemed to smile on me, because they sent 14 days of the sort of meteorological conditions during which—as an old aviation saying goes—'even the birds walk'... Dipl.-Ing. Ziegler (known to us pilots as 'Gretchen' Ziegler) had the task of making the first take-offs with this custom ride.[21] As far as I know, Messerschmitt's chief pilot 'Karle' Baur also completed a few flights with it, but it was a completely pointless undertaking.

"Karl Baur, with whom I took part in several Rhön gliding competitions in the 1930s, advised me in his rude manner: 'Flying it will not give you any insights other than that it's extremely dangerous and in no way suitable for active service. And you don't even need to fly it to know that. I can tell you all of that with great precision!'

"Gretchen Ziegler had already conducted flight tests with this engine in Rechlin, where he managed to make more than 20 take-offs with the V1 in order to find out and eliminate control errors... The Me 328 was nothing unfamiliar to Ziegler in terms of engines nor the primitive nature of the airframe. However, he was unable to do anything more than extended gliding flights after being towed up behind an He 111. Taking off under our own power was unthinkable. Self-start or something similar was planned, but this only existed on paper.

"After waiting in vain for 14 days for the weather to improve, I wrote my report based on the detailed information provided by Karl Baur and Gretchen Ziegler. I was never sent to Hörsching again after that, especially because the Me 328 project was eventually put to bed."

ME 328/DO 217 MISTEL

Based on what happened next, it would seem that Späte's negative report—when circulated more widely—was highly influential and may have ultimately dealt a death blow to the Me 328, in its 'flying artillery' form at least. In the meantime however, efforts were already being made to correct some of the issues that the test pilots had identified.

One of the primary responsibilities of the DFS since the beginning of the war had been to test aerial towing configurations as well as in-flight coupling and decoupling of two aircraft. The ability of a powered aircraft to facilitate the take-off of one or more unpowered aircraft, if it could be done successfully and without undue effort, had a range of military applications.

The towing configuration initially used for the Me 328 was a straightforward drag tow—but the DFS had been enjoying some success with a configuration known as 'Mistel', where one aircraft was positioned on the back of another.

On December 7, 1942, a DFS report was published by the Gliding and Aircraft Design Department entitled Investigations into Starting Possibilities 8-328, "Mistel-Tow" 8-328 on Do 217.[22] This outlined a plan to mount the Me 328 atop a Do 217 for take-off, with the former detaching mid-flight. Such an arrangement would, at a stroke, eliminate the hazardous nose-high towed take-off run which successive pilots had identified as the type's most undesirable feature even when flown as a simple unpowered glider.

According to the report: "The investigations were based on the flight performance data of the Dornier company on the Do 217 E and Do 217 K as well as the preliminary results of wind tunnel model data on the DFS 8-328."

The analysis found that in the Mistel configuration it made little difference to the take-off run whether the carrier aircraft was the E or K model, so "further performance calculations are therefore carried out for the Do 217 E as a readily available machine".

When it came to separating the Me 328 from the Do 217 cleanly in flight, it had been determined that the latter's cruising speed of 400km/h would be sufficient. Attention had then focused on giving the 328 more lift so it could pull away vertically. It was noted that "this could be achieved by increasing the angle of attack of the 8-328 shortly before release. But that would complicate the attachment points. It is more expedient to achieve the desired increase in lift coefficients by extending the landing flap. In terms of strength, there are no concerns as the landing flap is designed to operate at 500km/h plus gust stress at full deflection, so that the permissible stress during take-off is far from being reached".

The necessary calculations had been carried out assuming that the Me 328 had both its engines and a bomb attached. It was further assumed that the Do 217's propellers were only operating at 0.75% efficiency but nevertheless at a flight speed of 380-420km/h and an altitude of 3km "safe take-off is guaranteed". Safe separation was even possible at ground level but in this case the carrier's speed would need to be slightly higher at 460km/h, with the Do 217 using emergency power.

The report summary stated: "The rough calculation shows that a take-off of the fully-laden 8-328 in 'Mistel' configuration can be carried out perfectly. The strength of the 8-328 is completely sufficient for the required speeds. The arrangement allows you to take off from any large airfield and does not require any special additional equipment. The main advantage of this starting method,

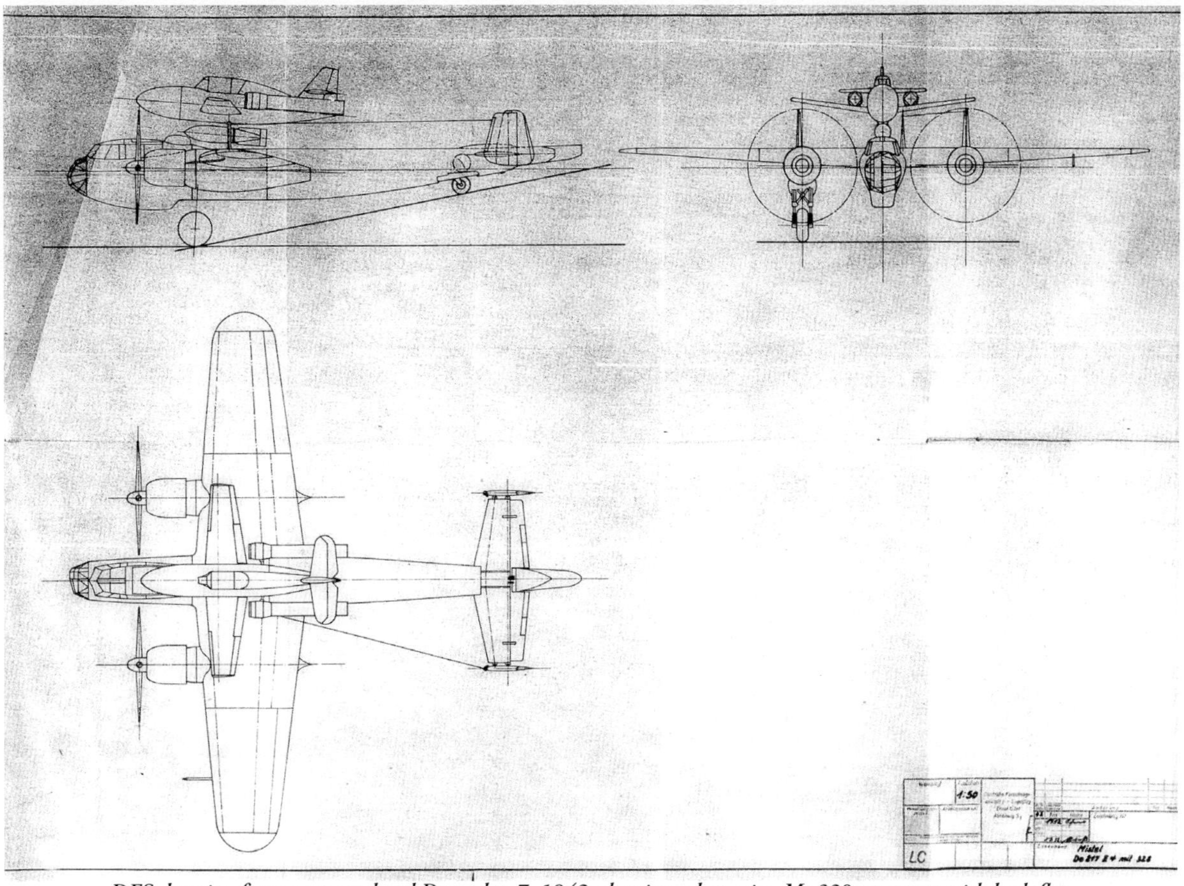

DFS drawing from a report dated December 7, 1942, showing a low-wing Me 328 prototype with both flat-windowed canopy and rear fuselage-mounted pulsejets carried on the back of a Dornier Do 217 E-4 for take-off.

however, is that a long take-off run in a heavily-loaded uncontrollable machine through the carrier aircraft's propeller wash is avoided and thus a jettisonable chassis, which can be expected to cause some difficulties with the bomb attached, becomes superfluous."

A Mistel take-off would still require the use of a medium bomber every time a single Me 328 needed to take off, just as it had with the towed configuration, but it did represent a big step forward in terms of flight safety and therefore viability for the project as a whole.

Three days later, on December 10, the Air Ministry composed an order outlining a new development and procurement programme prompted by "the unconditional demand for the qualitative superiority of German Air Force equipment over that of the enemy" under the codename 'Vulkan' or 'Volcano'.[23] The order, signed by Milch, stated: "The tasks carried out under this code have absolute priority within the Air Force. The programme includes jet-powered aircraft and remote-controlled vehicles, including the associated equipment and ground organisation necessary for their operation.

"The extension of the authority of the codename 'Vulkan' to the area of all armaments has been requested from the Reich Minister for Armaments and Ammunition [Albert Speer]. The development of some of the following devices is already underway at urgency level DE. The codename 'Vulkan' is intended to cover the procurement of these devices in particular, for which further preparations must be made as before."

The programme was said to cover the "Me 163 single-seat jet-powered interceptor; Me 262: single-seat fighter aircraft with two jet engines; He 280: single-seat fighter aircraft with two jet engines; Me 328: single-seat wooden fast bomber with two Argus pulsejets for coastal defence; Ar 234: single-seat reconnaissance aircraft with two jet engines" as well as various glide bombs, the V-1, a number of jet engines and some rocket engines.

The specific description of the Me 328 as being "for coastal defence" suggests that the Air Ministry was, at this point, at least nominally on board with the concept of the aircraft as outlined by Voigt three months earlier—as a launch system for the SC 500 RS rocket bomb against enemy shipping, perhaps during an invasion scenario. The Me 328 had found its purpose, the Air Ministry was backing it and the ongoing programme of development being jointly pursued by Messerschmitt and the DFS was smoothing out the rough edges. Späte's report, however, was a ticking timebomb…

4

JSF TO THE 'STOP' ORDER: DECEMBER 1942 TO SEPTEMBER 1943

By mid-December 1942 it appeared as though the stage was set for the 'special campaign' of emergency Me 328 production that Voigt had pleaded for so urgently in his September report.

The Vulkan programme was being established to ensure a ready supply of resources for jet projects, including the 328, and the Air Ministry continued to back the 'flying artillery' concept with ongoing support for the SC 500 RS rocket bomb. Furthermore, recognising that Messerschmitt continued to be overburdened with development tasks, the Ministry pursued another of the proposals bullet-pointed in Voigt's report — further outsourcing.

Voigt had suggested four potential production centres for the project: his company's own Regensburg factory, glider specialists Jacobs-Schweyer (JSF) at Darmstadt, Schempp-Hirth at Göppingen, and the newly established Graf Hagenburg factory at Sonthofen.

It was stated that JSF had been picked during a meeting on October 2 – and that Messerschmitt was considering building more Me 328s itself at Leipheim. The company would take over flight testing of the Me 328 V2 and V02 at Lechfeld as soon as possible but the DFS would continue in the meantime. Once the Me 328 V3 was ready, the DFS would use it as a development vehicle for the parasite Me 328.[1]

On October 27, a further meeting heard that preliminary approval had been granted for the construction of 300 Me 328s, with jig construction and the first 20 aircraft getting DE priority. A plan for this work was to be submitted to the Air Ministry by November 15.[2]

The partnership between JSF and Messerschmitt was fleshed out in a production proposal report labelled Programm Me 328 B—Bau von 300 Flugzeugen, dated December 15, 1942, and signed by both Jacobs himself and Messerschmitt's commercial director Rakan Kokothaki.[3]

According to the proposal's introduction, "the Me 328 B aircraft is a special development intended for use as a 'fast bomber' at low altitude. It was developed from the Me 328 A without any significant aerodynamic or size deviations, but with a simplified wooden construction".

The Me 328's construction was already fairly simple, but Messerschmitt had attempted to take this even further. Basic construction materials had been boiled down to "the cheapest possible materials", "in-demand materials" had been avoided at every turn and "the shortest possible production and throughput time" had been a consistent goal.

The report went on: "Due to the desired modular design

of the aircraft, it will be possible to carry out a final assembly of the individual airframe and equipment blocks easily, so that the disassembly can be carried out by a few specialists in a short time at any location, without any mechanical equipment". The Me 328 B was to become something of a flat-pack aircraft by design.

All of this was "based on the wish expressed by the Air Ministry GL/C-E 2 in Me 328 Protokoll Nr. 4, to produce a large number of Me 328 aircraft as fast bombers for use during the summer of 1943 using special measures in accordance with the 'Warschau-Süd' action. The task for these aircraft is: flying coastal artillery, invasion control and preparation for a major attack.

"The implementation of the intended programme is only possible under the condition that the deployment of the series production model aircraft begins before the completion of testing. When placing an order for delivery by the end of 1943, the client must therefore assume the risk that, in the event of significant setbacks in flight testing, delivery will be postponed beyond the planned dates. To protect against setbacks from testing, a comprehensive wind tunnel test (model scale approximately 1:1) is being prepared in an accelerated manner."

The report then outlined the current production status of the Me 328 prototypes: "Experimental and test aircraft—two [Me 328] aircraft from DFS-Ainring have been completed using mixed construction (wings made of wood, fuselage made of tubular steel with wooden skin); another eight are under construction. Furthermore, one aircraft made of welded sheet steel construction with wooden wings [has been] completed by Messerschmitt AG. The testing is in its early stages. Since the start of design and production of the Me 328 B can no longer wait until flight testing is completed, the following is required before series production begins: 1 x 1:1 scale model for wind tunnel tests, 3 x airframes without fixtures and fittings and with limited strength for rail take-off tests; 1x construction and visual mock-up; 1 x completed airframe without control surfaces for stress testing. These airframes, as well as the entire design, equipment design and construction, the entire production and, if possible, the final assembly, are [to be] carried out by JSF-Darmstadt under the supervision of Messerschmitt AG.

"Series aircraft—(complete production at JSF-Darmstadt) the production of 300 aircraft is currently planned. There will be: 1. [A] construction lot [of] 20 aircraft with makeshift jigs. 2. [A] construction lot [of] 280 aircraft with limited interchangeability. All 300 aircraft will be equipped as standard.

A table included in the report made it slightly clearer what all this meant; Messerschmitt's welded sheet steel Me 328 was, as mentioned, the V02, while the DFS-Ainring mixed construction aircraft were the Me 328 V1 to V10 prototypes. The construction batch of 20 assigned to JSF were also described as 'V-Serie' or prototypes—Me 328 B V1 to V20. This presumably meant that they would be used with various different equipment, bomb rack, bomb sight, skid and other loadouts to test those specific pieces of kit—a familiar way to utilise the initial run of prototypes for any new German aircraft type.

And finally, the batch of 280 aircraft was described as the 'Vor-Serie', the pre-production series.

LIST OF DEMANDS

Having outlined what was proposed, the report then set out what amounted to a list of demands—the essential political support, materials and manpower required to make it happen.

For starters, "the prerequisite for the timely delivery of these 300 aircraft is that no subsequent changes to the task or technical requirements occur during the course of the programme". Every German aircraft development programme up to this point had been plagued by on-the-fly change orders and requirement revisions, either from the Air Ministry or even directly from the Luftwaffe. And every German aircraft manufacturer abhorred this usually time-wasting, frequently ill-considered and occasionally contradictory interference. Firmly nipping this temptation to meddle in the bud right from the outset would vital to the fast delivery of the Me 328.

Secondly, if the Me 328 proved to be a hit with the Luftwaffe and it was clear that more would be needed, then "the decision to extend the programme ... must be made at least five months before the expiry of the currently planned programme in order to avoid a larger gap in output. If there are no changes in the follow-up programme in terms of [the] airframe and equipment, it will be possible to increase the planned final output of 75 aircraft per month to 100 with the same workforce".

If the Air Ministry wanted the full 300 Me 328s by March 1944, then "the implementation outlined in the project description of December 15, 1942 [must be] approved by the Air Ministry on January 4, 1943". And the initial batch of 20 prototypes would have to be given the much longed-for DE priority classification.

In fact, "the preliminary development decision and the material preliminary decision for [the] series must be received by Messerschmitt no later than December 20. The urgency classification must be in place by the beginning of January 43".

JSF would need some firm political backing too, specifically "ensuring that the current development staff [remain at] JSF-Darmstadt for the duration of the programme". Furthermore, just getting the necessary documents and blueprints together would require "1 x very good equipment designer, 1 x very good technical organiser/engineer, 2 x connection engineers, 2 x operating engineers, 1 x test engineer, 2 x lead designers, 6 x designers, 6 x draftsmen, 3 x structural engineers and 20 x skilled workers".

For the actual construction side, 15 jig makers were needed along with 15 skilled carpenters, and for final assembly JSF needed "2 x special fitters for the engine, 5 x inspectors, 1 x fitter for electrical systems, 1 x technician for radio systems, 1 x technician for general equipment". A total of 170 foreign workers had already been requested and "promised by the Darmstadt employment office".

Beyond this, the partners wanted an air base "with an assembly and storage hall and the necessary accommodation rooms, [which] must be assigned by March 1943 (e.g. Lechfeld, or another air base east of the Berlin-Munich line). The systems required for the launch, i.e. either Madelung [Kl 12] catapult, rail launch or concrete runway and tow planes for tow launch, must be secured and set up there by May 1943".

Lists of required machinery as well as the sums of cash needed for heating, lighting and other expenses were also appended.

ME 328 B

The proposal featured a technical outline of the Me 328 B which "represents a special development from the Me 328 A task. While the 328 A is still in development in the role of the parasite fighter, the version as a fast bomber with limited tactical operational possibilities was preferred in accordance with the current military requirements". However, a much more detailed description of this significantly revised design had been published a day earlier as part of a 'Projektübergabe' document produced by Messerschmitt.[4]

The most significant change from the Me 328 A to the Me 328 B concerned the wings. According to the Projektübergabe, "the wing was created by enlarging the middle section by 600mm from the wing of the Me 328 A (wing area of 7.5sqm, according to DFS construction documents). In addition, the following changes will be made for manufacturing reasons: a) Front edge of the spar perpendicular to the direction of flight. b) Flaps constant chord with constant profile. c) Aileron constant chord with constant profile. A large end cap (removable) is provided to optionally increase the wing surface area".

Me 328 spec comparison

	Length	Height	Wingspan	Wing area
Me 328 B (14.12.42)	7.05m	2.87m	7m/8.6m	8.5/9.4sqm
Me 328 B (25.11.42)	7.05m	2.85m	7m	8.5sqm
Me 328 (1.9.42)	6.83m	?	?	?
Me 328 (26.6.42)	?	?	?	7.5sqm
Me 328 Jäger Ausf. I (31.3.42)	6.83m	2.1m	6.4m	7.5sqm
Me 328 Jäger Ausf. II (31.3.42)	8.63m	2.1m	8.5m	12sqm
Me 328 Bomber Ausf I (31.3.42)	6.83m	2.5m	6.4m	7.5sqm
Me 328 Bomber Ausf. II (31.3.42)	8.63m	2.5m	8.5m	12sqm
P 79 V1 (21.12.41)	?	?	?	7.5sqm
P 79 (21.12.41)	?	?	?	5sqm

The latter feature meant that the base wingspan of 7m could be increased to 8.6m if desired, along with a surface area increase from 8.5sqm to 9.4sqm. The report noted that "a further increase in area should be possible by enlarging the mid-section after the first delivery programme has been completed".

Perhaps most strikingly, the Me 328 B's wing position relative to the fuselage had been elevated. This provided additional clearance for the underwing pulsejets and put the wing roots closer to the lip of the cockpit canopy.

The wing dihedral was set at four degrees but again, this "should be changeable during testing". The wing root fillets were also changeable and the wing slat gap was adjustable by replacing the associated supports. Evidently "the tail fin was created by enlarging the Me 328 A tail unit (design DFS)" and "the Me 109 G tailplane, which has not been modified in terms of shape and size, is used; a version made of wood is also an option if the weight is acceptable".

The circular cross section fuselage had a maximum diameter of 1.2m and comprised four separate assemblies: nose housing two fuel tanks and towline attachment point, front fuselage including cockpit, central fuselage housing two more tanks and tail section with control surfaces. The two front tanks had a 15mm armour plate sandwiched between them and a second plate of the same thickness was positioned at the front of the cockpit section. The wing was a single continuous component, with the bare spar in the centre, which was lowered into a cutout in the rear portion of the front fuselage section during assembly. This put the spar immediately behind the pilot's seat and the wings themselves on either side of him. The extendable skid, featuring a modified Fw 200 tailwheel spring

Artistic depiction from the Me 328 B Leichtes Schnellkampfflugzeug presentation booklet of December 15, 1942.

strut and designed for a safe impact load of 8,000kg, was housed directly below the cockpit.

Surprisingly, "the rear part of the fuselage, which is separably connected to the centre piece, should be able to be blown off together with the end of the fuselage in an emergency. For this purpose, a detonating cord is laid three times around the circumference in the area of the separation point". So if the pilot needed to bail out, everything behind the cockpit/wing section could be explosively jettisoned.

Inside the cockpit canopy at the front was a 90mm armoured disc "which should also serve as a rollover bar" and there was a hinged window on either side of the canopy, which was designed to open, close and be jettisoned like that of the Bf 109.

As usual, particular attention was paid to the take-off and landing processes: "When taking off, the skid remains retracted (starting on the wheeled dolly) and is locked in this position. After unlocking, the [skid] extension takes place automatically using its own weight; After reaching the final [landing] position, which is determined by a stop, the shock absorber engages. A [cockpit] display is required so the pilot can check that the shock absorber is extended and locked in its final position.

"The take-off procedures should include either a towed launch, a catapult launch with a Madelung catapult or a catapult launch on a self-propelled [Rheinmetall-Borsig manufactured] rail launch vehicle. A three-wheel nose-wheel dolly is used for the first two methods (the project documents for this will be delivered later)."

The rail launch vehicle was said to be "under construction" and it was stipulated that "all mountings for devices, fuel tanks, engines, etc. must be designed so that the acceleration forces are absorbed. The individual mountings of the equipment (radio devices and instrument) on the supplied bases and base plates are already designed accordingly. The pilot receives a headrest with a band [to be] placed around the forehead. There is also a safety device for locking the stick in the form of a toggle or something that can grasp the stick during the catapult process, whereby the pilot must still be able to move the stick in the direction of pulling up".

The two Argus pulsejets were expected to provide 400kg thrust each and would be installed under the wings in parallel to the fuselage. They had to be "mounted elastically" and "the aim is to install the engines in a way that they can be jettisoned (particular care must be taken to ensure that the tail unit is not damaged in the process). The engines are cooled by the airstream (air duct between the engine and the underside of the wing, approx. 30mm at the narrowest point). The wing must be insulated against radiant heat using thermal protection (reflector with an asbestos intermediate layer)".

A push-button sparkplug/ignition coil system was provided and the engines would be "started when taking off on the launch carriage using compressed air (acting on the valve box). The fuel is supplied by the pumps, which themselves are run off a power source installed on the starting car (detachable external connection)". The Seppeler generators would keep the pumps going in flight.

The pilot got most of the usual single-seater cockpit instruments and gauges with a FuG 16 Z Y radio system and FuG 25a transmitter-receiver plus heater and electrical lighting. It was planned to provide space for a seat cushion parachute, a medical pack in the tail section and a flare gun in a holster to the pilot's right.

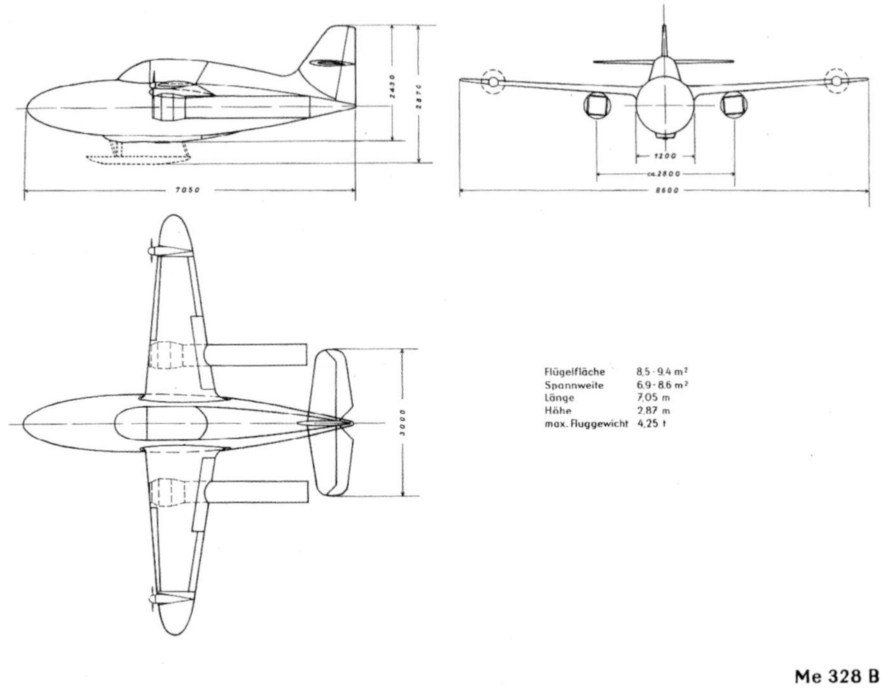

Three-view drawing from the Me 328 B booklet, showcasing the high wing position relative to the fuselage, the underwing pulsejets, the externally mounted skid, wingtip Seppeler generators—and old-style canopy.

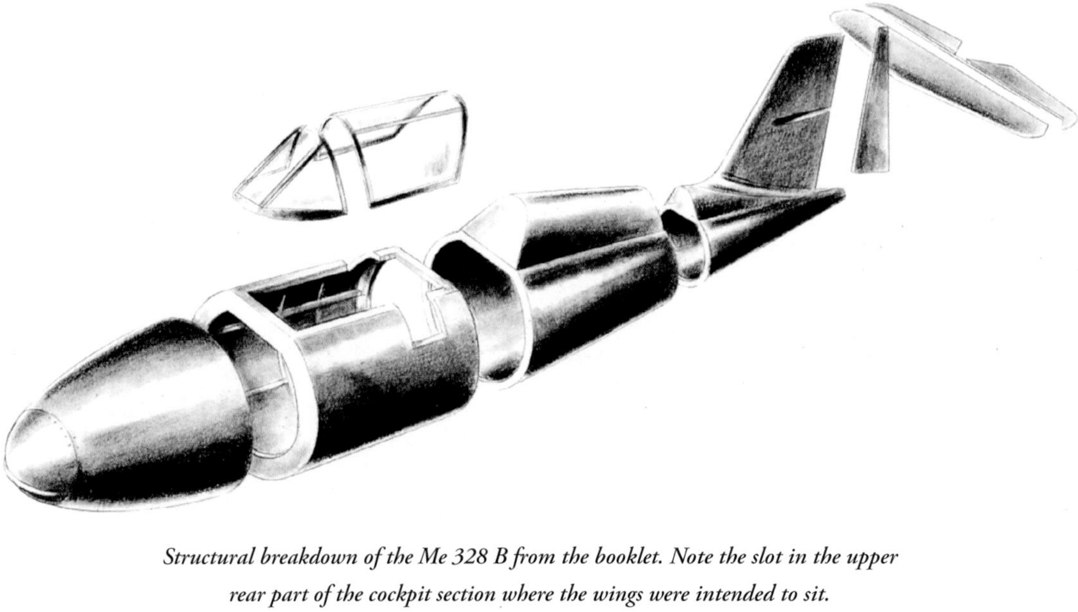

Structural breakdown of the Me 328 B from the booklet. Note the slot in the upper rear part of the cockpit section where the wings were intended to sit.

The aircraft was designed to carry bombs or other droppable loads of between 250kg and 1,600kg, and "the structural design must also make it possible to load the RS bombs that are being developed and to fire them from the airframe". The standard bomb rack, a Schloss 1000 or ETC 500 XI b, was to be installed in a U-shaped frame fitted to the skid cutout when the skid was in the retracted position. It was also possible to fit a Schloss 2000 XIII—necessary for carrying the SC 500 RS. Targeting would initially be done using a Revi 16b on the armoured windscreen but "in terms of space, it is possible to install a suitable bomb-aiming system (e.g. BZA 30), but its use is dependent on a) the timely completion of the development and procurement of that system and b) the installation option that is being considered".

PULSEJET FLIGHT TEST RESULTS

In addition to Programm Me 328 B—Bau von 300 Flugzeugen and Projektübergabe Me 328 B, a third description of the type was issued on December 15, 1942—a heavily

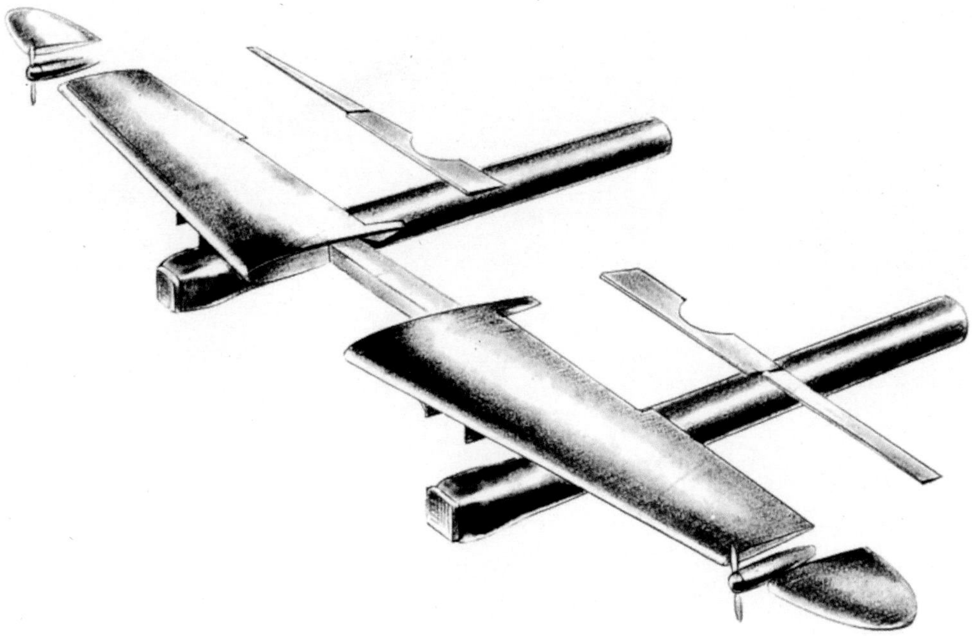

The wings that were to slot onto the Me 328 B fuselage shown in the other drawing.

Another artistic depiction from the December 15 booklet—this time on the ground with the skid extended.

illustrated presentation booklet printed on high quality card stock entitled Me 328 B Leichtes Schnellkampf-flugzeug.[5] It offered no further information but certainly demonstrated, as if further demonstration were needed, the effort Messerschmitt was prepared to put into securing a production contract.

Two days after these three hefty documents emerged from Messerschmitt, the DFS produced a report of its own entitled Preliminary Results of Flight Testing with Argus Jet Engines.[6] While much of it was concerned with recounting the usual information about what pulsejets were, what Argus's variant consisted of and how it worked, it did also supply some information about how the flight tests had actually gone.

A key difficulty, naturally enough in hindsight, was finding a way of mounting the extremely hot, loud and vibratory pulsejets to an aircraft. The difficulties involved in this seemingly simple task were clear right from the outset as the organisation's engineers attempted to prepare the pulsejet-powered DFS 230 for flight: "The pulsejets on the LS[7] are suspended under the wings. The first attachment was carried out using the supports provided by Argus.

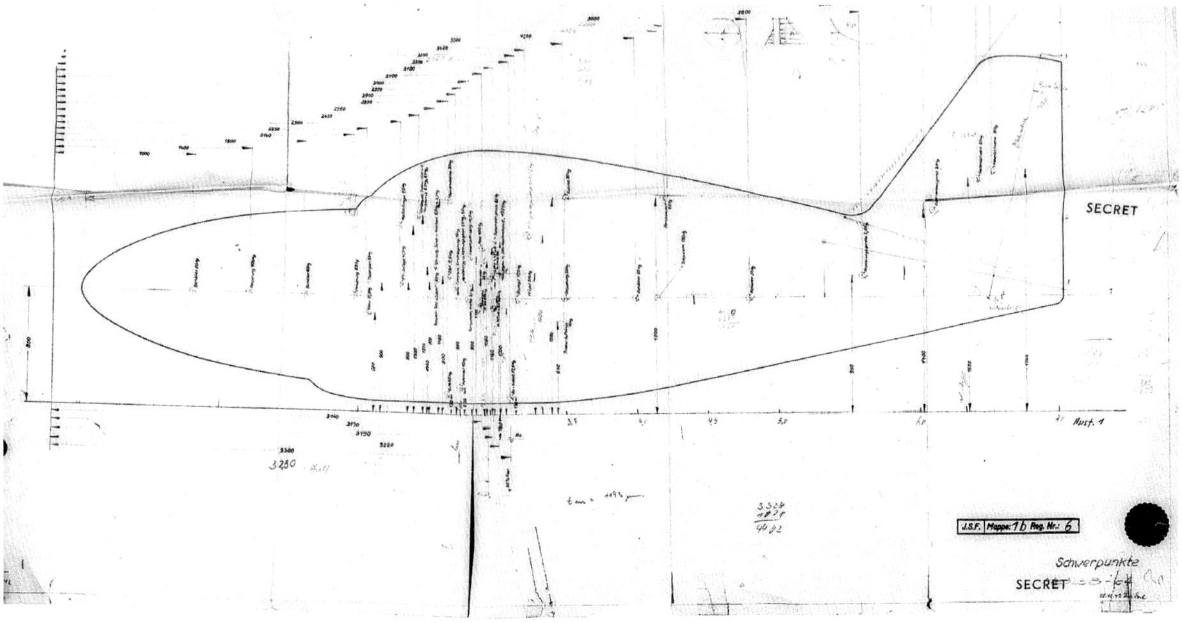

One of the earliest known JSF Me 328 B drawings, dated December 18, 1942, and showing centre of gravity measurements.

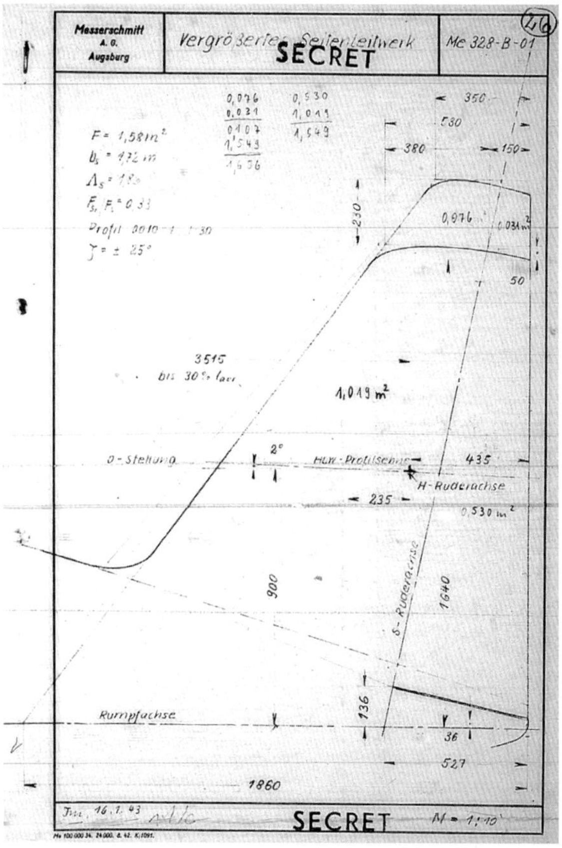

Messerschmitt proposal to increase the fin height on the 'Me 328 B-01'—seemingly never put into practice. The drawing is dated January 16, 1943.

This suspension proved to be inappropriate as the engines moved around too much during operation. To avoid this, clamps were attached to the engine. However, when the engines were in use, the weld points tore off. In addition, the direct contact between the clamp and the engine resulted in strong heat transfer to the suspension points.

"For these reasons, the DFS welded four U-shaped bolts onto the engine and attached the suspension struts to them. The distance between the engine and the base plate of the U is approximately 10mm. The air flowing through the slot cools the fittings well, so that ball bearings could be installed in the struts for later experiments without any concerns."

Another difficulty resulting from the immense heat radiating outwards from the engines was both the casings of the engines themselves and their supports losing their strength, deforming and cracking. This issue could not be conclusively resolved.

When it came to attaching pulsejets to the Me 328, "the pipes were hung under the wings like on the LS. Experience with the LS showed that the distance from the wings could be significantly reduced. It is now 25mm. The horizontal forces were transferred through bolts to vibration-damping rubber rings and thus to the supporting rib.

"With the LS it was determined that the pressure wave propagating at the end of the engine pipe placed a lot of strain on the parts of the aircraft in this area (tearing off the skin, loosening the mouldings, loosening the door handle and the door framework). On the Me 328, the engine exhaust is approximately 1m behind the wing [trailing edge]. The fuselage skin and sometimes also the tail unit are affected by the pressure wave. Since the pressure wave will be even stronger with the 300kg [thrust] engines, it seems advisable to attach the engine in such a way that the pressure wave can no longer act on the machine. For this reason, a suspension on the fuselage is provided in such a way that the end of the engine exhausts approximately 50cm behind the trailing edge of the tail unit".

It was ruefully noted that the pulsejets' performance was affected by altitude, the velocity of the aircraft, fuel flow and the preload and condition of the spring valve on the inlet—but that "naturally, these variables could not be completely assessed in the short flight test period to date in terms of their influence on engine performance, so that the results reported cannot claim to be absolutely accurate. Nevertheless, given the interest currently shown in pulsejet engines, it seems appropriate to announce these results. In some cases, the influence of a number of factors on engine performance only became apparent during flight testing.

"The large number of these variables requires a detailed, extensive series of measurements, which cannot be carried out with the current test vehicle. In the meantime, a second cargo glider has already been equipped by DFS with thrust measuring devices for two pulsejets, which enable the measuring points to be doubled without additional time expenditure. In order to be able to carry out the testing at high speeds, the same measurement system is installed in a Me 328 so that the speed range from 120km/h to 500km/h can be measured. The suspension and measuring device for the second LS and the Me 328 are designed so that the larger engines (465mm pipe diameter) can also be measured."

It is not clear from this whether reference is being made to fitting the Me 328 V2 with pulsejets or one of the incomplete prototypes still under construction.

The day after the report was issued, December 18, 1942, Willy Messerschmitt wrote a memo to Voigt and Seitz addressing the issue of how to fit the Me 328's pulsejets: "Due to the high drag of bomb racks ... it is absolutely necessary that a precautionary lining is provided between the wing and the engine from the first aircraft onwards. Under certain circumstances, this lining can be made entirely or partially of insulating material so that the heat from the engine is not transferred to the wing. In addition, ventilation will have to be provided through a carefully designed cowling at the front with an outlet at the rear in the fairing. The main difficulty will be that the fairing itself must be made conveniently retractable by providing a horizontal parting at which the upper and lower parts of the fairing move relative to one another so that the thrust against the wing can be measured."[8]

Having not yet received the DFS report, it is clear that Messerschmitt still assumed the Me 328's engines would be carried beneath its wings rather than being attached to the fuselage with a view to mitigating tail damage.

NO SECOND 'WARSCHAU-SÜD'

The aircraft was briefly discussed during the GL meeting on January 16, 1943.[9] This was chaired by Wolfgang Vorwald, head of the Technical Office, rather than Milch and at one point he brought up some observations from the commander of the Luftwaffe test centres, Oberstleutnant Edgar Petersen: "Now I have one more thing to pass on from Petersen, which concerns the He 177. It is a matter that now affects [Technical Office departments] CE 3 and CB 3. Another 177 with 610, an A-3 machine, came from above, I think yesterday. He considers it most urgent that the steam separator and the common oil circuit are now in order, as are the alternating engines, because this will significantly reduce the risk of fire. Eisenlohr, I ask that you investigate the matter urgently."

Wolfram Eisenlohr was the head of engine development at the Air Ministry and the stenographer noted his response in the transcript: "Yes!"

Vorwald: "Then, as his last wish before he left, he told me that Messerschmitt needed to be pushed harder again. These are the 262 and the 328. They do next to nothing about them because they claim that the designer's demands they constantly made were not met. These demands are downright ridiculous. He should kick people out of his project office and not keep coming here with these projects. The constant planning is useless. This passing of time this way doesn't get us anywhere; but it's the things that are [already] there that matter."

It would appear from this brief exchange that the items on Voigt's list of demands for a second 'Warshau-Süd' style 'special campaign' focused on the Me 328 had not been—and were not going to be—delivered by the Ministry. Indeed, Voigt's supercilious attitude and criticism of the Ministry seem to have gone down like a lead balloon and achieved exactly the opposite of what he wanted. As such, while the Me 328 was still regarded as desirable,[10] it would not be receiving the highest priority status nor the resources Voigt and Messerschmitt deemed necessary for a fast full-scale production turnaround.

Exactly when this decision was made is unclear but certainly the success of the Vulkan programme, as outlined just over a month earlier, had depended on "the extension of the authority of the codename 'Vulkan' to the area of all armaments". In effect, the Reich Minister for Armaments and Ammunition, Albert Speer, and his cadre of production specialists were being called upon to agree that the aircraft and equipment covered by Vulkan, including the Me 328, took priority over all over armaments—tanks, ships, rifles and so on. And it would appear, perhaps unsurprisingly, that they did not agree to this. The Vulkan programme had by now already disappeared from the historical record, never to be heard of again.

Ten days later, on January 26, 1943, the Me 328 was back on the agenda again as part of a production programme study—the GL meeting this time being chaired by General der Flieger Egon Doerstling with Milch still absent.[11]

The Technical Office's Oberstingenieur Georg-Bernhard Alpers introduced the topic: "Next sheet: jet fighter! They are planned according to the requirements. The deadline still has to be arranged very carefully with the companies because we are familiar with the [background] documents on this."

Doerstling replied: "This paper is more of a study than an actual programme. Maybe it's even a bit arbitrary."

Alpers: "It has been examined in terms of capacity, but in terms of timing it will only be clear if you can say from the airframe standpoint that it will happen. And I believe it will. The rest is uncertain because the testing of the engines for series production has not yet been progressed that far. This is the Me 328."

The head of aircraft at the Technical Office, Georg Pasewaldt, interjected: "May I ask that it be written 'jet aircraft'. The 328 is not a jet fighter. It is intended to be a short-range bomb carrier. It cannot be described as fighter-bomber. The matter is still undercooked."

The discussion then moved on to the Me 163 interceptor as well as the Me 262 and He 280 jet fighters. Based on Pasewaldt's description of the Me 328, it may be that he had read or was aware of Späte's negative assessment (see Chapter 3).

A new production plan, presumably associated with the study Doerstling was talking about, was issued by the Air Ministry on February 10, 1943.[12] Titled 'Flugzeug-Programm Studie 1015', it basically included the proposal to build 300 Me 328s outlined by Messerschmitt in December 1942. The first example would be due for delivery in June 1943, two more in July, five in August, 12 in September, 20 in October, 30 in November, 40 in December, 50 in January 1944, 65 in February and finally 75 in March 1944. An appended note stated that production could then continue at a rate of 75 per month as required.

This was, however, just a study and Messerschmitt was clearly facing some serious production capacity shortfalls.

Milch chaired the Ministry department heads meeting on February 11,[13] during which he tabled a radical solution to this thorny problem: "The Messerschmitt company's design capacity will be extremely strained for the next few years due to the current tasks (Me 209, 328, 163, 262, 410). The Field Marshal [Milch] considers a division of these tasks necessary, in the sense that Messerschmitt should preferably concentrate on the Me 209 and 410 and jet aircraft may be moved to a separate factory under the leadership of Lippisch and [flying wing specialists Reimar and Walter] Horten.

"[Industry and Speer Ministry representative Karl] Frydag suggests the Siebel company for this, as they would have good operational management to carry out the new constructive work. Likewise, industrial separation for the design and production of jet engines from the plants with piston engines is considered necessary. The entire workforce now engaged in this work would have to be concentrated in these plants. Corresponding investigations in this direction still need to be carried out and dealt with in a future meeting."

THE MANNED MISSILE

Meanwhile on February 7-8, Dr Theodor Benzinger, director of the aeromedical department at the Luftwaffe's Rechlin test centre, had given a presumably lengthy presentation to two of the Luftwaffe's highest-ranking and most-respected research specialists: Ministerialdirigent Adolf Baeumker, who was chancellor of the prestigious Deutsche Akademie der Luftfahrtforschung (DAL) and Georgii of the DFS on the possibility of using 'manned missiles'.[14]

A summary of this presentation, produced by Benzinger nine months later, said: "The war situation, which keeps our opponents dependent on supplies by sea, justifies and demands attacks on shipping targets using the most extreme means. The last of these is the manned missile, whose pilot voluntarily sacrifices his life.

"This new form of warfare for Europe cannot be achieved with measures that deviate from the old principles of Prussian-German soldiery. Rather, it should be developed from these principles. The soldier is used to voluntarily exposing his life to a high probability of death. Every day, without contradiction, he submits to providence's decision about his existence or non-existence. If he has to endure enemy fire without acting, his own abilities remain completely uninvolved in this fateful process.

"Nothing else is required of him if the final decision of fate about life and death is made before the fight, if, according to the content of the proposal that follows, a lottery is held shortly before the battle.

"A force will be formed from volunteers, among whom those who have [already] been severely affected by fate make up a significant proportion, whose members will voluntarily undertake a one-way deployment. The mission begins with submission to the lottery, which selects one person from five or more men to pilot a manned projectile.

"After this decision there is no going back. Those who were not chosen should return with honour to a new and possibly better life. The chosen one fulfils his mission. He deserves a hero's veneration and his family members deserve the nation's constant, active gratitude.

"Including the solemn act of election, there should only be a short time, counted in minutes or at most a few hours, which the chosen person spends dealing with the certainty of death. It is the duty of the leadership to look for means that will calm his mental struggle and maintain his performance during this time. Experiences from the history of medicine give hope that there are remedies that can do this to a certain extent. However, at best one can expect this to bolster the inner strength which the spirit of this force [of volunteers] awakens and keeps awake in the community of comrades under a commander who is determined to die.

"The conditions of this style of fighting seem very harsh. [But] in reality, it saves great blood sacrifices and suffering, which is balanced against the short spiritual struggle of a few people and their painless death."

Nothing initially seems to have come from Benzinger's suggestion to call on disgraced or depressed pilots to draw straws for a heavily medicated suicide mission—but it certainly wasn't forgotten.

THE ME 328 SIDESHOW

By mid-February 1943 the Me 328 Warschau-Süd-style special campaign was dead in the water. It remained to be seen whether the Air Ministry would ever green-light the plan for 300 examples as it ran through its theoretical production studies and tried to work out what aircraft would be needed for the near-future Luftwaffe.

Yet work on the Me 328 project continued, albeit with a low priority. Towed take-off flight testing of the Me 328 V2 had been brought to a halt at Hörsching, with the DFS now making preparations to experiment with Me 328/Do 217 Mistel take-offs.

According to Felix Kracht, during interrogation immediately after the war, Mistel take-off "offers special advantages for the tests of new models as the risk of landing is reduced considerably. Coupling links detachable through mechanical action, and those which act through a charge of explosive, are used according to their purposes. The first mentioned have the advantage of being able to be used many times during test flight but their manufacture entails a considerable amount of work ... mechanically working links took ten weeks for their construction (March to May 1943). They were used without alterations during towing tests of the Me 328 and Do 217 K".[15]

It also appears that the original proposal made to the Air Ministry, that the DFS would construct a full series of ten Me 328 prototypes, was never rubber stamped. So while the Me 328 V1 and V2 had certainly been built by the DFS—and there is clear evidence that the V3 and V5had been worked on—there is no known evidence that work was ever started on the V6-V10 at Ainring.

At the same time, Me 328-related wind tunnel tests were being carried out at various institutes and JSF at Darmstadt was putting together jigs and tools needed for the first two Me 328 B prototypes. It was simultaneously conducting stress tests on sets of Me 328 A wings—presumably units built by the DFS at Ainring that were no longer needed. Berlin-based Argus was attempting to extract more power from its engines and Messerschmitt was very slowly completing the still-unfinished Me 328 V02 at Augsburg[16] while distractedly overseeing and liaising with the others.

And there were plenty of distractions for Messerschmitt. The company had been under contract, since early 1941, to prepare the Luftwaffe's next generation piston engine fighter—the Me 309—for production. This aircraft, which was to be powered by either a DB 603 or Jumo 213, was abruptly cancelled in January 1943 as a result of political wrangling and in its place Messerschmitt offered another design: the Me 209. This aircraft, supposedly composed of 50% existing Bf 109 parts, would preserve the company's existing 109 production lines; but with the exclusive 309 contract dissolved, a window of opportunity opened for rival company Focke-Wulf, which could now promote the Ta 153 (a redesignation of the Fw 190 D) as a viable and attractive alternative to the new 209.

Even as this unexpected new round of competition was getting under way, Messerschmitt managed to outright lose another extremely lucrative contract—to build the Luftwaffe's new fast bomber. Towards the end of 1942 it had seemed as though the twin-fuselage Me 109 Z, again composed largely of existing 109 components, would take the contract but at the last moment Dornier had pitched the single-fuselage push-pull prop Do P 231 and this had defeated the 109 Z before going on to receive the designation Do 335.

The future of the rapidly aging Bf 109 had been cast into doubt by these events and worse was to come as Ministry interest in the previously sidelined twin-jet Me 262 began to grow. There were some in officialdom who began to wonder whether the 109 should be cancelled entirely so that Messerschmitt could concentrate on the 262 instead. Such a move would undo at a stroke all the painstaking

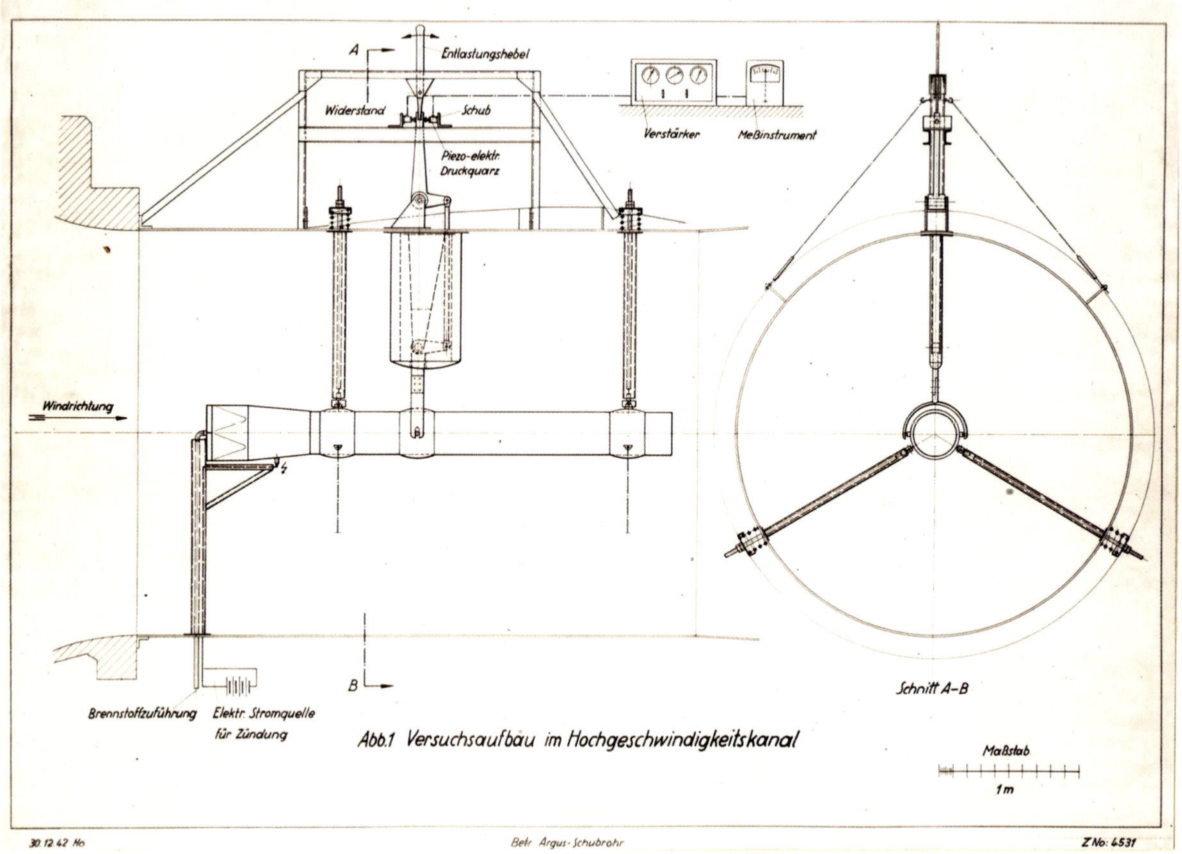

Zobel's pulsejet test rig at the LFA, as depicted in his February 22, 1943 report.

measures Willy Messerschmitt had already put in place to preserve the 109 and would necessitate massive upheaval and untold difficulty in trying to take the Me 262 from a ragtag handful of neglected prototypes to a viable mass production machine.

Within this rapidly evolving landscape, the 'undercooked' Me 328 became a sideshow.

A BATTERY OF TESTS

The practical phase of the DFS's extensive series of wind tunnel tests on an adaptable Me 328 model, which had begun on April 8, 1942, finally concluded on January 20, 1943.[17] There had been 11 periods of activity between those dates, totalling 44 days of trials. A mountain of data had been collected but most of it related to models fitted with the pre-Me 328 B low-wing configuration and no report was immediately forthcoming.

Starting on January 28, 1943, Theodor Zobel at the Luftfahrtforschungsanstalt Hermann Göring experimental institute at Braunschweig (the LFA) had conducted a second round[18] of aerodynamic tests on various configurations of the Argus VSR 9—the 610mm diameter pulsejet designed to produce 400kg thrust.[19] There would be two phases of testing in the institute's 2.8m high-speed wind tunnel this time, from the 28th to February 3, then from February 9 to February 20. The results were then reported on February 22, representing an incredibly quick turnaround.

Unfortunately for all concerned, Zobel's conclusions were not encouraging: "A means of increasing fuel pressure at [already] high pressures without impairing the combustion function of the [pulsejet] pipe has not yet been found.

"The safest means of further increasing thrust is to reduce drag by further improving the shape of the pipes or using suitable [aerodynamic] fairings. In connection with this, the [correct] shaping of an attachable inlet cowling is essential.

"The shape of the combustion chamber seems to play a crucial role in improving the functionality of the pipes. A further increase in the air flow rate in the existing combustion chamber through a larger [spring] flap box has so far not been successful.

"Increasing the useful thrust achieved with the VSR 9 v tube with a new pipe designed for a static thrust of 400kg did not bring any progress, since the increase in drag associated with the change in shape of the tube cancelled out the increase in thrust."

On March 3, 1943, Rudolf Seitz produced a comparison between the Me 262 and an 'Me 328 C', also described in the same document as 'Me 328 (Bomber)'.[20]

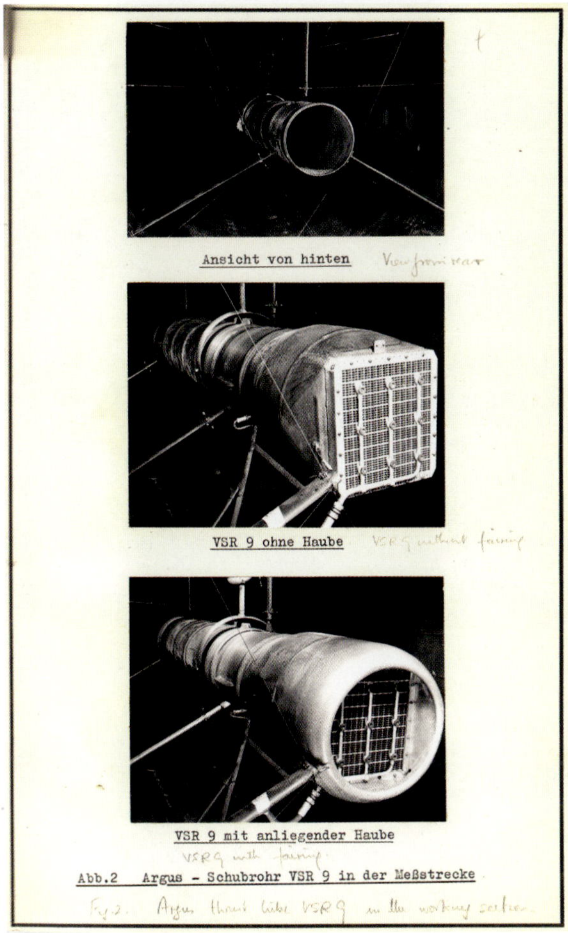

A series of three photos showing the Argus VSR 9 pulsejet tube from the rear (top), a forward view without the fairing showing the spring-valve grid and fuel injection pipework (centre), and with the aerodynamic fairing attached (bottom).

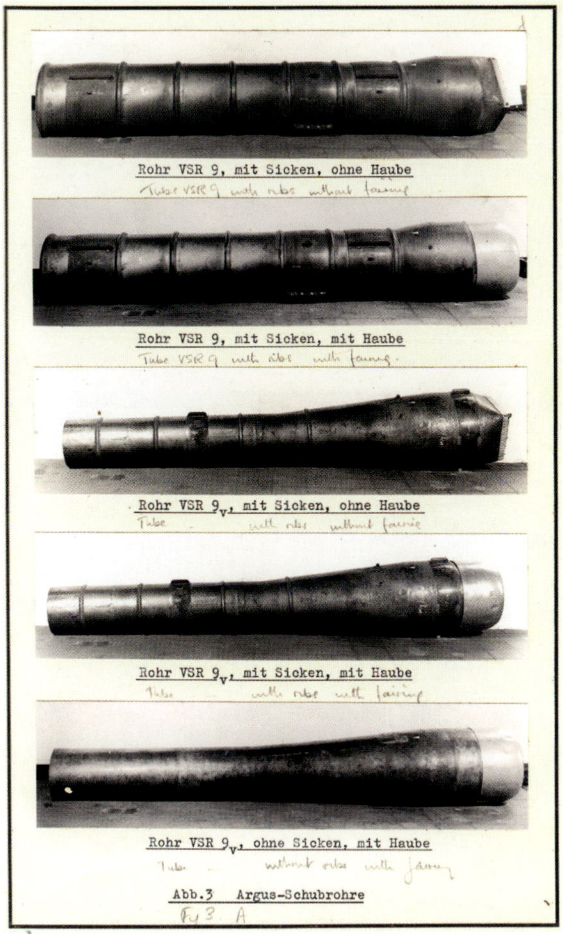

Photos showing the pulsejets tested by Zobel—the basic VSR 9 with ribs and no fairing (top) and with ribs and with fairing (second top); the VSR 9 v with ribs and no fairing (centre), the VSR 9 v with ribs and with fairing (second bottom) and the VSR 9 v with a full fairing covering both the inlet and ribs.

No drawing was appended and it is unclear what this new Me 328 would have looked like but it was certainly the largest example proposed so far—with a wing area of 18sqm, compared to 8.5sqm (or 9.4sqm) for the Me 328 B of two and a half months earlier. The Me 262's wing area was given as 21.6sqm.

The new design's fuselage surface area was 30sqm, compared to the Me 262's 31.6sqm, or a whopping 39sqm if 'extended'. Tailplane surface area was 3sqm compared to 4sqm and the fin was 1.8sqm compared to 2.9sqm. Even the empty weight was a big increase on anything proposed before—3,300kg (the Me 328 B was 1,510kg empty) compared to the Me 262's 4,250kg.

The major selling point appears to have been fuel tank capacity; the Me 328 C could carry 1,670kg compared to the Me 262's 1,320kg or 2,500kg in 'extended' form. Even when fitted with additional fuel tanks the Me 262's maximum possible capacity could only reach the 1,800kg mark.

Seitz noted that if configured with the same fuel capacity—1,500kg—without bombs, the Me 328 C's range would be 17.7% better than that of the Me 262. With their actual unmodified fuel capacities (1,670kg versus 1,320kg) the Me 328 C's range would be 47% better. And the range of the 'extended' Me 328 compared to the unmodified Me 262 was 84% better.

Without a drawing it is impossible to say how the Me 328 C/Me 328 (Bomber) of March 3, 1943 was configured and similarly no information was presented which might offer a clue as to what propulsion system the Me 328 C used.

It is possible, however, that even at this early stage the Me 328 C/Me 328 (Bomber) was a single-jet design. This would reduce fuel consumption considerably compared to the twin-jet Me 262 and compared to the immensely thirsty pulsejets with which the Me 328 was usually associated. The Me 328 C designation disappears at this point—though the notion of a turbojet-powered Me 328 does not—only to reappear seven months later, after the pulsejet Me 328's cancellation.

Second page of pulsejet test pieces—VSR 9 v with ribs, without fairing and with four scoops (top), VSR 9 v with a different full fairing (second top), VSR 9 ab with covered ribs but no inlet fairing (centre), VSR 9 with ribs covered and with a different inlet fairing (second bottom) and VSR 9 ab with ribs and with yet another different inlet fairing (bottom).

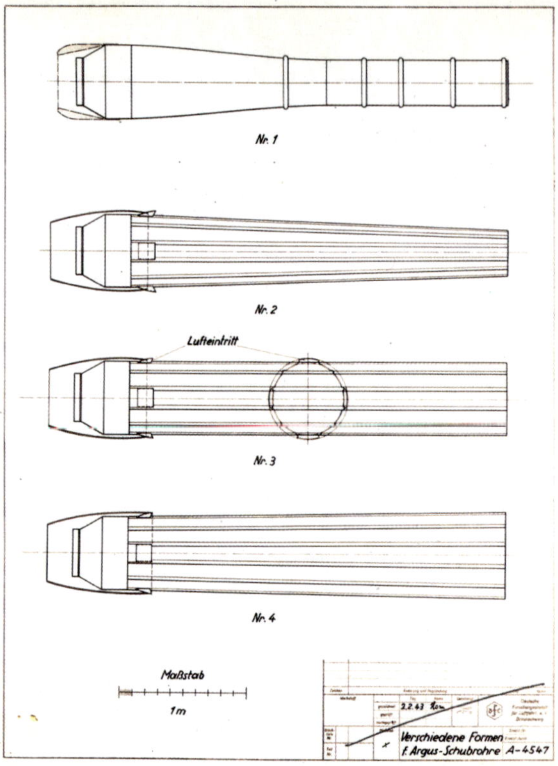

Various different pulsejet designs supplied to the LFA, depicted on February 2, 1943.

Using a single jet to power an airframe that was almost the same size as an Me 262 and full of fuel seems like a recipe for severely limited performance, yet if this design was still intended for a Mistel, towed or catapult take-off then a wheeled undercarriage would theoretically be unnecessary, resulting in a significant weight saving. Certainly, giving the Me 328 C/Me 328 (Bomber) an 18sqm wing area would help it detach safely from its tow or carrier aircraft.

Meanwhile, with analysis of the first 44 days of mostly low-wing model tests still pending, the DFS embarked on a new series of wind tunnel tests using an Me 328 model on March 2, 1943.[21] This model "which was designed with an extended fuselage and with the wings in high position with an anhedral of two degrees, was measured with the engine bodies on the wing underside. Studies with various wing root fillets, with wing slots near the wing roots and with sheet metal strips on both sides of the cockpit canopy should show the influence of the aerodynamic crossflow".

At the end of March, a report was produced by the Bauaufsichts-Leitung des RLM (BAL)—the Luftwaffe's production inspection authority—on the month's activities at JSF, including work on the Me 328.[22] This noted that jig and tool construction for the Me 328 B V1 and V2 prototypes was 30% complete and was due to be finished by May 31, 1943. Stress testing on the Me 328 A wing was 60% complete.

Tests had also been conducted to determine the sensitivity of Me 328 B wings to gunfire.

The DFS wind tunnel tests carried on into April before concluding for a second time, on April 22. A week later, Zobel commenced his third series of tests on Argus pulsejet designs.[23] Since his previous report of February 22, three of Germany's foremost aerodynamicists had been brought on board to design a new cowling for the VSR 9. The director of the Aerodynamische Versuchsanstalt (AVA), Alfred Betz, and his colleague Dietrich Küchemann—a specialist on intake shapes—had submitted two designs and a third had been put forward by the director of the DFS's aerodynamics department Paul Ruden. All three were duly fabricated to the appropriate size and fitted to Argus pulsejet tubes—which Zobel then tested.

After a month of relative inaction, the BAL report

Highly polished wind tunnel model used by Messerschmitt circa March 5, 1943, during comparative tests against models of an Me 262 and Me 309. The room in which it was photographed can be seen, distorted, in the reflection.

Underside of Messerschmitt's reflective Me 328 wind tunnel model.

Top view of the Messerschmitt Me 328 wind tunnel test model.

on JSF's activities for April recorded that jig and tool preparation for the Me 328 B V1 and V2 was now 60% complete, but the expected completion date of this work had slipped by more than two weeks to June 15, 1943.[24] Further Me 328 A wing bending and torsion tests had been conducted and Me 328 B wing test pieces were being constructed so they could be fired on with 20g and 50g explosive ammunition.

A drawing produced at JSF on April 20, 1943, showed a redesigned cockpit canopy for the Me 328 B—with a more rectangular windscreen, another feature that would clearly differentiate the design from the earlier Me 328 A types going forward.

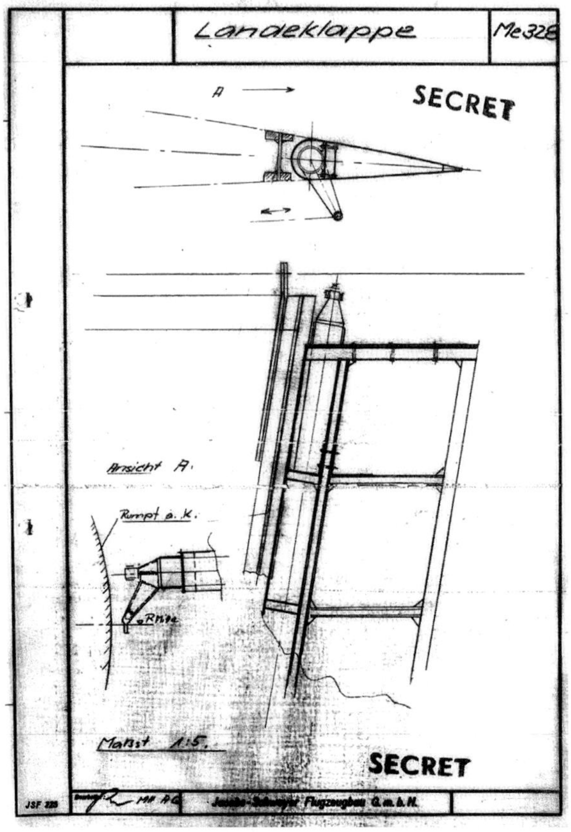

Me 328 B landing flap design drawing from Jacobs-Schweyer Flugzeugbau dated April 6, 1943.

ME 328 MISTEL - FIRST FLIGHT TEST

May 1943 was a pivotal month for Messerschmitt, with Milch, Göring and Galland agreeing to phase out construction of the Bf 109 in order to replace it entirely with the Me 262.[25] This should have been a triumphant moment for the company, but instead it was looked upon as a disaster since it would mean scrapping plans for the Me 209, shutting down the vast 109 production lines along with their monstrous supply chains, throwing the company's complex networks of contractors and subcontractors into chaos and starting everything again from scratch. Willy Messerschmitt's long-cherished modularity concept, where

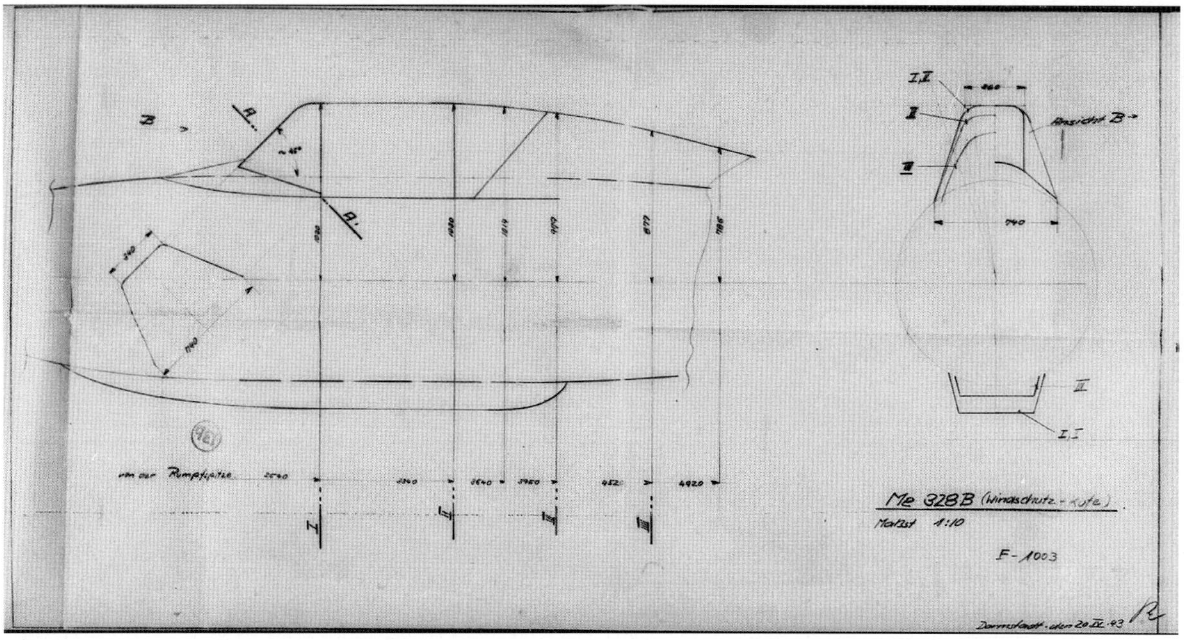

JSF design dated April 20, 1943, showing the Me 328 B's new rectangular windscreen and skid.

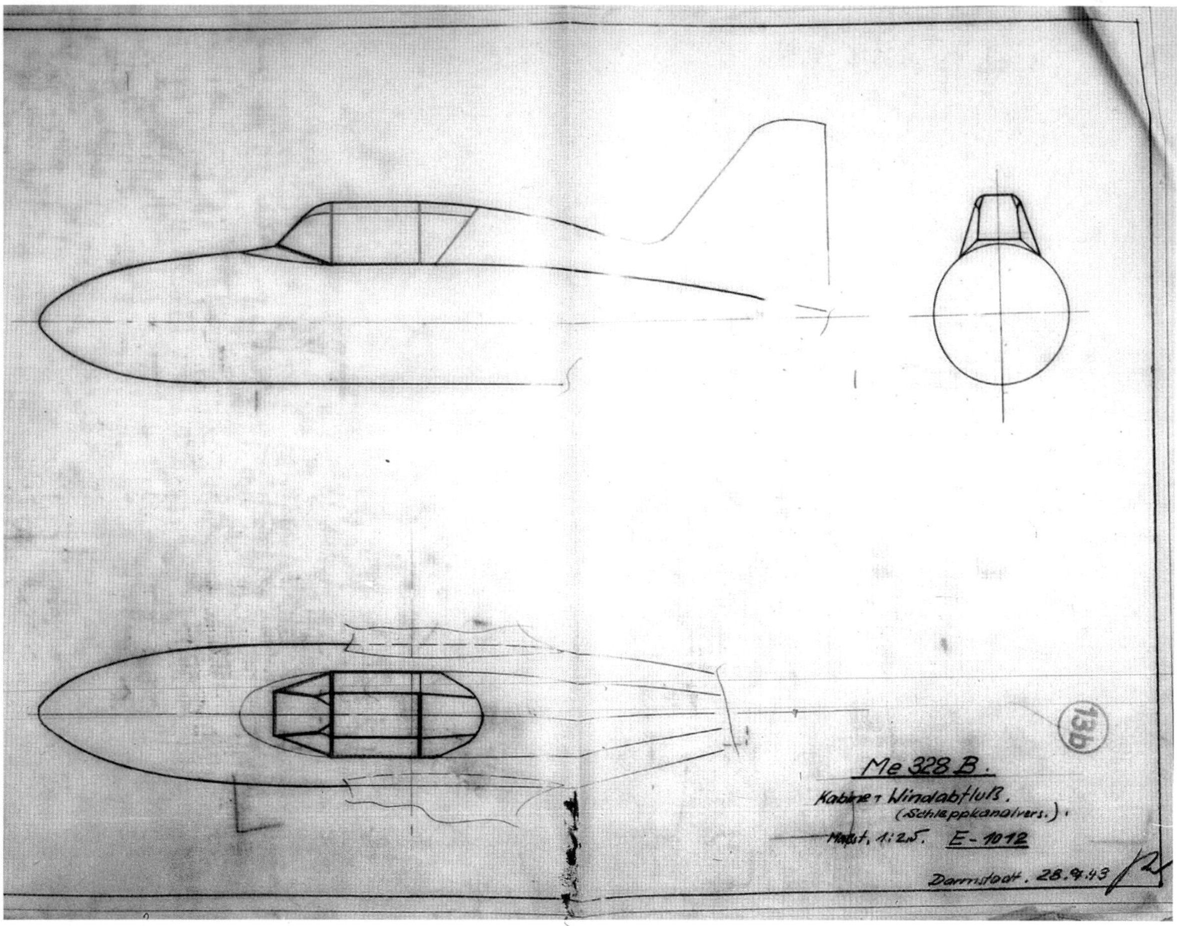

The distinctive new canopy designed by JSF/Messerschmitt at Darmstadt for the Me 328 B. The drawing is dared April 28, 1943.

aircraft to suit different roles could be created from modular parts—such as making the Me 109 Z fast bomber out of regular 109 parts—would also be derailed.

While this pressure point was forming elsewhere, Rudolf Ziegler reportedly made the first Me 328 Mistel take-off, albeit from the cockpit of the Do 217 carrying it, on May 18. It would appear that this was just the first of many take-offs and landings where the still-airworthy

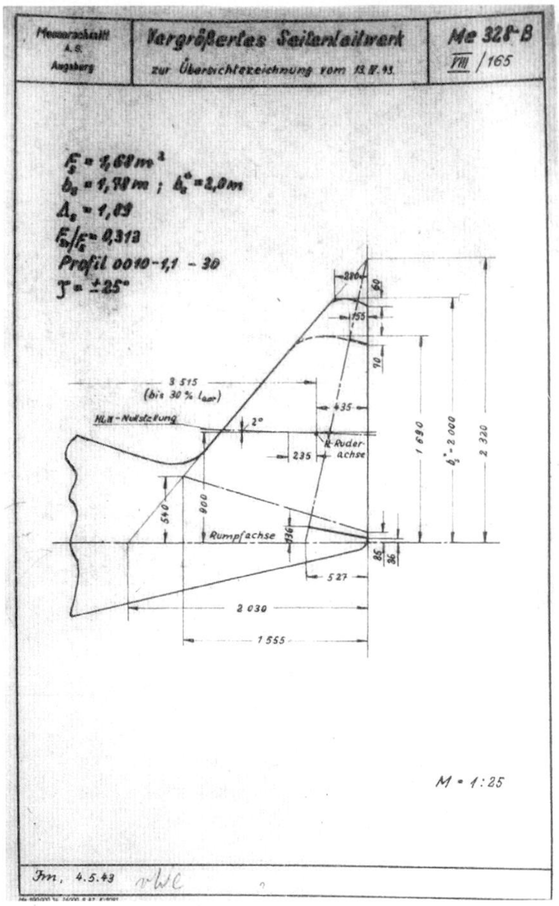

This Messerschmitt drawing from May 4, 1943, shows ongoing efforts to redesign the Me 328 B's fin.

from the Me 328 A wing tests.[26] It was found that the wings did not meet flexural stress fracture safety requirements—and the ailerons could not even cope with a standard load. The wings' torsional strength was deemed adequate, however.

Meanwhile, a Messerschmitt satellite office had been established at Darmstadt, the intention being to oversee JSF's work on the Me 328 more closely as well as carrying out original design work on the type in situ. The earliest known product of this was a report on the Me 328 B's weights and centre of gravity produced on May 26.[27]

Based on this report, it would appear that the intention was still to build the Me 328 B largely in the form outlined in the various descriptions of mid-December 1942. Sketches showed the aircraft with a high wing position and it was stated that wing area was 8.5sqm or 9.4sqm with wing end caps, the same as before. However, each prototype was said to have two skids rather than one.

Separate tables showed weights for the Me 328 B V1 and V2, then the Me 328 B V3 to V6, then the Me 328 series production model. The main difference between the V1/V2 and the rest was a complete lack of armour, fuel tanks, fuel systems, generators, radio and other operational equipment. A very light weight value was given for engines and attachments—perhaps indicating mocked-up engine tubes, rather than actual engines.

The BAL report on JSF's progress for May began by noting that "Me 328 [B] V1 should be reported to BAL as ready on August 1, 1943".[28] However, this seemed increasingly unlikely since "there is a major shortage of metal workers in the experimental construction, which

Me 328 V2 remained attached to the carrier throughout while measurements were taken and recorded.

Three days later a report was produced by JSF's Hagemann, overseen by Heinrich Pieler, drawing conclusions

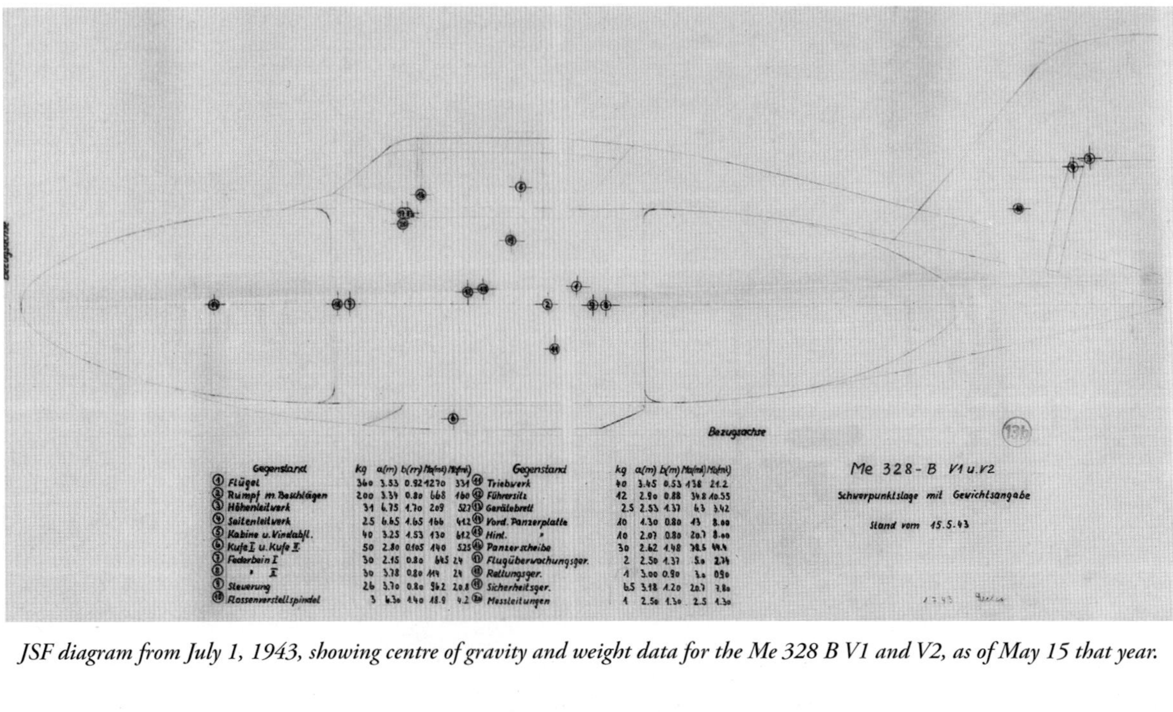

JSF diagram from July 1, 1943, showing centre of gravity and weight data for the Me 328 B V1 and V2, as of May 15 that year.

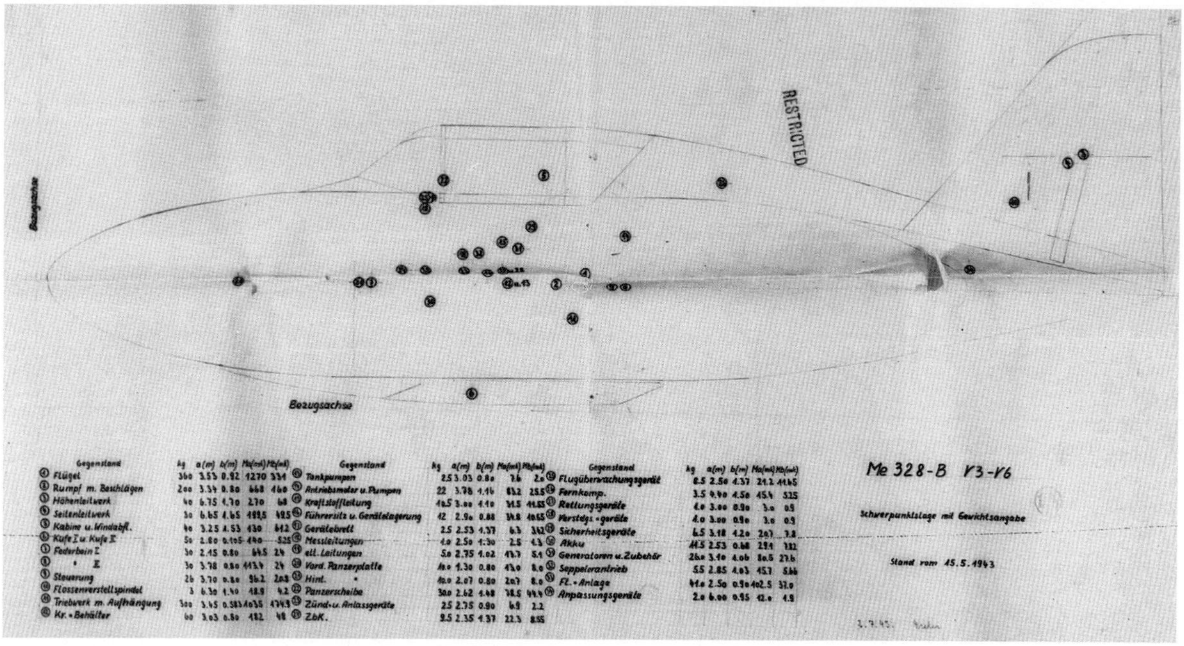

Centre of gravity and weights for the Me 328 B V3-V6 from JSF.

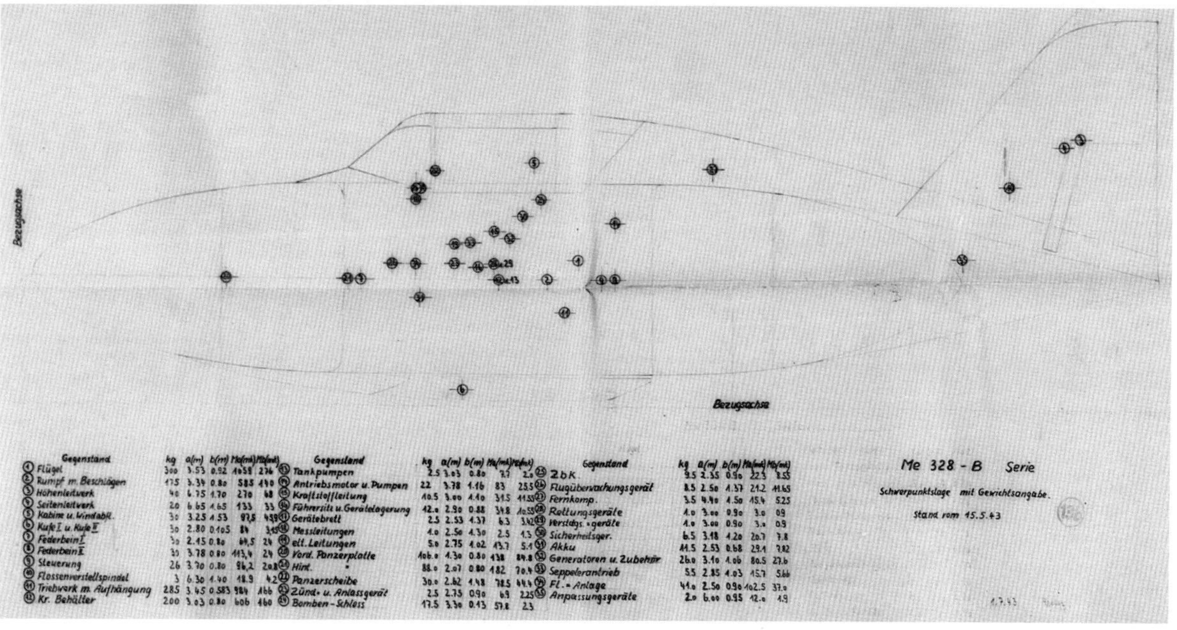

Me 328 B series production model centre of gravity and weight data from JSF.

seriously jeopardises deadlines. An attempt is being made to compensate by bringing in foreign workers at short notice". An application had been submitted to the Air Ministry but the workers "could not be assigned".

Progress on the jigs and tools for Me 328 B V1 and V2 had slowed to a crawl, being reported as just 5% further along compared to the previous month—at 65% complete. The expected completion date had slipped again, this time to July 15, 1943. The Me 328 A wing stress tests had been completed but those Me 328 B wing test pieces for 20g and 50g explosive ammunition firing tests were still under construction.

Throughout June, the DFS pilots at Hörsching continued to fly experimental take-offs with the Me 328 V2 on the back of a Do 217. Whether any separation attempts were made at this stage is unclear but it would appear not.

ME 328 MISTEL – FIRST SEPARATION

On June 24, Messerschmitt's aerodynamics department at Augsburg issued a report on its own wind tunnel tests with an Argus pulsejet engine, which in the accompanying diagrams was labelled "Me 328 engine".[29] Measurements of the engine were made in its unpainted, as-delivered, form both with and without the accompanying

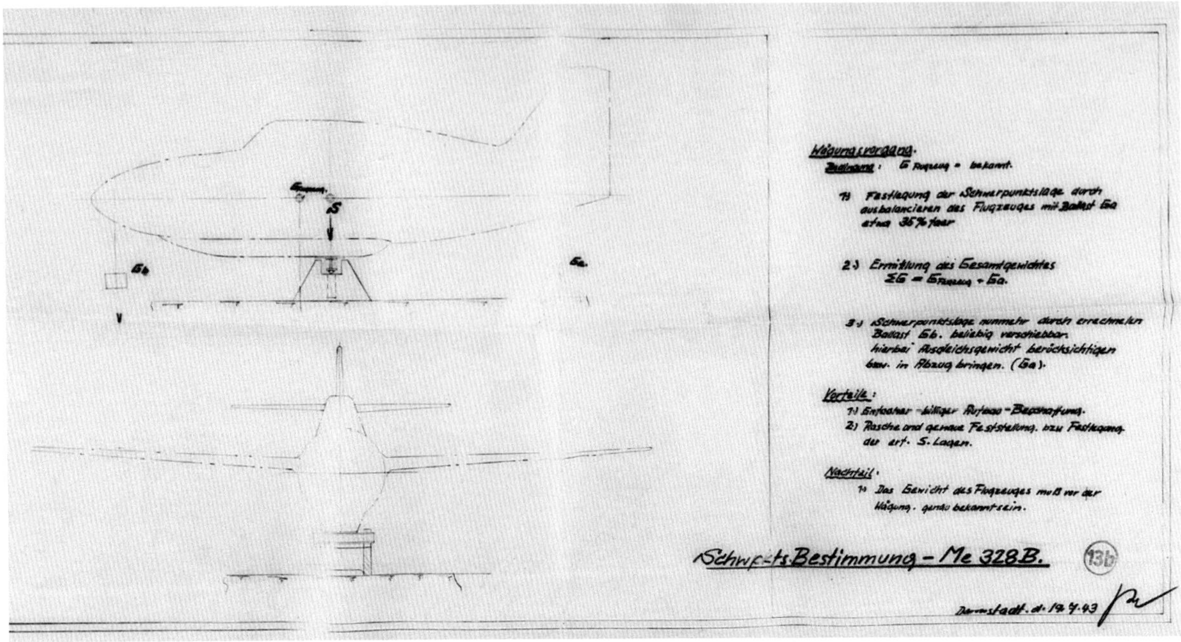

Diagram dated July 19, 1943, showing centre of gravity testing at JSF.

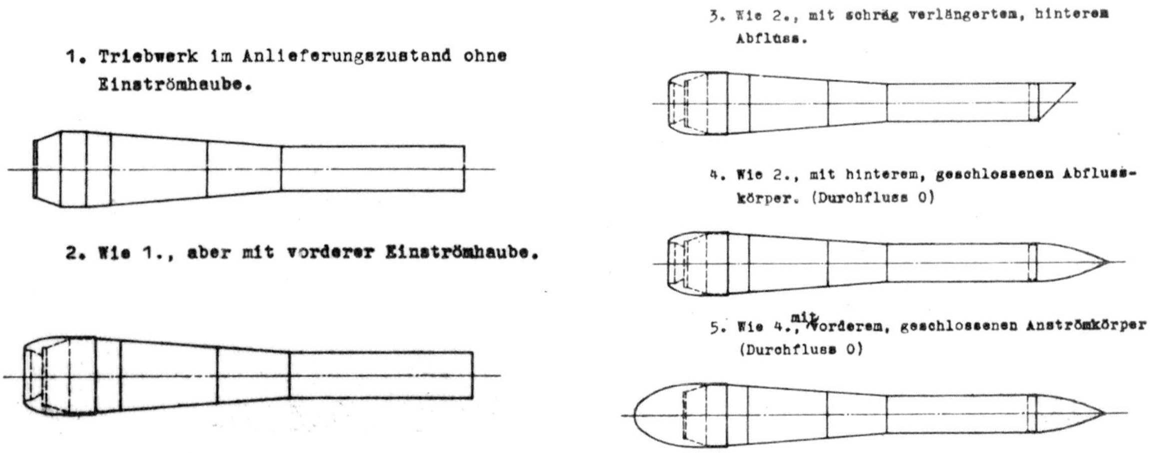

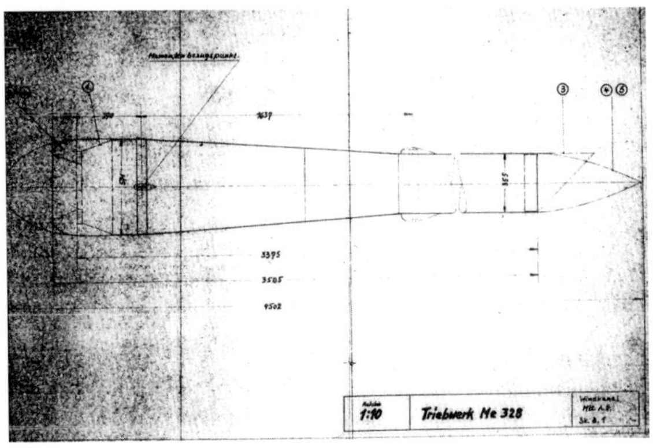

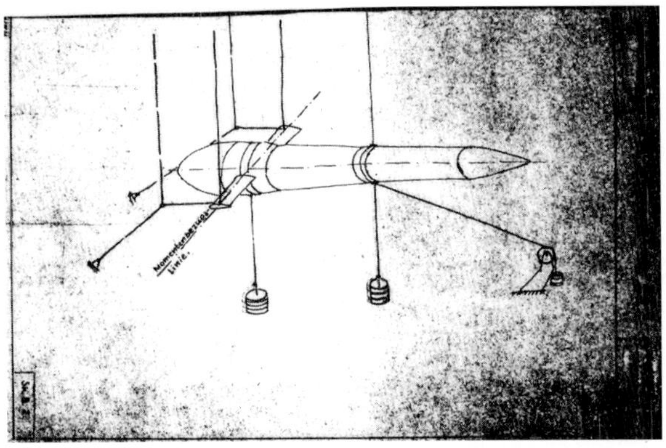

Diagrams from Messerschmitt's report on its own wind tunnel tests with various Argus pulsejet arrangements.

Argus-supplied intake cowling, and with and without the engine's overall aerodynamic fairing. The fuel line in the forward part of the cowling protruded from its outer contour by about 30mm so this was tested with and without an aerodynamically-shaped covering of plasticine to determine what drag penalty it incurred either way.

It was found that total drag of the bare engine tube was four and a half times greater than for the tube with its fairing in place. And the exposed fuel line did indeed significantly increase drag compared to the covered fuel

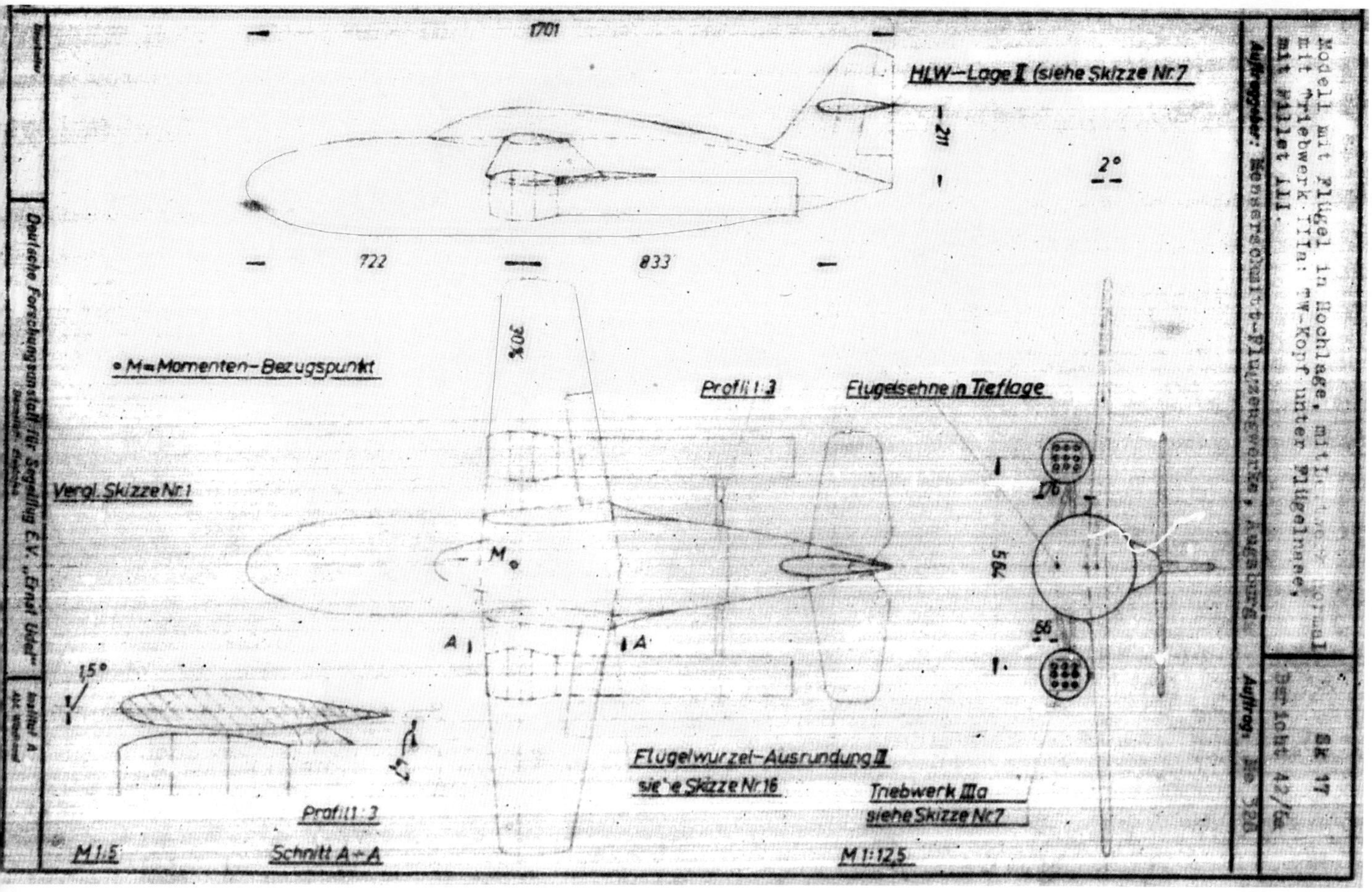
1701
HLW-Lage II (siehe Skizze Nr.7
211
2°
722
833
30%
M=Momenten-Bezugspunkt
Profil 1:3
Flügelsehne in Tieflage
Vergl. Skizze Nr.1
176
564
M
66
A
A
1.5°
Flügelwurzel-Ausrundung III
siehe Skizze Nr.16
Triebwerk IIIa
siehe Skizze Nr.7
Profil 1:3
M 1:5
Schnitt A-A
M 1:12,5
Deutsche Forschungsanstalt für Segelflug E.V. „Ernst Udet"
Modell mit Flügel in Hochlage, mit Leitwerk normal
mit Triebwerk IIIa: TW-Kopf unter Flügelnase,
mit Fillet III.
Auftraggeber: Messerschmitt-Flugzeugwerke, Augsburg
Sk 17
Bericht 42/6a

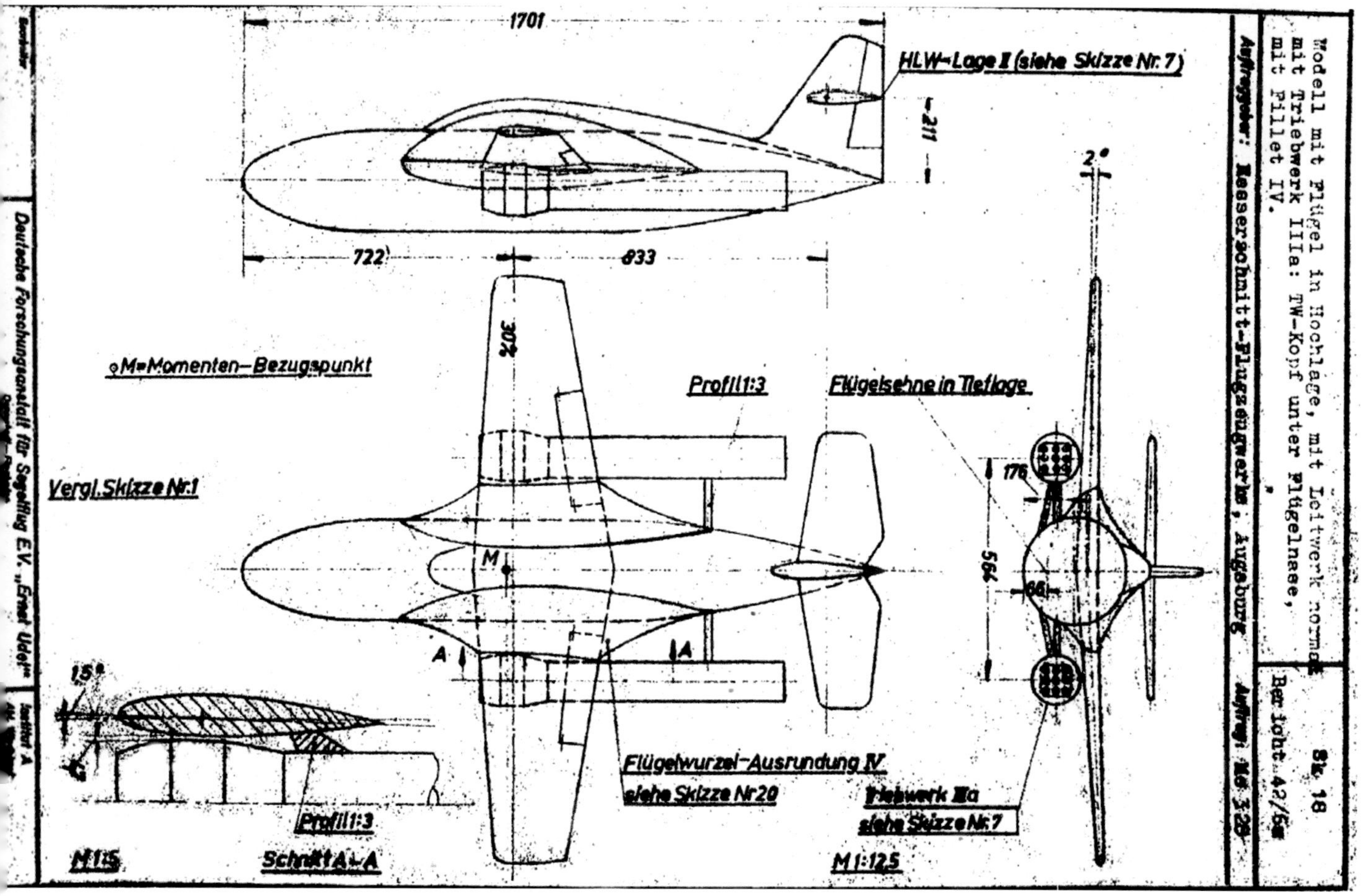
1701
HLW-Lage II (siehe Skizze Nr.7)
211
2°
722
833
30%
M=Momenten-Bezugspunkt
Profil 1:3
Flügelsehne in Tieflage
Vergl. Skizze Nr.1
176
564
M
66
A
A
1.5°
Flügelwurzel-Ausrundung IV
siehe Skizze Nr.20
Triebwerk IIIa
siehe Skizze Nr.7
Profil 1:3
M 1:5
Schnitt A-A
M 1:12,5
Deutsche Forschungsanstalt für Segelflug E.V. „Ernst Udet"
Modell mit Flügel in Hochlage, mit Leitwerk normal
mit Triebwerk IIIa: TW-Kopf unter Flügelnase,
mit Fillet IV.
Auftraggeber: Messerschmitt-Flugzeugwerke, Augsburg
Sk 18
Bericht 42/6a

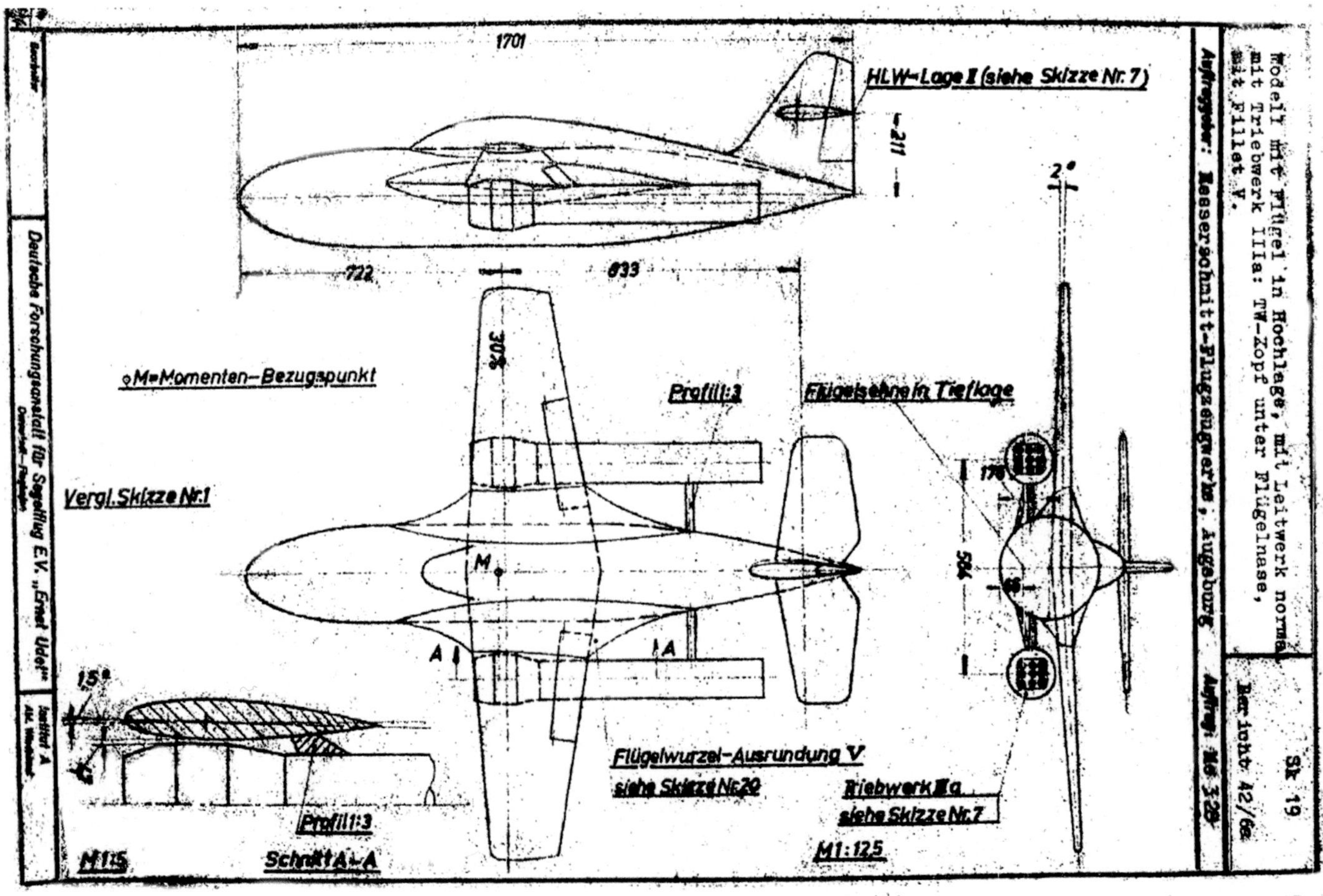
1701
HLW-Lage I (siehe Skizze Nr. 7)
211
722
833
M=Momenten-Bezugspunkt
Profil1:3
Flügelsehne in Tieflage
Vergl. Skizze Nr.1
M
A
Flügelwurzel-Ausrundung V
siehe Skizze Nr.20
Triebwerk IIIa
siehe Skizze Nr.7
M1:125
Profil1:3
Schnitt A-A
M1:5
Deutsche Forschungsanstalt für Segelflug E.V. „Ernst Udet“
Modell mit Flügel in Hochlage, mit Leitwerk normal
mit Triebwerk IIIa: TW-Zopf unter Flügelnase,
mit Fillet V.
Auftraggeber: Messerschmitt-Flugzeugwerke, Augsburg
Sk 19

line. These results, however, do not seem to have revealed anything too surprising—nor anything that had not been discovered by wind tunnel tests of the same engine elsewhere. Indeed, Zobel's third round of Argus pulsejet wind tunnel tests came to an end on June 26, though the results would not be reported for another three months.[30]

Four days earlier, on June 22, the DFS published its first report on Me 328 wind tunnel tests—not the main report on the tests conducted between April 8, 1942, and January 20, 1943, but an addendum to that based on the second round of testing from March 2 to April 22.[31] Presumably there was greater urgency to publish the results of these tests since they were based on models representing the high-wing Me 328 B form, rather than the low-wing Me 328 A.

In addition to studying the effects of the high wing position, the tests also examined a variety of wing root fillets and wing slots, while using metal strips to examine crossflow on the canopy.

At the end of June, the BAL reported that the ready-to-fly date for the Me 328 B V1 had slipped to August 20, 1943, and "there is still a large shortage of skilled metal workers for the experimental construction, which seriously jeopardises deadlines. An attempt is being made to compensate by bringing in external manufacturers at short notice. The procurement of alloys continues to cause great difficulties. Due to a failure on the part of the on-call management to secure driving permits and a lack of tyre allocation, parts from suppliers can only be delivered by train with a large delay".[32]

Construction of jigs and tools was now 80% complete and progress on actually constructing the Me 328 B V1 had started and was 10% complete. Those Me 328 B wing test pieces for firing tests remained 'under construction'.

The Me 328 made its last known appearance during an Air Ministry management meeting during one chaired by Milch on July 9.[33] The fairly recently appointed Inspector of Bombers, Oberst Dietrich Peltz, was attempting to secure some production of the Arado Ar 234 as a bomber and Milch was telling him that it wouldn't be straightforward and that the Ar 234 wasn't really suitable for his needs anyway.

Milch said: "The whole thing isn't ready right now. Unfortunately, all the questions that should have been answered can't be answered right away. [To Walter Friebel] What's its range at low altitude?"

Friebel: "800 to 900km."

Milch: "That's not much."

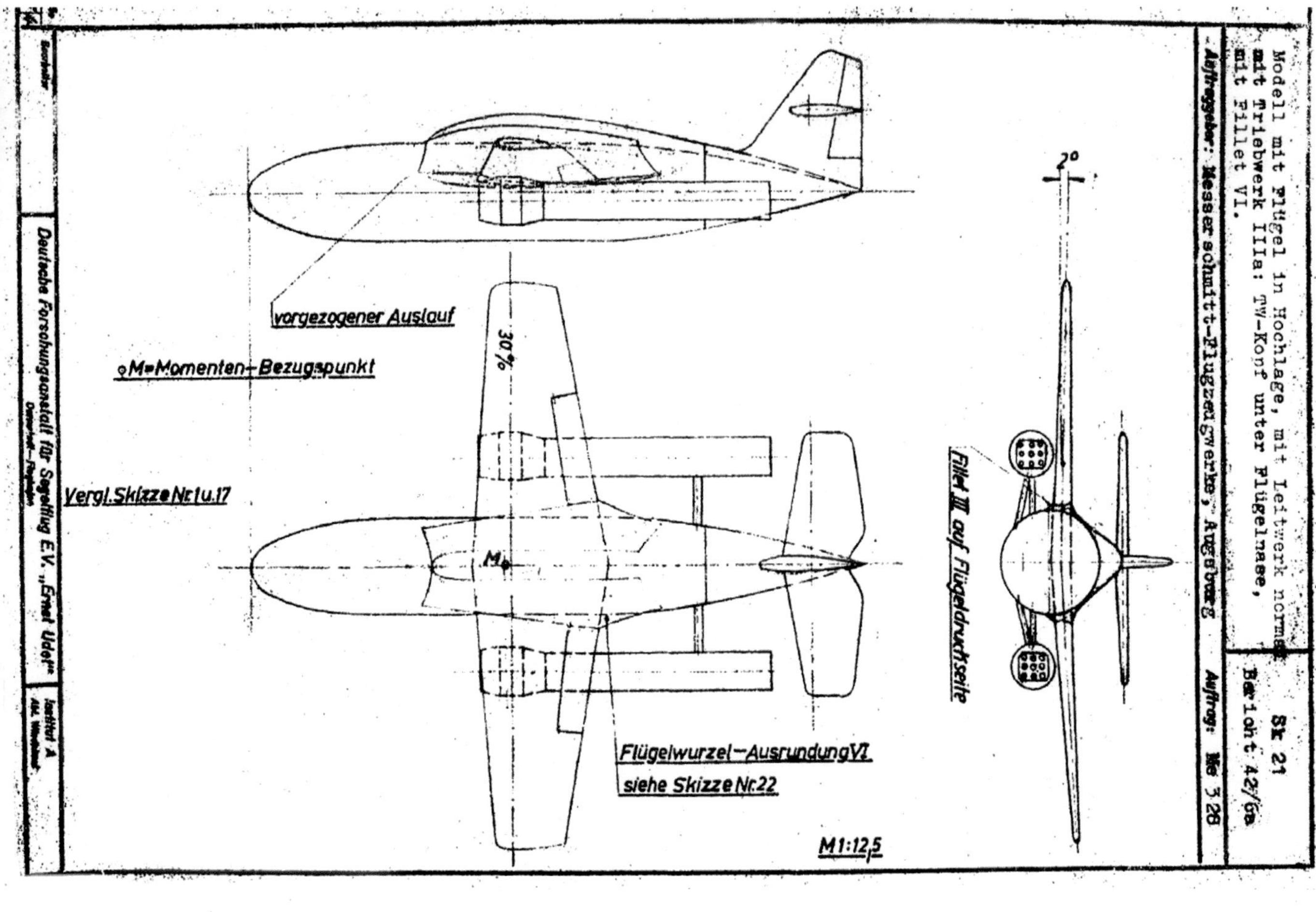

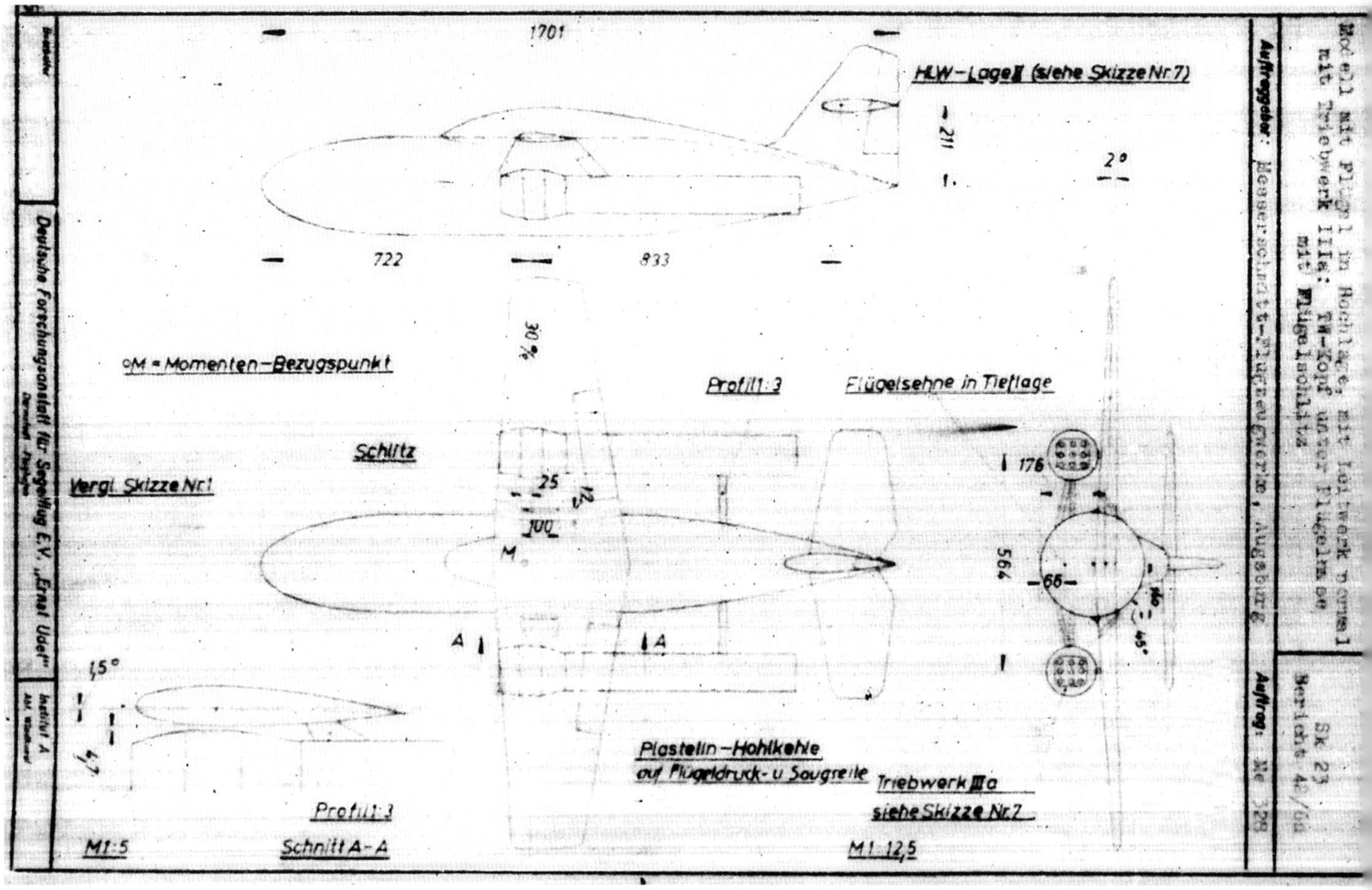
HLW-Lage II (siehe Skizze Nr.7)
oM = Momenten-Bezugspunkt
Profil 1:3
Flügelsehne in Tieflage
Schlitz
Vergl. Skizze Nr.1
Plastelin-Hohlkehle
auf Flügeldruck- u Saugseite
Triebwerk IIIa
siehe Skizze Nr.7
Profil 1:3
M1:5
Schnitt A-A
M1:12,5
Deutsche Forschungsanstalt für Segelflug E.V. „Ernst Udet"
Auftraggeber: Messerschmitt-Flugzeugwerke, Augsburg
Auftrag: Me 328
Sk 23
Bericht 42/6d

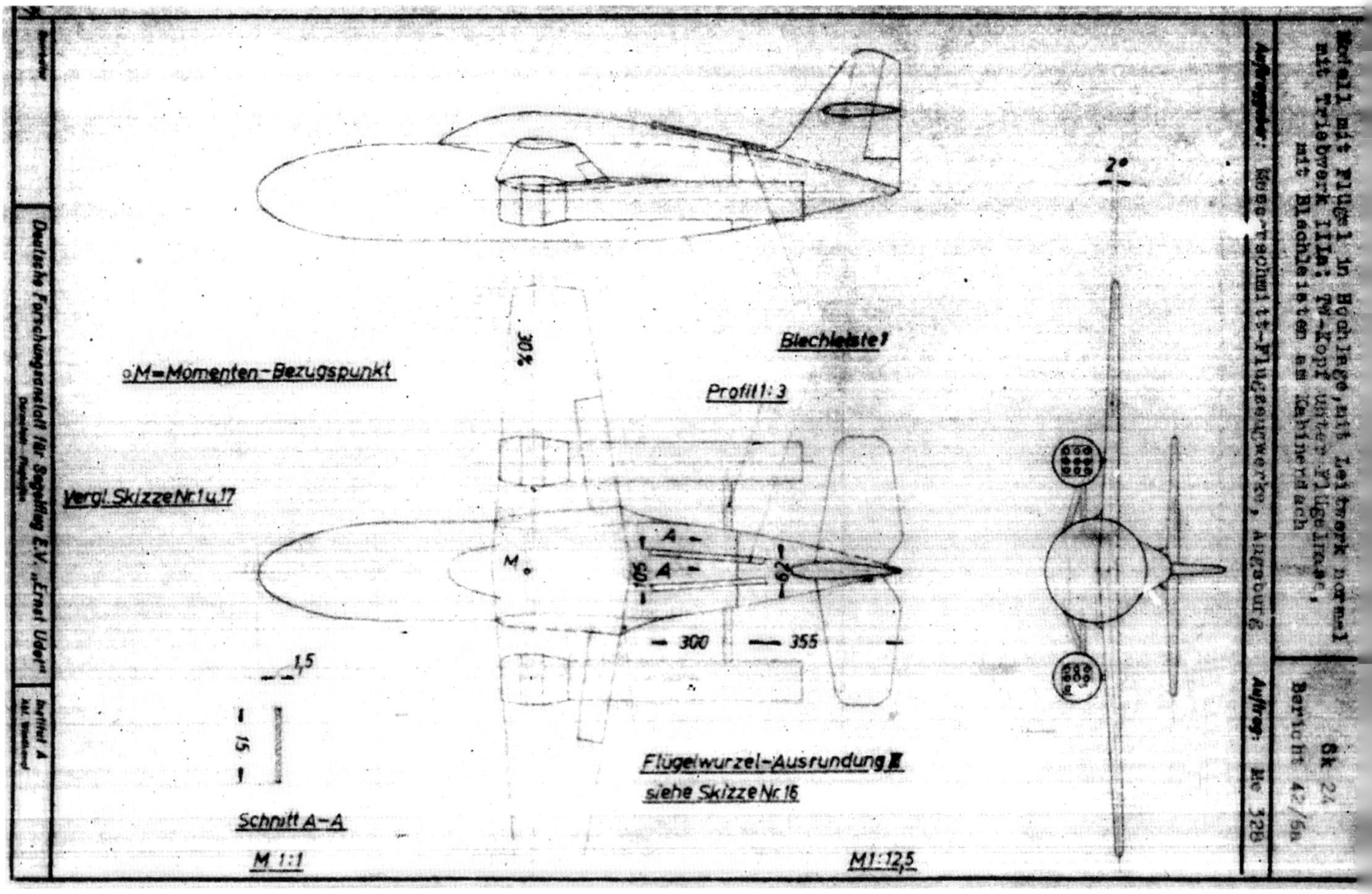
oM=Momenten-Bezugspunkt
Blechleiste I
Profil 1:3
Vergl. Skizze Nr.1 u.17
Flügelwurzel-Ausrundung II
siehe Skizze Nr.16
Schnitt A-A
M 1:1
M1:12,5
Deutsche Forschungsanstalt für Segelflug E.V. „Ernst Udet"
Auftraggeber: Messerschmitt-Flugzeugwerke, Augsburg
Auftrag: Me 328
Sk 24
Bericht 42/6a

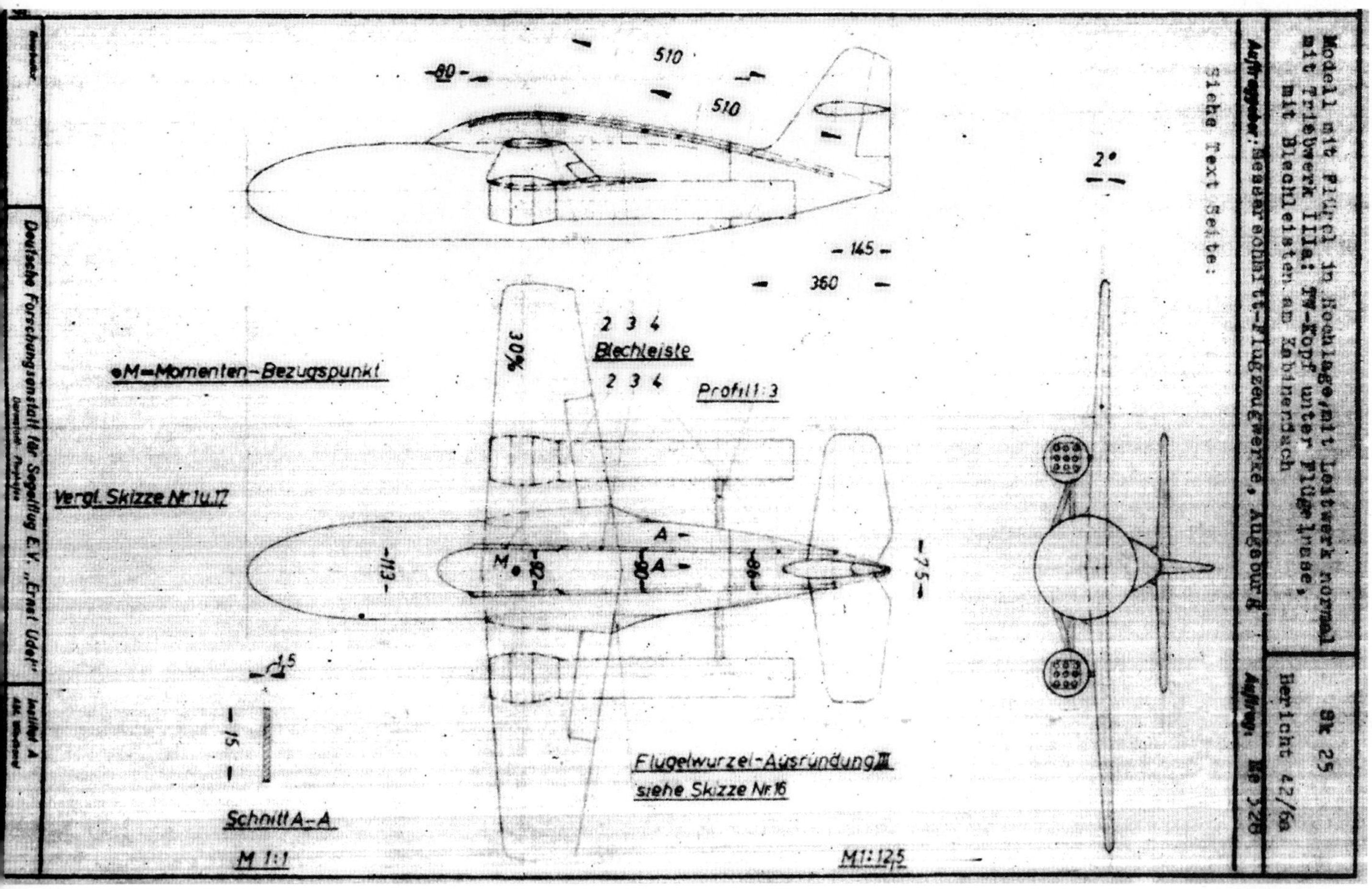
●M=Momenten-Bezugspunkt
Vergl. Skizze Nr 1u.17
Blechleiste
Profil 1:3
Schnitt A-A
M 1:1
Flugelwurzel-Ausrundung III
siehe Skizze Nr.16
M1:12,5
Deutsche Forschungsanstalt für Segelflug E.V. „Ernst Udet"
Sk 25
Bericht 42/6a
Auftrag: Me 328
Auftraggeber: Messerschmitt-Flugzeugwerke, Augsburg
Siehe Text Seite:

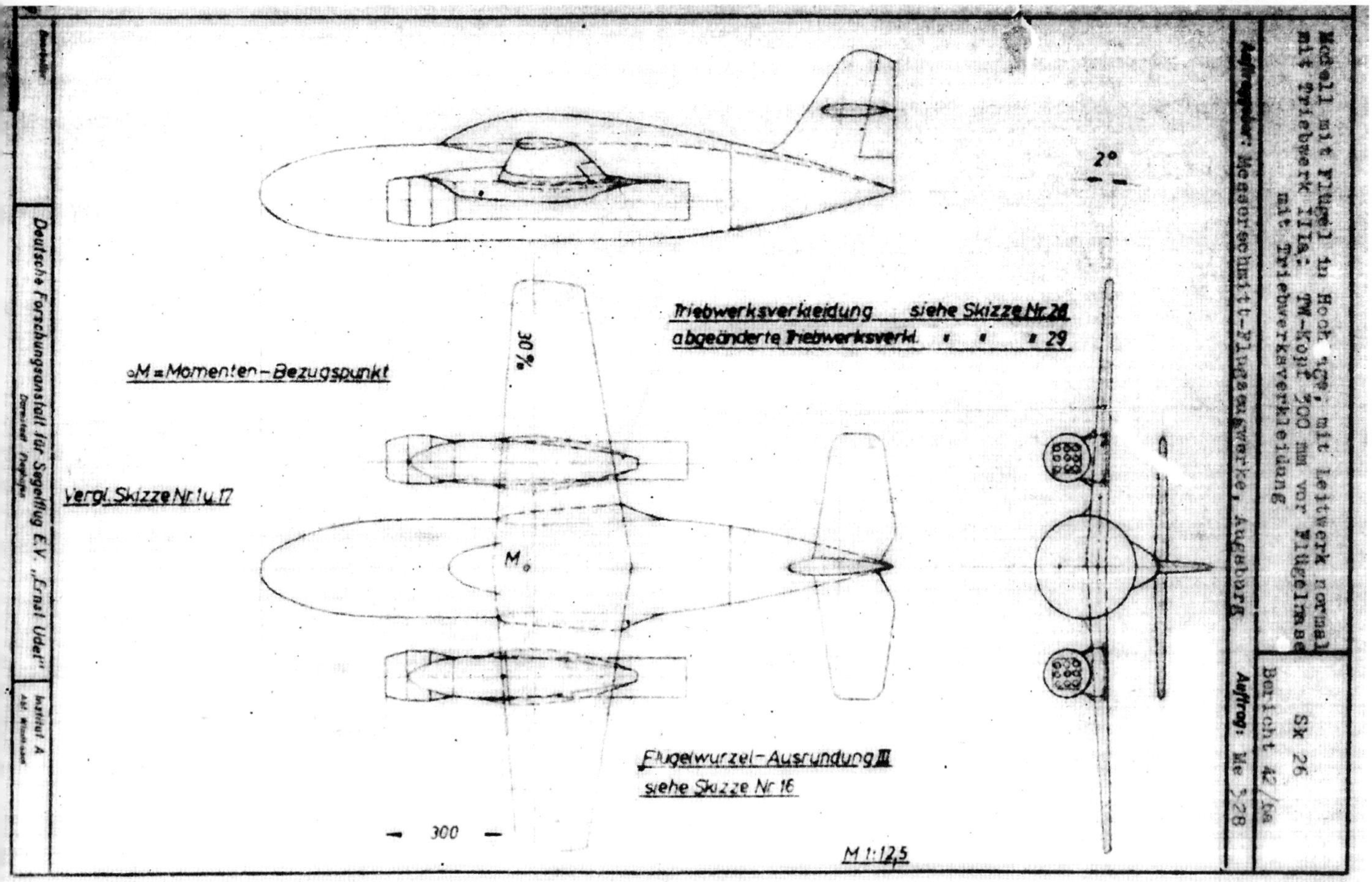
○M=Momenten-Bezugspunkt
Vergl. Skizze Nr 1u.17
Triebwerksverkleidung siehe Skizze Nr.28
abgeänderte Triebwerksverkl. " " " 29
Flugelwurzel-Ausrundung III
siehe Skizze Nr 16
M 1:12,5
Deutsche Forschungsanstalt für Segelflug E.V. „Ernst Udet"
Sk 26
Bericht 42/6a
Auftrag: Me 328
Auftraggeber: Messerschmitt-Flugzeugwerke, Augsburg

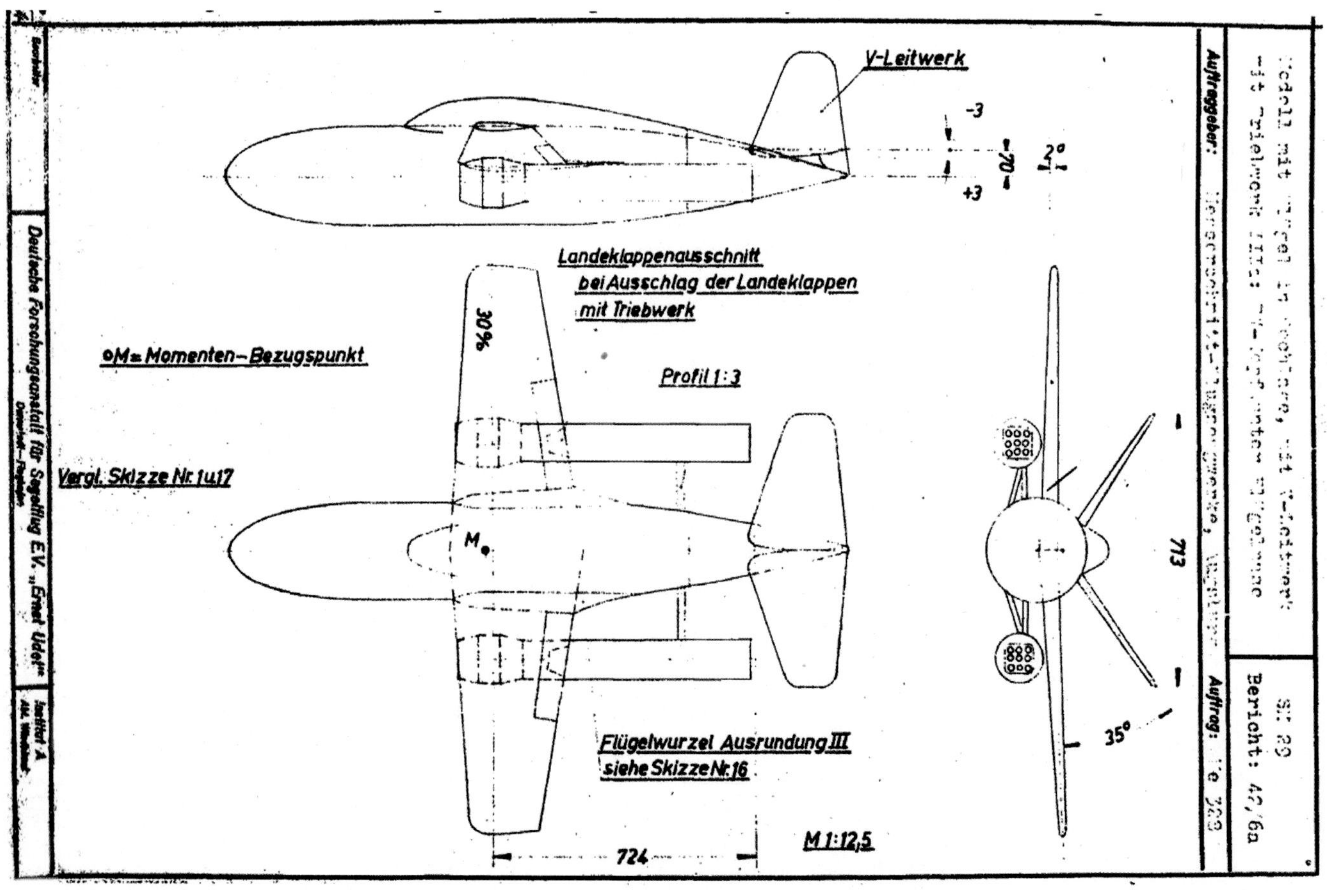

Nine different high-wing Me 328 configurations were wind tunnel-tested by the DFS between March 2 to April 22 and the results were published as Bericht 42/6a on June 22—ahead of earlier tests made using models with the low-wing configuration. Each of the nine has a 'Skizze' or Sketch number, these being Sk 17, Sk 18, Sk 19, Sk 21, Sk 23, Sk 24, Sk 25, Sk 26 and Sk 29. Photos also exist showing the test models used for the Sk 19 and Sk 29 forms, with very large wing root fairings and a V-tail respectively.

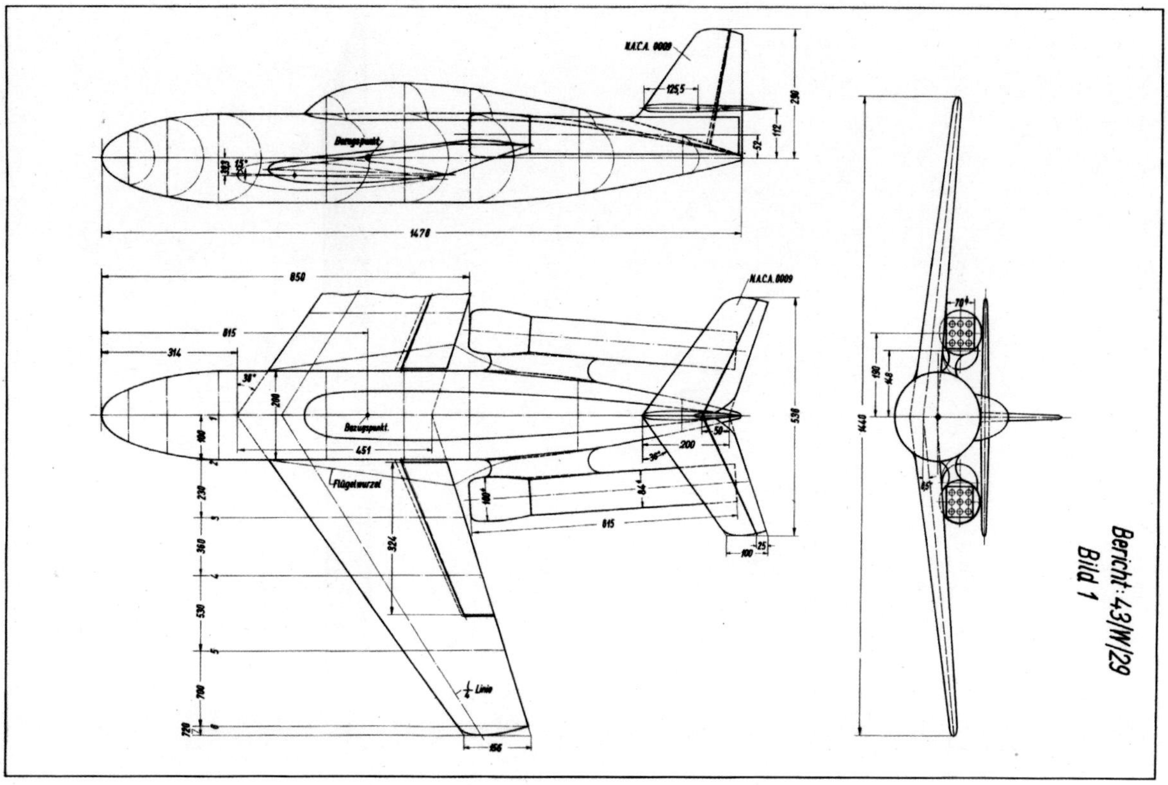

AVA drawing from a report dated July 14, 1943, showing a wind tunnel test model of an Me 328 with extended fuselage and a swept low-wing configuration—plus rear fuselage-mounted pulsejets.

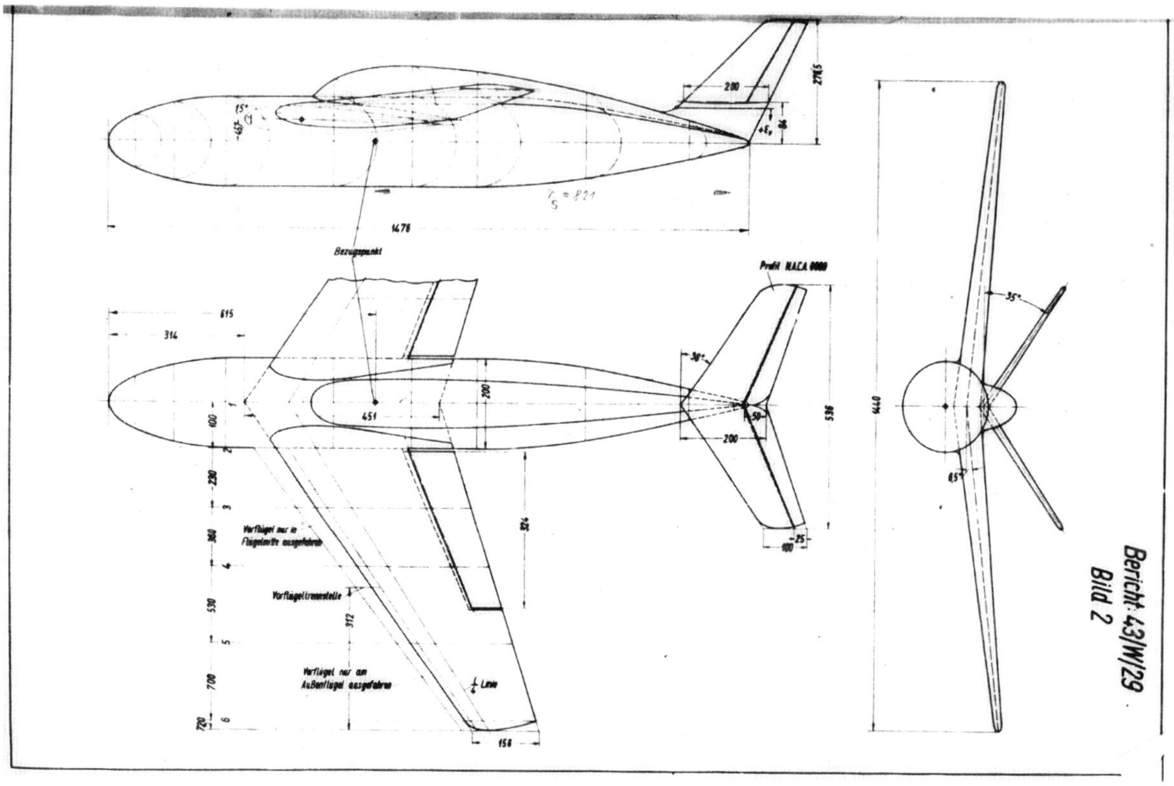

The second AVA test model from the July 14, 1943, report—a high-wing design, retaining the lengthened fuselage and swapping the swept cruciform tail for a V-tail. The engine position for this design is unclear however.

Georg Pasewaldt: "Very little. But it has the advantage of absolutely straight flight at this speed."

Milch: "At what speed?"

Pasewaldt: "750km/h."

Friebel: "750 to 780km/h."

Milch: "The same high up and low down?"

Hoffmann: "No, faster high up."

Milch: "Peltz says you can take any sled and stick something underneath it—a few turbojets."

Pasewaldt: "We created these small Me 328s for the fast bombing mission, which were actually intended [from the outset] as bomb carriers [unlike the Ar 234, which was made for reconnaissance]. This is the machine with the Argus pulsejets. It's not yet ready to be offered. We had the machine back then, you, Friebel, or your predecessor in office..."

Friebel: "She was presented to the Inspector of Fighters at that time. Oberst Peltz doesn't know her. It is a wooden aircraft with two Argus pulsejets. It has low penetration range, 750km, at 650 to 700km/h ground speed."

Milch: "What's she taking with her?"

Friebel: "A 500kg bomb. Self-start is not possible. The aircraft must be towed or catapulted."

But Peltz appears to have had little interest in the Me 328 and would not be dissuaded from his goal. Completely ignoring the points just raised, he responded instead: "Is it not possible to produce a number of the Ar 234, e.g.

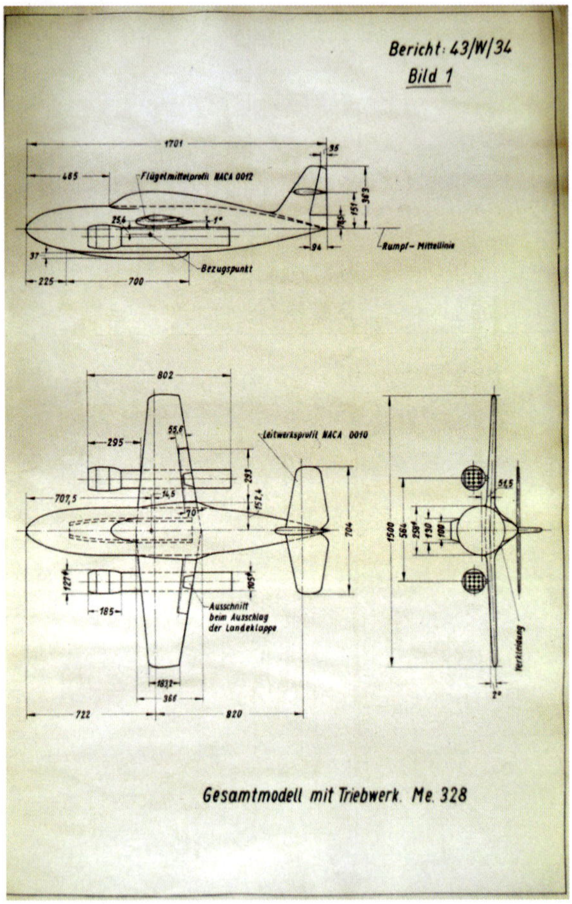

High-wing Me 328 model used by the AVA during wind tunnel tests of the rail-launch configuration. The report in which it appears is dated July 16, 1943.

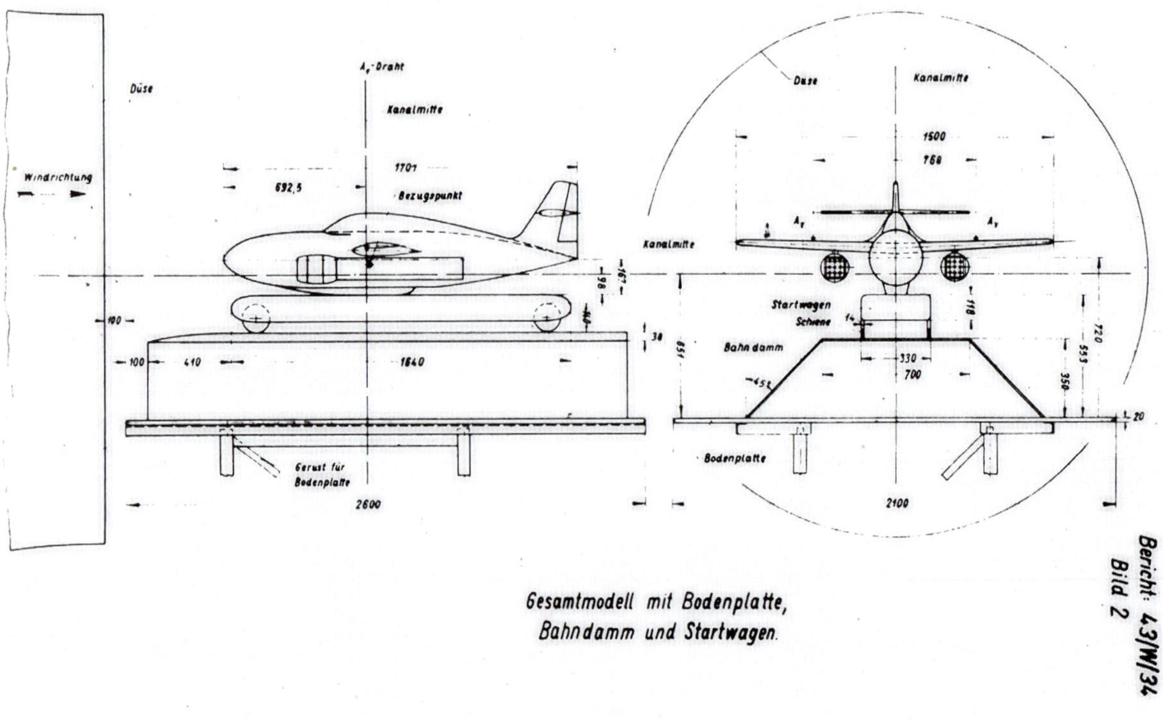

Diagram from the July 16 AVA report showing the Me 328 model positioned on a small rail car, on tracks atop an embankment, ready for launch.

Photograph of the rail-launch Me 328 model on its own in the AVA's wind tunnel at Göttingen.

The rail-launch Me 328 model with its rail car. The configuration was tested at various take-off angles.

Tests were conducted on the rail-launch Me 328, plus rail car, with a facsimile of a railway embankment factored in.

100 examples?"

And the conversation moved off in a different direction, never returning to the Me 328.

At Hörsching, it was apparently recorded on July 14 that a successful Me 328/Do 217 Mistel separation had been carried out by the DFS, with Klöckner at the controls of the Me 328 V2. That same day yet another report was published on Me 328-related wind tunnel tests. Not only had such tests been carried out by the DFS, Messerschmitt itself and the LFA, but the AVA at Göttingen had been working on it too.

The tests were conducted using a 1:5.5 scale model of the Me 328 with swept wings and measurements were taken with these in both high and low positions relative to the fuselage. The model was also variously reconfigured with a conventional or V-tail and with or without pulsejet forms attached to the rear fuselage.

The fuselage shape was very similar if not identical to the extended form with the old rounded canopy appearing in the Messerschmitt Flugzeuge mit Strahlrohren report of March 31, 1942, but the wings were new.

RAIL-LAUNCHED ME 328

Just two days later, on July 16, 1943, the AVA published a second Me 328 wind tunnel test report—this time on a 1:4.26 scale model with high-set straight wings and associated models of a railway embankment, base plate and railway line take-off trolley.[34]

While no contemporary documents are known to exist which detail plans to rail-launch the Me 328, it would appear that this was largely the same concept applied at roughly the same time to the Me 163. Details of the Me 163 version were explained by Lippisch to his interrogators in England shortly after the war as follows: "It was at one time proposed to launch the Me 163 from standard gauge railway lines. To this end special trains were to be made up which could be readily taken to selected points on the railway system. Each train was to comprise special trucks for carrying the Me 163, and the necessary fuel and spares, and accommodation was also to be provided for pilot and ground crew. There would also have been a special launching trolley for the aircraft.

"At selected points the track was to be prepared by the addition of a third central rail of appropriate length. The launching trolley was to be propelled by Borsig rockets and when it had attained the necessary speed the Me 163 would become airborne. Thereafter the trolley was to be arrested by hydraulically operated brakes engaging the central rail.

"Experiments were carried out to develop a suitable trolley but the design produced was unduly heavy so that a large proportion of the trust of the rockets was expended in accelerating the trolley. The scheme was tried at Peenemünde towards the end of 1943. A length of rail was laid down and launching tests were carried out using wood mock-ups of the Me 163. No launch was ever attempted with an aircraft, and the scheme was abandoned partly on account of the weight of the trolley."[35]

Up to the last week of July 1943, it had seemed as though the Me 262 would replace the Bf 109 as the next main fighter of the Luftwaffe. However, those attending the Air Ministry management meeting on July 27 were surprised to learn that this decision had been completely undone. The Me 262 was reduced to an "additional requirement" to the main production programme—which would see the Me 209 becoming the Luftwaffe's main fighter instead.[36]

JSF'S ME 328 B

The Messerschmitt office at JSF produced a timescale for Me 328 B prototype completion on July 20, 1943.[37] As part of 'deadline group A', the Me 328 B V1 glider was scheduled for completion on September 1, 1943, while engine tests were to begin earlier—on August 25.

Deadline group B included the completion of the Me 328 B V2 which was "being prepared for the installation of engines and is being brought forward compared to the original planning". It also included the construction of a basic airframe for take-off tests designated Me 328 SV1 and various stress test pieces. Deadline group C included Me 328 B V3 and take-off test airframe Me 328 SV2. Deadline group D was the Me 328 B V4 and Me 328 SV3, while deadline group E was the V5 and F was the V6.

The BAL report on JSF's activities for July cited the same September 1, 1943, date but the earlier problems with shortages of skilled metal workers, difficulty in procuring alloys, and failure to secure driving permits and fuel for deliveries persisted. The jig and tool preparation was now 95% complete and construction of the Me 328 B V1 had reached 50%. One Me 328 B wing piece for 20g and 50g ammo testing was finished and two more were now being fabricated.

While manufacturing at JSF was clearly not going well, the nascent Me 328 B design itself was continuing to evolve—taking it further and further away from the Me 328 A type. The biggest difference between the 'A' and the new 'B' remained the wing position—low for the 'A', high for the 'B'—though a little less high now than originally envisioned back in December 1942. Changes now also been made to the cockpit canopy, the landing gear and the overall shape of the fuselage.[38]

While the Me 328 V2's flat-windowed cockpit canopy had an unusual triple triangle arrangement up front—a V-shaped windscreen in the middle with a regular triangular panel on either side—JSF, or perhaps the Messerschmitt team at JSF, had come up with a canopy featuring a rectangular central windscreen plus a low fairing at the base which blended it into the nose more smoothly.

The Me 328 A's landing skid was like a single ski blade, housed internally directly below the pilot, which extended parallel to the fuselage on struts. The JSF Me 328 B system featured two externally-mounted landing skids, one below the nose and the other below and slightly behind the pilot. Rather than coming down like ski blades, they were hinged at the front and swung down at the rear only, rather like the flaps on a wing—so that the sprung trailing edge of each flap hit the ground first, providing two points of contact and presumably a greater cushioning affect compared to the original arrangement.

And there would be no need for a take-off trolley for the Me 328 B. Instead, the aircraft had a low tricycle undercarriage—a 380x150mm nosewheel and two 770x270mm mainwheels—which would be jettisoned on take-off. This would be both lighter than a full trolley and safer in the event of the wheels failing to fall away correctly, since they would create less drag and be less of an impediment to an emergency landing.

Allowing the landing flaps to sit on the fuselage underside, rather than within it, gave the Me 328 B a somewhat stubbier and more portly appearance than the Me 328 A even though it was 35cm longer overall at 7.18m compared to 6.83m.[39] This impression wasn't helped by a raised spine which blended the taller canopy into a larger fin to the rear. The nose was also somewhat reprofiled, sloping away from the pilot to a slightly more pointed tip—perhaps to provide slightly improved visibility in a nose-high attitude.

ME 328 V2 WITH REAR FUSELAGE PULSEJETS

The DFS activities summary for the period up to August 1 confirmed that the Mistel take-off method was working for the Me 328 and that a number of flights had been carried out with pulsejets attached to the rear fuselage.[40] It is not explicitly stated that these flights involved the Me

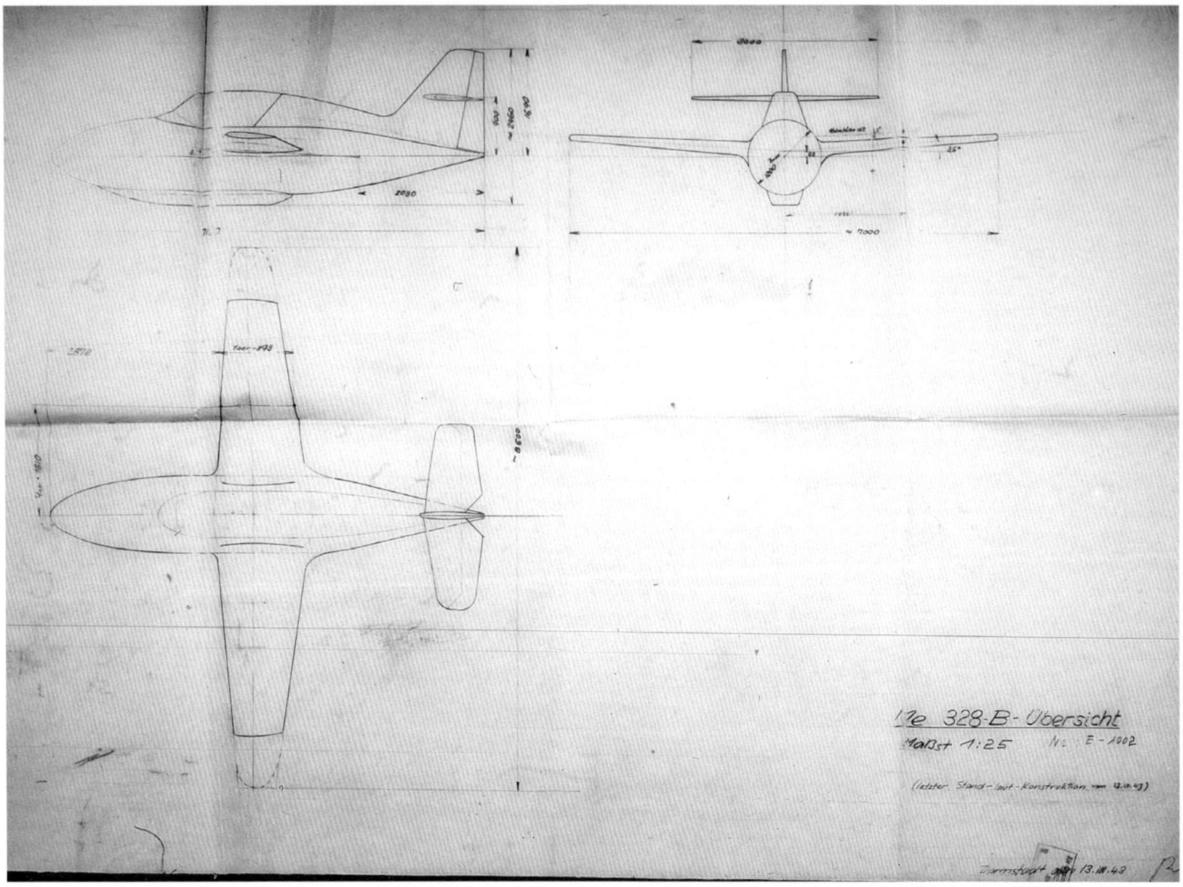

Three-view drawing of the redesigned Me 328 B circa July 14, 1943. The aircraft is slightly longer and slightly taller overall than it was on December 15, 1942. The nose profile is different, the canopy is different and the skid is different and the wing position is more central relative to the fuselage.

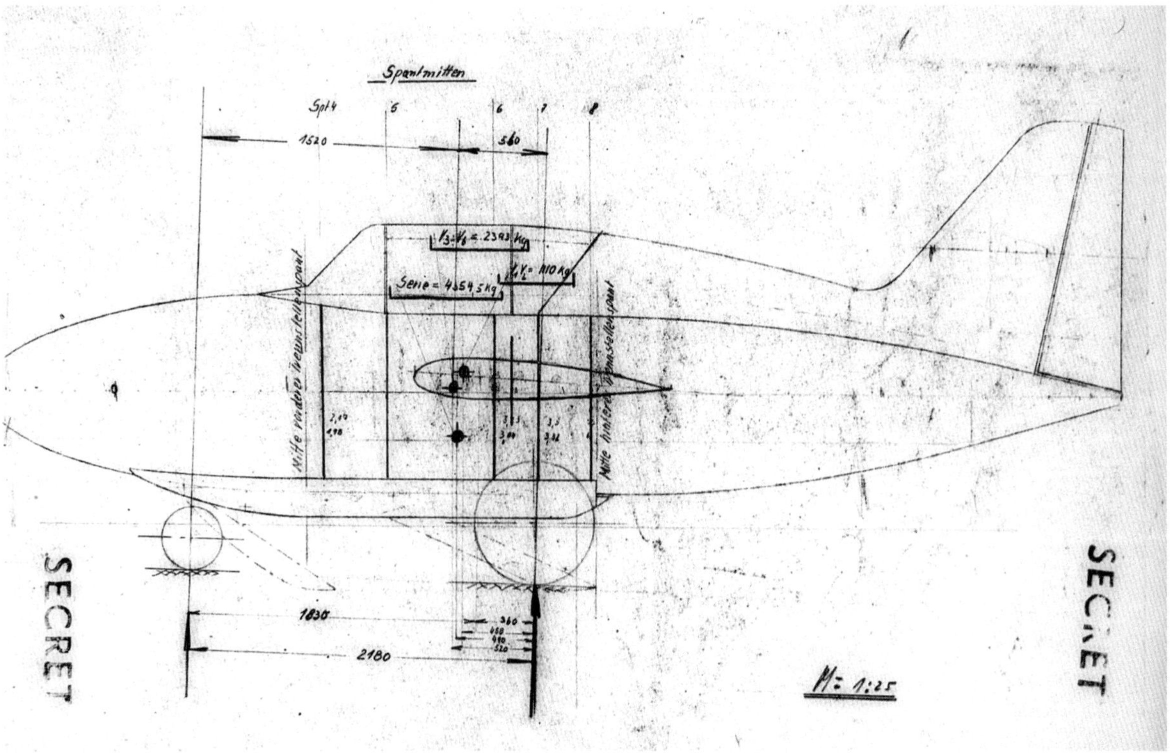

Me 328 B diagram from July 1943 showing the design's revised undercarriage — two flap-type skids arranged in tandem with jettisonable tricycle undercarriage wheels.

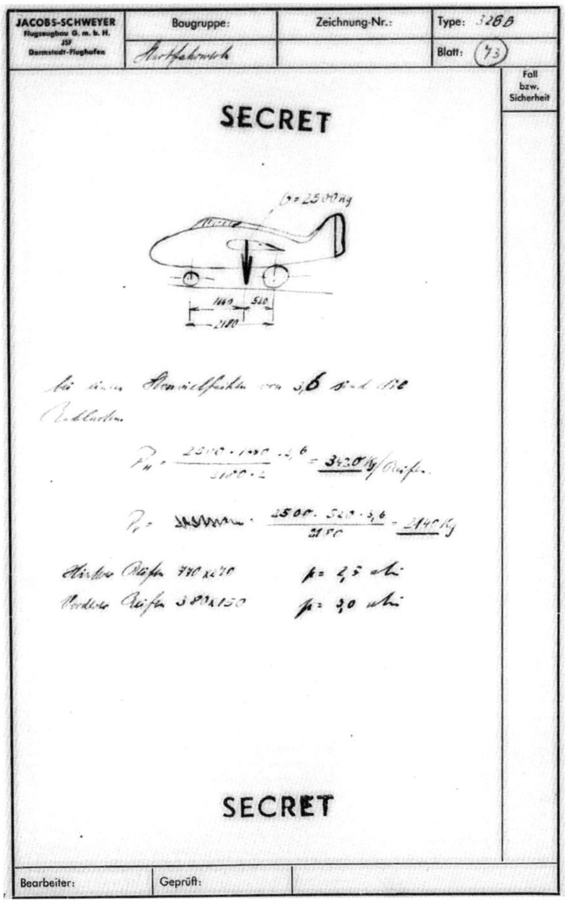

JSF diagram showing work on the new wheeled undercarriage.

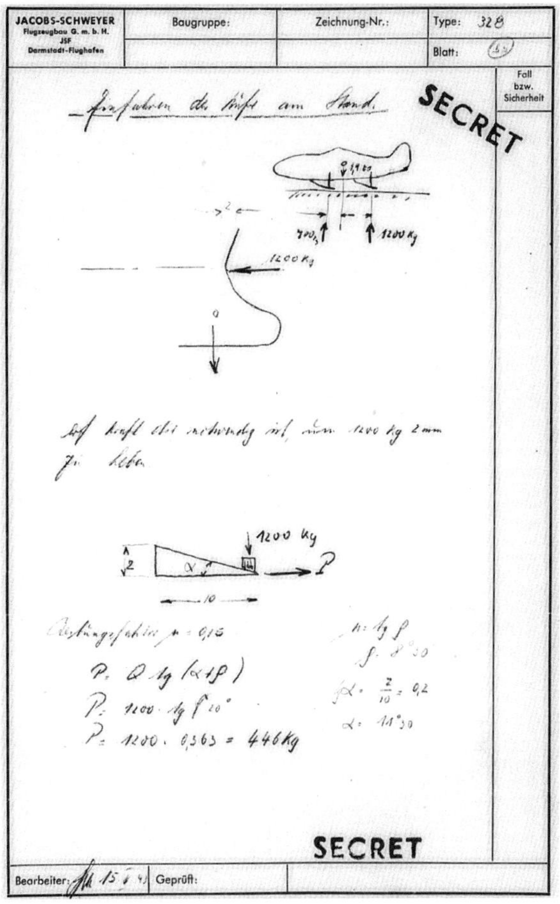

Another diagram from JSF, dating from July 15, 1943, showing the twin landing skid arrangement. On landing, the trailing edge of each skid would contact the ground.

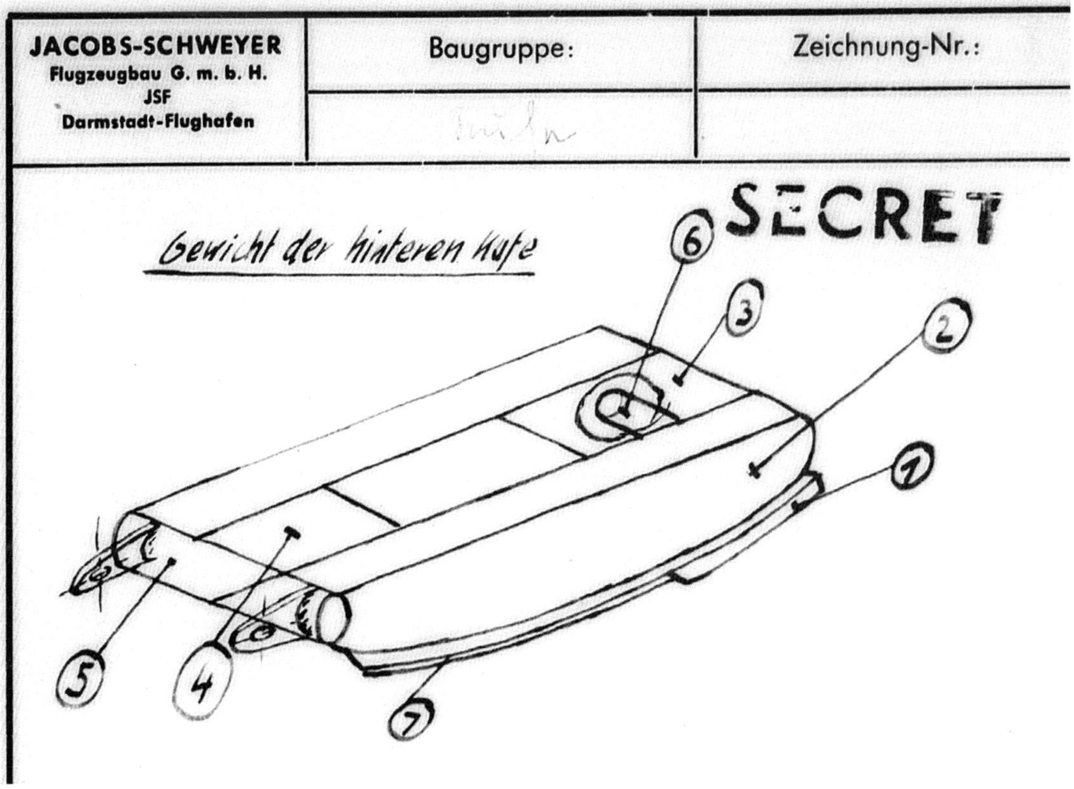

JSF sketch showing the design of the Me 328 B's rear skid, hinged at the front.

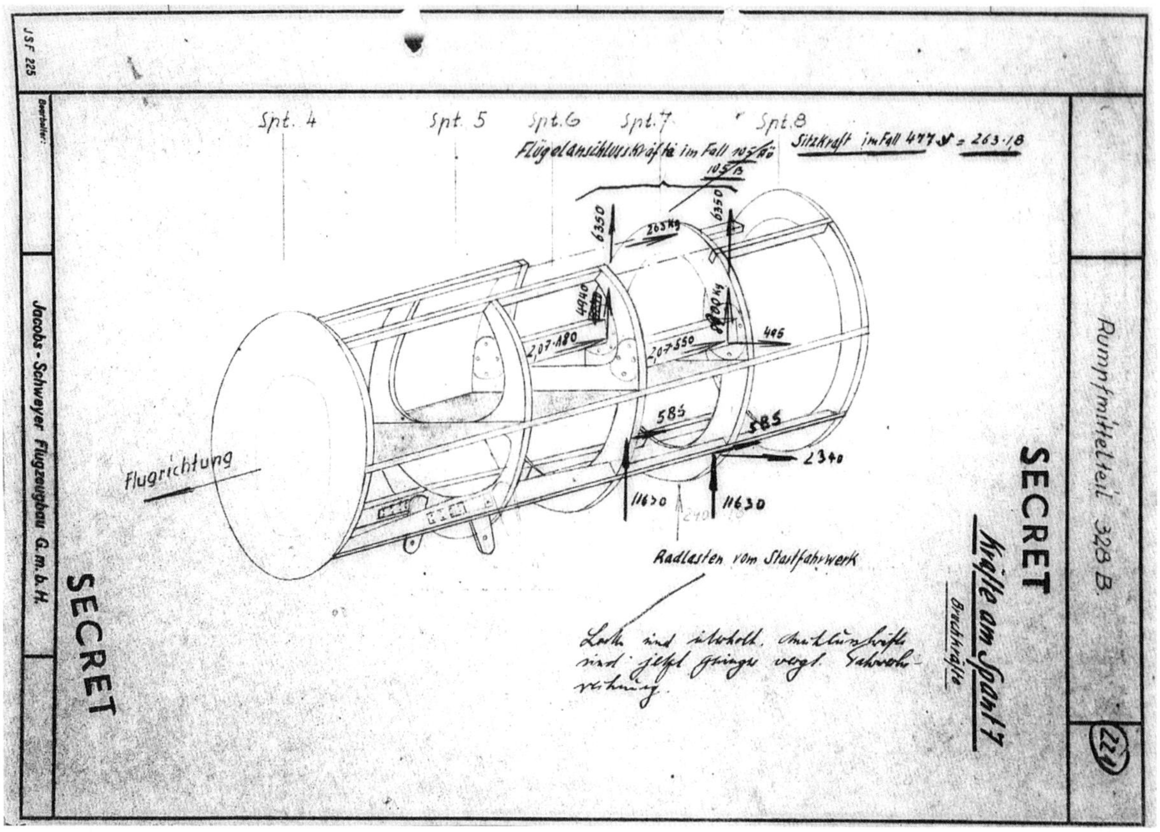

Diagram showing the five structural frames comprising the Me 328 B's fuselage centre section. The attachment points for the rear skid appear at the bottom of Frame (Spt) 5. The cockpit would sit between Frames 5 and 6, with the wings slotting in between Frames 6 and 7 from above.

328 V2—but this was, and had been for a long time, the only airworthy Me 328 prototype.

It said: "Me 328 (P 1079). During the reporting period, the Mistel tow was examined for the Me 328. It turned out that this type of towing was the suitable take-off method for the Me 328. The team is absolutely capable of flying blind. Uncoupling is no problem up to the highest flying weights. After some deficiencies in the landing gear were corrected, the new VSR 9 sk pipes were installed, but all of them were destroyed after a short time.

"Afterwards the older tubes VSR 9 ad [pipes] were tried and several flights were carried out with them. The impairment of the flight characteristics caused by the pulsejets arranged at the tail is acceptable. The question of the fuel system has not yet been completely satisfactorily solved, as the existing taps and filters are not designed for such large delivery quantities."

No detailed accounts of these flights are known to exist, but it would appear from this brief summary that the Me 328 V2 had been fitted with pulsejets on its rear fuselage, had taken off on the back of a Do 217, had successfully separated in mid-air, and had then flown under pulsejet power before making a successful landing—and it had done it on multiple occasions judging by the fact that two different pulsejet variants had been tried.

TURBOJET ME 328 PROGRESS

Seitz travelled to Dessau on August 4, 1943, to meet Anselm Franz, head of Jumo 004 jet engine development at Junkers, to discuss the 'Me 328 B mit 1 x TL Jumo 004 B'.[41]

As mentioned, the Me 328 C designation had originally been applied to this design back in March but it appears to have fallen out of favour by this point. Much of the discussion focused on two key areas: the undercarriage and the engine intake. The turbojet-powered Me 328 had been designed with its single Jumo 004 in a ventral position—under the fuselage—and Seitz had evidently planned on fitting a sprung flap-type skid to the compressor housing as the aircraft's landing gear. Arado already had a similar skid arrangement for the turbojets under the Ar 234 A's wings.

However, it was reported that "after asking Herr [Walter] Uhlig of Arado, it emerged that Arado only provided support skids on the engine, so that [installing] fittings on the compressor housing for connecting a landing skid with higher forces was not an option".

It also appears that the jet-propelled Me 328 had been designed with a nose-type intake and that the jet engine

DFS display model of the Me 328 V2 fitted with pulsejets. This model, captured by the Allies after the war, shows the distinctive V-shaped windscreen, nose-mounted Seppeler generators and rear-fuselage mounted pulsejets of this unique aircraft.

The Me 328 V2 mounted on the back of its Do 217 K-3 carrier aircraft, with its elevators down—presumably at Hörsching. The visible attachment struts appear quite sturdy, so perhaps this was prior to a non-separation test flight.

Another view of the Me 328 V2 on its carrier, this time with the engines running.

Side view of the Me 328 V2, coded RL+TY, with bare-rib pulsejets attached to its rear fuselage and Seppeler generators on its nose.

The Me 328 V2 mounted on its carrier aircraft as viewed from the rear. These pulsejets appear to have an aerodynamic fairing over their ribs.

Another view of the Me 328 V2 on its carrier. Note the arrangement of slender bracing struts holding the aircraft in position. The attachment points were mechanically actuated for release, rather than making use of explosive bolts.

The Me 328 V2 in flight atop the Do 217 K-3 carrier. Again, this time the pulsejets are wearing a full fairing.

itself was to be installed at an angle. The meeting report noted that "the inlet for fresh air into the engine at the tip of the fuselage indicated in the sketch was said by Herr Dr Franz to be risk-free, although he pointed out that due to the inclined arrangement of the engine, the inlet fairing may need to be removed. It would have to be reshaped accordingly".

But at least "Jumo is of the opinion that the engine arrangement shown does not present any difficulties with regard to the jet blast acting on the end of the fuselage". In other words, the engine's exhaust was positioned below the aircraft's tail but this was unlikely to cause any problems.

ME 328 V02 SACRIFICED

By now the lone Messerschmitt-made Me 328 prototype, the steel-skinned Me 328 V02, had finally been completed. Given all the changes that had been made to the Me 328 V2 during its nearly 12 months as an airworthy flight test vehicle, this aircraft was something of a throwback—its cockpit canopy, while not identical to that of the Me 328 V1, also had a rounded windscreen. And it had been designed to accommodate pulsejets beneath its wings, whereas the DFS had long since determined that a tail-mounted configuration gave better results.

Perhaps because it was now so outdated, the Me 328 V02 was not rolled into the flight test programme. Rather, it was sent to the Peenemünde test station and used for static pulsejet running tests—so that the effects of an underwing installation on a completed airframe could be studied in controlled conditions.[42]

The resulting report was published on August 17, 1943, and provides valuable insights into the seriously deleterious effects of pulsejet propulsion on an aircraft. It began: "To test the pipes themselves, their fuel supply and their suspension, the pipes were initially in operation with interruptions for about 10 minutes. During this time there was no tail unit on the aircraft. After attaching a tail unit, the pipes were in operation intermittently for about 75 minutes, mostly at full load, at times at partial load (thrust about 200kg per pipe). The tests were then stopped in order to save fuel, as no significantly new results could be expected, and will be continued after the star-shaped pipe ends have been attached. So far the pipes have been running as delivered.

"Since the necessary injection pressure could not be produced with the Leistritz pumps (these pumps were driven by small electric motors via gears and flexible shafts), a pressurised container with around 580 litres [of fuel] was installed outside the machine. The contents were supplied via two pipes using an older model Argus regulator. Injection pressure was 2-2.4 atmospheres at

The steel-skinned Me 328 V02 prototype built by Messerschmitt. The aircraft appears to have originally been configured as a glider and is not equipped for pulsejet operation in flight.

A forward view of the Me 328 V02 shows a complete absence of the Seppeler generators that would be essential to run the fuel pumps for pulsejet-powered flight.

full load. The working frequency of the pipes, which was measured with a stroboscope, fluctuated between approximately 40-45Hz.

"The results of the testing were as follows: 1) Tailplanes with sheet metal panelling. After the first run, which lasted 15 minutes, some of the rivet holes had already broken out slightly. The damage was very noticeable due to the build-up of soot, but had no influence on strength. As the tests continued, the number of rivet holes knocked out increased, so that finally almost all of the rivet holes on

The pulsejets installed on the Me 328 V02 for ground testing were completely unfaired—lacking both inlet cowlings and overall skin. It appears that the aircraft was tested to destruction at Peenemünde.

the underside were knocked out. Even after 75 minutes, however, the damage was nowhere so severe that the load-bearing capacity had suffered. The rivets themselves are still firmly seated in the stiffening profiles underneath the skin.

"In conclusion, it should be said that the present design of the tailplanes (Me 109) has proven itself well and can be assumed to have a service life of a few hours. The commander, who was present at times during the tests, had expected the tail unit to be destroyed in a maximum of 10 minutes."

This last sentence suggests that the unnamed 'commander' who didn't stick around to watch the whole sequence of tests, absolutely believed that the Me 328 V02 was being tested to destruction—which further suggests that no future flight testing was planned for the Me 328 V02. It was simply being sacrificed for the purposes of a one-off experiment.

Next up was the effect on the fabric covered elevators: "The elevator is also still usable at the end of the experiments. Some of the eyelets used for ventilation were torn out at the beginning of the tests; the fabric was probably already damaged by the sharp edges of the eyelets. However, the holes did not tear any further afterwards. After about 50 minutes, the paint on the underside showed strong cracks and then mostly peeled off, especially in the middle, so that the covering became loose. This could perhaps be remedied by using a different varnish that penetrates the fabric better, or by stretching the fabric firmly before painting. The paintwork on the top is undamaged."

Then there was the effect on the wooden fin: "At the end of the tests, the fin was undamaged except for small cracks in the glue on the rear, which may have been there before or may have occurred during transport. On the other hand, after about an hour, a piece of skin on the rudder about the size of a hand was torn off on one side. At the end of the tests, part of the skin was missing on both sides and two ribs were loose. However, the appearance of the cracked glue points certainly indicates poor gluing, which, under the influence of the negative pressure waves, led to the rapid destruction of the gluing and then the skin."

The mid-wing engine mounts had apparently "proven themselves well" since "strong vibrations cannot be detected on the pipes". One of the rubber mounts used had melted but "this is unlikely to happen in flight, especially if the tube is positioned a little lower". There was a bigger problem however, since "the wing begins to vibrate noticeably, mainly torsional vibrations. These are probably partly transmitted through the air, but partly also through the suspension. An attempt must therefore be made to see how a more flexible suspension, possibly with more or less strong damping, affects the transmission of these vibrations".

What had not been mentioned up to this point was

the fact that some brave or foolhardy individual had actually sat in the Me 328 V02's cockpit throughout the 75 minutes of testing. Under 'impact on the pilot', the report stated: "The noise pollution within the cabin is tolerable, and the sealing can also be improved somewhat. What is more unpleasant is that all parts of the airframe vibrate strongly and for this reason the control stick cannot be kept still. A softer engine suspension could also have a beneficial effect in this sense."

The Argus pulsejets themselves "generally ran well" but the test crew had found it difficult to get them started. After the first run, water had been used to cool the glowing hot pipes—creating clouds of steam. This had failed to dissipate fully by the time the next test was due to begin and when the crew tried to restart the engine the steam was sucked into the inlets, resulting in a failed start. Once they were going again, they ran for 35 minutes without issue—then "the rear end of the right pipe, which had become more and more egg-shaped, tore open about 20cm in the longitudinal direction and then across. The edges of the cracks were badly battered. The cracks were then welded and the weld held. Flow lines can be seen along the entire length of the pipes, inclined at about 75 degrees to the longitudinal axis. At the end of the experiments, about a third of the valves [the shutters over the inlet] were more or less damaged, some are missing. The contact surfaces of the destroyed flaps are knocked out".

And what of the metal fuselage—the only one of its kind in existence—that had taken more than a year to prepare in Messerschmitt's own experimental workshop? Well, "towards the end of the tests, some cracks and holes appeared in the area behind the cabin, approximately at the level of the pipe exhausts and behind them. The transition panel to the tailplane has a long crack along the stiffener at the bottom edge and part of one of the inserted ribs has broken off.

"A hatch cover near the end of the fuselage is severely damaged (after about 50 minutes); one of the four latches has come off and the webs above the attachment points of the latches have torn off. This could have been due to the loose fit of the cover, as the other covers are undamaged. Apart from a few slightly loosened screws (including on the cockpit canopy), the screw connections held up well. The bearings on the tail unit are somewhat worn, as shown by the black colour of the grease, but there is no noticeable play or damage to the linkage anywhere".

The ultimate fate of the Me 328 V02 is unknown but given the damage its bespoke components had suffered during testing, and the expectation of the 'commander' that it wouldn't survive the tests anyway, it seems likely to have been scrapped.

JSF'S VANISHING FRENCHMEN

Following his meeting with Franz on the turbojet Me 328, Seitz seems to have pursued another line of development for a single-jet fighter—one composed of parts and assemblies from other aircraft. This 'new' design was given the project number P 1095 and a partial surviving drawing of August 19 shows it to have loosely the same configuration of the turbojet 328, with a single underslung Jumo 004. Another undated drawing shows a side and top view of the P 1095, the side view clearly indicating that the tailfin could come from either an Me 262, and Me 209 or an Me 328.

Unlike the turbojet Me 328, the engine was positioned precisely in parallel to the aircraft's thrust line, rather than being installed at an angle, the cockpit was further forward, the fuselage more slender and the wings set low. An undated text description of the P 1095 made no mention of Me 328 parts, stating that the aircraft was to be composed of Me 262 wings and cockpit with the tail coming from the Me 209 and the undercarriage coming either from the Me 262 or Me 209. In any case, the material that was to be borrowed from the Me 328 appears to have been little to none.

The BAL report on JSF's activities for August stated that once again the completion date for the Me 328 B V1 had slipped—to October 15, 1943—and there were yet more elaborate excuses as to why this was the case.[43] Evidently "the timely completion of the prototype Me 328 B is influenced by the simultaneous start of the series for the wooden Me 109 fin". The Me 328 B, once a priority job, was being shoved aside to make way for more pressing war-critical work.

But that wasn't the half of it. The report went on: "The postponement is caused by: 1) Loss of 38 semi-skilled workers, 26 of them in metal construction. These 38 men are French civilians who went on vacation between the end of May and July and did not return despite intervention from the employment office and the Gestapo. 2) Due to difficulties in the procurement of materials and parts due to inadequate means of transport. 3) Enemy action on the Messerschmitt Regensburg aircraft factory (destruction of the Me 109 parts required for 328). 4) Enemy action on Mannesmannröhren, Hamburg (conditional redesign of the canopy). 5) JSF lacks an operations engineer who would give initiative and authority to the production of the 328 in the company."

By now, the jigs and tools for building the Me 328 B gliders were finished. The corresponding jigs and tools

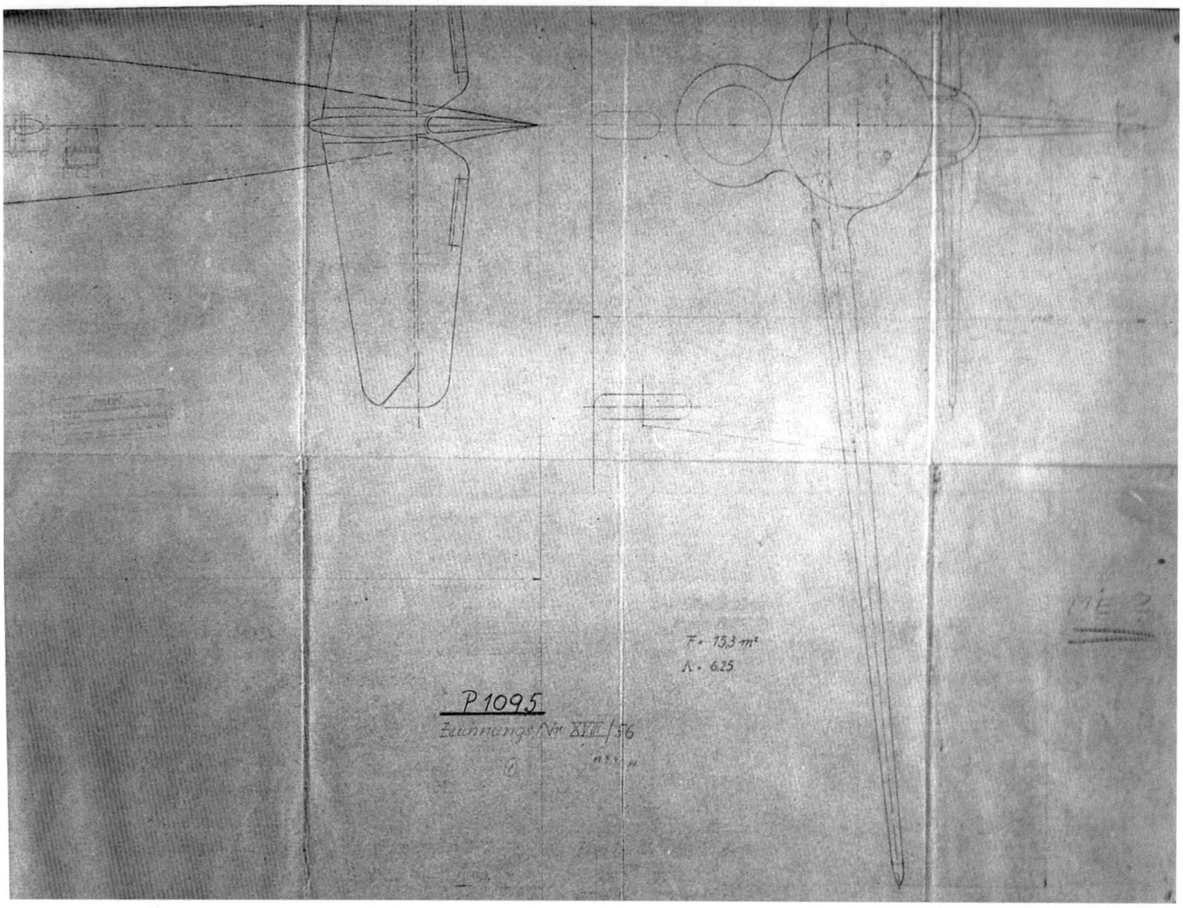

A fragment of Messerschmitt drawing XVIII/56, dated August 17, 1943, showing the P 1095 single-jet fighter—seemingly a relative of the turbojet-powered Me 328 design.

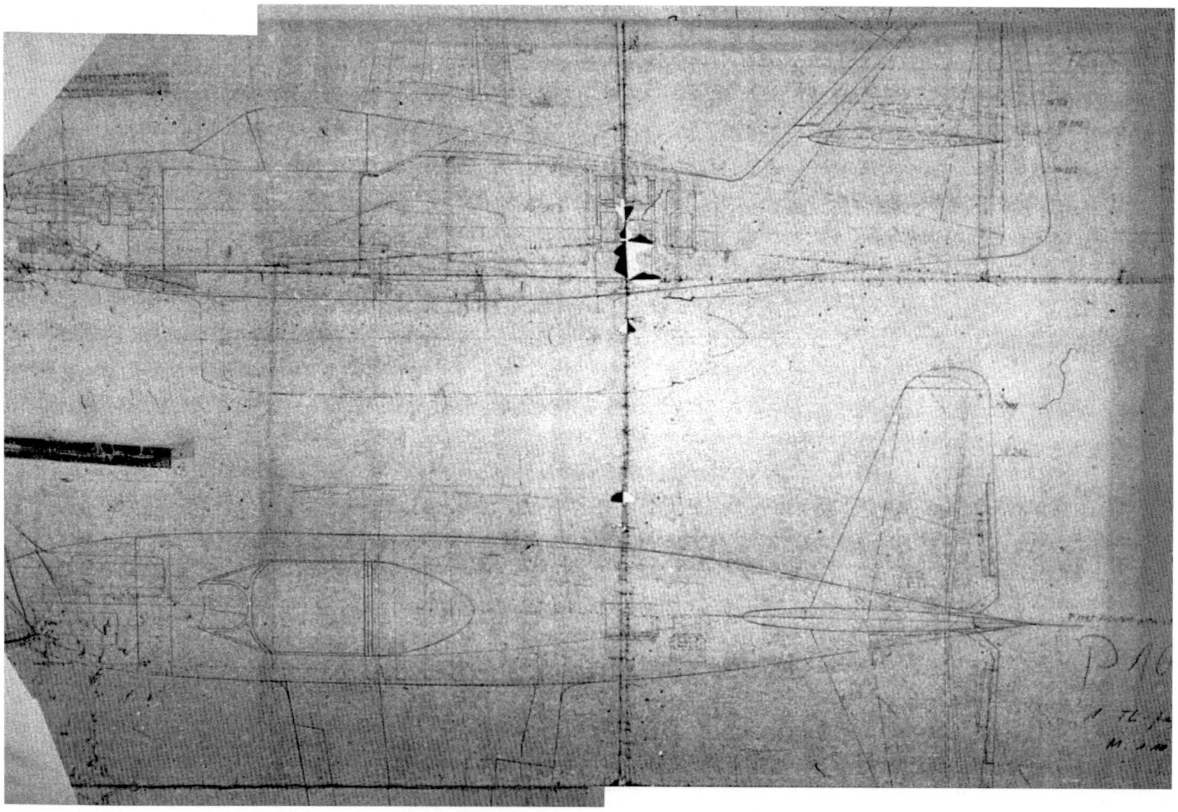

Undated side and top views of a different Messerschmitt P 1095 design. Labels to the rear indicate that Me 328, Me 209 and Me 262 components were all considered for the fin.

for making powered Me 328 Bs were 90% finished. The actual Me 328 B V1 was said to be 80% complete, while the V2 was 30% complete. The three wings intended for firing tests had been finished and one had already now been shot up, with a report on the results evidently having been produced.

HANNA GOES TO HÖRSCHING

Famous test pilot Reitsch had been badly injured in a crash while testing a Messerschmitt Me 163 in October 1942 and had been in hospital for five months. Then from March 1943, to July 1943, she spent some time convalescing and occasionally meeting up with some of Germany's most powerful individuals—such as Göring and Heinrich Himmler.

Between July and November 1943, according to her own account, she "returned to [her] task of test pilot". But for Reitsch this never seems to have amounted to an actual job. One day in August 1943, she recalled, "I came across two old friends. One of them was an aeronautical medical specialist, and the other, a very skilful and experienced glider pilot." The aeromedical specialist was Theodor Benzinger and the pilot was Oberleutnant Heinrich aka Karl-Heinz Lange.

During this meeting it seems Benzinger and Lange explained the same self-sacrifice concept to her that Benzinger had pitched to Georgii and Baeumker back in February and she found the idea appealing. Indeed, according to the logbook of her 'hack' Bücker Bü 181 Bestmann,[44] Reitsch flew from Regensburg to Ainring on August 30, 1943, staying there for two nights, before flying from Ainring to Hörsching on September 1. She remained at Hörsching for just over five hours before flying back to Ainring. Whether she saw the Me 328 V2 and its Do 217 mount during this trip is unknown—but she would presumably have been aware of it at this time.

August 30 had also finally seen the publication of the first round of wind tunnel tests conducted by the DFS between April 8, 1942, and January 20, 1943, using models to represent a wide range of low-wing configurations and just one high-wing arrangement.[45] This data, while interesting from an academic standpoint, was now largely irrelevant since Messerschmitt had shown no inclination to return to a low-wing layout.

Just three days later, on September 3, 1943, the order was given to cease work on the Me 328.[46]

Drawings from DFS Bericht 42/6 of August 30, 1943, showing 12 different wind tunnel configurations and model components tested from April 8, 1942, and January 20, 1943. As with Bericht 42/6a, each of the drawings has a 'Skizze' or Sketch number, these being Sk 1 to Sk 16. Photos also exist showing the test models used for the Sk 2, Sk 3, Sk 4, Sk 6, Sk 7 and Sk 11 forms. Of the 12 different configurations, all feature the old low-wing layout except for Sk 12.

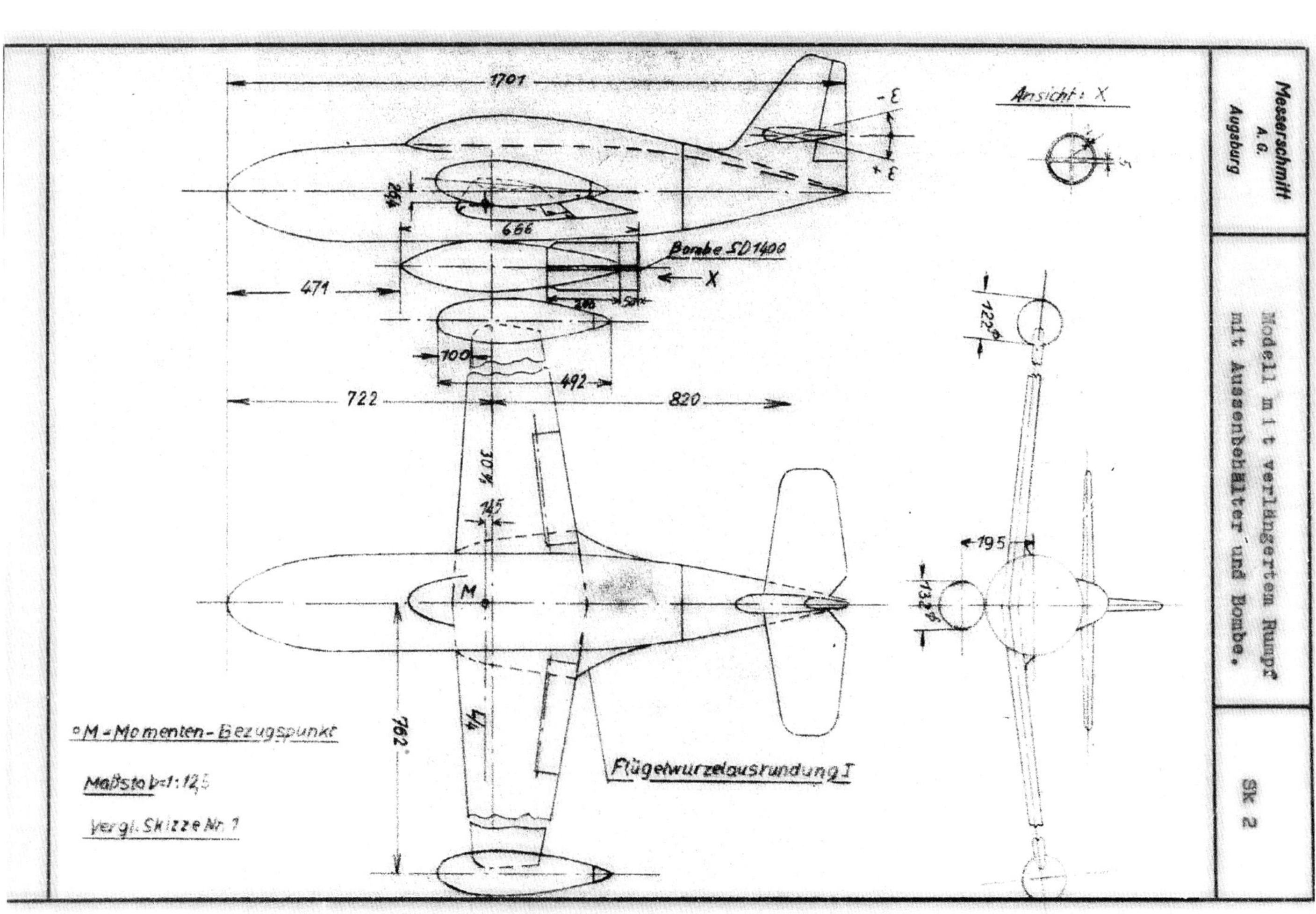

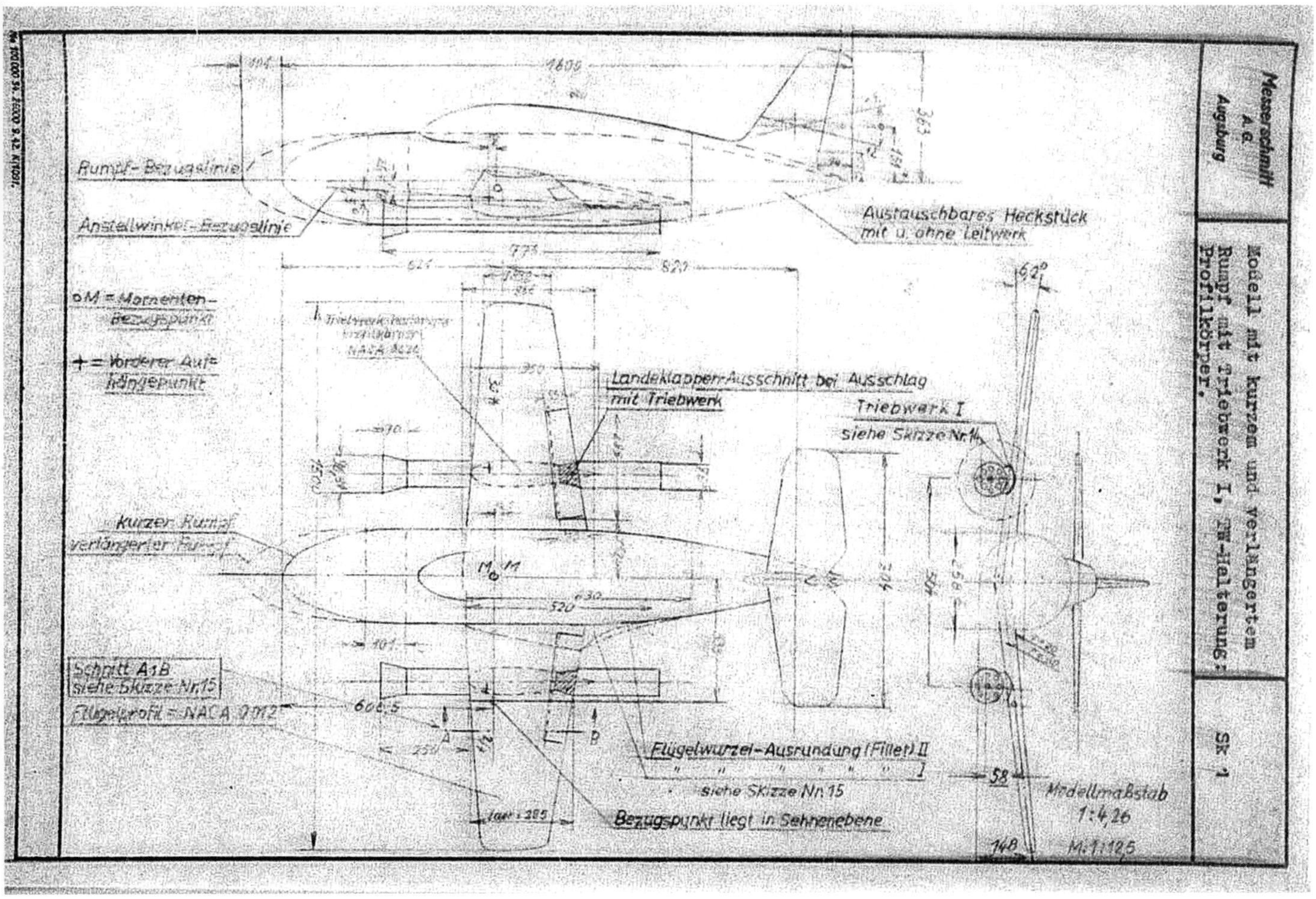
Messerschmitt A.G. Augsburg
Modell mit kurzem und verlängertem Rumpf mit Triebwerk I, TW-Halterung, Profilkörper.
SK 1
Rumpf-Bezugslinie
Anstellwinkel-Bezugslinie
Austauschbares Heckstück mit u. ohne Leitwerk
oM = Momenten-Bezugspunkt
+ = Vorderer Aufhängepunkt
Landeklappen-Ausschnitt bei Ausschlag mit Triebwerk
Triebwerk I siehe Skizze Nr.14
Kurzer Rumpf
verlängerter Rumpf
Schnitt A-B siehe Skizze Nr.15
Flügelprofil = NACA 0012
Flügelwurzel-Ausrundung (Fillet) II
siehe Skizze Nr.15
Bezugspunkt liegt in Sehnenebene
Modellmaßstab 1:4,26
M.1:12,5

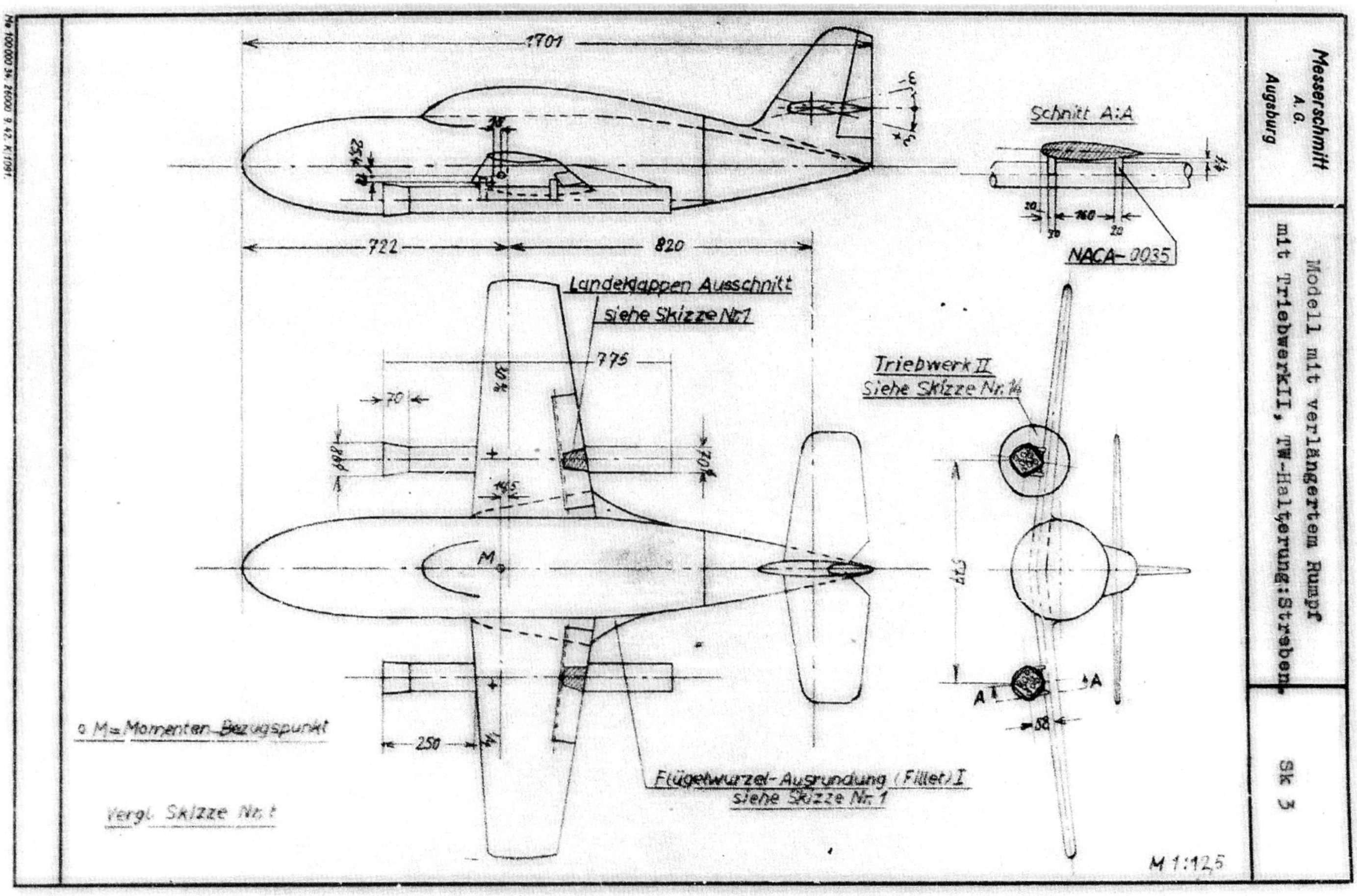
Messerschmitt
A.G.
Augsburg
Modell mit verlängertem Rumpf
mit TriebwerkII, TW-Halterung:Streben
Sk 3
1701
722
820
Schnitt A:A
NACA-0035
Landeklappen Ausschnitt
siehe Skizze Nr.1
775
70
Triebwerk II
siehe Skizze Nr. 14
M
o M= Momenten-Bezugspunkt
250
58
Flügelwurzel-Ausrundung (Fillet) I
siehe Skizze Nr. 1
Vergl. Skizze Nr. 1
M 1:125

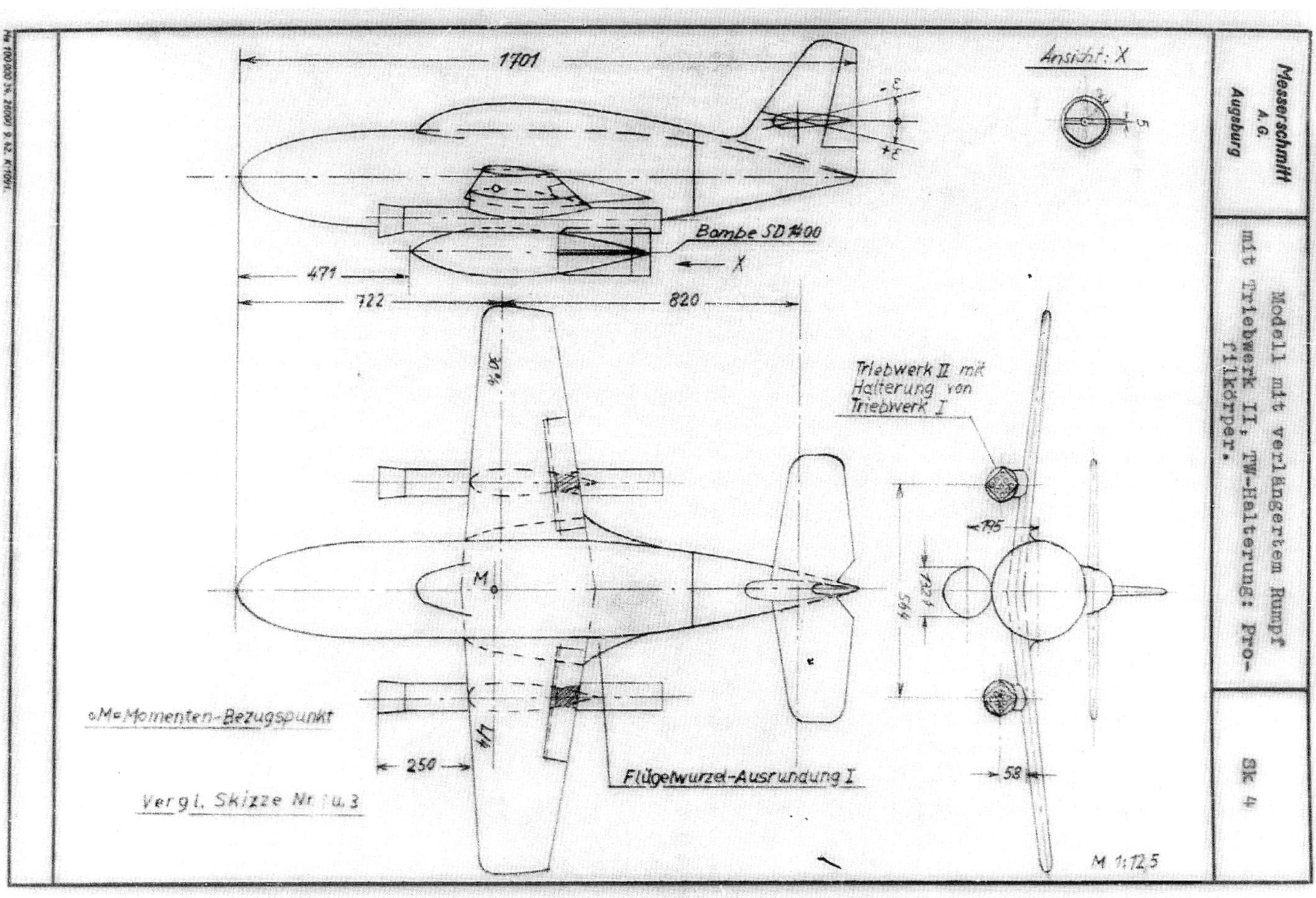
Messerschmitt A.G. Augsburg
Modell mit verlängertem Rumpf mit Triebwerk II, TW-Halterung: Profilkörper.
Sk 4
1701
Ansicht: X
Bombe SD 1400
471
722
820
X
Triebwerk II mit Halterung von Triebwerk I
195
564
M
M=Momenten-Bezugspunkt
250
Flügelwurzel-Ausrundung I
58
Vergl. Skizze Nr 1 u. 3
M 1:12,5

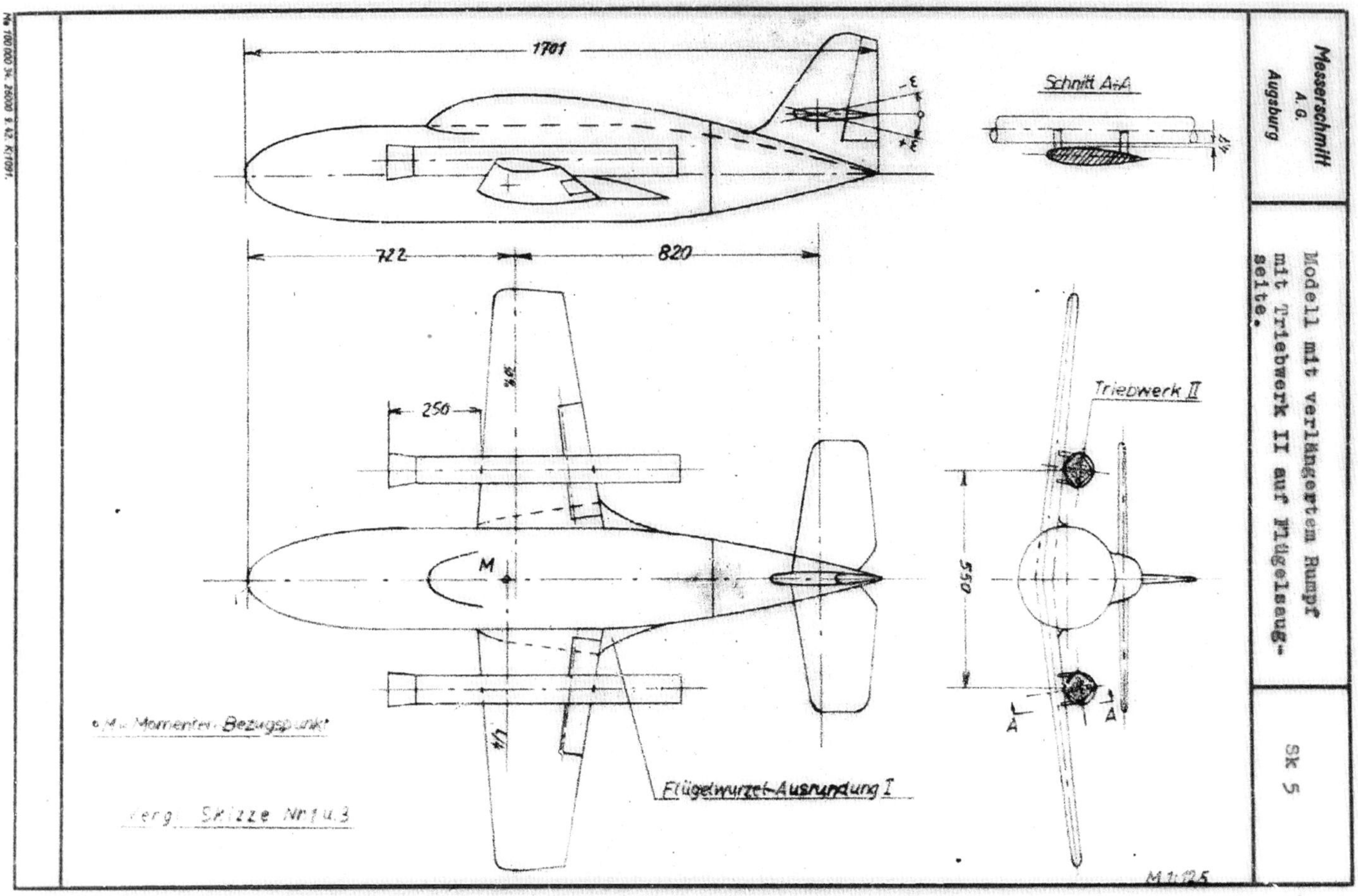
Messerschmitt A.G. Augsburg
Modell mit verlängertem Rumpf mit Triebwerk II auf Flügelsaug-seite.
Sk 5
1701
722
820
250
550
Schnitt A-A
Triebwerk II
M
M = Momenten-Bezugspunkt
Flügelwurzel-Ausrundung I
A
A

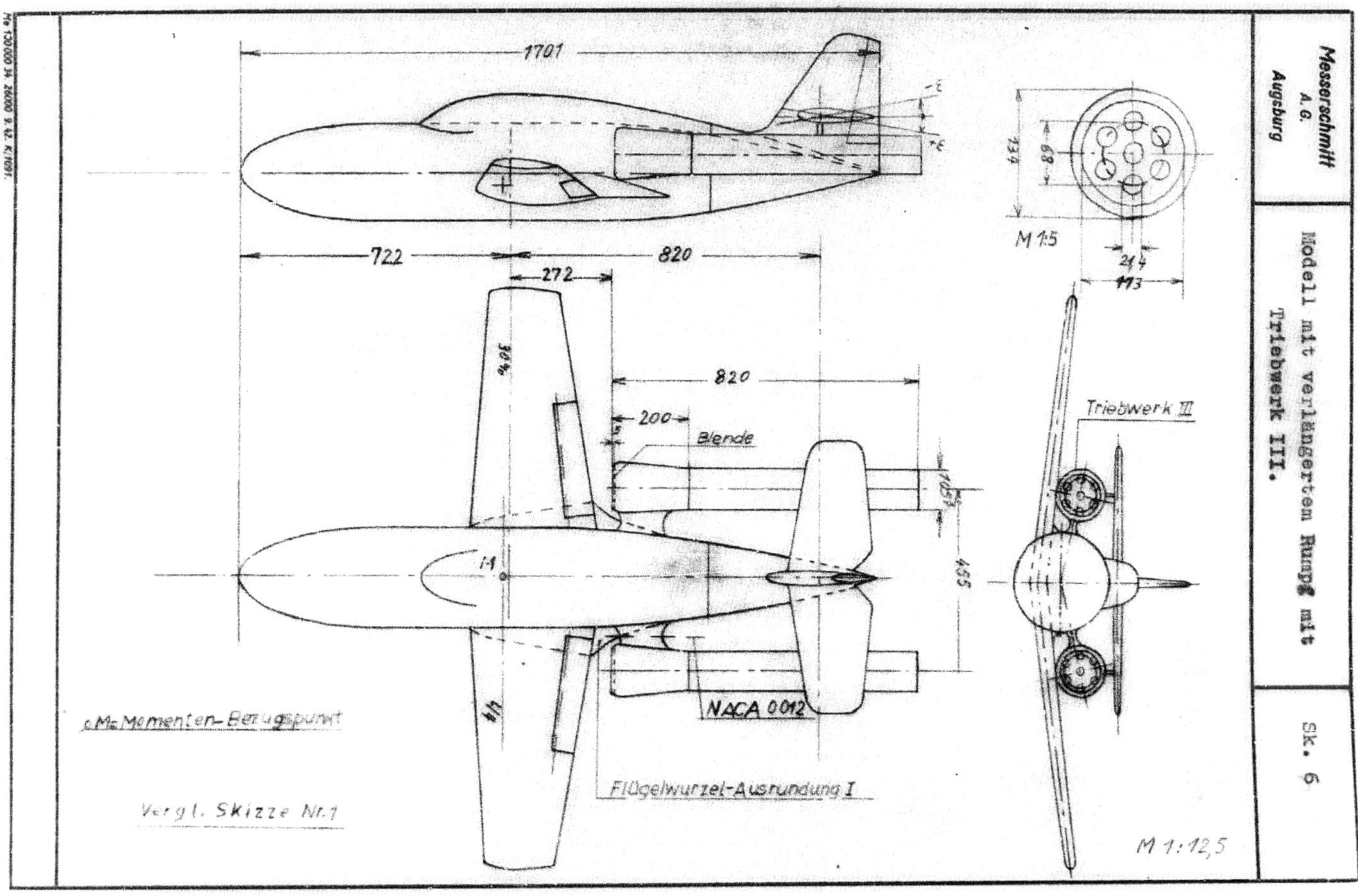
Messerschmitt A.G. Augsburg
Modell mit verlängertem Rumpf mit Triebwerk III.
Sk. 6
1701
722
820
272
200
Blende
Triebwerk III
NACA 0012
Flügelwurzel-Ausrundung I
Vergl. Skizze Nr.1
M 1:5
M 1:12,5

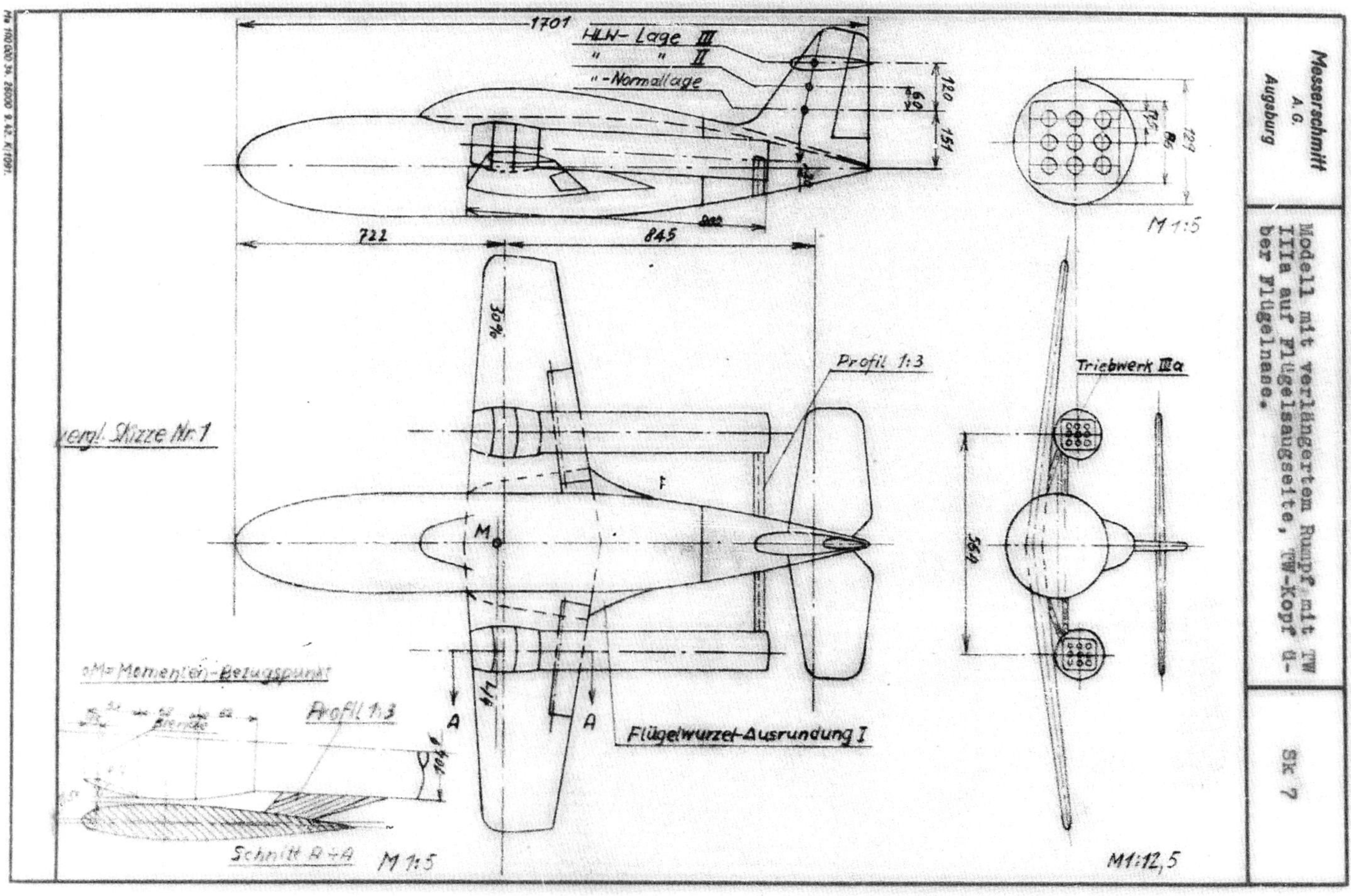
1701
HLW- Lage III
" " II
"-Normallage
722
845
Profil 1:3
Triebwerk IIIa
vergl. Skizze Nr. 1
M
M=Momenten-Bezugspunkt
Profil 1:3
Flügelwurzel-Ausrundung I
Schnitt A-A
M 1:5
M 1:5
M1:12,5
Messerschmitt A.G. Augsburg
Modell mit verlängertem Rumpf mit TW IIIa auf Flügelsaugseite, TW-Kopf über Flügelnase.
Sk 7

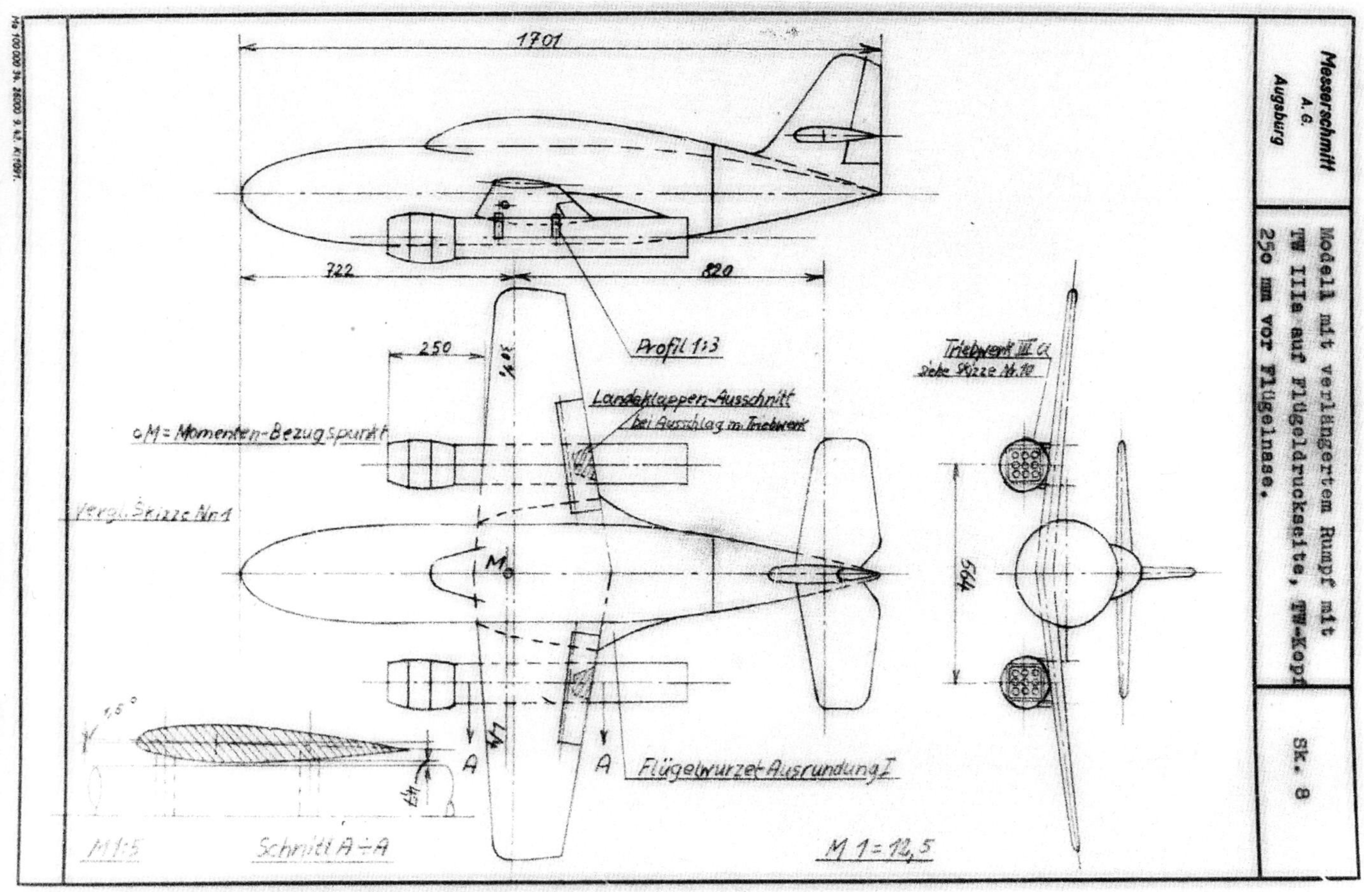
1701
722
820
250
Profil 1:3
Landeklappen-Ausschnitt
bei Ausschlag m. Triebwerk
oM = Momenten-Bezugspunkt
Vergl. Skizze Nr. 1
Triebwerk III a
siehe Skizze Nr. 10
564
A
A
Flügelwurzel-Ausrundung I
M 1:5
Schnitt A÷A
M 1 = 12,5
Messerschmitt A.G. Augsburg
Modell mit verlängertem Rumpf mit TW IIIa auf Flügeldruckseite, TW-Kopf 250 mm vor Flügelnase.
Sk. 8

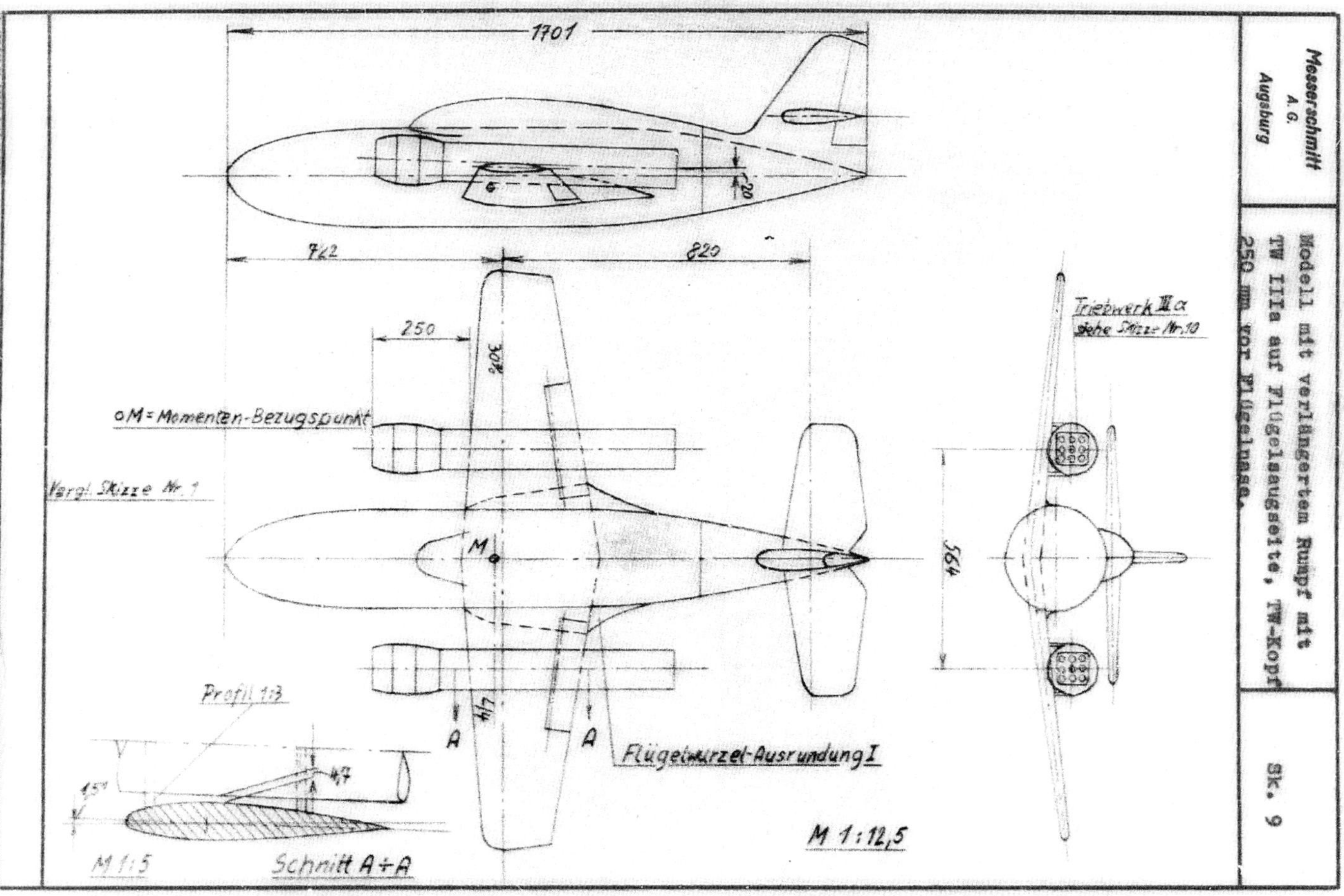
1701
722
820
250
oM = Momenten-Bezugspunkt
Vergl. Skizze Nr. 1
Triebwerk III a
siehe Skizze Nr. 10
564
Profil 1:3
A
A
Flügelwurzel-Ausrundung I
M 1:12,5
M 1:5
Schnitt A÷A
Messerschmitt A.G. Augsburg
Modell mit verlängertem Rumpf mit TW IIIa auf Flügelsaugseite, TW-Kopf 250 mm vor Flügelnase.
Sk. 9

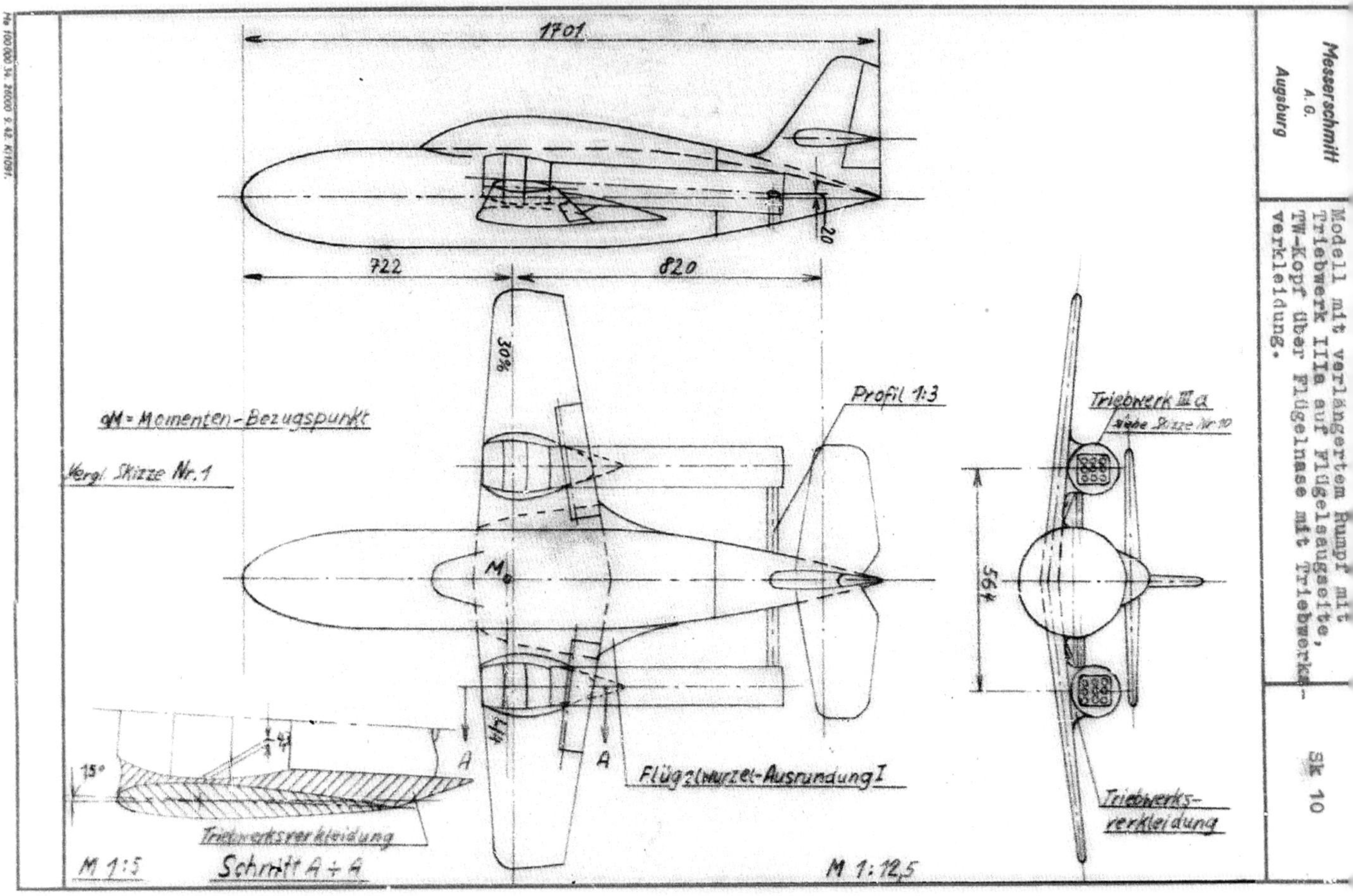
1701
722
820
20
30%
oM = Momenten-Bezugspunkt
Vergl. Skizze Nr. 1
Profil 1:3
Triebwerk III a
siehe Skizze Nr. 10
564
Flügelwurzel-Ausrundung I
Triebwerksverkleidung
Triebwerks-
verkleidung
M 1:5
Schnitt A – A
M 1:12,5
Messerschmitt
A. G.
Augsburg
Modell mit verlängertem Rumpf mit
Triebwerk IIIa auf Flügelsaugseite,
TW-Kopf über Flügelnase mit Triebwerks-
verkleidung.
Sk 10

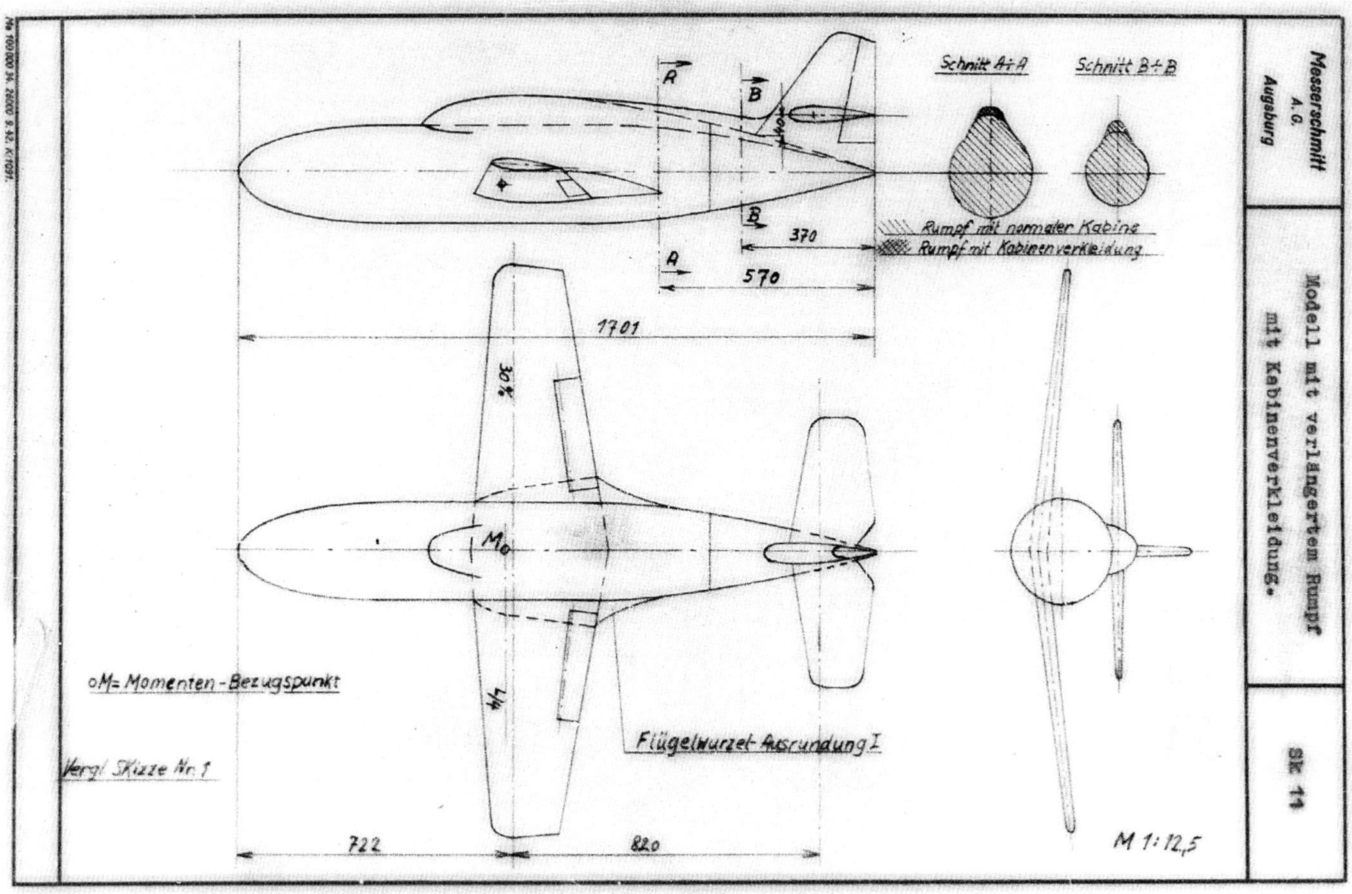
Messerschmitt A.G. Augsburg
Modell mit verlängertem Rumpf mit Kabinenverkleidung.
Sk 11
Schnitt A÷A
Schnitt B÷B
Rumpf mit normaler Kabine
Rumpf mit Kabinenverkleidung
370
570
1701
30%
oM= Momenten-Bezugspunkt
Flügelwurzel-Ausrundung I
Vergl. Skizze Nr. 1
722
820
M 1:12,5

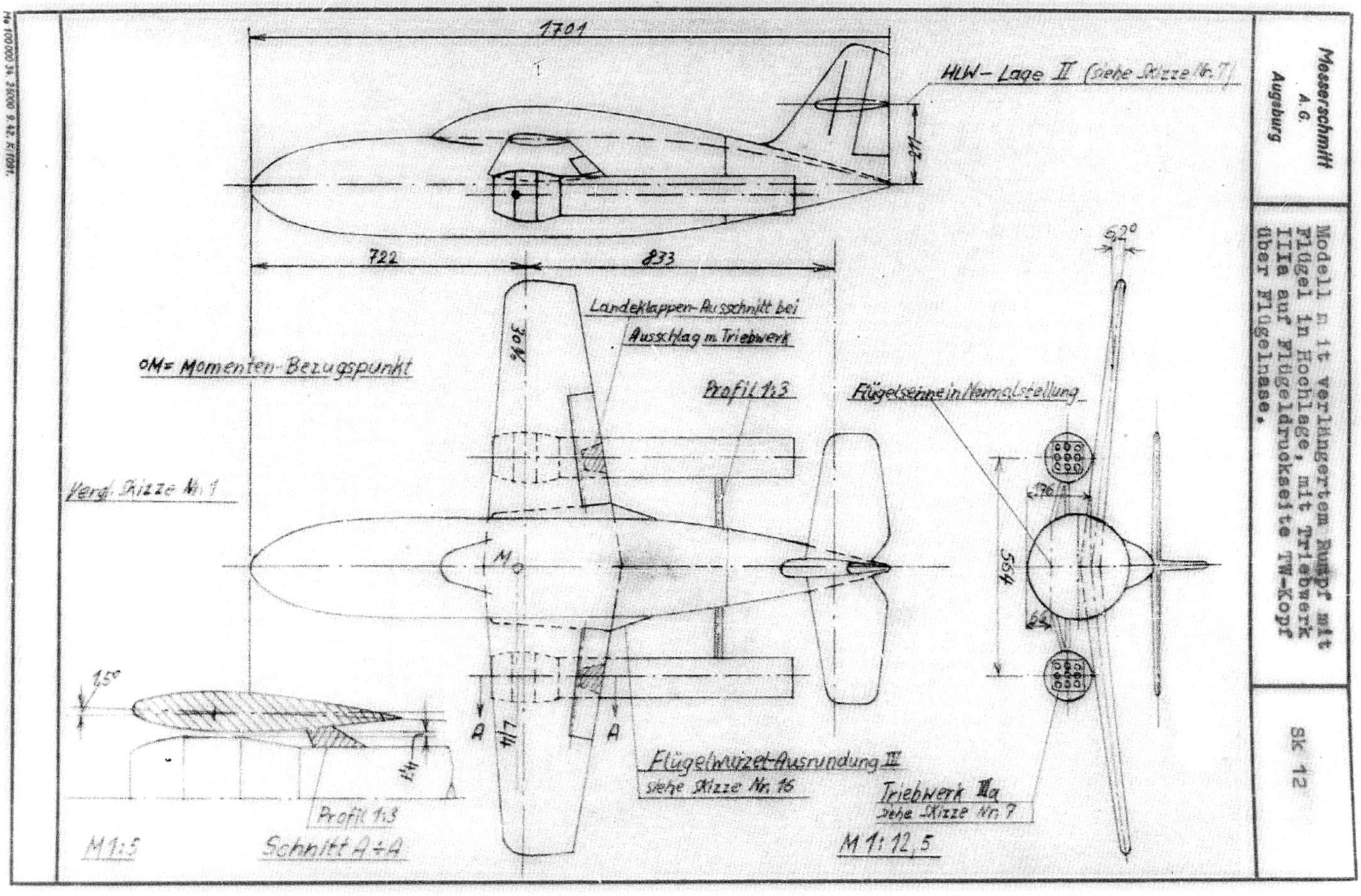
Messerschmitt A.G. Augsburg
Modell mit verlängertem Rumpf mit Flügel in Hochlage, mit Triebwerk IIIa auf Flügeldruckseite TW-Kopf über Flügelnase.
Sk 12
1701
HLW – Lage II (siehe Skizze Nr. 7)
722
833
Landeklappen-Ausschnitt bei Ausschlag m. Triebwerk
oM= Momenten-Bezugspunkt
Profil 1:3
Flügelsehne in Normalstellung
Vergl. Skizze Nr. 1
Flügelwurzel-Ausrundung III
siehe Skizze Nr. 16
Triebwerk IIIa
siehe Skizze Nr. 7
Profil 1:3
M 1:5
Schnitt A÷A
M 1:12,5

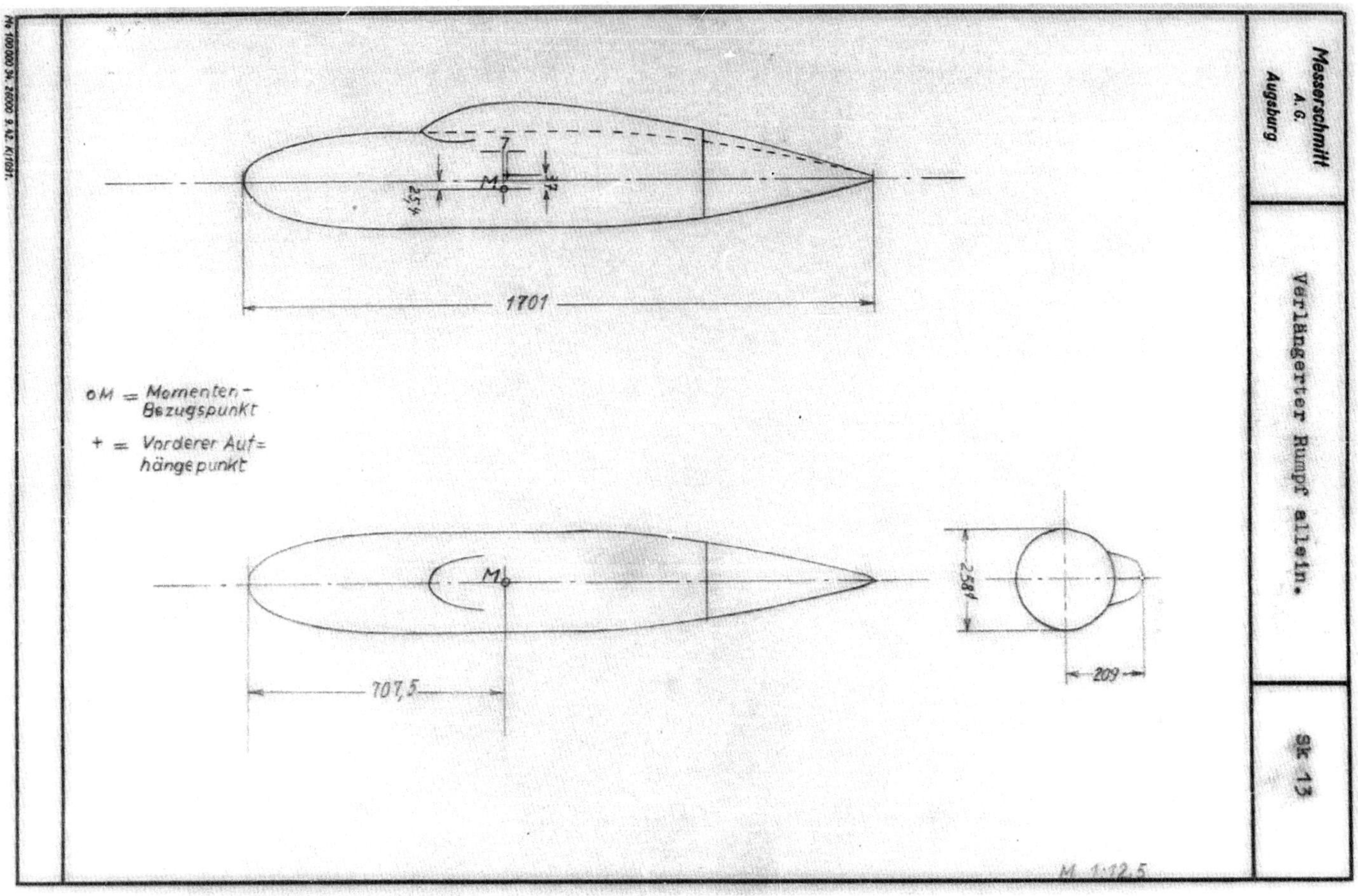
Messerschmitt A.G. Augsburg
Verlängerter Rumpf allein.
Sk 13
1701
oM = Momenten-Bezugspunkt
+ = Vorderer Auf=hängepunkt
707,5
258
209
M 1:12,5

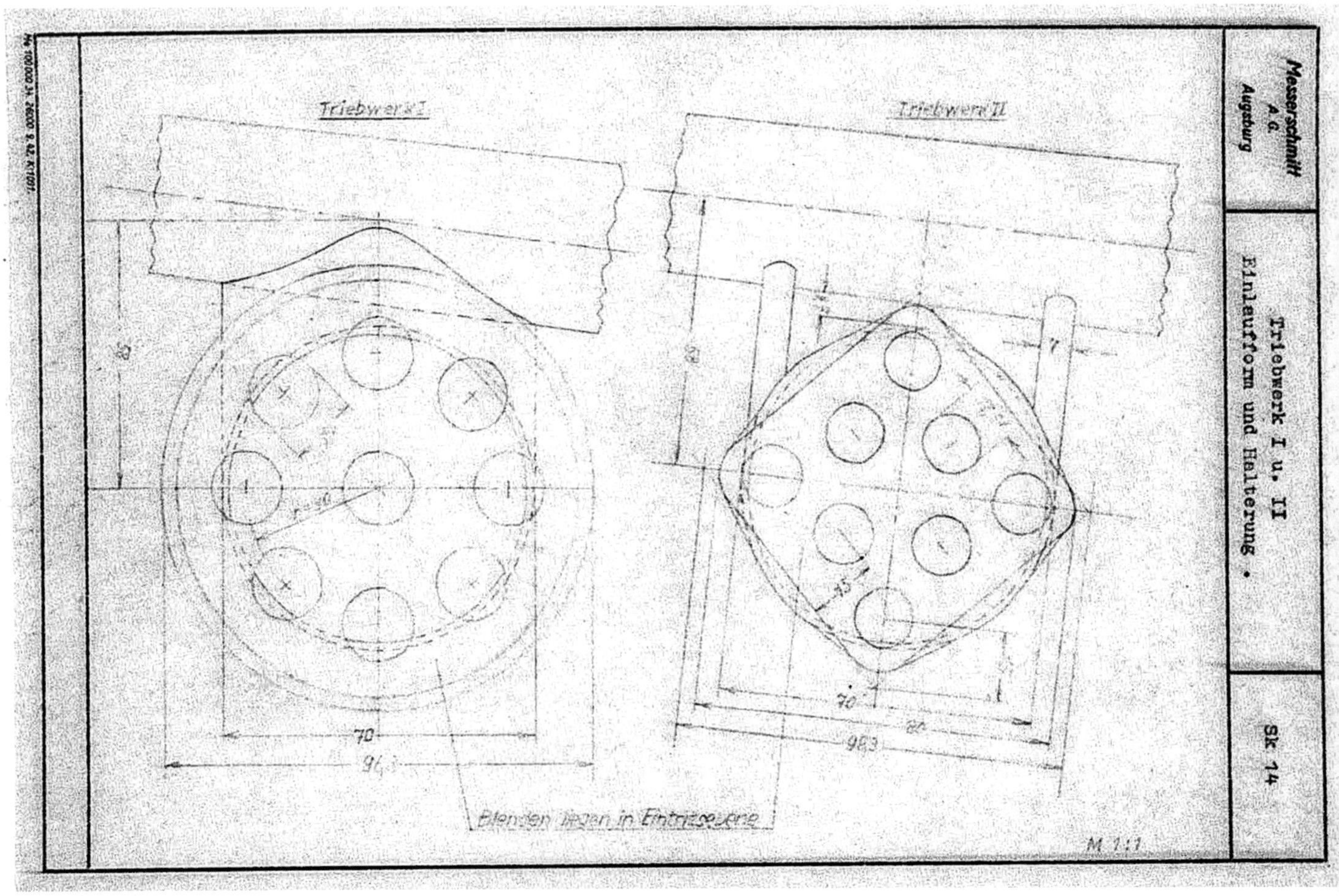
Messerschmitt A.G. Augsburg
Triebwerk I u. II
Einlaufform und Halterung.
Sk 14
Triebwerk I
Triebwerk II
70
98,3
Blenden liegen in Eintrittsebene
M 1:1

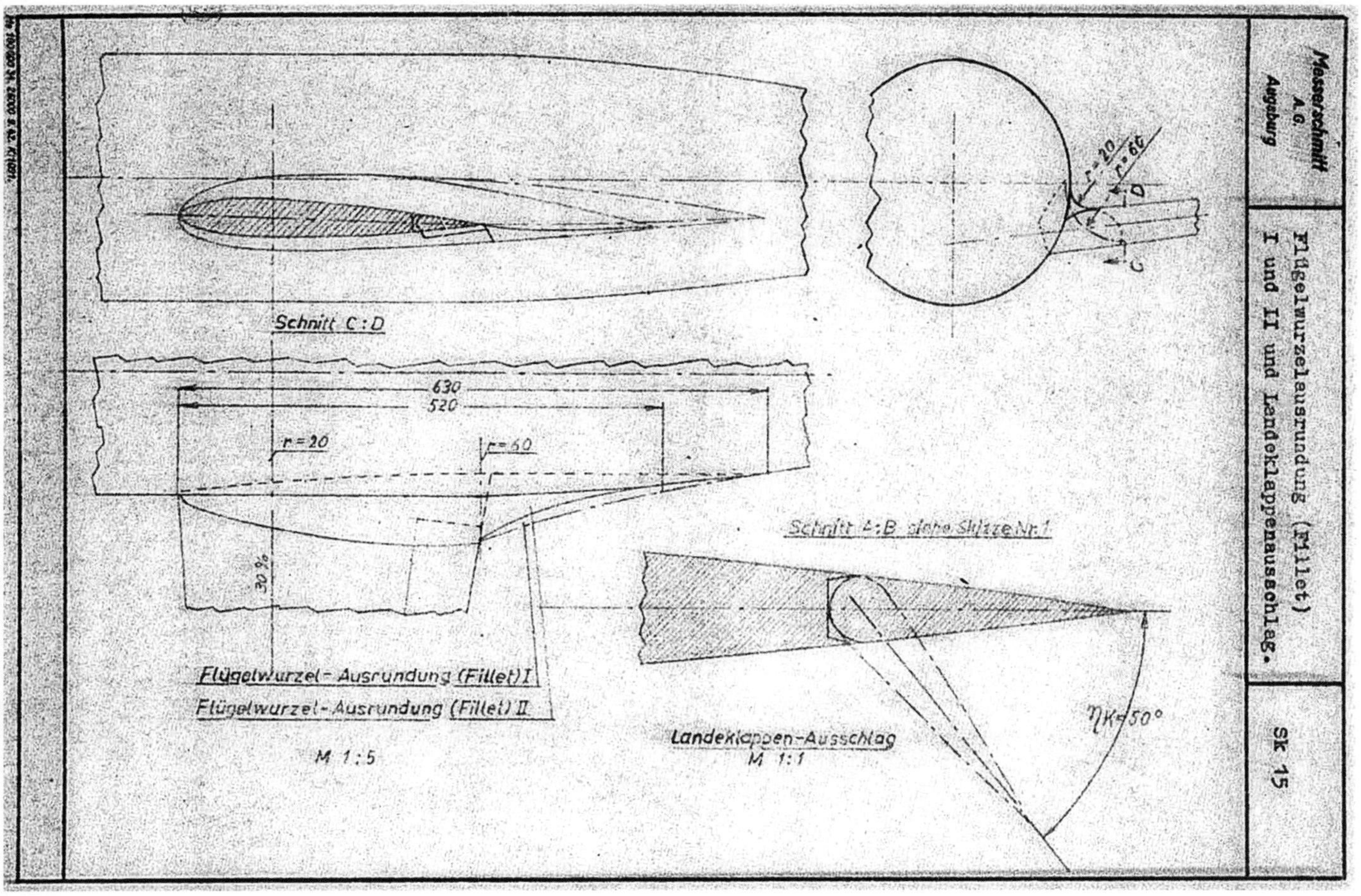
Messerschmitt A.G. Augsburg
Flügelwurzelausrundung (Fillet) I und II und Landeklappenausschlag.
Sk 15
Schnitt C:D
630
520
r=20
r=60
30%
Schnitt A:B siehe Skizze Nr.1
Flügelwurzel-Ausrundung (Fillet) I
Flügelwurzel-Ausrundung (Fillet) II
M 1:5
Landeklappen-Ausschlag
M 1:1
ηK=50°

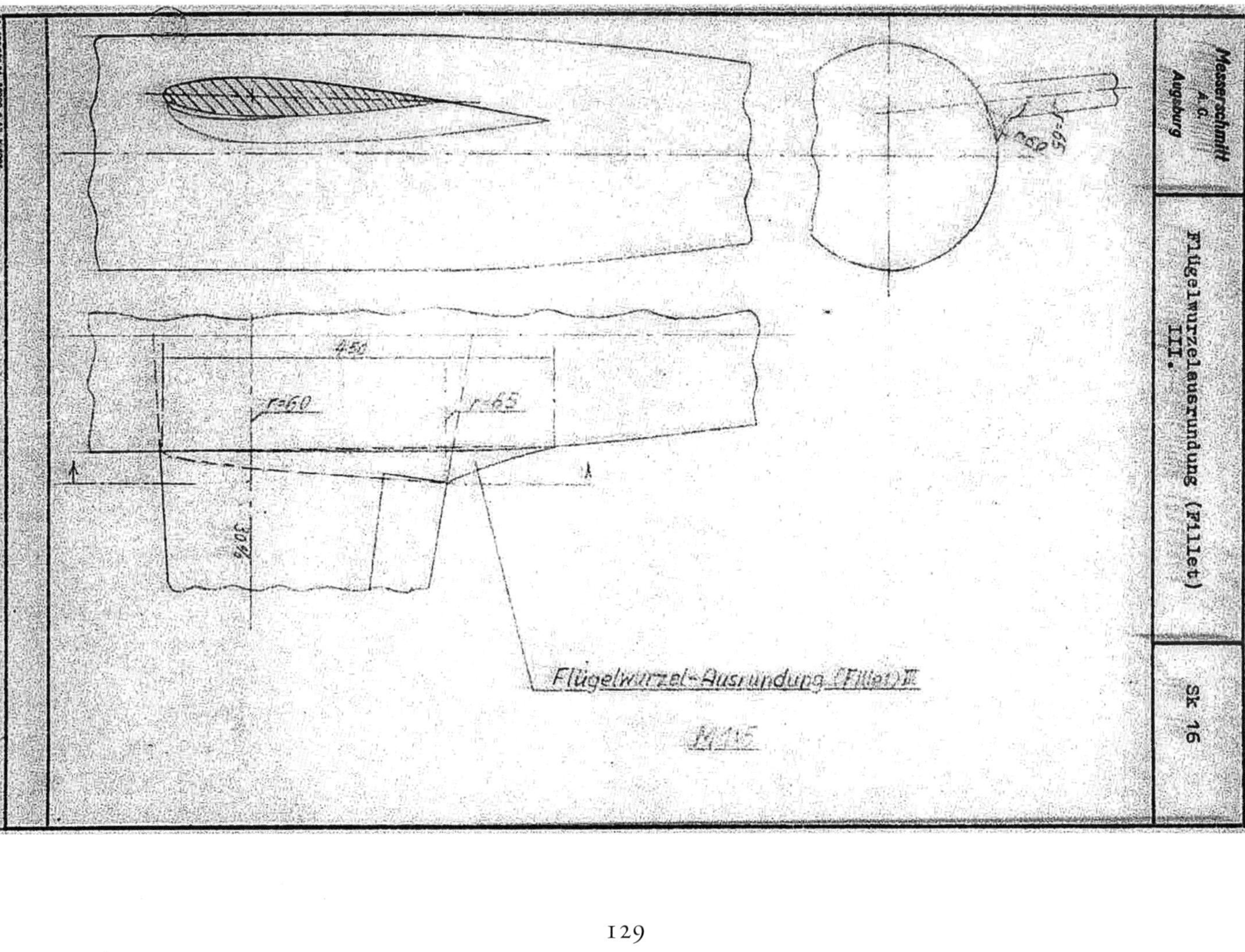
Messerschmitt A.G. Augsburg
Flügelwurzelausrundung (Fillet) III.
Sk 16
450
r=60
r=65
30%
Flügelwurzel-Ausrundung (Fillet) III

5

'SELF-SACRIFICE' AIRCRAFT: SEPTEMBER 1943 TO NOVEMBER 1944

Just three Me 328s had been completed by September 3, 1943: the long since destroyed Me 328 V1, the most-likely-now-destroyed Me 328 V02 and the long-serving Me 328 V2.

Then there were another five Me 328s known to be in various stages of completion. The DFS had been working on three[1] – the Me 328 V3, V4 and V5—and JSF had nearly completed one, the Me 328 B V1, while managing to get 30% of the way through building a second, the Me 328 B V2.

So when the order to stop work on the type was given, only one complete Me 328 existed along with five unfinished examples.

While the development project had been scrapped, the Air Ministry had given permission for both the Me 328 B V1 and V2 to be completed by JSF along with one basic airframe for stress testing and three more for take-off tests.[2] Similarly, the DFS does not appear to have been barred from finishing its three in-progress builds, but rather decided to suspend work on two of them itself, the V4 and V5, leaving only the Me 328 V3 to be completed.

When—if—all in-progress Me 328s were completed, then there would be a grand total of four Me 328s in existence, with only six ever having been made.

ZOBEL'S FINAL VERDICT

The LFA published the results of Zobel's third round of testing on Argus pulsejet forms on September 24, 1943.[3] Three different variants had been tested—designated VSR 9 ad (which the DFS had already test flown on the Me 328 V2 back in July 1943), VSR 9 ak and VSR 9 ai. In addition to the new cowlings designed by Betz, Küchemann and Ruden, Zobel had assessed two different types of choke/spoiler—a shaped block which sat behind the spring-valve to guide the air/fuel mix entering the engine.

Despite his gloomy conclusions at the time, there had evidently been some improvements by the end of the second round of tests. However, Zobel was now reasonably certain that no further significant improvements would be possible.

He wrote: "The fundamental improvements in the Argus pulsejets came to a certain conclusion with the results published in part two. This considerable progress was obtained by enlarging the chokes and so the throughput of air. The effective thrust could be increased further by reducing the external drag of the tube. Further, suitable cowlings resulted not only in decreased drag, but also an improvement of the conditions of [air] flow, which led also to an increase of the effective thrust.

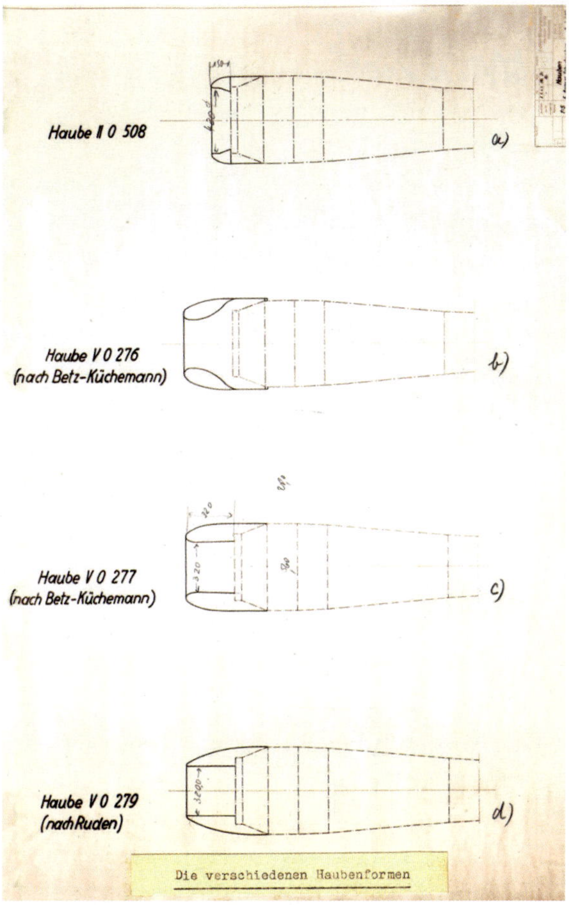

Diagram from Zobel's report showing the three different pulsejet intake forms designed by Betz, Küchemann and Ruden in profile.

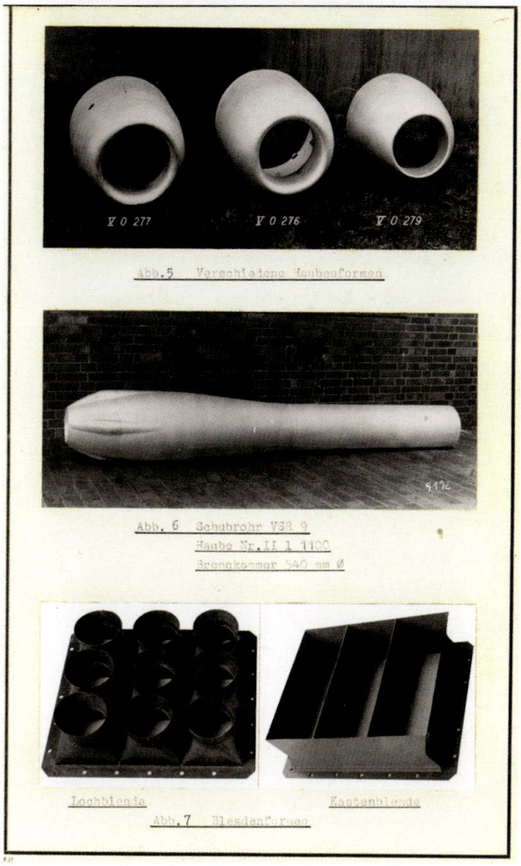

Photos showing the physical models of Betz, Küchemann and Ruden's intakes tested (top), VSR 9 with another different intake (middle) and the different air/fuel mix-guiding chokes/spoilers tested by Zobel (bottom).

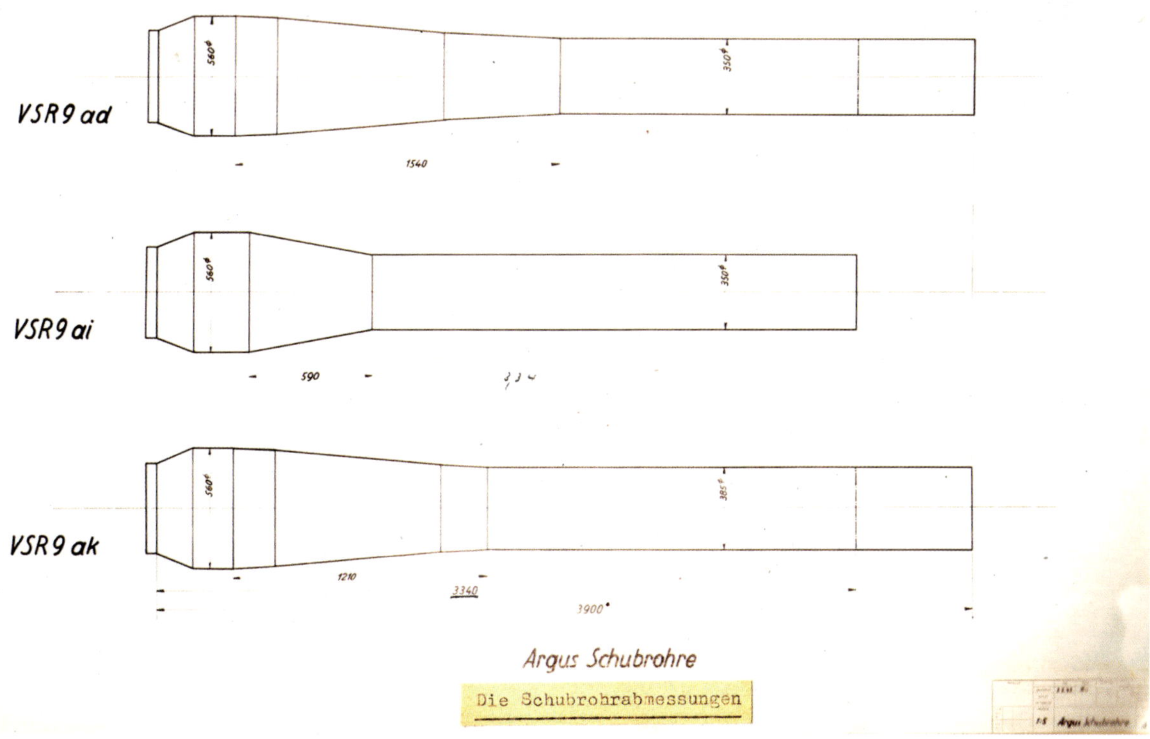

The three Argus pulsejet variants tested—VSR 9 ad, which the DFS had already flight tested, VSR 9 ai and VSR 9 ak.

"It is probable that the essential improvements made up to now have reached their physical limit. This supposition is confirmed by the results published in the present report. They show that by further measures it is only possible to obtain incremental improvements, and then only with difficulty."

He noted that while a full aerodynamic nacelle around the engine might help, "a special outer cowling of the whole tube in order to diminish the drag is not wanted at present for reasons of cooling and because of the increased expense".

Although the intakes designed by Betz, Küchemann and Ruden did improve airflow, none of them stood out as better than the others and they ultimately did little to improve the engine's performance.

ME 328 AS 1-TL-JÄGER

September 20 saw the Messerschmitt group at Darmstadt producing a drawing labelled 'Me 328 T V1', which showed a stretched Me 328 B fuselage and cockpit with a single Jumo 004 turbojet housed within an underslung nacelle. The undercarriage consisted of a nosewheel, which could be fully retracted into the aircraft's oddly-shaped nose (the result of essentially chopping away the lower portion of the regular Me 328 B nose to provide space for the turbojet intake), and mainwheels which were mounted to the sides of the fuselage and withdrew partially into it. No armament was shown.

Shortly after the Me 328 stop order had been given on the 3rd, Seitz had apparently written a memo on the project's development which proposed a continuation based on the single-jet variant.[4] Willy Messerschmitt wrote back to him on September 29, 1943, to say that "a final decision as to whether the [Me 328] aircraft with the single jet engine should be further developed at an accelerated rate and put into series production depends on the following conditions: 1) The probability that the flight characteristics will not cause any difficulties. 2) Precise planning of the entire process, including series preparation, to the point at which at least 100 examples per month are produced. 3) The performance of the aircraft a) with fixed wheeled undercarriage, b) with retractable wheeled undercarriage. 4) The capacity available to deploy the series aircraft.

"This examination must be carried out as quickly as possible, although I would like to point out that it must be treated very carefully. If this result shows that large numbers can be created in a relatively short time, which, with sufficient defensive armament, will have better flight performance than the best enemy piston engine aircraft—the flight performance could still of course be worse than that of the 262".

This response was copied to Messerschmitt chairman Friedrich Seiler, commercial director Rakan Kokothaki, Voigt and production specialist Bley. And it seemingly resulted in a number of hastily prepared performance and production graphs and calculations from Seitz on October 1, 1943,[5] with the Me 328 C designation now finally making a return. These indicated that the aircraft's wing area was 10.85sqm and its take-off weight was 3,000kg.

Two further general arrangement drawings of the Me 328 C followed on October 6, showing that while the nosewheel remained fully retractable, the mainwheels had become completely fixed within aerodynamic fairings attached to the inner wings. The aircraft's length was given as 7.68m—presumably indicating a 50cm section inserted into the centre of the aircraft to stretch it out. Wingspan was 9m and a pair of MK 103 cannon were depicted housed in bulged fairings on the sides of the forward fuselage on either side of the turbojet.

Meanwhile, the BAL report on JSF for September[6] mentioned the Me 328 C for the first time, noting curtly: "Me 328 C. Engine 1 x Jumo TL 004 B-2. In project in progress. Project completion by October 4, 1943."

It would appear that October 6 was the last point at which any work was undertaken on the type and it must be assumed that it was cancelled shortly thereafter.

On a mildly more optimistic note, the BAL report also noted that "the deadline for the completion of the Me 328 B V1 on October 15, 1943 is expected to be met" though an air raid on September 23 had resulted in some damage. No further work had been carried out on jigs and tools but the actual Me 328 B V1 was said to be 98% complete while the V2 languished at 30% complete, no progress apparently having been made on that either. Vibration testing on "one end of the fuselage with tail unit" was 90% finished.

The BAL report for October, however, stated that "development of the Me 328 B type has been halted. The following will be built: V1 as a glider. V2 with engine. One stress test airframe. Three take-off test airframes (primitive design)". A little further work on the V2 jigs and tools had been done, taking them to 95% complete and the Me 328 B V1 had inched forward to 99% finished. Even the Me 328 B V2 had seen some progress, reaching 45% complete. The Me 328 C was now listed as "project stopped".[7]

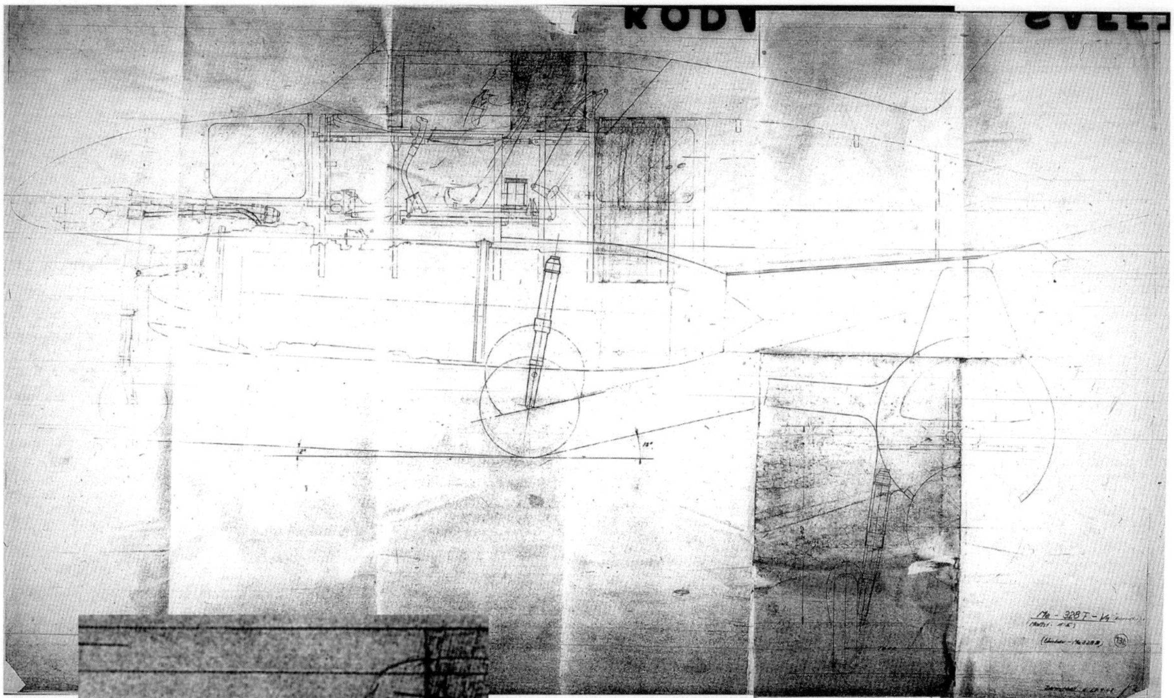

The single-jet Me 328 T V1 of September 20, 1943. Much of the Me 328 B's fuselage was to be retained, though the lower forward fuselage would be cut away to provide an unobstructed intake for the engine. Note the pilot picking his long nose—perhaps a humorous reference to the aircraft's shape.

RISE OF THE FANATICS

This might have been where the story ended, as the DFS and JSF became increasingly swamped with other tasks—pushing their unfinished Me 328 prototypes to the back of their respective workshops. It would then be only a question of how much longer the Me 328 V2 could last.

But the end of the Me 328 as an Air Ministry-backed future light bomber for the Luftwaffe coincided with a period of increased activity on the part of suicide attack promoters Benzinger and Lange and their new convert, Hanna Reitsch.

According to a report[8] on Reitsch's interrogation: "In the early fall of 1943, something that began to resemble an organisation began to develop. At this time the group numbered between 30 and 40 young aviation enthusiasts. They were not tired of life, nor otherwise potential suicides, for they were healthy young men, many of them fathers and husbands, who believed that through their deaths, which eventually need total hardly more than a thousand, many thousands of soldiers and civilians could be saved … The first semblance of organisation was headed by … First Lieutenant Lange, Medizinrat Doctor Theo Benzinger … and Hanna Reitsch.

"These three began to draw up the aims and plans in October 1943. Lange, who at that time belonged to XI Fliegerkorps, did all the paper and organisational work, Dr Benzinger performed the medical and psychological research which would enable the human body to be in full command of its faculties and possessed of the necessary calmness and clearness of mind up to the last moment of the actual suicide attack, while Reitsch was to undertake the flying training and test flying of the plane developed."

At around the same time, two members of the Luftfahrt-Forschungsanstalt München (LFM)—the Munich Aviation Research Institute—independently wrote up a paper on preparing to launch suicide attacks titled Proposal for Setting up an Air Force Formation for Effective Point Target Combat, dated it October 1943, and sent copies out to Baeumker, Georgii, Benzinger and Dr Eduard Fischel—head of the DFS Institut für Flugausrüstung (Institute for Flight Equipment) who specialised in guided weapons.[9]

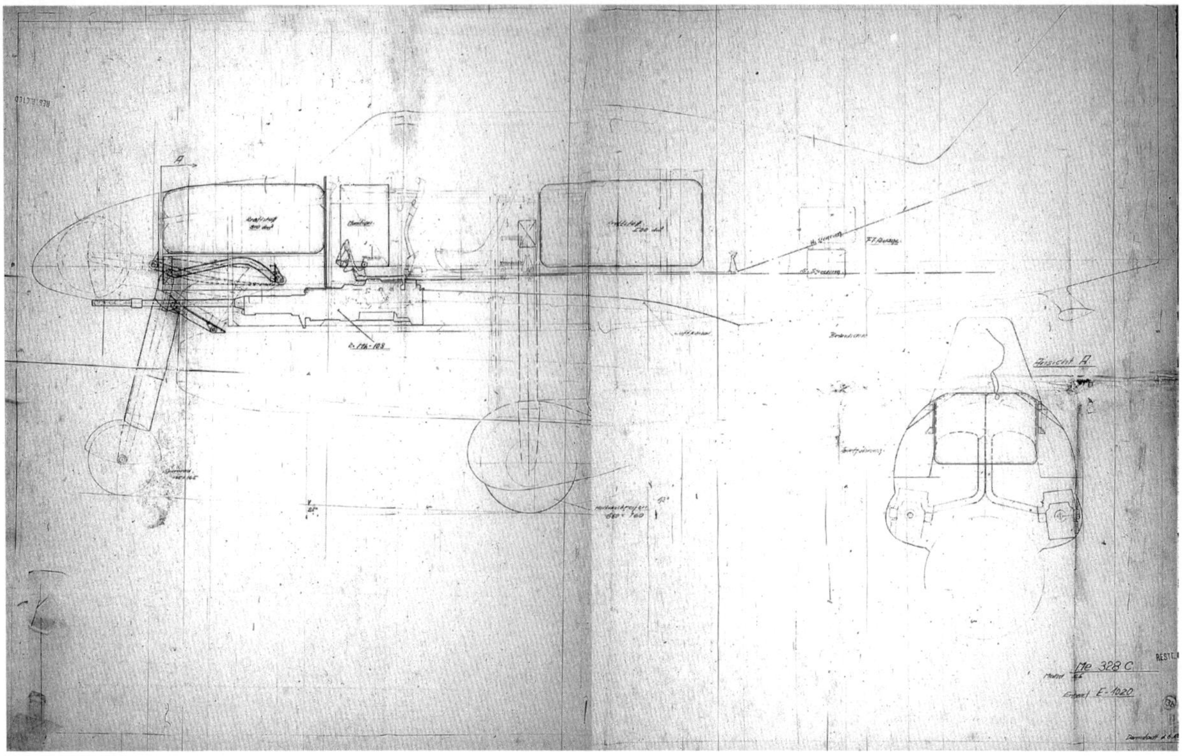

The design of the Me 328 C fighter, dated October 6, 1943, differed from the Me 328 T V1 in having its fixed undercarriage attached to its wings rather than its fuselage—and had the barrels of its two MK 103 cannon protruding from its nose. Note the stretched cockpit canopy compared to the Me 328 B as seen in Chapter 4.

Where Benzinger's pitch, as delivered to Baeumker and Georgii, had stressed the notion of a 'noble sacrifice' bolstered by drugs, this document by institute chairman Dr Ulrich K. Henschke[10] and Professor Peters described something even darker.

It began along the increasingly familiar lines: "Today's war situation urgently demands a safe weapon that can be used in large numbers within a short period of time against point targets, especially against ships. The most effective means of destruction and the easiest way to carry it out is undoubtedly to use a human-controlled aircraft or a human-controlled bomb, sacrificing the pilot."

But evidently the suggestions made along those lines up to this time hadn't gone far enough. So, "a proposal is made below that has been worked out in psychological and technical detail, the implementation of which will ensure a mass deployment of soldiers at the necessary level. With appropriately generous support and appropriate powers, human recruitment and training as well as technical development could be achieved in a short time.

"The advantages of using such a formation are clear: firstly, it would be possible to safely destroy point targets and thus deliver a decisive blow against the enemy's war, supply and merchant fleet. Secondly, supported by appropriate propaganda, it would be an important boost to one's own people's morale, and the enemy is given a secret horror of the determination and willingness to sacrifice of the German soldiers and the German people. However, such a propagandistic expectation only appears advantageous when sufficient secrecy is no longer guaranteed".

The authors suggested that earlier 'self-sacrifice' ideas had failed because they had always tried to give the volunteers concerned a chance of survival during the operation—however slim that might realistically be. As such, "we are therefore only taking a small step when we consciously incorporate chance into the fate of the individual soldier. This leads to the basic idea of our proposal: volunteers who join the formation are given a 50% chance of survival, but this is determined by chance in the form of a lottery, which decides immediately before the deployment which of two applicants has to sacrifice themselves".

Somewhat horrifically, a key aspect of the proposal was giving volunteers the least possible opportunity to save themselves. The best vehicle for the mission was said to be an unpowered guided bomb—because the pilot, prone or seated beneath a canopy that would be bolted down from the outside after they got in, would be completely unable to land it safely.

According to Henschke and Peters: "In our opinion, only human-controlled bombs can be considered for mass use. These bombs could be designed either as gliding bombs … (modelled on remote-controlled gliding

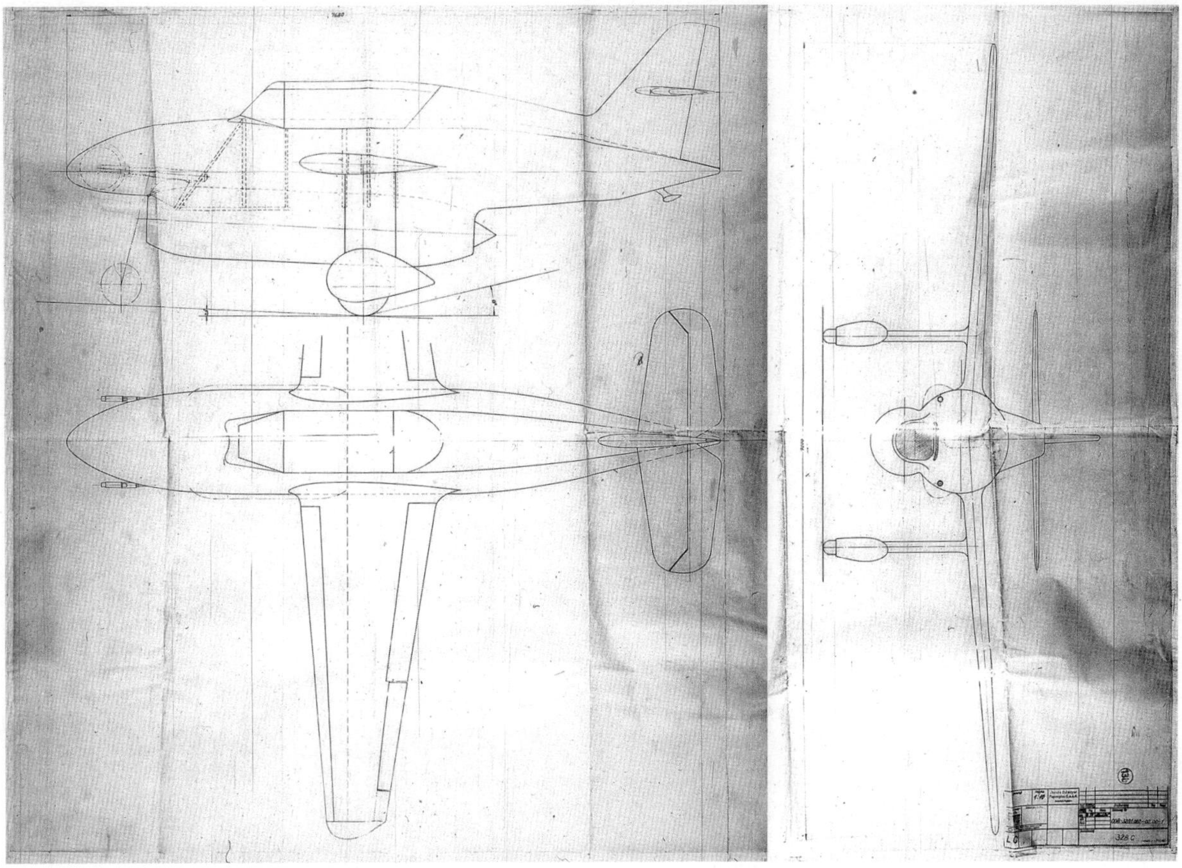

Me 328 C drawing, from October 6, 1943, focusing on the MK 103 30mm cannon installation, with bulged fairings to provide the necessary room. A little more detail of the nosewheel retraction system is also show.

bombs) or as vertically falling bombs (modelled on the FX [Fritz X]). Given the greater tactical freedom, glide bombs appear more advantageous as a first solution. Later we would also have to develop a vertical [drop] bomb that is particularly intended for use against large warships (hits in the funnel)."

Piloted bombs weighing 1,000kg could be carried by an Me 410, a Do 217 could take a 3,000kg bomb, an He 177 up to 6,000kg—preferably two bombs of 3,000kg each. And "for very small bombs, the pilot must lie down in the prone position with their head in front—above or below the explosive device—offering the best view. Placing the man directly in the front of the bomb does not seem beneficial because of the reduction in the bomb's penetrating power and for psychological reasons.

"Positioning under the explosive device could also be considered, with viewing and aiming carried out through a periscope. In all of these positions, control is best done with your hands only. In bombs over 1,500kg, a sitting position is also possible, but the advantage of the somewhat more favourable position for steering comes at the cost of poorer visibility, so that a periscope is also necessary to look down. Oxygen and heating must be provided. Entry is via a door that can be locked from the outside on the ground only."

WHO LIVES AND WHO DIES

Henschke and Peters considered that volunteers for death might come forward "to a small extent ... out of a high ideal", while others might want "the new, interesting and unusual task out of a desire for adventure or related motives". Others "would come from among the wounded and sick", still more might want medals, glory and material benefits but "for the most part ... the applicants will be recruited from circles who are dissatisfied with their current situation and who—no matter the cost—want a change". These were prisoners or refugees, who be attracted by "the superior conditions and the superior benefits".

Individuals with skills needed elsewhere or who cared for children would be rejected except in exceptional cases—as would people "with strong nervousness as well as unreliable and antisocial elements. In terms of physical abilities, the only important thing is sufficient visual acuity, which can be achieved with glasses. Special requirements for physical dexterity and mental gifts are not necessary, as the technical tasks to be performed can be easily learned by every normal person".

Training would last two months and would mostly consist of learning different ship types and practicing steering while positioned inside the vehicle on the ground, watching a film of a ship getting closer and closer through a periscope. Later, "the entire practice bomb is placed in an elevator in order to imitate the acceleration that occurs immediately after it is dropped. The whole process can therefore be imitated in reality, something that can almost never be achieved with other training in aviation".

There was even a fanciful proposal for conducting training drops onto a canvas target on the water using a practice 'bomb' which then floated back to the surface for retrieval.

Psychological conditioning would also take place during the two months. The volunteer would be made to break all contact with things that were familiar to them, so "particular care must be taken when selecting books, films, speech topics, etc." They would receive preferential treatment including a special uniform, good food, a release from minor duties, good sleeping quarters and a good living space.

Time not spent training would be spent in leisure pursuits, particularly sports, and the volunteer would be promised posthumous honours plus "a person chosen by him is promised a monthly pension in addition to the surviving dependents' pension. Likewise, every child he leaves behind receives a monthly pension up to the age of 18". But this was only if they actually sank a ship; "neither is granted if the man fails".

The 50% who 'won' the lottery after the two months, and survived, would get a bravery award plus "special benefits (e.g. exemption from further military service or special leave with a holiday allowance or a lifelong pension)".

The weird community of isolated volunteers imagined by Henschke and Peters would live in relative luxury but without any familiar psychological anchor points. They would be arranged into groups of ten people—each group being "matched in terms of background and education" and "it is often made clear to this group that only five of them will escape with their lives ... [but] the acquittal only occurs if the other five chosen by lottery do not fail. Otherwise, the other five are used as replacements". This threat was supposed to foster a sense of camaraderie and "all impulses of cowardice must be combated ruthlessly. Nothing can be more shameful than shying away from a task that others are also carrying out".

Deployment would take place immediately after the two months. Each group of ten would be taken to the airfield on a transport under the supervision of an officer. Straws would then be drawn and the losers would go straight into their bombs, but "a difficulty arises when the carrier aircraft does not find a worthwhile target and returns to base with the bomb. In this case, the man is of course exposed to a particular strain until the operation is repeated. You have to consider whether you should use him again, give him another chance to draw or release him. Anyone who resists the operation after the draw will be shot immediately".

Among the "suggested discussion points" appended by Henschke and Peters were whether to use a motorised aircraft, glider or bomb for the attack, whether small bombs were worth using, which types of carrier aircraft to use, which applicant groups should be given preference, whether the applicants should be conditioned to the drawing of straws and "use of pharmacological agents".

Also appended was a sketch showing the type of guided bomb design the authors were thinking of—effectively a torpedo with a cockpit to the rear and large wings.

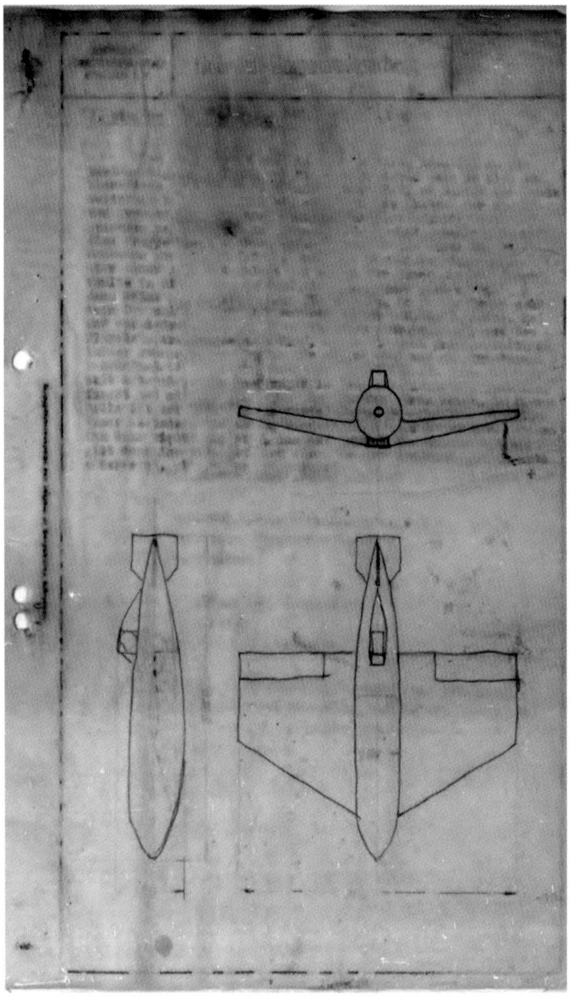

The proposed LFM design for a manned glide bomb. In this page from a microfilmed document at NARA, the original design appears to have been crudely overdrawn for clarity. Close inspection reveals aspects of the underlying original—such as the pilot depicted in the cockpit and the lines marking its dimensions.

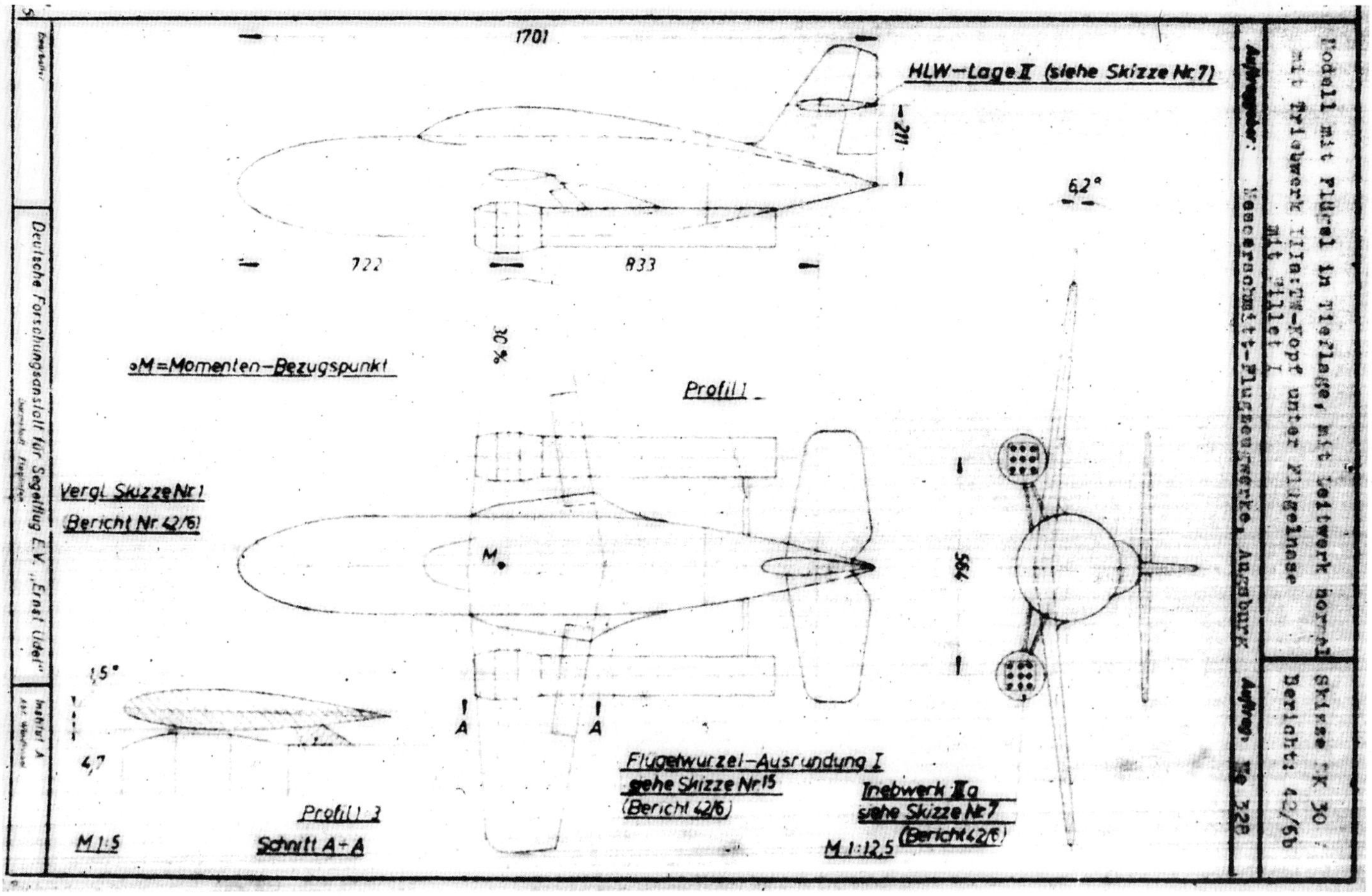

DFS diagram, Skizze Sk 30, depicting a low-wing model tested from July 30 to August 9, 1943.

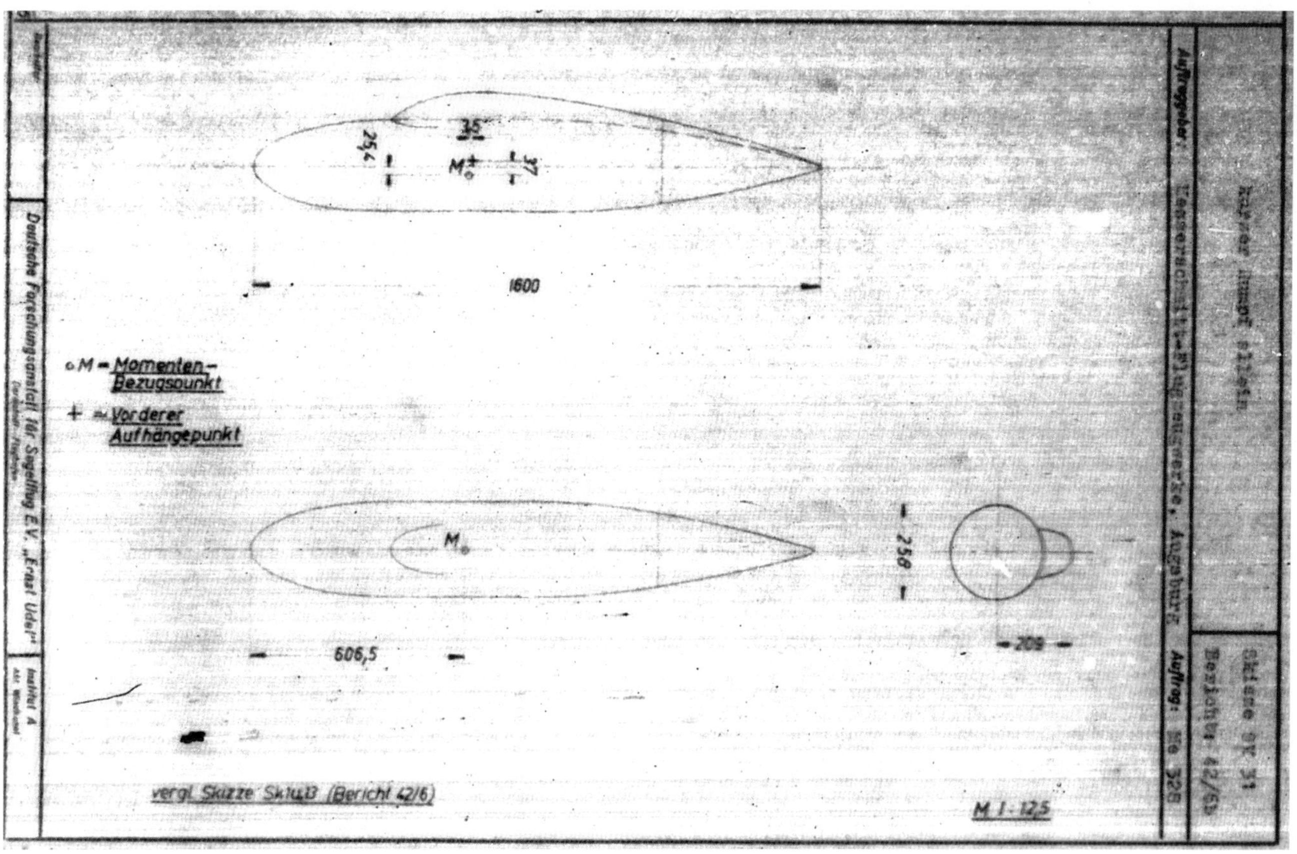

Skizze Sk 31 showing Me 328 model components used in DFS wind tunnel testing during the summer of 1943.

JSF AND DFS CONTINUATION

The final part of the DFS's long-running series of wind tunnel tests on Me 328 models came to an end with the publication of Bericht Nr. 42/6b on October 26, 1943, covering tests undertaken between July 30 and August 9, 1943. These had evaluated a long-wing variant with a wing dihedral of 6.2 degrees, which allowed the pulsejets to be positioned below them but still attached to the rear fuselage.[11]

Baeumker wrote to Georgii on November 18, 1943,[12] to say he'd received the Henschke proposal and that "compared to Benzinger's ideas presented to me earlier, the proposal represents an improvement in that it avoids pharmaceutical means to create a psychological state that is favourable to self-sacrifice, and because it gives the men involved in the attack a greater chance of saving themselves.

"Personally, I take the following position on the thoughts of both gentlemen: the successes of the Japanese can be explained on a basis of metaphysical ideas. These processes can perhaps be compared with certain soldierly ideas of the Roman warriors and have something in common with the spiritual world of fanatics who are willing to go to extremes and who then usually lack a connection to the external environment.

"Under no circumstances can such achievements arising from psychological ideas be ethically compared with the results of the effects of medical means. They arise on a different level and do not come from the thoughts of the doctor or engineer. The basic ethical attitude of the German soldier corresponds entirely to the high standards of the Japanese. Like him, the German is also ready to give up his life for the fatherland at any time.

"However, as a rule he lacks the connection to a world beyond after death, i.e. to the metaphysical area. The result of this is that he should be given a certain chance of preserving his life in the event of a successful attack, which the Japanese soldier has already renounced in many known and documented cases if he believes that he can thereby preserve his 'immortality'."

The only problem Baeumker saw with the Henschke-Peters proposal was actually its most fundamental concept: "In my opinion, the most important thing missing … is the technical possibility of jumping out of the bomb that was directed at the target by human hands. Whether such a possibility exists at all without a very significant reduction in the chances of success would have to be tested technically. I don't think it's out of the question. Those deployed would of course have to forego their personal freedom, as their capture would be unavoidable. Even under the aforementioned circumstances, the risk of use is still extremely high and will justify every technical step to reduce it."

At the end of November, the monthly BAL report on JSF noted that with regard to the Me 328, "since the company no longer has any workers available due to series construction of the [Bf] 109 fin (wooden construction), the Air Ministry will decide later this week what else JSF will build". Unsurprisingly, the Me 328 construction situation had not changed since October.[13]

A month later, BAL reported that JSF had received a new direction from Messerschmitt on December 14, stating that only the Me 328 B V1 glider would now be built by Jacobs-Schweyer. The Me 328 B V2, fitted out for pulsejet operation, would instead be manufactured "by JSF's subcontractor" along with two additional sets of wings and the stress test airframe.[14] JSF had actually made a start on the take-off test airframes but these would now be scrapped.

Meanwhile, the DFS was apparently also continuing to carry out limited Me 328 work despite the stop order. According to the organisation's summary report for the period up to December 1943, "[wind tunnel] investigations on the Me 328 and Hs 293 F continued. For the first type, the influence of the engine position and various wing shapes on the low-wing aircraft model were determined, in particular with a wing dihedral angle of 6.2 degrees. Further six-component measurements were carried out on a model with an extended fuselage".[15]

And, "in connection with the Me 328 project, changes to the pulsejet suspension were suggested based on the frequency measurements. To check the obtained values, static vibration tests were carried out, which were repeated after changing the pulsejet suspension for verification purposes. The flight test is still pending. Work on a controlled pulsejet tube continued. It can be expected that the first operational bench tests can begin during the next report period".

The single skid landing gear of the Me 328 A type was clearly a problem—which was why the Me 328 B's twin tandem flap-type skid system had been developed. The DFS also reported that, "the landing gear of the Me 328 has proven to be unsuitable in the long term and must be replaced by a new one, the design and construction of which was carried out during the reporting period".

This would appear to suggest that a new landing gear had been specifically designed for use with the Me 328 A type; something different from what had been applied to JSF's Me 328 B. The report does not elaborate further but this new gear had been fitted to the Me 328 V3, the DFS's only in-construction prototype.[16] It has been suggested that the Me 328 V3 made its first flight on December 15, 1943—15 days into the next reporting period—but this is unverified.

Lastly, this same report appeared to offer some indication as to exactly why the DFS was still involved with the Me 328 and why tests with the Me 328/Do 217 Mistel take-off system had continued. Under the heading "Grossbombe Ju 88/Bf 109 ('Beethoven')", it stated: "This task was carried out and completed during the reporting period. In terms of flight mechanics, controlling the team [a Mistel pair comprising an unpiloted Ju 88 controlled from the cockpit of a Bf 109 attached to its back] from the Bf 109 presents no problems. In terms of performance, the team is much better than expected.

"The structure of the Ju 88 intended by the Junkers company turned out to be inappropriate and was fundamentally redesigned based on the experience of the Do 217/Me 328 team. There were no difficulties with decoupling up to the maximum permissible ... speeds."

The Me 328 V2/Do 217 Mistel arrangement had evidently been used as a basis for the Bf 109/Ju 88 Mistel system, codenamed Beethoven, which would actually see active service before the end of the war.

BYPASSING MILCH

January 12, 1944, saw the LFM submitting a brief document to the Luftwaffe research command entitled The Technical Implementation Possibilities for Human-Controlled Bombs.[17] No author was identified but the distribution list for copies included Henschke, so it may have been written by his co-conspirator Professor Peters.

It simply reiterated the notion that offering the pilot a chance of survival during the mission—rather than by lottery just before it—was counterproductive since it would result in design compromises in the chosen vehicle and could easily reduce its accuracy as the pilot would be preoccupied with getting out alive, rather than guiding the bomb all the way into its target.

Crucially, for the first time this document notes that the bomb "can be smaller (up to around 1,000kg total weight) and designed as a normal glider, which offers considerable advantages both in development and in attachment to carrier aircraft". A reference was also made to a memo from the DFS on these points.

The BAL report on JSF for January had no good news, since the company's subcontractors "which are supposed to assemble the Me 328 B V2 machine are not taking on the work". And the Me 328 B V1 remained unfinished.[18]

A JSF memo from February 14, 1944, noted that during recent stress testing it had come to light that part of the Me 328 B V1's framework was "welded very poorly" and "there are therefore serious concerns about the safety of the fuselage structure". The section in question had apparently been manufactured by another JSF subcontractor—Kahl of Aschaffenburg. As a consequence, "the JSF control is therefore forced to block the aircraft from flight operations. The Messerschmitt Office, Darmstadt, is asked to order three new pieces for the designated section (two for installation in V1, one for material testing). Furthermore, the control asks that all welded parts manufactured by the Kahl company, Aschaffenburg, for the above aircraft type either be scrapped or made available to the control for a further check".

While JSF had been gamely continuing on with the Me 328 B V1 and the LFM had been pushing its own spin on the suicide mission, Hanna Reitsch had been attempting to drum up high-level backers for her group's rival suicide mission manifesto. According to the report on her interrogation, "Reitsch's first duty ... was to present the idea to various Luftwaffe authorities in order to win official support for the project. But here the first opposition came in such overwhelming force that it began to appear that extraordinary steps would have to be taken to even achieve a hearing by the proper authorities.

"The idea was at first passed off as fantastic and the result of abnormal mental hallucinations of people tired of life who were looking for a martyr's end in the pages of German history. Worst of all, no one could be sufficiently impressed to even permit a hearing of the plans already completed. Reitsch claims that the group did not want to present their idea to Hitler until all the technical details had been worked out. This would have been the job of the German Air Ministry, headed by Feldmarschall Milch.

"When Reitsch finally obtained an interview with Milch, he too belittled the plan and flatly declared that the idea was impossible. Reitsch begged that the plan at least be examined by competent authorities before judgement was passed. This was granted, but Reitsch immediately suspected that the grant was only made to close the issue in the hope that the plan would die a normal death.

"After waiting for some weeks without any results forthcoming from her discussion with Milch, Reitsch, by virtue of her reputation and position in German air circles, gained a hearing at the German Academy of Aeronautics [the DAL] in whose power it lay to call together the necessary scientists, technicians and experts in aeronautical combat tactics. The Academy was able to do this without requesting permission from Milch, and were required merely to inform him of what they intended to do."[19]

Sure enough, on February 25, 1944, Baeumker in his position as chancellor of the DAL wrote a note to Milch on the subject: "The problem of the use of manned missiles, which was presented to the Generalfeldmarschall by another party, has been brought to the Academy several times in the most confidential and cautious manner. It was suggested that the question be discussed from a technical and scientific point of view in the presence of some Luftwaffe officers who are likely to be ultimately responsible for the task or implementation."[20]

He said he felt that the notion of a manned missile was in line with the DAL's founding decree, which stressed innovation, though he himself remained sceptical. This last point seems to have been rather stretching the truth, since Baeumker appears in reality to have been one of the suicide mission's most ardent and influential supporters.

He told Milch that plans to set up a small working party, including some Luftwaffe officers, had been drawn up to assess the manned missile project. And "if, in [your] opinion, the above suggestion is absurd, the Academy will take every suggestion given into account as far as possible or even drop the entire idea".

Baeumker then listed some "leading personalities" who he knew had already been informed of the suicide mission without the DAL's involvement—Generaloberst Robert Ritter von Greim, Peltz, and Gauleiter Karl Hanke—but "since [they] were probably only [involved in] discussions of military ideas that do not belong to the work area of scientific and technical tasks, a suggestion for their participation was omitted".

His list of potential working party members included Vorwald, Georgii, ballistics expert Hubert Schardin, Benzinger, Lippisch, Galland, Jacobs from JSF, Oberleutnant Lange, Oberst Walter Marienfeld, Oberst Heinz Heigl (commander of special operations unit Kampfgeschwader 200), Robert Lusser from Fieseler, Generaladmiral Karl Witzell, Obersting. Dietrich Schwencke of the Air Ministry and Hanna Reitsch.

ME 328 B V1 COMPLAINTS

JSF finally submitted the completed Me 328 B V1 to the BAL for inspection in mid-February 1944 and a report listing numerous complaints was handed back to JSF's Messerschmitt office on February 18. The office then prepared a detailed response, effectively refuting each complaint, and submitted it on March 1.[21] To begin with, it noted that many of the individual complaints had already been raised previously by Messerschmitt's own inspector, Herr Willi, and these were in the process of being resolved at the time of BAL's inspection.

It was pointed out that the cockpit height was sufficient; the canopy emergency release lever had been placed close to the canopy glass on purpose; the cockpit was not designed to be rainproof since it wouldn't be flown in the rain and would always be parked under cover; the pilot's bailing out procedure had been tested using a mock-up and was fine; the landing flap position display wasn't in the pilot's direct field of vision but he could see it on the left if he just turned his head a little; the actuation levers were still being labelled; clearance of the control stick against the armoured glass was fine and "the trigger lever on the stick can be omitted since the aircraft will not have any firearms in the future"; the side and horizontal fin gap panelling had originally been made of aluminium but Willi had complained and "it was replaced with sheet steel cladding [so] there is probably no longer any risk of deformation"; the position display for the rear landing skid had been deliberately positioned the way it was (out of the pilot's direct line of sight again) to ensure its mechanical reliability; it was acknowledged that the [jettisonable] nosewheel support was too light but "it is suggested that the design be left as is, since the Me 328 B V1 will use Mistel take-off in the majority of cases"; no engines would be fitted; a medical pack was included; a flare gun wasn't needed; drainage holes were provided and finally—the fittings to enable attachment for a Mistel take-off had been installed.

The end-of-month BAL report noted that "complaints from BAL are currently being processed" and further stated that "the work on V2 and stress test airframes ... will be taken over by Kittelberger Bregenz".[22] Like many other glider and light aircraft manufacturers, Flugzeugbau Kittelberger of Bregenz, Neu Amerika, Austria, on the shore of the Bodensee, had long since become a military subcontractor and presumably had a modicum of spare capacity, at least on paper, to take on the job of finishing off the Me 328 B V2.

HITLER AND THE SUICIDE PLAN

During her postwar interrogation and again in her autobiography, Reitsch stated that Georgii called a meeting of the DAL working party to evaluate the suicide mission concept and "after a lengthy discussion this group reached the following conclusions: 1) That the plan was operationally sound. 2) That a manned flying bomb was to be used with the further recommendation that this be the Me 328 which already existed and would thereby save valuable construction and development time.

"3) That a 2,000lb bomb-torpedo should be used and installed in the nose of the plane, which would then be steered into the water at such an angle that the torpedo would explode directly under the keel of the vessel".[23]

She seems fervently to have believed that this happened prior to February 28, 1944. In her interrogation, she states that she applied for an interview with Hitler and was called to the Berghof at Obersalzberg near Berchtesgaden on the 28th. In her book, she states that "an unlooked-for opportunity presented itself. I received a summons to attend at the Berghof, Hitler's mountain chalet, to be presented with a certificate to mark my award of the Iron Cross (First Class)".

According to the interrogation, the interview lasted three hours and was witnessed only by Hitler's adjutant Oberst Nicholas von Below. In his autobiography,[24] von Below remembered: "The three of us took tea in the large hall. Hanna Reitsch quickly seized the opportunity to speak on her favourite theme of the day and suggested that a suicide squad be formed in Germany and if necessary deployed. She informed Hitler of the early preparations which were already in hand and asked for his blessing. Hitler was completely opposed to the idea of self-sacrifice. He spoke out against the idea at length, referring to the new military weapons under development by the Kriegsmarine and Luftwaffe and the imminent introduction of the new jet fighter."

In the account Reitsch gave to her interrogators: "He claimed that it was not in keeping with the character of the German people, and that such a plan had never been put into practice in all of German history." Reitsch was distraught but she "did win Hitler's permission to allow the development and planning to go on so that when he considered the proper time had come, the plan could immediately be put into operation. The interview closed with Hitler's remark that he did not want to be bothered with the idea again until he gave the order and declared the time as ripe".

KG 200 AND TANK GET INVOLVED

Oberst Heigl of KG 200 seems to have been aware of the suicide mission well in advance of his inclusion on Baeumker's working party list since, on March 1, he personally produced a list of requirements for the 'manned glide bomb'.[25]

He wanted something that would guarantee safe destruction of the target (described as "battleships, aircraft carriers, large cargo ships, dams, large power plants, crucial core parts of an arms industry, etc."), would be quick to build and would be easy to use and versatile.

Its physical form would have the aerodynamic shape of a high-performance glider, the option to attach different bomb forms depending on the target, small wings and a tail unit. In flight it needed to be sufficiently manoeuvrable to compensate for a moving target, fast enough to avoid enemy fighters, able to begin its attack run far away from the target and suitable for carriage either "under a suitable flighter or as a 'Mistel' on a suitable carrier machine".

Equipment-wise, it needed basic flight instruments, a comms link to the carrier aircraft, a suitable targeting device, dive brakes or brake parachute, an "adjustable thrust device" and a parachute for the glide bomb pilot so there was a "possibility of rescue by parachute jump in the event of engine failure, fighter attack, flak hit"—even though the vehicle wouldn't have engines as such.

The explosives needed to be high quality, safe to transport, capable of functioning after hitting water and equipped with a suitable detonator. 'Desirable' features included a seated position for the pilot to "avoid lying on your stomach for long periods of time, which is tiring", thrust devices with longer duration and "further development of the device in such a way that the man controlling the bomb has the best possible chance of being rescued". Lastly, he wanted a trainer version that could be landed. Heigel then sent the list to Georgii on March 10.[26]

Focke-Wulf chief executive Kurt Tank, who was another vice president of the DAL, wrote to Baeumker with his views on March 9, which Baeumker then passed to Georgii.[27]

He wrote that while, in principle, self-sacrifice could be worthwhile "if it achieves a decisive effect on the war ... the term 'decisive to the war' is unfortunately somewhat worn out and is often used for devices and operations that are not". In this case, if "one speaks of decisiveness in the war, then respect for the life of the individual comrade and the entire community requires that those with the highest level of responsibility, check precisely—and very carefully—whether what is achieved with the planned operation is in reality ... decisive for the war". And if it wasn't, then "allowing or demanding self-sacrifice would be a careless crime against the precious blood of the German people". Alternatively, if "there lie within reach of our air force targets whose destruction can decide the war in a short period of time" and it was absolutely certain they would be destroyed if a manned bomb was used, "then this action should be started under all circumstances".

WORKING PARTY

Georgii wrote to Heinz Kensche of the Deutschen Versuchsanstalt für Luftfahrt (DVL) on March 16 to say that the DAL working party on the manned glide bomb would take place from 3pm on Monday, March 27, at the Haus der Flieger, Prinz Albrecht-Strasse 5, Berlin.[28] In his letter, Georgii wrote: "As agreed, a short report on the technical development of the manned gliding bomb is provided for you. The invitations that are currently available to the State Secretary are still being sent to you. However, I ask you to prepare for your presentation now. You can obtain documents about the 328 from me or from Herr Kracht."

This letter is the earliest known contemporary evidence that the Me 328 was indeed now being considered as the most appropriate vehicle for the suicide mission. According to the report on Reitsch's interrogation, "the German Air Ministry was ordered by the Chief of the General Staff to supervise and direct the technical preparations. To head this work a staff engineer, Heinz Kensche, an outstanding glider expert, was selected. Kensche was one of the volunteers and applied for membership of KG 200 after signing the suicide pledge".[29]

Also on the 16th, Georgii wrote to Hubert Schardin of the Technische Akademie der Luftwaffe, summoning him to the working party meeting.[30] His letter said: "You will provide a short report on the effectiveness of high-explosive bombs against warships to introduce the discussion of the problem of the manned glide bomb. The report should not take more than 15 minutes. I would be grateful if you would prepare for the meeting now."

Lippisch had been booked to give a talk on the technical possibilities, development time needed and manufacturing capacity available for manned glide bombs and was also helping with the organisational duties. He wrote to H G Snay of the Forschungsanstalt Graf Zeppelin, also on the 16th, ordering him to prepare a report: "You should give a short report on 'what happens when jettisoned objects are immersed in water'. The report should not take longer than 15 minutes. A screening of the film is necessary. The invitation to this meeting, which is only valid for you personally and is classified as a 'secret command matter', may not be disclosed to any other person".[31]

Two days later, Georgii sent another invitation out, this time to Oberst Viktor von Lossberg.[32] His letter included reassurances that everything was above board: "The working session is taking place with the express permission of Generalfeldmarschal Milch. The Chief of the General Staff of the Luftwaffe, General Korten, is also aware of the matter and largely supports it." Galland, who was due to give a presentation on expected losses of carrier aircraft to enemy fighters during the approach and return flight, got the same letter on the same day[33] as did Heigl, the latter additionally being asked to give a report on his manned glide bomb requirements.[34] Jacobs was also invited and ask to bring his Me 328 documents with him because Kensche urgently needed them.[35]

On March 23, Georgii suddenly realised that no one had bothered to invite Hanna Reitsch—who he'd heard had been forced to request an invite—nor Oberleutnant Lange nor von Griem, so he wrote to the DAL's general secretary, asking for them to be included.[36] Other attendees would include Benzinger, Baeumker, Vorwald, Kracht, Inspector of Bombers Oberst Walter Marienfeld, commander of the Luftwaffe test centres Oberst Edgar Petersen and Witzell.

GLIDE BOMB ME 328

The meeting duly took place on March 27 and Georgii penned a report on the outcome, which was published on March 31.[37] The mission had been outlined as before and "the meeting concluded that the most suitable airframe for the manned gliding bomb would be that of the Me 328. The Me 328 was developed by the DFS on behalf of Messerschmitt as a fighter-bomber. The airframe has already been flight-tested and has good flight characteristics. Jacobs-Schweyer Flugzeugbau, Darmstadt, was already involved in the production.

"Me 328 was cancelled about six months ago … [but] is quite suitable for use as a manned glide bomb in terms of glide ratio, speed range and payload. The speed range is between 350km with a glide ratio of 12 and 700km with a glide ratio of five. The flight weight is 3.7 tons; 2.5 tons of explosive charge can be carried. With the glide numbers 12-5, distances from the attack target of up to 30km can be selected. The manned glide bomb is brought in for the attack using the Mistel arrangement.

"The flight weight already takes into account that the explosive charge must have armour protection of 10mm thickness. The advantage of using the Me 328 as a manned gliding bomb is that only a small amount of additional construction work has to be done to install the explosive charge. Series production could begin after a short time (around three months). In addition, the existing airframes of the Me 328 could soon be used for training the flight crew after installing dual controls. A detailed project on the use of the Me 328 as a manned glide bomb is currently being developed and can be submitted by April 7.

"The Institute for Aircraft Construction of the DFS can be used for the construction work still required to install the explosive charges in the Me 328. In order to ensure the early use of manned glide bombs, an early decision on the use of the Me 328 and the award of an order for the necessary additional designs would be necessary".

The distribution list for this report consisted of Milch, Generalmajor Kurt Kleinrath, Vorwald, Technical Office chief Siegfried Knemeyer, Galland, Marienfeld, von Lossberg and Heigl.

On the same day, Seitz produced a document entitled SO-B [Selbstopferungsbombe or Self-Sacrifice Bomb] Mission with Me 328 B—Technical Assessment and Suggestions.[38] This noted that "the development of a manned gliding bomb and the delivery of it close to the target by carrier aircraft is technically possible without major difficulties. A method for safely transporting ordnance near the target is the Mistel method (piggyback) and has been tested (trials DFS). Due to scheduling reasons, any new development of a glider is not possible.

"Existing aircraft suitable for the task should be mentioned: Me 109, Fw 190, Me 163, Me 328 B. The first three types are cancelled because they are urgently needed for the defence of the Reich. The Me 328 B model seems well suited for this task [since]: a) The model was developed as a fast bomber with jet propulsion and was designed for high wing loadings. b) The model has been thoroughly tested at DFS in the first test series (Me 328 A), particularly as a glider, with the exception of very high wing loads. c) A first test model of the final version of the Me 328 B has been completed as a glider and is to be flown in in the very near future (further work on the fast bomber task was stopped in October 1943 as part of the measures for Reich defence).

"d) In order to meet the demand for cheap and bomb-proof production that was a priority at the beginning of its development, the model is made entirely of wood, with the exception of the steel spar of the wing. Its completion therefore only puts a very small amount of strain on otherwise urgently needed metal capacity. e) The engines on the wing were intended for the fast bomber task; for the task at hand, use as a glider does not mean any significant change to the airframe. f) The aircraft has very small dimensions (wing area = 9.5sqm); the fuselage has a very considerable usable volume of 2.5 cubic metres. The Do 217, Ju 188 and He 177 [can be] used as carrier aircraft".

In terms of what changes would be needed to tailor the Me 328 B to the suicide mission: "If the basic requirement is that the existing Me 328 B model does not undergo any significant changes (engine system, fuel system, landing gear, landing skid, landing flaps are omitted without changing the overall structure of the airframe), the following options are available for the task. Version 1: In the front and rear parts of the fuselage, which were previously intended for fuel storage, explosives are stored in an armoured shell. Version 2: A bomb torpedo 1800 is attached to the underside of the unchanged glider (the fuselage remains empty). Version 3: A high-explosive charge is accommodated in the nose of the fuselage. In the rear of the fuselage there is a PC 1400 bomb or something similar."

A drawing had been appended showing an Me 328 B-0, with the same date as the report, but this appears to have been lost.

The armoured shell featured in Version 1 was to be a steel jacket 10mm thick, which would weigh 500kg. Up to 5,000kg of explosives could be accommodated "in extreme cases" but a normal load would be 2,500kg including the shell—said to be sufficient to destroy a merchant ship, destroyer or aircraft carrier.

In the normal Version 1 load case, take-off weight would be 3,600kg with a wing loading of 380kg per square metre. The best glide angle was said to be 1:13 and maximum range when carried by a DB 610-powered He 177 was 3,100km at an altitude of 5,000m and a speed of 400km/h. Version 2 would have a take-off weight of 2,900kg, a wing loading of 305kg/sqm and an optimal glide angle of 1:10. Version 3 was regarded as a "further development" and the numbers had apparently, therefore, not yet been crunched.

Seitz considered that the programme would begin with "preliminary tests: retesting Me 328 A at DFS; testing Me 328 B at JSF and DFS; training [on] Me 328 B prototypes (water ballast 2,200 litres to represent high wing loadings); Mistel tests on Do 217 and He 177; water channel tests for BT dropping".

This would be followed by further prototype production: "Creation of 10-20 Me 328 B prototypes in the previous version as a glider (with landing skid and wheeled gear) remaining construction work and stress tests at JSF or DFS with additional workers. Annotation: Since February 1944, the production of further Me 328 B prototypes with the jigs created by JSF has been running at Flugzeugbau Kittelberger, Bregenz."

The last step would be series production: "Start-up by Messerschmitt AG/JSF; production at GWF [Gotha], Hartwig-Sonneberg, Kittelberger etc. Accommodation of the production facilities in bomb-proof shelters (ravines and grottoes in the mountains)."

The report was distributed to Georgii, Reitsch and Willy Messerschmitt.

JACOBS' CONFESSION

The JSF update report from BAL for March noted that the Me 328 B V1 was now ready for delivery pending clarification of spar reinforcement work. The Me 328 B

V2 and stress test airframe were under construction at Kittelberger.[39]

At the same time, the DFS published a status report covering the period from December 1, 1943, up to March 31, 1944, which provided further details on this seemingly estranged branch of 328 development: "Me 328—the completion of V4 and V5 was postponed due to other work. The modified landing gear was installed in the V3, the suspension of the Argus thrust tubes was modified again and equipment for measuring the forces occurring between the aircraft during Mistel flights was installed. Flight testing is scheduled to resume shortly."[40]

According to Hanna Reitsch's interrogation report, "Kensche designated Reitsch to undertake the testing of the Me 328 and to supervise the flying training of the volunteers as soon as the Me 328 had been declared acceptable".[41] But in the meantime Kensche and Lange apparently travelled to Hörsching and both flew an Me 328—presumably the V2—on April 13, 1944. Kensche went first, taking off at 11.10am, detaching from the Mistel combination after 20 minutes then gliding for ten minutes to land at 11.40am.

Oberleutnant Lange took off at 3.05pm and landed at 3.32pm, with seven minutes having been spent gliding.

According to the JSF BAL report for April, the Me 328 B V1 was loaded onto a rail car on May 1, 1944, to set off on its journey to Hörsching for flight testing.[42]

All of the work done on the suicide mission up to this point presupposed that the Me 328—after such a long time in development and after more than year, on and off, of flight tests—was basically ready for mass production. However, JSF director Hans Jacobs was painfully aware that his company had spent nearly a full year giving BAL excuse after excuse as to why progress on the Me 328 B was so slow. Documentation and drawings had failed to keep pace as the hand-crafted Me 328 B V1 prototype steadily became more and more different from the design for which DFS flight test results were actually available. And there remained many unanswered questions about the most basic structural design details.

Yet Jacobs had sat and watched quietly as these extraordinary meetings took place and plans were laid by the most powerful and influential men—and woman—in German aviation to place this aircraft at the heart of the suicide mission programme.

Finally, on May 3, Jacobs wrote a letter to Kensche revealing the true state of the aircraft.[43] He explained first that the Me 328 B V1 incorporated a fundamental design flaw: "The V1 ... [has] a wing spar made of steel with a 60kg strength, instead of 90kg, which could not be procured. Due to this fact, the aircraft is limited to a flying weight of 2.3 tons. [And] in my opinion, Kittelberger is not in a position to complete [the Me 328 B] V2 in the next few months because he has neither sufficient organisation, metal processing nor experience.

"Almost all of the stress tests are still missing for the aircraft because we were unable to complete the stress test airframe. However, based on the experience available here, there will certainly [need to] be significant changes to the design and series production after the fracture tests.

"The documents are not ready for series production, as only the V1 has been built as a glider based on these drawings. In addition, there will be significant redesigns for the special task [i.e. manned glide bomb operations]."

He said that even if the go-ahead was given by mid-May, the full set of documents needed for series production wouldn't be ready before the end of July—and then only "if an experienced design office is employed".

A stress test airframe fitted with the required 90kg strength steel spar did not exist—and testing couldn't start until it did—and it would take four to five months to build the jigs needed for series production.

He went on: "Based on the above situation, we can at best start series production in November/December [1944], so that the first aircraft would come out at the beginning of next year. However, a factory with sufficient capacity would have to be used for the jigs and construction of the aircraft, otherwise significant figures could not be produced in the first months of next year."

Worst of all, none of this could happen at all unless the Me 328 B was given priority over the Luftwaffe's fighter programme—since otherwise the 90kg strength steel needed for the wing spar of every aircraft would be unobtainable. He ended the letter with: "The above statements are only intended to point out the possible difficulties so that the General Staff does not make false assumptions. A copy of this letter goes to flight captain Hanna Reitsch."

No one in their right mind would give Me 328 production priority over the Luftwaffe's fighter programme and Jacobs knew it.

ZIEGLER ON THE ME 328 B V1

It took nine days for the Me 328 B V1 prototype to reach Hörsching, with the handover scheduled for May 9. The aircraft was there, accompanied by JSF's supervision and control manager, but the handover couldn't initially take place because his counterpart from Messerschmitt failed to show up. According to his travel report,[44] the JSF man then discovered he'd been misinformed and that the

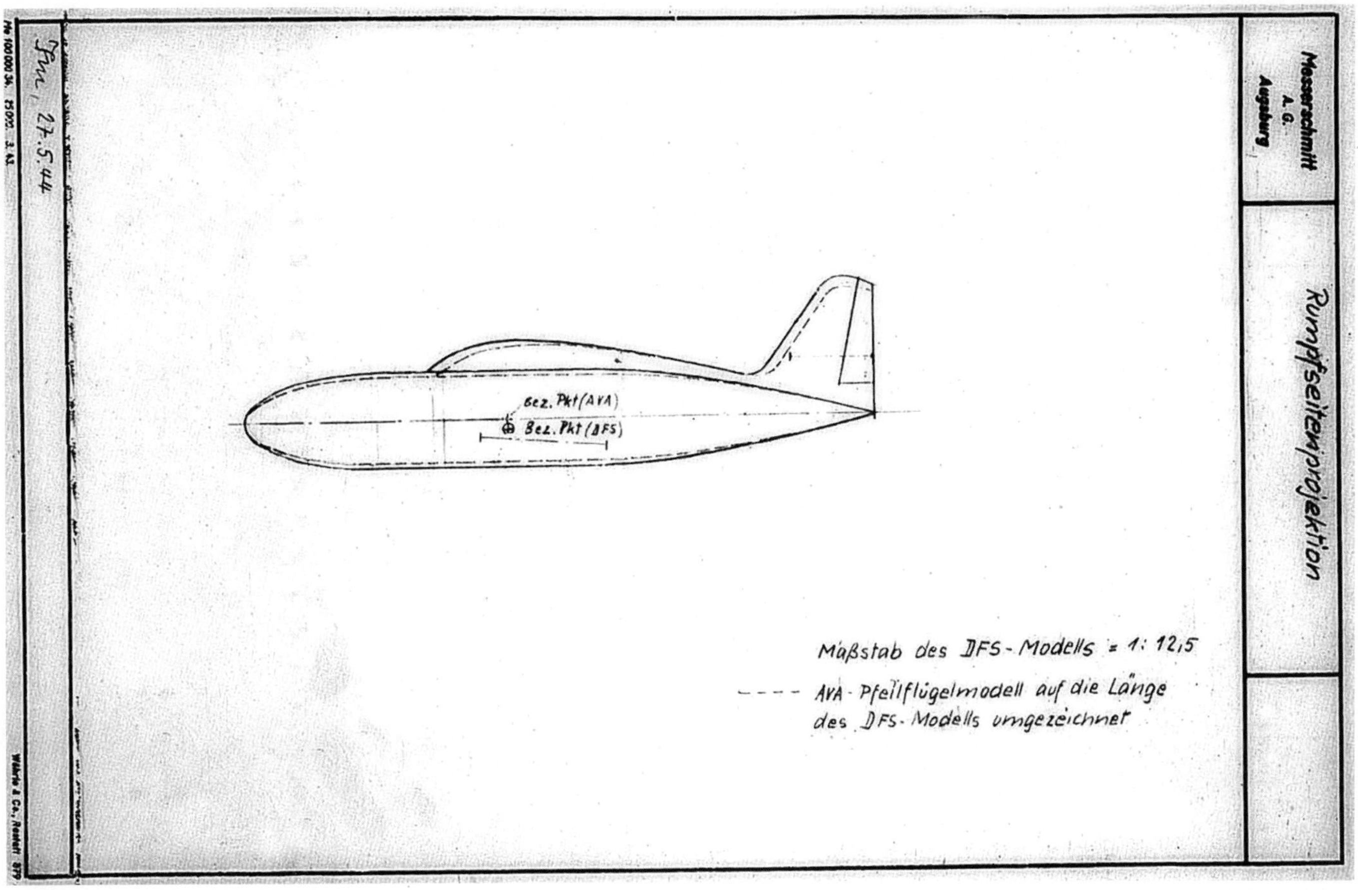

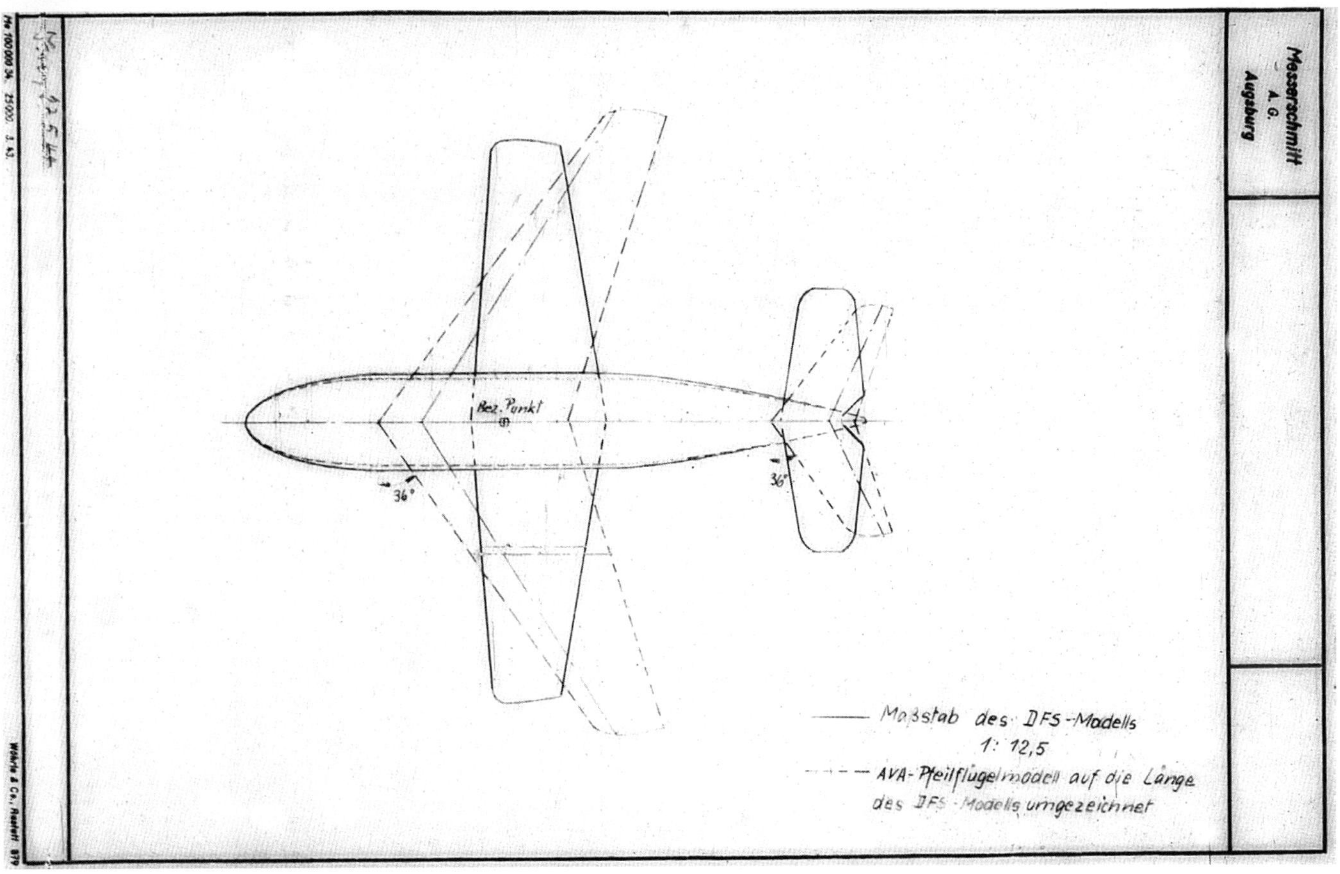

Even as late as May 27, 1944, Messerschmitt had apparently not given up on the long-fuselage version of the Me 328. These drawings show a comparison between the straight-wing long-fuselage model tested by the DFS and the swept-wing long-fuselage model tested by the AVA.

handover wasn't meant to take place until static vibration testing had been done.

While he was waiting, Rudolf Ziegler the DFS test pilot who, by all accounts, had spent the most time in the Me 328 V2, showed up and explained the findings of a report he'd made on the Me 328 B V1. The JSF man wrote: "During a discussion with the test pilot, Herr Dipl.Ing. Ziegler DFS, I learned of some complaints and suggestions for improvement that he had, based on his test flights with similar aircraft.

"First, the canopy release mechanism does not appear to be reliable as the canopy is pushed up at the rear end, giving it a negative angle. In an emergency, there is a risk that the hood could slide into the cabin and trap the pilot. According to Herr Ziegler, such an accident occurred.

"Second, the arrangement and design of the pilot's seat appears to be inadequate in terms of strength. The result is injuries to the pilot due to the pilot's seat breaking. Third, the armoured glass should be removed for the flight tests, as it prevents the pilot from wiping the windscreen if it fogs up.

"The Mistel fittings [on the Me 328 B V1] cannot be used because the structure on the carrier aircraft can never be rigid enough for each point to actually take on the theoretically assigned forces. There is therefore a risk that a lateral force will trigger the rear suspension point. It is therefore likely that only a rope tow take-off will be carried out; it is to be expected that the nose wheel will be severely damaged with each release.

"Lastly, according to the experience there [at the DFS], the connections for the pulsejets are by no means sufficient, apart from the fact that flight tests have shown that the location of the attachment points on the main spar [i.e. on the wings] is not possible. For the aircraft type V1, some of the complaints mentioned above are probably not so critical, as the aircraft is [to be] flown without power. However, they should be mentioned to provide an indication for the development of further prototypes."

Ten Me 328 prototypes appeared on the Air Ministry's prototypes production plan of May 15 but with a note appended which said "further progress is still unclear. Delivery, however, by the end of 1944".[45]

DFS TO JSF TO GOTHA

A third organisation was now commissioned to take charge of Me 328 development and production—Gothaer Waggonfabrik (GWF), more commonly known as Gotha. It had been responsible for manufacturing the Go 242 transport glider and therefore must have seemed like a good fit for the Me 328 B in unpowered manned bomb configuration.

A representative or representatives from the company visited JSF in late May or early June to meet with department chief Herbert Lück and, intermittently, Jacobs himself to gather information about the project.[46]

Unfortunately for them, Lück seems to have known very little and Jacobs wasn't around long enough to correct him. He erroneously claimed that the Me 328 A had never flown and that no Me 328 had ever flown under pulsejet power. He also said that the Me 328 B V1 had made a single Mistel flight on a Do 217. Apart from that, he could provide only basic information and frequently deflected questions by saying that only the DFS or Messerschmitt could provide the answer.

These details were noted down back at Gotha as a retrospective travel report on June 5—the same day that, according to the BAL report for June, the Me 328 B V1 was finally accepted and taken over by Messerschmitt's BAL representative at Hörsching.[47]

A meeting between GWF glider designer Hans Wegerich, Voigt, Seitz and Behrbohm at Messerschmitt's newish Oberammergau design offices from June 20 to June 21, 1944,[48] then just between Wegerich and Seitz from June 21 to June 22,[49] proved much more productive.

Wegerich noted that the project was covered by "special secrecy" and the Seitz was introduced to him as "the special person responsible".

Seitz explained that Gotha was to "become the parent company for the type [but] currently Herr Seitz is still acting supervisor and middleman between the companies involved. All documents must be obtained from JSF and DFS. Flight tests with the first examples are still taking place at DFS. JSF gives our designers any necessary instructions for the planned changes for further work in Gotha".

The first job would be to develop and build eight new prototypes—the Me 328 B V3 to V10—as training gliders.

These "must be designed in accordance with V1 and V2. For the first seven examples, fittings, shells and frames should be ready at Kittelberger". However, a host of changes would be necessary. The existing wooden seat would need to be reinforced to cope with crash landings during training ("Herr Seitz suggests a double thickness of plywood in the seat shell and reinforcement of the fittings, of course also on the fuselage side. Safety must be proven by breaking tests"); a longitudinal slot needed to be added below the front window with an adjustable cover for ventilation and the existing clear vision panel needed to be moved to the opposite side of the aircraft; the ailerons needed alterations; the control surfaces needed adjusting in light of the aircraft's unpowered state; it had to be ensured that an external load of 1,300kg could be carried beneath the aircraft while bearing in mind the positioning of the DFS-developed Mistel take-off framework; a cable tow coupling needed to be installed; the rudder depth needed to be reduced; the canopy release needed to be reworked and simplified and the landing flap ratio needed to be doubled.

A key change affected the jettisonable nosewheel gear. This was to become "permanently attached and only the main landing gear is designed to be jettisonable. However, it should be investigated whether the nosewheel can be made pivotable using simple means to make it easier to transport the machine on the ground".

The landing gear needed to be reverted back from the two-skid Me 328 B design to the single skid of the Me 328 A and "it should be investigated whether the storage of the front skid can be moved from the front part of the fuselage to the middle part of the fuselage. The chassis load assumptions must be obtained from Jacobs-Schweyer". The skid retracted/extended display in the cockpit needed to be made easier to read and the wing spar needed to be reworked. Wing slots needed to be extended across the entire wingspan and all fittings and fixtures baked into the design for attaching engines needed to be deleted.

Beyond the eight new prototypes, the Me 328 B V11 onwards would be the 'operational aircraft'—the manned glide bombs themselves. Seitz told Wegerich that the operational 328 B would have the 10mm armoured shell up front as well as the option to carry explosive charges or a "special cargo" internally or an underslung bomb torpedo. And a host of features included on the trainers could be deleted: the leading-edge slats, the landing flaps and the skids, including all their associated fittings, control lines etc.

Evidently, "in general, every conceivable simplification is desired for the operational machines. The connection of the frames to the spar, for example, can be made significantly cheaper".

TIRED OF WAITING

Attempts were then made to extract the relevant drawings from both the DSF and JSF but this proved to be somewhat problematic. Gotha received a letter from the DFS on June 27 saying that Messerschmitt had asked for drawings of the Mistel framework and front cable tow coupling on the Me 328 B to be forwarded on. But "since the Me 328 B was built by Jacobs-Schweyer ... DFS asks you to request the drawings from this company.

"However, DFS would [also] like to draw your attention to the fact that the Mistel couplings installed by

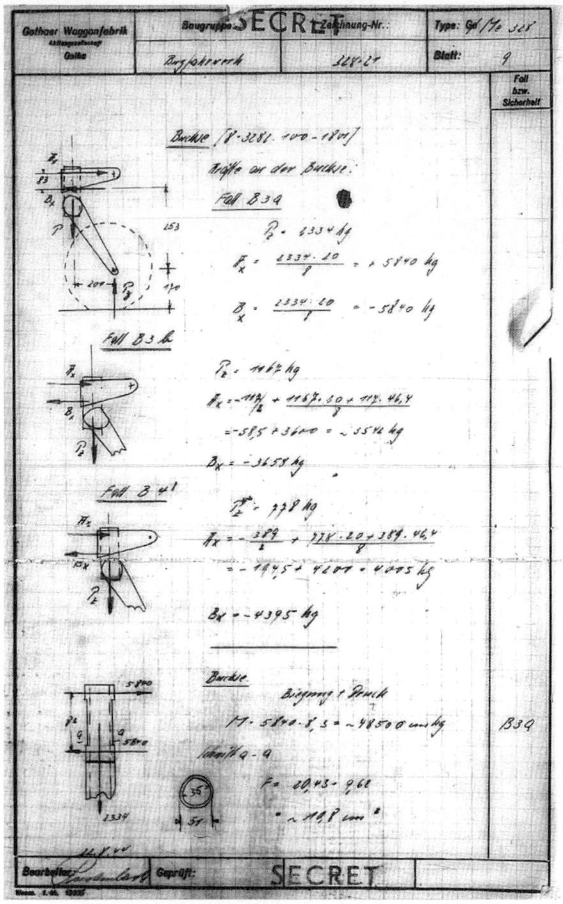

Design work carried out at Gotha on the Me 328 B's fixed nosewheel, dated August 22, 1944.

Jacobs-Schweyer do not meet the requirements and asks you to let us know whether DFS should inform you of the arrangement of the couplings as tested in the Me 328 B.

"No binding information can be given at the moment about the changes in the controls, as these must first be determined as part of flight testing. For the special application it is to be expected that the tail units themselves will also have to be changed".[50]

Gotha's engineers and designers met on July 3 to discuss progress on the training glider design.[51] Maximum take-off weight—with 2,700kg of ballast, was given as 4.2 tons. Maximum gliding speed was 700km/h. Seitz's instructions concerning the wooden seat, ventilation, clear vision panel, nosewheel, skid and so on were reiterated but evidently what Messerschmitt wanted doing with the skid wasn't possible.

The wing spar would remain a steel piece with 60kg strength and plans to order enough material for ten aircraft were laid.

Within 11 days, it was reported that Gotha had been asked to design and build a "dual control system for two-seater training operations" but this wasn't feasible, as it would then eliminate the possibility of using the aircraft with [the correct] ballast". The company had also

Gotha drawing showing the then-current state of the Me 328 B's undercarriage design — two flap-type skids and jettisonable mainwheels, but with a fixed nosewheel. The drawing is from August 21, 1944.

been told that "the Ju 88 S-3 and Ju 388 are possible carrier aircraft". A GWF representative had been sent over to Ainring to examine the Mistel framework designed by the DFS.[52]

The whole process of getting the Me 328 into a fit state for use as a manned glide bomb was taking way too long for Reitsch and the other suicide mission supporters by this point. According to her interrogation report: "Unexplained difficulties and delays prolonged the construction until it began to appear to Reitsch and her volunteers that there was some sort of official sabotage afoot to delay or prevent the suicide project. When it began to appear that long months would still be required before the Me 328 was available in any sufficient quantities, the suicide group began to look about for some sort of a makeshift plane that would still fulfil the purpose and, most important, be immediately available. The decision was reached to use a manned V-1.

"It was decided that the V-1 could be properly modified to suit the purpose in a matter of weeks. This modification programme began at once under the code name 'Reichenberg' and was kept highly secret so that even the V-1 workers directly concerned with the modification did not suspect the real nature of their work. The V-1 alteration programme was put under the supervision of Director Lusser of the Dipl.Ing. Fiedler Construction Bureau, which was located at the Henschel firm in Berlin-Schoenfeld. In a frantic 14-day period of work the V-1 was rebuilt into four separate types to fulfil both the training and mission requirements. In less than three weeks the four types were ready for test flying.

"The fuselage of the V-1 was not greatly altered; the important changes required in modifying the plane were the installation of a pilot's compartment and the necessary instruments."

Reitsch offered no timeline for when the group switched their focus from the Me 328 to the V-1 flying bomb but in her autobiography she recalled that as early as April 1944 the idea to use it had come from Waffen-SS special forces officer Otto Skorzeny. She later recalled attending the first test flight of the modified V-1 with Skorzeny at Lärz "on a warm summer's day" and that in October 1944 she was injured in an air-raid on Berlin, with Kensche 'standing in' for her as test pilot of the V-1.

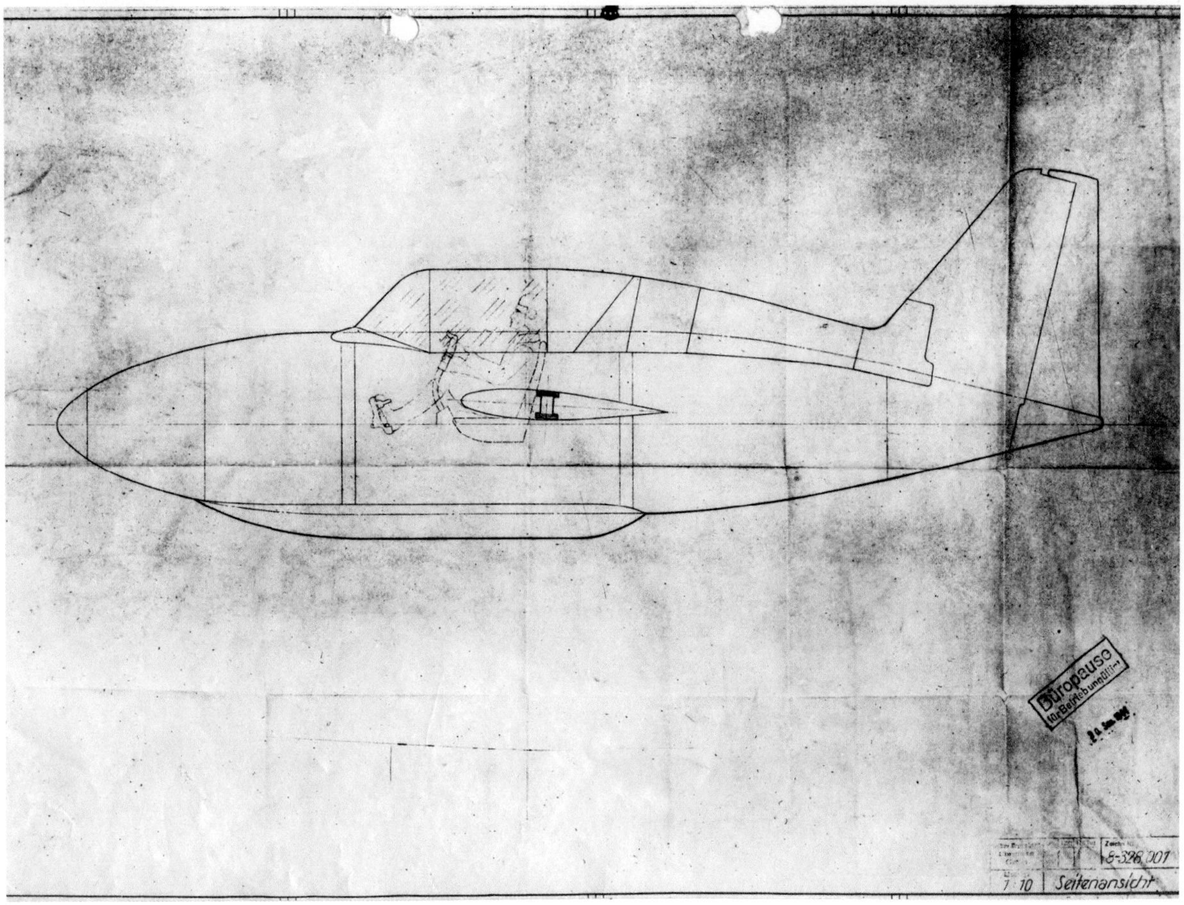

The final known depiction of the Me 328—a rather basic Gotha drawing stamped September 20, 1944.

TO THE END

Even though the suicide mission fanatics had long since grown tired of waiting and gone elsewhere, Gotha doggedly continued its work on revising the Me 328 B design along the lines indicated by Seitz into the autumn of 1944.

Towards the end of August or during early September, GWF engineer Heiss travelled to Junkers' technical office at Nordhausen to meet with Dr Fritz Haber and discuss using the Ju 88 S or Ju 388 as a carrier for the Me 328.[53] In his report, written on September 7 after his return to Gotha, he wrote: "The order to deploy the Me 328 on Ju 88 was discussed in detail. Dr Haber knows the Do 217 arrangement from Ainring and he once flew it there. In general, Dr H. has concerns about the planned 328-Ju 88 combination in relation to the power available. Junkers has three engines available for the take-off [i.e. two on the carrier and another on the aircraft being carried], alternating between Me 109 or Fw 190 on Ju 88 and [this] requires a take-off distance of 800-1,000m. He wants to talk about it with Herr Fl. Haupting. Kensche.

"At Junkers, the separation of the two machines is not carried out with a clutch [as with the DFS process] but exclusively with explosive bolts: the control line is also blown up. The explosive bolts are available to us if required.

"After looking through the [potential attachment] points on the Ju 88, it was found that points on the front and rear spars as well as secondary points in the main spar level (middle of the fuselage) can be used for us, the rear point in the middle of the fuselage for the support strut will probably have to be developed by us ourselves. For this purpose, fuselage drawings must be requested from Junkers; I brought the documents for the aforementioned ones with me."

Surviving documents show Gotha carrying out load tests on Me 328 ailerons during late September,[54] load tests on the landing flaps during early October,[55] a Kittelberger-manufactured Me 328 seat during late November ("the seat as delivered did not meet the strength requirements. The tests were stopped as the seat was replaced with a standard seat")[56] and lastly a rudder on November 21, 1944.[57]

This abrupt drop-off in work on the Me 328 at Gotha coincides with an uptick in work at the company on preparing prototypes of the Horton Ho 229, which had also now been palmed off on Gotha, and it would seem that by December the manned glide bomb—the final version of the Me 328—had at last been abandoned.

According to the report on Reitsch's interrogation,

"technical development and construction of the Me 328 and V-1 suicide versions ... continued until March 1945" but this seems unlikely, except in the sense that various bits and pieces of Me 328 may have remained at Gotha's workshops until then.

What happened to the surviving Me 328 airframes? Kracht, interviewed at the DFS's Prien facility on July 1, 1945,[58] told the Americans: "Altogether three planes were produced. The first one was wrecked through the vibrations of the propelling units, while the other two were destroyed in Hörsching on the 5th of May, 1945."

Presumably he was referring to just the three DFS-made airframes: the Me 328 V1, V2 and V3. The Messerschmitt-made Me 328 V02 is believed to have met its end at Peenemünde, as outlined above, but the fate of the Me 328 B V1 and whatever bits and pieces of the Me 328 B V2 eventually got manufactured is not known for certain. A photograph is said to exist showing a fire-damaged high-wing Me 328 B type captured by the Allies at Ainring but assuming these are the remains of the Me 328 B V1, it is unclear why it was there. Perhaps it was due to have its Mistel attachment points reworked, or it may have been relocated for storage when it proved ill suited to the DFS Mistel take-off technique. In any case, none of the five completed prototypes are known to have been captured in one piece.

(Opposite) One of the few Me 328 artifacts to survive the war: a steel and aluminium wind tunnel model of a high-wing B-type discovered at "a plant for manufacturing wind tunnel models" in a castle near Wallerstein, Bavaria, presumably Schloss Wallerstein, on June 11, 1945. The three images are from USSAFE Technical Intelligence Report No. A.447. The short and bulbous underwing objects, protruding ahead of the wing and not much behind, look rather like bombs — maybe SC 1000s without their tail cones — suggesting that this is a representation of the suicide attack glider variant

PA

PA

SUMMARY

UNLIKE THE Me 262, which was always intended as a fighter, the Me 328 only existed in the first place as a pulsejet vehicle. It was not a response to any military requirement, nor was it designed to suit any particular role. Rather, it was a technology demonstrator in search of a purpose – and as such it became a blank canvas onto which successive parties could project their ambitions.

The head of Messerschmitt's Project Office, Woldemar Voigt, initially saw it as an alternative to the Me 163, and therefore as a means of frustrating and defeating the efforts of Alexander Lippisch's rival Abteilung L during their petty inter-office rivalry back in 1941.

Willy Messerschmitt then took advantage of its compact dimensions to make it part of his ambitious proposal for attacking America with fleets of long-range carrier aircraft and parasite bombers, before the ball bounced back to Voigt. This time Voigt invoked the name of the Führer in pitching the Me 328 as 'flying artillery' and the focal point of a 'special campaign' which would elevate his office and provide privileged access to manpower and materials.

Finally, the suicide attack fanatics entered the picture with their ambitions of sacrificial glory. The Me 328 was presented as an aircraft that not only fulfilled their requirements but which was also ready to enter series production without further ado.

With hindsight it can be said that the Me 328 was entirely unsuitable for use as an interceptor; Messerschmitt's parasite attack bomber proposal was little more than a fantasy and the aircraft's development had become so convoluted by 1944 that it was never going to enter production fast enough for the fanatics. It could be argued that Voigt's 'flying artillery' concept had some merit (though whether the SC 500 RS rocket bomb would ever have entered mass production is another story), but it could also be convincingly argued that the inability of the finest minds in German aeronautical science to overcome the pulsejet's inherent problems and improve its performance killed any such notion stone dead. And there was also the not-so-small matter of the negative effects that the pulsejet's noise and vibrations evidently had on both airframes and pilots despite all efforts to negate them.

Going back to March 1942, handing responsibility for the Me 328's design and development over to the DFS at that time was perhaps the smartest move Messerschmitt could have made. The DFS was a long-established, well-funded and consequently well-equipped organisation with many highly-trained and highly-experienced personnel on staff. And it specialised in glider research, which was perfect since the Me 328 could not take off under its own power and had to be taken aloft by whatever means as a glider.

Over the course of many months, flight and wind tunnel testing determined areas of weakness in Messerschmitt's original design and the DFS's own workshops were apparently able to manufacture replacement or improved parts as needed.

The canopy was fully revised from the first prototype to the second, changing the aircraft's looks significantly. The generator props were moved from the wing roots to the nose and the pulsejet attachment points were shifted from the wings to the rear fuselage – so that the engines exhausted behind, rather than beside, the tail.

Their output remained woefully inadequate but the long-term survival of the Me 328 V2 despite being tested with pulsejets suggests that the rear fuselage position was a 'success'.

By December 1942, the DFS version of the Me 328 was gradually shaping up to be, if not a good aircraft, then at least a somewhat viable one. But unfortunately for all concerned, Messerschmitt retained the final say on the Me 328's design. Mounting the pulsejets on the rear fuselage appears to have been a point of fundamental disagreement – with Messerschmitt never accepting the DFS's assertion that an underwing position simply didn't work because it resulted in unacceptable damage to the tail.

So when Voigt made his grandiose push for a 'special campaign' it was with a new design that differed significantly from the one that the DFS had expended so much time and effort on improving. The initial Me 328 B proposal completely ignored the new flat-windowed canopy design that had been undergoing flight tests for at least a month by that point – and which Messerschmitt's own test pilot, Baur, had recommended be included.

It retained the underwing pulsejet position which the DFS already considered unsuitable; changed the wing position from low to high and changed the fuselage shape, invalidating much of the wind tunnel data already accrued on the low wing position by the DFS; and made the landing skid protrude from the underside of the aircraft rather than tucking up inside it.

Design and development was then handed over to JSF—which though run by the famous Hans Jacobs had no wind tunnel nor flight testing facilities of its own. It lacked the DFS's prestige and found it difficult to obtain materials. It also seems to have lacked the high-quality staff found in such abundance at the DFS. As a result, the project slowed to a crawl. Messerschmitt set up an on-site branch of the Project Office but this seems to have accomplished little other than a series of changes which evolved the Me 328 B further and further away from the original design. Meanwhile, scientists such as Zobel at the LFA had already concluded that Argus's pulsejets had reached their physical limit and the long hoped-for 400kg thrust tube was permanently out of reach, despite some incremental improvements.

When the supporters of the self-sacrifice manned glide bomb concept were deciding what vehicle to use, DFS director Georgii undoubtedly spoke up in favour of the Me 328 because his organisation had been ironing out its kinks as a glider for two years by that point. But using 'his' Me 328, the low-wing 'A' type, was out of the question as far as Messerschmitt was concerned because the Me 328 B represented the 'current' state of the aircraft. There is a certain logic to this, in that the DFS Me 328 had been hand-made and while its problems had gradually been resolved over time, the drawings necessary to replicate all those 'fixes' had not been made. Similarly, there were no jigs for building more Me 328 A types.

In theory, JSF had spent more than a year preparing the B type for mass production. All of its changes would have been accompanied by the appropriate drawings and documents—and there would be sufficient jigs and tools available to start production immediately. Except... they hadn't and there weren't. JSF had been unable to do its job and the Me 328 B's situation was the same as or even worse than that of the Me 328 A by March 1944.

The sensible thing to do at this point might have been to forget the Me 328 B and go back to the Me 328 A design, working on the basis of the copious data already gathered by the DFS. But this was unthinkable to Messerschmitt, still the controlling authority, and instead Gotha was handed the Me 328 B, the sole prototype of which might never have even flown, along with a list of further design changes that would be needed before testing could begin—let alone the manufacture of more airframes.

Gotha got started but seemingly made little real progress and the project appears to have been dropped by the end of November 1944.

As a postscript, it is worth mentioning some work carried out by the Forschungsanstalt Graf Zeppelin (FGZ) at Stuttgart at around this time.[1] The research institute was working with the Forschungsinstitut für Kraftfahrwesen und Fahrzeugmotoren (FKFS) to design a wire-guided anti-aircraft missile powered by two Argus As 014 pulsejets. The FKFS had noticed something curious while working on the pulsejet installation—if the two tubes were positioned side by side, the oscillations were reduced, the tubes became quieter and their operation was "more consistent with that of a single tube".

According to a postwar report compiled by Ulrich Hütter of the FGZ, the FKFS believed that if "the tubes were installed appropriately in a well-shaped fuselage, significant thrust and performance gains could be achieved at high speeds". The FGZ had evidently tested this theory on an experimental rig and the "double pipes ran quite satisfactorily on the test stand, even with a large plywood intake in the shape of the planned fuselage nose in front [of them]".

Plans were laid to build an aircraft powered by two pulsejets positioned next to one another within a fuselage, however Hütter noted that "although the wing and tail structure of the He 162 fighter, which were being mass-produced in many woodworking workshops, were to be used, it was clear that the problems were increasing in scope and that the originally planned quick solution was out of the question. Attempts to build manned aircraft with pulsejets have been made several times, e.g. manned Fi 103 with enlarged wings, Junkers 'Lilli' with 500mm diameter pipe, DFS/Messerschmitt 235 [328] with two freely suspended As 014 tubes. But this has failed again and again because neither the pilot nor the more sensitive parts of the aircraft can cope for a tolerable period of time with the severe vibrations that occur. There is damage to coverings and skin, to control systems and instruments, the pilot's windscreen becomes difficult to see through when the engines are running and the pilot's memory and concentration suffer greatly."

This evidence would seem to suggest that there had, in fact, been a way forward for a pulsejet-powered Me 328 all along—but Messerschmitt, the DFS, the LFA, the AVA, Argus and all the rest simply never discovered it. Nothing remains of the project today besides a scant handful of documents and a general perception among those who study aviation history that the Me 328 was bad news.

APPENDIX I

HORACE 'REX' KING ON THE ME 328 B

Many of the documents covering the development of the Me 328 were destroyed during the war, particularly those of the DFS, but British intelligence nevertheless managed to put together a reasonable – if not entirely accurate – summary of its features and history by August 29, 1945. The following is the full text of Horace 'Rex' King's A.I.2.(g) Report No. 2356 Me 328 B Light High-Speed Bomber, minus the images referenced and the performance tables presented at the end.

1. The Me 328 B was developed from the Me 328 A, a front view of which is shown herewith. The design is of interest because it represents the first serious attempt to apply Argus As 014 impulse duct propulsion units to a piloted aircraft. Although full specifications had been drawn up by the end of 1942 the Me 328 B never went into production. It is known that damage to the tail resulted from the pulsations of the jet units and that the first prototype crashed for this reason.
2. The aircraft shown in the sketch (top) was intended to be used as a light, high-speed bomber for daylight operations against strongly defended targets and more particularly as "flying coastal artillery" for defence against Allied landings. Virtual immunity from fighter interception was to be ensured by high speed at low altitude which would also make it a difficult target for ground defences, particularly in view of its small size. The design is simple throughout to ensure cheap and rapid production.
3. Examination of papers captured from the Jacobs-Schweyer aircraft factory at Darmstadt has revealed some details of the Me 328 experimental aircraft, a development of which may have been intended for use as a flying bomb or ramming aircraft.
4. Previous mention of the Me 328 was made in official German documents of 1942, and some conflicting descriptions have been given by prisoners of war.
5. In March 1943, Jacobs-Schweyer began their experimental programme on the 'V' ('Versuchs' = experimental) series of the Me 328 B sub-type. Apparently the A sub-type was used only for static and destruction tests. Of the B sub-types the V1 was a glider for flight testing of the general design; thus the development was analogous to that of the Me 163, which was originally tested as a glider before installation of the power unit. The V2 is powered by the Argus Rohr As 014 impulse duct units of 660lb thrust. (The Argus Rohr is the propulsion unit of the FZG 76 flying bomb).
6. The Me 328 C was to be fitted with one Jumo 004 B-2 turbojet unit, but the project was abandoned in October 1943.
7. The V1 of the B sub-type was ready for flying trials in March 1944, after modifications which included the strengthening of the wing main spar. In June 1944, the V2 and a further ten 'V aircraft were manufactured by Kittelberger of Höchst Bregenz.
8. The only technical details available in the captured documents pertain to the B sub-type and are given below:

FUSELAGE

1. The wood fuselage is of circular cross-section throughout with a maximum diameter of 3ft 11in. It is made in four parts, namely nose; cylindrical centre section; rear fuselage; and conical tail end. On assembly bulkheads are interposed between the various sections. The upper portion of the centre-section is recessed to receive the one-piece spar for the shoulder wing, and on the underside of this section are fitted the retractable landing skid and bomb carrier.
2. Two self-sealing tanks of equal capacity occupy the whole of the nose space and two identical tanks, but in reverse positions, are housed in the rear fuselage. The pilot's cockpit is in the centre-section together with most of the instruments and equipment. There is a space beneath the pilot's seat which could be utilised for additional fuel or for the stowage of anti-personnel bombs.
3. There is a 15mm armour bulkhead between the two nose fuel tanks and an armour ring 10 inches wide and 15mm thick between the nose and centre sections. Further protection for the pilot is afforded by an 80mm bulletproof windscreen. The cockpit cover is hinged on the starboard side and the wood fairing as shown in the general arrangement drawing is extended as far as the rear of the fuselage where it blends with the fin. A balloon cable-cutter is fitted

to the nose.

4. The fuselage is of semi-monocoque construction and has a plywood skin; reference is made to 'Polystal' and 'Kaurit' as bonding media for the skin.
5. The cockpit has a bullet-resisting glass screen (not fitted in the V1) and a jettisonable cockpit cover. The pilot's seat was found to be weak in construction resulting in danger of injury to the pilot due to breakage. This may imply the intended use of a pilot-ejecting device.
6. A standard Me 109 metal tailplane is used. Mention is made of a modification to one of the fuselage frames of the V1 for giving clearance to the tailplane incidence gear. This resulted in a weakening of the structure by 22% and a consequent limitation of the maximum speed to 370mph. No armament was apparently intended for the B sub-types.

WING AND TAILPLANE

1. Few details are given of the wing, which is believed to be of wood. It is of "exceptionally small dimensions" and difficulties were incurred in the location of inspection plates for the aileron linkage. Two-position flaps are fitted and are used for take-off as well as landing; a flap indicator is incorporated, although the flap setting can be ascertained visually from the cockpit.
2. The tapered wing is of wood construction throughout, including the single spar. The camber-changing flaps are out away to clear the propulsion units. They can be deflected through a maximum angle of 50 degrees. Outboard of the propulsion units are fixed leading-edge slots, and balloon cable-cutters extend along the full length of the leading edges.
3. Long-span and short-span versions were proposed, the long span being shown in the drawing. The short span is identical except that the wing-tip sections are omitted and the fairings of the wind-driven generators form the end caps. The spans are 28ft 2½in and 22ft 7½in and the corresponding winf areas 101 sq ft and 91.5 sq ft respectively.
4. Adjacent to the power units the undersurface of the wing is protected by asbestos-covered plates.

POWER UNITS

1. Two Argus 109 014 propulsion units are flexibly suspended under the wing and are quickly interchangeable. In emergency they can be jettisoned by explosive bolts. For added strength the jet tubes are enclosed in outer tubes at the mounting points. Initially it was proposed to install units of 660lb thrust were to be substituted when available. It is stated that the thrust varies directly with atmospheric density and falls to zero at 33,600ft.
2. Fuel is delivered to the units by electrically driven pumps, the current supply being taken from an accumulator on the undercarriage until the wind-driven generators come into operation. Special Argus regulators meter the fuel in accordance with the speed and altitude.

EMERGENCY EXIT

1. On account of supply difficulties a catapult seat was not to be fitted. Instead there was to be an arrangement whereby the whole of the rear portion of the fuselage behind the pilot's seat could be jettisoned by explosive bolts to facilitate bailing out.

LANDING SKID

1. The aircraft is landed on a central skid of composite wood and steel construction which incorporates a braking arrangement. Part of the skid surface at the rear is cut away to accommodate the bomb carrier. Landing shock is absorbed by a modified Fw 200 oleo leg fitted with a roller which runs on a track on the upper surface of the skid. At take-off the skid is retracted and locked against the underside of the fuselage so that although the bomb is carried by the skid the load is transferred to the main structure. The skid can only be lowered after the bomb has been dropped.
2. The aircraft is supported on the jettisonable undercarriage (employed for take-off) on two spherical sockets in the wings and a third point at the rear of the fuselage. There are three alternative methods of take-off:-

    1) Borsig rocket-propelled rail carriage.
    2) Three-wheel carriage and cable-type catapult.
    3) Three-wheel carriage and towing aircraft.

3. A reliable informant has reported the use of two landing skids arranged in tandem; the captured documents refer to retracting gear and a visual indicator for the rear skid. Oleo legs are apparently used to absorb the landing impact and operate at a pressure of 400lb/sq in for the normal version of the Me 328 with a landing weight of 4,200lb, and a pressure of 140-210lb/sq in for the V1 (glider), which has a landing weight of 3,100lb.
4. A jettisonable tricycle undercarriage is used for take-off from the ground.

LAUNCHING

1. The Me 328, or one version of it, is intended to be air-launched, but it is not clear whether it is to be carried above, below or partially inside the aircraft. The connections to the structure of the carrying aircraft were apparently not used for launching the V1 in flying trials because of breakage of the rear fitting. The documents state that "for the time being (1943), only towed take-off will be used."

APPENDIX II

GERMAN VERSION OF THE SUICIDE WEAPON

During the initial phase of gathering intelligence on the Me 328 shortly after the end of the war, Allied intelligence had learned of its proposed use as a "use as a flying bomb or ramming aircraft" – see Appendix I. Curious to know more, they found a veritable fount of knowledge on the topic in test pilot Hanna Reitsch. Though not, in fact, the key proponent of the plan by any means, her already high profile meant she would subsequently become widely associated with it. This is her account, as filtered through Interrogation Report No. 187, itself based on a report by American chief interrogator Captain Robert E. Work.

Interrogation Report No 187
Ref No AIU/IS/10
7 Oct 46

British Intelligence Objectives Sub-Committee
Target Nos. C4/328, C5/287, C25/641

Main interest: German Version of the Suicide Weapon (Gp. 2) (M.O.S.A.P.)

1. **Introduction:** It appears that the Japanese did not control the market on the "Kamikaze" suicide-weapon type of warfare. The Germans had made considerable strides of their own in the development of a more typically Teutonic version of suicide air tactics. The German style differed considerably from that utilized by the Japanese and although it never progressed as far as actual operational use, it did represent considerable effort and planning. Hitler does not appear to have been a pronounced enthusiast of the plan but he did grace the project with a type of negative support, inasmuch as he did not utterly forbid further development and planning when the idea was presented to him by Hanna Reitsch.
    a) Reitsch appears to have been one of the founders of the movement and in spite of serious opposition from various sources it seems clear that the idea, both technically and spiritually, was developed to a considerably high degree. The following account is the story of the German suicide idea from its conception to its final organizational and functional collapse, as Reitsch was able to observe it through her close relation and participation in the project.
    b) It is possible that her story may throw some light on this comparatively little known project of the German Luftwaffe.
2. **The plan:** In 1943 many people in Germany, Reitsch claims, were becoming thoroughly convinced that only extraordinary measures would actually bring the war to a successful conclusion for the Reich. Among these, who were so convinced, was a small group of idealists who combined their idealism with the acute realization that the war was lost unless a sudden, decisive blow could be struck against the Allies that would, in a matter of days, force defeat upon the enemy. It was believed that this could be done by totally disrupting and destroying the invasion of the continent that everyone was already momentarily expecting. If this invasion could be definitely defeated, it was felt that the Allies would realise that Germany was militarily secure in her continental fortress and would then sue for peace. To accomplish this the idea of a "suicide squadron" was born, with which it was intended to meet the serious and extraordinary situation with a powerful and extraordinary weapon. It was intended then to devise a weapon, some sort of a man-controlled flying bomb, that would destroy and sink at a ratio of one vessel per flying bomb, all the larger naval craft that were so important in protecting and covering an invasion force.
3. **The participants:** The group of men who were brought together by this idea came from all walks of life, from army and civilian status alike. They were motivated, Reitsch claims, by the pure desire to give their lives for the existence of their country. They had carefully studied the progress of the war and realized that time was counting heavily against a German victory. They also realised that the best in German arms and manpower had already been lost on the battlefields and felt that only an effort such as they proposed could possibly turn the tide with any real effectiveness. Their only demand was that as long as they had offered their lives

for the Fatherland, they be given a weapon that would be certain to achieve the end for which they were prepared to die. They had their own ideas of what this weapon should be and among them they possessed the necessary skill to help develop it. Reitsch, from the beginning, was considered the chief test pilot, who through her experimental flights was to play a big part in evolving the final aircraft and training the participants to fly it.

4. **The organisation:** The first, faint beginnings of the idea go back almost to the beginning of the war. In the early fall of 1943 something that began to resemble an organisation began to develop. At this time the group numbered between 30 and 40 young aviation enthusiasts. They were not tired of life, nor otherwise potential suicides, for they were healthy, young men, many of them fathers and husbands, who believed that through their deaths which eventually need total hardly more than a thousand, many thousands of soldiers and civilians could be saved.
   a) The group was led by a First Lieutenant Heinrich Lange, whom Reitsch describes as the sparkplug of the whole idea, without whose principles and driving energy the project would never have gained the strength it did. The group was not known to any but a very few, and only vague rumours of fantastic suicide tactics spread through the populace. Most of the volunteers were former or active glider pilots and some had never flown powered aircraft.
   b) Meetings were held by this small group, which Reitsch usually attended, until they felt that the idea was sufficiently developed to present to the proper leaders and Luftwaffe officials for utilisation so that actual construction of the required aircraft could begin.
   c) Before they carried their programme to higher authorities they reached several understandings. First, there must be no danger that the leaders would misunderstand the "holiness" of their plan. Secondly, they wanted a sincere investigation of their idea, to be followed by technical and tactical assistance that would make their mission possible. Thirdly, they wanted the whole matter handled as quickly as possible because of the desperateness they already saw in the military situation. And lastly, they wanted to be placed under a command, be it Göring, Himmler, or whoever, who would assure that the operational use of their weapon would be utilised in the spirit it was intended.
   d) The first semblance of organisation was headed by the above named Lieutenant Lange, Medizinrat Doctor Theo Benzinger, leader of the Institute for Medical Aeronautics at Rechlin, and Hanna Reitsch. These three began to draw up the aims and plans in October 1943. Lange, who at that time belonged to XI Fliegerkorps, did all the paper and organisational work, Dr Benzinger performed the medical and psychological research which would enable the human body to be in full command of its faculties and possessed of the necessary calmness and clearness of mind up to the last moment of the actual suicide attack, while Reitsch was to undertake the flying training and test flying of the plane developed.

5. **Immediate opposition:** Reitsch's first duty, however, was to present the idea to various Luftwaffe authorities in order to win official support for the project. But here the first opposition came in such overwhelming force that it began to appear that extraordinary steps would have to be taken to even achieve a hearing by the proper authorities. The idea was at first passed off as fantastic and the result of abnormal mental hallucinations of people tired of life who were looking for a martyr's end in the pages of German history. Worst of all, no one could be sufficiently impressed to even permit a hearing of the plans already completed.
   a) Reitsch claims that the group did not want to present their idea to Hitler until all the technical details had been worked out. This would have been the job of the RLM (German Air Ministry), headed by Feldmarschall Milch. When Reitsch finally obtained an interview with Milch, he too belittled the plan and flatly declared that the idea was impossible. Reitsch begged that the plan at least be examined by competent authorities before judgement was passed. This was granted, but Reitsch immediately suspected that the grant was only made to close the issue in the hope that the plan would die a normal death.
   b) After waiting for some weeks without any results forthcoming from her discussion with Milch, Reitsch, by virtue of her reputation

and position in German air circles, gained a hearing at the German Academy of Aeronautics, in whose power it lay to call together the necessary scientists, technicians, and experts in aeronautical combat tactics. The Academy was able to do this without requesting permission from Milch, and were required merely to inform him of what they intended to do.

6. **Technical examination of the suicide weapons:** The meeting to evaluate the technical and tactical capabilities of the suicide idea was called by Prof Dr Walter Georgii, Director of the German Aeronautical Research Council.
   a) Present at this meeting were:
      1) An explosives expert.
      2) A torpedo expert.
      3) Navigation and radio technicians.
      4) Ship engineers and naval exports.
      5) Experienced airplane designers and constructors.
      6) Representatives of the Luftwaffe Fighter Command.
      7) Representatives of the Luftwaffe Bomber Command.
      8) Representatives of the Office of the Air Surgeon.
   b) Reitsch was not familiar with the individual names of these committee members.
   c) After a lengthy discussion this group reached the following conclusions:
      1) That the plan was operationally sound.
      2) That a manned flying bomb was to be used with the further recommendation that this be the Me 328 which already existed and would thereby save valuable construction and development time. (A few months later this was changed in favour of a manned V-1 for the purpose.)
      3) That a 2,000 pound bomb-torpedo should be used and installed in the nose of the plane, which would then be steered into the water at such an angle that the torpedo would explode directly under the keel of the vessel. The plane was expected to shatter upon impact with the water, killing the pilot instantly and allowing the bomb to tear loose from the plane to continue under the keel of the vessel where it would explode with a time fuse that would be set in motion upon impact with the water.
   d) After the meeting was adjourned, the technical possibilities of the weapon having been theoretically proven, all that remained to be done was to convince the leaders, including Hitler, that the weapon should be considered practical and given official support. The problem of giving the leadership into proper hands now also came to a head. The group of volunteers had long since agreed among themselves that Göring, because of the lack of leadership he had already shown, was not the one who should control the project.
7. **Presenting the suicide plan to Hitler:** To solve both the problems of getting the plan accepted and the naming of proper leadership, Reitsch applied for an interview with Hitler and was called to the Berchtesgaden Berghof on the 28th of February 1944, where in the presence of the Führer's Luftwaffe Adjutant, Oberst von Below, she held a three-hour discussion with the Führer.
   a) Hitler at once objected to the self-sacrificing idea. He claimed that it was not in keeping with the character of the German people, and that such a plan had never been put into practice in all of German history. Reitsch's rejoinder was that the present situation was such that it allowed no comparison with anything that history had to offer and that the present situation was so precarious and dangerous that only by drastic emergency measures could they possibly hope to turn the tide. To this Hitler remarked, quite emphatically, that the situation was not precarious and that the time for such unusual measures had not yet come, and that if it ever should come, he himself would give the order to put such a plan into execution.
   b) Reitsch claims that she was totally distraught during the interview because she felt that there was not a moment to lose and that it would be senseless to use the volunteers at a time when even the suicide weapon could not hope to turn the battle.
   c) Reitsch did win Hitler's permission to allow the development and planning to go on so that when he considered the proper time had come, the plan could immediately be put into

operation. The interview closed with Hitler's remark that he did not want to be bothered with the idea again until he gave the order and declared the time as ripe.

8. **Presenting the plan to the GAF General Staff:** The next step was to lay the whole matter before General Korton, Chief of the General Staff of the GAF, (later killed through the assassination attempt of 20 July 1944). Korton made light of the idea, but because of the left-handed support Hitler had given the plan, he was compelled to give his own half-hearted assistance. He appointed a member of his staff, a Colonel Heigl, to take command of the project. Heigl commanded Kampfgeschwader 200, the Luftwaffe bomber wing responsible for all sorts of special and highly secret activities, such as spy-dropping and intruding into Allied formations with captured aircraft. At this time too, Göring was informed of what had already been done. But the Reichsmarschall never bothered to call in any of the leaders or investigate the plan's possibilities. At first the appointment of Heigl was met with complete trust by Reitsch and the other volunteers, but it soon developed that he was completely the wrong man for the position.
9. **The suicide pledge:** At this time (March 1944) the group numbered about 70 to 80 men and the real framework of an organisation began to develop. Recruiting was very select and, for the time being no open efforts were made to gain new members. A pledge had been written and each new, accepted candidate was admitted to the circle of volunteer suicides only after he had affixed his signature to it. The approximate wording of the pledge was: "I hearby volunteer as a pilot of the manned glider bomb. I am convinced that this action will end with my death."
10. **Reitsch's position in the movement:** Reitsch claims to have stood first on the list of volunteers although she did not join the organisation as an actual member, preferring to maintain the freedom that her rather unusual position in German aviation gave her. Her reason for this is that she felt she could be of greater use outside the organisation because of the position she held with Hitler, Himmler, etc., in the event that something went wrong with the operational control of the project. Dr Benzinger also remained outside of the organisation, although Reitsch claims that he worked ceaselessly in perfecting his medical and psychological plans and was at all times prepared to join the volunteers in the execution of their mission.
11. **Misuse of the idea:** In KG 200, under Colonel Heigl, the self-sacrificing idea was falsely conceived from the beginning and the pure idealism that Reitsch claims for the volunteers was badly misused by Heigl and others. Almost at once the volunteers suspected that Heigl was glad of the opportunity to control such a weapon, believing that through it he hoped to reach some sort of military achievement for which he, a non-volunteer, would then win the glory and credit. The details of Heigl's mismanagement and the later non-idealistic conceptions that were given the idea, were carefully recorded by Lieutnant Lange. Reitsch suggests the complete evolution of the project and the contamination it underwent after it was turned over to KG 200 could best be obtained either from Lieutenant Lange or from the daily journal he kept at the time.
12. **Heinz Kensche, technical advisor:** The German Air Ministry was ordered by the Chief of the General Staff to supervise and direct the technical preparations. To head this work a staff engineer, Heinz Kensche, an outstanding glider expert, was selected. Kensche was one of the volunteers and applied for membership in KG 200 after signing the suicide pledge. Kensche designated Reitsch to undertake the testing of the Me 328 and to supervise the flying training of the volunteers as soon as the Me 328 had been declared acceptable.
13. **The Messerschmitt Me 328:** The Me 328 was originally intended as either a fighter or a fighter-bomber. It was developed jointly by Messerschmitt and DFS (Deutsche Forschungsanstalt für Segelflug), the German Glider Research Institute at Ainring, Germany. Originally it was intended to power the Me 328 with two Argus-Schmidt assemblies, but after the first experiments, development of the plane was stopped by the RLM.
    a) For the self-sacrificing project the Me 328 was to be used without powerplant as a piloted glider bomb. It was a small, one-seater plane, with very short wing-spread, approximately 4 to 5 metres. Its gliding range at 155 miles per hour was about five to one and at a speed of 465 miles per hour approximately twelve to one. Test flights to prepare it for the suicide flyers were made at Hörsching airfield in Austria near Linz.
    b) The Me 328 was not a self-starting plane and

was carried aloft by a Dornier 217, attached on top of the wings of the carrier plane. From here the pilot of the Me 328 could release himself from the Dornier and lift himself away from the larger plane. The test releases were made at heights varying between 9,000 to 18,000 feet. The Me 328 was tested in all forms of manoeuvres and aerobatics at speeds of 81/87 miles per hour to speeds of 465 miles per hour. Aerodynamically this plane did not compare favourably with most of the other German aircraft but for the purpose it was now intended, its capabilities were more than sufficient. The aeronautical characteristics most important for the intended use of the plane were:

1) Excellent visibility.
2) Ample cockpit space to afford the pilot sufficient room and comfort in controlling the aim.
3) Excellent manoeuvrability.
4) Good flight stability.

c) In the degrees required the Me 328 fulfilled all of these requirements. These tests at Hörsching airfield were completed in April 1944.

d) Thereupon the Flugzeugbau Gothaer Waggonfabrik in Gotha, Thuringia, was ordered to undertake the assembly-line production of the plane. Unexplained difficulties and delays prolonged the construction until it began to appear to Reitsch and her volunteers that there was some sort of official sabotage afoot to delay or prevent the suicide project. When it began to appear that long months would still be required before the Me 328 was available in any sufficient quantities, the suicide group began to look about for some sort of a makeshift plane that would still fulfil the purpose and, most important, be immediately available. The decision was reached to use a manned V-1.

14. **Manned V-1 as a suicide plane:** It was decided that the V-1 could be properly modified to suit the purpose in a matter of weeks. This modification programme began at once under the code name "Reichenberg," and was kept highly secret so that even the V-1 workers directly concerned with the modification did not suspect the real nature of their work. The V-1 alteration programme was put under the supervision of Director Lusser of the Dipl.-Ing. Fiedler Construction Bureau, which was located at the Henschel firm in Berlin-Schoenfeld. In a frantic 14 day period of work the V-1 was rebuilt into four separate types to fulfil both the training and mission requirements. In less than three weeks the four types were ready for test flying.

15. **V-1 types for the suicide project:** The fuselage of the V-1 was not greatly altered, the important changes required in modifying the plane were the installation of a pilot's compartment and the necessary instruments. The following four types were developed:

a) A single seater with sledge runners, without power plant, to be used as a glider for solo-flying training purposes.

b) A two-seater, dual control, without power plant, to be used as training plane for student and instructor.

c) A single seater with power unit, landing gear, and ailerons.

d) A single seater with power unit and no landing assembly, to be used on the operational missions.

16. **Test flying the V-1:** Reitsch claims that her offers to test-fly the V-1 were at first ignored by the Luftwaffe Testing Division in favour of using their own pilots for the job. Two pilots from the Division were assigned and both crashed, uninjured at the first landing. Then when both were seriously injured at the second attempt, Reitsch was called in and allowed to continue the test-hops.

a) She was assisted in this by Heinz Kensche. After about ten flights Reitsch was injured in a Berlin air raid. Kensche was then assisted by a Lieutenant Starbati, who was killed when his V-1 crashed in one of his early flights.

b) Starbati was replaced by a Sergeant Schenk who was also killed on a test-flight. Kensche himself narrowly escaped death when he bailed out as the V-1 fell out of control due to excessive vibrations at very low altitude. Reitsch claims that the cause of these accidents was at first impossible to determine. Later tests showed that they were due to the vibrations set up by the full power action of the Argus-Schmidt power units. This was also the first inkling of why at least 30% of the unmanned V-1s launched against England crashed due to mechanical failure before they reached their target. Extensive work was being conducted to eliminate this constructional defect when the war ended.

c) In spite of the danger and high fatality rate, these tests were considered successful and complete satisfaction was expressed by Reitsch that the V-1 would do for the suicide mission. It was felt that an average pilot would have no difficulty in properly manipulating the V-1, as the only danger was connected with landings and these were not required on the mission as landings were to be performed during the training programme chiefly by the very highly skilled instructors.

d) At first test flights were made without power unit. The V-1 was carried aloft by a Heinkel 111 in the same manner that the unmanned V-1s were launched against England after the launching sites were overrun by the invading Allied armies. The V-1 was attached to the right wing of the Heinkel between the right landing assembly and the fuselage. The pilot wore a throat microphone with which he communicated with the Heinkel crew and was released from the carrier plane by its pilot when the V-1 occupant gave the request. The landing was made at speeds which varied from 155 miles to 133 miles per hour and due to its steep angle of descent when flying without power, was extremely dangerous.

e) With power unit installed, the manned V-1 was even more dangerous. It was in testing these that both Lieutenant Starbati and Sergeant Schenk were killed. The intention was to train 4 or 5 men to land the plane safely. These would then be the instructors for the other and would themselves execute most of the landings. The end of the war, however, together with the previous deaths of several of the instructors prevented the completion of the programme.

17. **Training in V-1 tactics:** Elaborate plans for the shipping attack tactics were drawn up and substantial beginnings in this training had actually been made. The target ship was simulated by coloured smoke bombs which were released at an altitude of about 2,000 metres. Dives and approaches were then made to the cloud to test angles and necessary speeds. These clouds would maintain their density for quite some time and could be made to assume sizes that were but little larger than the larger naval vessels.

a) An intricate aiming device was also developed. This was a celluloid plate that enabled the pilot to compute the depth of the vessel below the water and then indicated how far from the ship the V-1 would have to crash into the water in order to allow the torpedo to pass beneath the keel of the vessel where it was to explode by the carefully timed fuse.

b) Reitsch claims that she is not fully conversant with the technical aspects of this aiming device but adds that competent engineers and technicians claimed a high degree of accuracy for it. The device was taken along in the suicide plane, but its biggest attribute was the results obtained in the Link-trainer type mechanism wherein the pilots could evaluate their points of impact for all types of major vessels through pure rote-memory.

c) The most important thing that had to be done carefully and accurately was to determine the distance from the ship that the V-1 was supposed to enter the water. The size and weight of the ship had to be judged exactly in computing this correctly. By a sliding scale on the apparatus before him the pilot was able to select his proper angle and maintain it correctly throughout his loss of altitude until his plane entered the water. The speed with which he was to make his descent was to be so great that anti-aircraft fire was to be practically useless in the ship's defence. Reitsch herself had tested the V-1 in dives at speeds in excess of 528 miles per hour. This impact was to literally disintegrate the V-1 and give the necessary impetus to the torpedo to continue on through the water at a pre-determined speed until it reached its proper position of explosion where the time fuse would automatically set it off. The pilot was to meet his end with typical Teutonic violence as the V-1 crashed into the water.

18. **The "too late" of German technology:** True, the technical development was not totally completed at the end of the war. This, however, cannot be chalked up as a technical failure. It was merely another example of the "too late" of German technology during the last years of the war. Had the war continued, the weapon would have been ready for operations that promised to be successful as all developments progressed with better results and

speed than any of the people involved had suspected possible. But even if the war had continued, it is likely that organisational difficulties would have prevented making operational use of the weapon long after it should have been ready in every other respect. Technically the Me 328 or the V-1 would amply have served the purpose. Operationally, the volunteers would have been ready for the execution of their missions. The only controlling factor was that both were "too late". The only serious handicap with which the movement had to contend, from its very conception, was the lack of appreciation and understanding with which the idea was met on the part of the Luftwaffe and other Nazi leaders.

19. **Improper "spiritual" evaluation:** An Air Force developed under the leadership of Göring was physically unable to properly evaluate or make intelligent use of such a weapon. Everywhere the idea was met with misunderstandings and ridicule.
    a) "That the spirit," Reitsch says, "with which Göring had infused the Luftwaffe was detrimental to our project was well known to all of us. We needed strong leadership, tempered with an idealism that matched our own. Most of all we needed a leader who saw the present military situation (March 1944) in the same degree of precariousness as we ourselves saw it. Unfortunately, very few of the higher Luftwaffe leaders appeared to entertain the slightest doubt that Germany would still win the war. We had hoped for some of this required leadership from Colonel Heigl but it soon became evident that he had no intention of being one of us and, worse yet, he placed individuals in responsible positions to plan and organise the project who had no more intention than he did to participate in the actual intention of the movement. No one held this against them, but the fact that such people should have had anything to do with the idea is added evidence of faulty Luftwaffe leadership. For instance, Heigl had an officer on his staff whose job was that of technical supervisor of the project.[1] Daily this officer proposed one fantastic idea after the other as to possible utilisation of the suicide volunteers. The volunteers were all ready to die, but only if by their deaths they were able to decisively turn the course of the war, and not to blow up some ammunition train on the Russian front as this technical supervisor repeatedly suggested. It appeared that everyone was ready to dream up mission after mission for our men to perform, all in utter conflict with the original idea of the movement. It appeared that the leaders we had been given felt that as long as they had men at their disposal who had indicated their willingness to die for Germany their only job was to find any sort of a mission, useless or otherwise, whereby they might be able to end their lives."

20. **Mistakes in training technique:** Reitsch describes as foolish even the way their training was begun. For days the volunteers were given simple physical exercises and pistol practice. All of which took valuable time in which they felt they could better be perfecting their flying and developing the proper psychological approach for their suicide mission.
    a) Lieutenant Lange, always the driving power of the movement, did what he could to save the idea and improve the method in which it was handled. But by virtue of his rank he could do nothing but obey orders and despair. He also tried to establish a flying programme that would properly train the volunteers but in this too he met with all sorts of difficulties until Reitsch again used her influence with the Luftwaffe Chief of Staff to get the programme established, again after the loss of considerable valuable time.

21. **Himmler's ideas regarding the suicide plan:** According to Reitsch it became clearer and clearer that the entire purpose of the suicide plan was slowly being destroyed by all of these mismanagements. In order to prevent this she asked for an was granted an interview with Himmler, who she hoped would be able to use his influence to bring some sort of order out of the chaos that was fast engulfing the movement. Himmler did not approve of the suicide idea as the group had developed it. He was not against the idea in principle, but preferred to use such men as were tired of living for one reason or another, were criminals, or incurably sick, all of whom could, by this grand suicide gesture, assure a place for their names for all time on the "honour scroll" of the German nation. If Reitsch and her volunteers were prepared to follow his suggestion he promised to furnish one of his own men in whose hands he felt the proper leadership of the project would be assured. Reitsch

immediately saw that this would be as bad as the mismanagement they were momentarily confronted with and was therefore compelled to turn down Himmler's offer.

22. **Situation at the time of the invasion:** At about this point the invasion of the west began and neither the Me 328 nor the V-1, nor the tactical training were ready for utilisation. The disappointment and heartbreak that Reitsch claims was felt by all those connected with the movement through idealistic motivation, was profound. Here the invasion that was to have been stopped by the "suicide squadron" had come too soon and after four to six days showed every indication of being successful. Immediately work on the project was speeded up but no one, with the exception of Lieutenant Lange and one or two others, had much heart left in the project.

23. **Introduction of the Fw 190 into the movement:** Several days after the invasion began and all efforts against it seemed doomed to immediate and dismal failure, Göring suddenly remember the existence of "his" suicide flyers. Colonel Heigl at once declared them available. The men themselves were astounded as they knew that no plane was yet available for the missions. Without consulting any of the group, Heigl and his technical assistants went quickly to work on plans to utilise a Focke-Wulf 190 that was to carry a 4,000lb bomb and was to be crashed into the target.
    a) Heigl reported to Göring that these Fw 190s would be ready in 14 days' time.
    b) To properly evaluate Heigl's promise it must be remembered that all of the volunteers were glider pilots and that some of them had never flown a motored plane except in the few hours of their recent training. And now in 14 days they were to fly high-powered fighter planes in extremely difficult manoeuvres.
    c) Additionally it must be remembered that no one had ever flown a Fw 190 with a 4,000lb bomb and no one could know if the landing gear and tyres would be strong enough, or if available runways were long enough, or most important, whether the Fw 190 would ever be able to leave the ground with such a load.
    d) Immediately following the news that Heigl had declared his suicide flyers as ready for operations in 14 days' time, came the even more overwhelming news that part of the volunteers would undertake the test-flights in the very next days and that if they should lose their lives in the test-drop their deaths would be recorded just as gloriously as if they had died in hurtling themselves at enemy naval craft. This was an expedient that grew out of the simple fact that no other test pilots could be found to attempt such a monstrous undertaking.
    e) Reitsch states that at this point any enthusiasm that might have been left among the volunteers quickly vanished and that only the love of the Fatherland and the hope that something useful might still be accomplished with the suicide plan, kept some semblance of organisation alive among the suicide flyers.

24. **Hitler intervenes:** Reitsch, still independent of any sort of military control, hoped to save something of the original intention and to accomplish this she again went to Himmler. When Himmler realised what was intended in using the Fw 190 he immediately took the story to Hitler, from whom an order was at once forthcoming forbidding the use of the Fw 190 as it had been intended and even more strongly forbidding the test-flying of this or any plane by the inexperienced suicide pilots. Together with this came a strong rebuke from Hitler to the commander of KG 200.
    a) Thereupon a normal, though highly speeded up, training programme in powered aircraft was inaugurated for the volunteers. One of the prime purposes of this training was an immediate transition programme to acquaint the men thoroughly with the Fw 190. From this it was fearfully suspected that some sort of intention still existed to utilise the suicide flyers in the use of the 4,000lb bomb laden Fw 190.

25. **The revised suicide pledge:** The suspicion that it was still the intention to use the Fw 190 was increased even more when a Major Semper, chief of staff of Colonel Heigl, destroyed the original pledge and substituted one that ready approximately as follows:
    a) "I hereby volunteer as a suicide pilot of any aircraft my superiors select. I am convinced that this action will end with my death."
    b) In order to railroad the volunteers into signing this pledge, Lieutenant Lange and ten of his closest companions were separated from the rest of the group and sent to another field. The pledge was read to them and through

the advice of Lange each man refused to sign. Then the pledge was read to the remaining 60 to 70 men, who were told that Lange and the small group had signed, whereupon, in allegiance to Lange, all of the larger group affixed their signatures to the new pledge.

c) As soon as the signatures of the 60 to 70 men had been obtained, Lange and his small group of companions were removed from KG 200 and offered to the 9th Flying Corps as competent fighter-bomber pilots. That this was merely an attempt to do away with Lange and his group was perfectly clear. They had just completed their primary training with the Fw 190 and each had accomplished only one practice bomb release, of which not a man had hit his target. This then was the training of men who were accepted as accomplished pilots by the 9th Corps.

26. **The movement gets a new commanding officer:** After these developments Reitsch spent almost all of her time in attempting to win better conditions and rectifying the wrongs already perpetrated. Dr Benzinger, who had remained with the movement from the beginning, now became so disheartened that he separated himself from the project altogether. As Reitsch knew that by virtue of the tricked pledges many of the volunteers were irrevocably committed to whatever misuse the leaders of KG 200 decided to put them, she tried a new tactic and through the help of Generaloberst von Greim, was able to have Colonel Heigl removed as commanding officer.

a) His successor as commanding officer of KG 200 was Lt Colonel Baumbach, a popular and highly successful combat leader, whose accomplishments were well known to Germans and Allies alike.

b) But even under Baumbach there was little that could still be hoped for by way of rectifying the errors that had been made in the management of the suicide squadron. Baumbach had far too many responsibilities to devote much time to the personal direction of the suicide flyers. The only actual accomplishment for which everyone was exceedingly grateful was that the insane 4,000lb bomb Fw 190 idea was quickly discarded.

27. **The end of the suicide movement:** In March 1945, with Baumbach still trying to achieve some workable plan for the utilisation of the suicide flyers that might even yet have had some effect on the current situation, it finally had to be admitted that the military situation was such that nothing could be hoped for from a full-scale suicide programme. The project was terminated and the volunteers sent to other tactical units where they might still be of some military value. Technical development and construction of the Me 328 and V-1 suicide versions had also continued until March 1945. This, too, was now closed out.

a) "And so," Reitsch concludes, "died an idea that was born of fervent and holy idealism, only to be misused and mismanaged at every turn by people who never understood how men could offer their lives simply for an idea in which they believed."

b) Reitsch's evaluation of the idea is that it might have been decisive had it been fully ready for utilisation at the time of the western invasion. After the invasion was a success she claims that it was clear to her, to Lt Lange, and other leaders that the proper time for its use was gone for all time.

c) It appears clear that she and others who were closely connected with the movement actually believed until the "premature" invasion that the "suicide squadron", properly used, could really have won the war for Germany.

28 Nov 45
Robert E. Work,
Captain, Air Corps,
Chief Interrogator,
Air Division, HQ, U.S. Forces in Austria,
Air Interrogation Unit.
DS 73737/1 (25)/R.11 300 9/46 R

ME 328 IN PROFILE

ALL ARTWORKS BY ZOLTÁN CSOMBÓ

Messerschmitt P 79/1 with single Schmidt pulsejet from Messerschmitt report circa August 1941.

Messerschmitt P 79/4 with single Schmidt pulsejet from Messerschmitt report circa August 1941.

Messerschmitt Me 328 Jäger Ausführung I with two Argus pulsejets, single Seppeler generator and 2 x MG 151/20, from Messerschmitt report dated March 31, 1942.

Messerschmitt Me 328 Jäger Ausführung I with four pulsejets, from Messerschmitt report dated March 31, 1942.

Messerschmitt Me 328 Jäger Ausführung I with swept wings and tailplanes plus wheeled undercarriage, from Messerschmitt report dated March 31, 1942.

Messerschmitt Me 328 Jäger Ausführung I with very short swept wings and landing skid, from Messerschmitt report dated March 31, 1942.

Messerschmitt Me 328 Jäger Ausführung II, from Messerschmitt report dated March 31, 1942.

Messerschmitt Me 328 Jäger Ausführung II, lighter version, from Messerschmitt report dated March 31, 1942.

Messerschmitt Me 328 Bordflugzeug from Messerschmitt report dated July 7, 1942.

Messerschmitt Me 328 Bordflugzeug m. Kreisflügel from Messerschmitt report dated July 7, 1942.

Messerschmitt Me 328 V1 in its original glider configuration, circa August 1942.

Messerschmitt Me 328 V1 with underwing pulsejets installed, circa August-September 1942.

Messerschmitt Me 328 V2 in its original glider configuration, circa November 1942.

Messerschmitt Me 328 V2 with unclad pulsejets installed and skid extended, circa May-July 1943.

Messerschmitt Me 328 V2 with pulsejets fitted with aerodynamic fairings, circa May-July 1943.

Messerschmitt Me 328 Skizze 17 high-wing design from DFS report dated June 22, 1943.

Messerschmitt Me 328 Skizze 18 high-wing design from DFS report dated June 22, 1943.

Messerschmitt Me 328 Skizze 19 high-wing design from DFS report dated June 22, 1943.

Messerschmitt Me 328 Skizze 21 high-wing design from DFS report dated June 22, 1943.

Messerschmitt Me 328 Skizze 23 high-wing design from DFS report dated June 22, 1943.

Messerschmitt Me 328 Skizze 24 high-wing design from DFS report dated June 22, 1943.

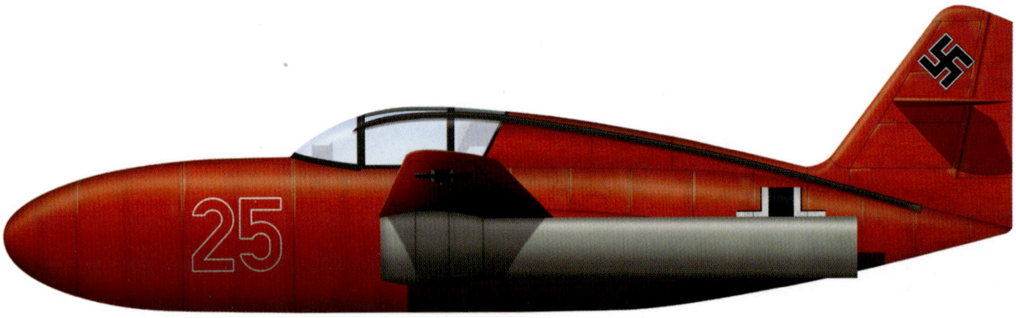

Messerschmitt Me 328 Skizze 25 high-wing design from DFS report dated June 22, 1943.

Messerschmitt Me 328 Skizze 26 high-wing design from DFS report dated June 22, 1943.

Messerschmitt Me 328 Skizze 29 high-wing and V-tail design from DFS report dated June 22, 1943.

Messerschmitt Me 328 with lengthened fuselage, swept low-set wings and conventional tail, from AVA report dated July 14, 1943.

Messerschmitt Me 328 with lengthened fuselage, swept high-set wings and V-tail, from AVA report dated July 14, 1943.

Messerschmitt Me 328 high-wing design on rail-launch wagon from AVA report dated July 16, 1943.

Messerschmitt Me 328 V02 as it appeared at Peenemünde circa August 1943, prior to static pulsejet testing.

Messerschmitt Me 328 Skizze 1 low-wing design with short nose, from DFS report dated August 30, 1943.

Messerschmitt Me 328 Skizze 1 low-wing design with long nose, from DFS report dated August 30, 1943.

Messerschmitt Me 328 Skizze 2 low-wing design with wingtip tanks and bomb (no engines), from DFS report dated August 30, 1943.

Messerschmitt Me 328 Skizze 2 low-wing design with wingtip tanks and bomb, from DFS report dated August 30, 1943.

Messerschmitt Me 328 Skizze 3 low-wing design from DFS report dated August 30, 1943.

Messerschmitt Me 328 Skizze 4 low-wing design from DFS report dated August 30, 1943.

Messerschmitt Me 328 Skizze 5 low-wing design from DFS report dated August 30, 1943.

Messerschmitt Me 328 Skizze 6 low-wing design from DFS report dated August 30, 1943.

Messerschmitt Me 328 Skizze 7 low-wing design with high-set tailplanes from DFS report dated August 30, 1943.

Messerschmitt Me 328 Skizze 8 low-wing design from DFS report dated August 30, 1943.

Messerschmitt Me 328 Skizze 9 low-wing design from DFS report dated August 30, 1943.

Messerschmitt Me 328 Skizze 10 low-wing design from DFS report dated August 30, 1943.

Messerschmitt Me 328 Skizze 11 low-wing design with reprofiled tail and larger fin (no engines) from DFS report dated August 30, 1943.

Messerschmitt Me 328 Skizze 11 low-wing design with reprofiled tail and larger fin from DFS report dated August 30, 1943.

Messerschmitt Me 328 Skizze 12 high-wing design with raised tailplanes from DFS report dated August 30, 1943.

Messerschmitt Me 328 T from design drawing dated September 20, 1943.

Messerschmitt Me 328 C from design drawing dated October 6, 1943.

Messerschmitt Me 328 Skizze 30 low-wing design with raised tailplanes from DFS report dated October 26, 1943.

Messerschmitt Me 328 B glider in pre-take-off condition with jettisonable undercarriage attached, from design drawing circa July 1943.

Messerschmitt Me 328 B glider in flight condition, with fixed nosewheel still attached but mainwheels jettisoned, from design description of June 1944.

Messerschmitt Me 328 B glider in landing condition with tandem flap-type skids extended, from design description of June 1944.

Messerschmitt Me 328 B self-sacrifice variant with torpedo, based on design description of June 1944.§

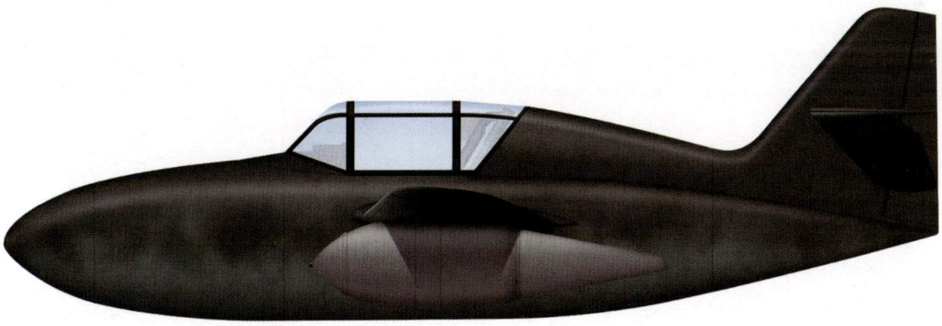

Messerschmitt Me 328 B self-sacrifice variant with underwing bombs, based on wind tunnel model photographed circa May 1945.

ENDNOTES

INTRODUCTION

1 Such as Berne Telegram No. 4523, dated September 21, 1944, from TNA AIR 40/206.
2 United States Strategic Air Forces (USSAF), more commonly known as United States Strategic Air Forces in Europe (USSAFE).
3 Given Voigt's testimony, it seems as though the cockpit is more likely to have been sound-proofed in an attempt to shut out the noise of the engines.
4 ADRC/T-2 2006/2 Air Technical Intelligence Review Report No. F-IR-6-RE Survey of Messerschmitt Factory and Functions, Oberammergau, Germany 31 July 1945
5 The only mentions over the course of 516 pages are during an interrogation of Voigt on July 26, 1945, and a line on a table labelled 'systematics in respect to aileron effect'. The interrogation report says merely: "Me 328 (single seat small jet bomber, VI engine). The Me 328 was not ordered in quantities."
6 Messerschmitt's archive at Oberammergau seems to have been captured mostly intact by American forces at the end of the war, with many documents concerning discontinued mid-war types such as the Me 264 surviving. Far fewer Me 328 documents made it into the Allies' collection of German reports and many of those that did came from JSF or Gotha. A huge part of the Me 328's history appears to have gone up in smoke with the deliberate destruction of documents at the DFS's Ainring headquarters shortly prior to its capture by the Allies. See CIOS Evaluation Report 92, 13 June 1945 Target: Deutsche Forschungsanstalt für Segelflug. Location: Ainring (Z 4026) & Prien (R 4528). Investigated by Maj. Harkinson, F/Lt. Ewans, Capt. Bratt. "1. Ainring – Undamaged by bombing, but a large amount of equipment had been dispersed to neighbouring villages. All important documents were destroyed."

C1. ORIGINS. 1928 TO FEBRUARY 1942

1 BIOS Final Report No. 1777 Item No. 26 Research and Development of Impulsive Ducts in Germany by A. K. Oppenheim, circa 1947
2 Ibid.
3 ADRC/T-2 2039/287 Das Schmidtrohr by Paul Schmidt. Note: This document is date-stamped June 15, 1945, but appears to have been written during 1944.
4 Compared to, say, a Messerschmitt Bf 109 which had a wingspan of around 9.9m depending on the variant.
5 AHB6/163 Argus Motoren, Die Vorgeschichte des „Flakzielgeräts 76", 12.4.44
6 Ibid.
7 It would later be designated 8-292. See ADRC/T-2 2260/801 DFS Stellungnahme zur Begutachtung des Gerätes 8-292 durch Herrn A. Lippisch Juli 1941
8 Defense Technical Information Center C-1179/29468 US Navy Project Squid Technical Memorandum No. Pr.-4 The Aero-Resonator Power Plant of the V-1 Flying Bomb by Ing. Guenther Diedrich translated by A. Kahane June 30, 1948
9 AHB6/163 Argus Motoren, Die Vorgeschichte des „Flakzielgeräts 76", 12.4.44
10 AHB6/163 Argus Motoren, EA II – Aktenvermerk Nr. 7/39, Betr. Besprechung bei Argus am 30.11.39 über „Luftstrahltriebwerke"
11 Defense Technical Information Center C-1179/29468 US Navy Project Squid Technical Memorandum No. Pr.-4 The Aero-Resonator Power Plant of the V-1 Flying Bomb by Ing. Guenther Diedrich translated by A. Kahane June 30, 1948
12 Such a fortunate combination, in fact, that nearly every later effort to improve upon it would be doomed to failure—though none of those involved with the powerplant during its early years realised just what a 'sweet spot' Diedrich had hit upon so quickly.
13 BA-MA RL3/780 RLM LC 7/III Gegenwärtiger Stand und künftige Entwicklungsarbeit auf dem Gebiete des Schnellfluges mit Strahltriebwerk 14.10.38
14 IWM FD4355/45 Vol. 4/246 Messerschmitt—Aktennotiz! Herrn Voigt, Probü, Mitteilung Nr. 9/41 10.1.41
15 ADIK 129/638 BMW Arbeitsplan für die L-Entwicklung im Geschäftsjahr 1941/42 7.2.41
16 ADRC/T-2 2217/585 Messerschmitt Flugzeuge mit Strahlrohren, various dates 22.5.41-1.8.41. It is worth mentioning here that these are preliminary figures specific to this particular time—they are the figures Messerschmitt was given at this point, and used in its considerations, and in no way reflect the actual values of the as-built engines which came later.
17 ADRC/MAP 5018/389 Me 262 mit Jumo 210 G (700 PS) + 2 x 500kg 11.5.41
18 ADRC/T-2 2217/585 Messerschmitt Flugzeuge mit Strahlrohren, various dates 22.5.41-1.8.41.
19 ADRC/T-2 5009/503 Hochstgeschwindigkeiten P 79/13 1.8.41
20 ADRC/MAP 5009/500 P 79 Gewichtsaufstellung Vergleich mit Me 109 F und Me 262 28.7.41
21 ADRC/MAP 5009/497 Polarenaufstellung P 79 Umrechnung aus Me 109 D 31.7.41
22 ADRC/MAP 5009/481 Messerschmitt Baubeschreibung P 79, 1.8.41
23 That designation, 'P 79/13c', was evidently used before the end of August 1941 by Woldemar Voigt in describing the P 79 to a third party. See IWM FD4355/45 Vol. 5/649 Messerschmitt Aktenvermerk Besprechung mit dem RLM Berlin, den 29. August 1941
24 Erinnerungen by Alexander M. Lippisch, Luftfahrtverlag Axel Zuerl 1977
25 Iowa State University Library Special Collections and University Archive MS-243 Box 17 Folder 42 Messerschmitt Projektbaubeschreibung Li P 05 27. August 1941
26 IWM FD4355/45 Vol. 5/649 Messerschmitt Aktenvermerk Besprechung mit dem RLM Berlin, den 29. August 1941
27 Indeed, Lippisch's P 05 description of August 27 already includes a reference to the 'Li 163', suggesting that this change had been requested by him and Udet was simply agreeing to it.
28 IWM FD4355/45 Vol. 5/649 Messerschmitt Aktenvermerk Besprechung mit dem RLM Berlin, den 29. August 1941
29 Risky because the rocket fuel required by these designs was highly volatile and extremely hazardous to work with—posing a very real threat to the life and health of both ground crew and pilots.
30 ADRC/MAP 5041/81 RLM Nr. 108/12.41 gKdos. Protokoll Betr.: Lastannahmenvorbesprechung Me P 1079. Vorg.: Besprechung am 17.12.1941. 30.12.41
31 ADRC/MAP 5041/79 Datenblatt P 79 21.12.41
32 BA-MA RL 3/1003 RLM Flugzeug-Programm Lieferplan Nr. 21 1.2.1942
33 ADRC/T-2 3372/1159 Messerschmitt Aktenvermerk Betr.: Projektauslieferung P 1079 V1-V3 (Elt. Ausrüstung) 3.2.42
34 ADRC/MAP 5002/383 Messerschmitt Projektbüro Festlegungen Me 328 (P 79) 10. Februar 1942
35 ADRC/T-2 3372/1167 Messerschmitt Aktennotiz Betrifft: Arbeitsunterbringung Me 328 (P 1079). Vorgang: Rücksprache bei Herrn Prof. Messerschmitt am 11.2.42. Augsburg, den 12.2.42
36 Ibid.
37 IWM FD4355/45 Vol. 4/493 GL/C-E 2 Nr. 1272/42 (I) Geh. Reidenbach an die Firma Messerschmitt A.G. Betr.: P 1079 17.2.1942
38 IWM FD4355/45 Vol. 4/492 Messerschmitt an das Reichsluftfahrtministerium Herrn Generaling. Reidenbach GL/C-E 2 Nr. 1272/42 (I) 17.2.42 P 1079 24.2.1942

C2. LIGHT FIGHTER AND MULTIROLE. MARCH 1942 TO AUGUST 1942

1 ADRC/MAP 5012/56 Messerschmitt Flugzeuge mit Strahlrohren Me 328, 31.3.42
2 ADRC/MAP 5042/302 DFS Windkanalmessungen am Modell Me 328 von H. Frosch Bericht Nr. 42/6. 30. August 1943
3 IWM FD4355/45 Vol. 1/220 Messerschmitt ‚Kameraden!' am 25.3.42
4 IWM Milch 13/115 GL-Besprechung unter dem Vorsitz des Staatssekretärs Generalfeldmarschall Milch am Dienstag, dem 14 April 1942, vorm. 10 Uhr, im Reichsluftfahrtministerium
5 IWM Milch 62/5190 Besprechungsnotiz Nr. 67/42 g.Kdos. Reichsjägerhof Rominten, 19.4.42
6 IWM Milch 13/175 Stenographischer Bericht über die GL-Besprechung unter dem Vorsitz des Staatssekretärs Generalfeldmarschall Milch am Dienstag, dem 21. April 1942, 15 Uhr.
7 IWM Milch Vol. 13/221 Stenographischer Bericht über die GL-Besprechung unter dem Vorsitz des Staatssekretärs

Generalfeldmarschall Milch am Montag, dem 27. April 1942, Vorm. 10 Uhr
8 *Willy Messerschmitt Pioneer of Aviation Design* by Erbert, Kaiser and Peters, p178
9 IWM Milch 13/306 GL-Besprechung unter dem Vorsitz des Staatssekretärs Generalfeldmarschall Milch am Dienstag, dem 5. Mai 1942, vorm. 10 Uhr im Reichsluftfahrtministerium
10 IWM Milch 62/5199 Besprechungsnotiz Nr. 77/42 g.Kdos. Insterburg, den 9.5.1942, 12.35-13.30 Uhr
11 IWM Milch 14/582 Stenographischer Bericht über die GL-Besprechung unter Vorsitz des Staatssektretärs Generalfeldmarschall Milch am Dienstag, dem 19. Mai 1942, 10 Uhr im Reichsluftfahrtministerium
12 In fact the Me 329 would not be abandoned at this time. Rather, it would outlive Croneiss himself, who died in November 1942, surviving into 1943. See ADRC/MAP 4002/336 Messerschmitt Projekt Me 329 Februar 1943
13 Defense Technical Information Center C-1179/29468 US Navy Project Squid Technical Memorandum No. Pr.-4 The Aero-Resonator Power Plant of the V-1 Flying Bomb by Ing. Guenther Diedrich translated by A. Kahane June 30, 1948. It seems more likely that, in fact, a Bf 110 was fitted with a pulsejet below its fuselage—not a Bf 109. Indeed, a photograph may exist showing just such a configuration. Certainly, Argus did employ a Bf 110 with a pulsejet installed above its tail.
14 ADRC/T-2 8031/275 Messerschmitt Flugbericht Nr. 772/1 3.7.42
15 IWM FD4355/45 Vol. 4/197 Messerschmitt an H. Fettermann, AB. Betrifft: Me 264. 26.4.41
16 Apparently on March 10, 1942. See Endnote 17 below.
17 ADIK 149/248 Der Oberbefehlshaber der Luftwaffe, Führungsstab I T Nr. 699/42 g.Kdos (1) H. Qu. 24.4.42 Betr.: Me 264. Bezug: St/GL Nr. 200/42 g.Kdos. v. 10.3.42
18 ADRC/T-2 3216/75 Messerschmitt Me 328 als Bordflugzeug, unter dem Gesichtspunkt der Leistungssteigerung des Flugzeuges, sowie wirtschaftlicher und sparstoffsparender Möglichkeiten für den Tragwerksbau. 7. Juli 1942
19 ADRC/T-2 2211/206 Messerschmitt Vorläufige Baubeschreibung des Fernstkampfflugzeuges Me 364 als 6motorige Weiterentwicklung der Me 264 Juli 1942
20 Testpiloten by Wolfgang Späte, Aviatic Verlag, 1993.
21 In his original German article for Späte, Klöckner here inserts a quote from Johann Wolfgang von Goethe's famous 1782 poem Erlkönig or 'King of the Fairies'—a story about a child killed by the titular supernatural being. At the end of the poem, the child's father races to rescue him, only to find him already dead. Klöckner's quote is the penultimate line: "Erreicht den Hof mit Mühe und Not" which literally translates as "He reaches the farm with effort and urgency". It could also be translated less literally, as "He reaches the farm desperate and exhausted". Klöckner's use of this quote is to illustrate his race to reach the toilet ahead of his flight, hence the use of an English substitute term here: "He reaches the farm by the skin of his teeth." It is implied that he gets there in time, barely—whereas the child's father in Goethe's ballad did not.
22 Air being pushed into the inlet by the forward motion of the aircraft through it.

C3. FLYING ARTILLERY TO VULKAN. SEPTEMBER TO DECEMBER 1942

1 IWM GDC 15/103 Messerschmitt Projektbüro Technischer Bericht TB Nr. 70/42 Me 328. Sonderaktion zur Entwicklung und Fertigung. Bericht Voigt 1.9.42
2 As mentioned previously, SS was the second highest priority that could be given to a German aircraft development programme. The highest was DE.
3 Rechlin E 7 RS Erprobungs-Nr. 52 763 Die 570kg-Raketenbombe SC 500 RS I als überschweres vom Flugzeug abschiessbares Raketengeschoss by Grauerholz 14.4.44, reprinted in its entirety in *Waffen Revue* Nr. 46, Journal-Verlag Schwend GmbH
4 IWM GWY 1486 Trial drops of SC 500 RS rocket-assisted bombs over the Lebasee on April 28, 1942
5 The Air Ministry Technical Office's GL/C-E 6 department dealt with projectile weapons and ammunition.
6 Sicromal, or SiCromAl, refers to a series of ferritic heat-resisting stainless steels with varying amounts of silicon, chromium and aluminium. It was evidently supplied by the Böhler company and German engine manufacturers such as BMW used it to make piston engine turbocharger components. It remains in use today with applications including furnace construction, high-temperature conveyors and heat treatment systems.
7 Deep drawing is where a sheet metal blank is shaped by the action of a mechanical punch pushing it into or onto a forming die.
8 IWM FD4355/45 Vol. 4/777 Messerschmitt an Herrn Brigadeführer Croneiss 15.9.42
9 AHB6-163 Argus Die Vorgeschichte des „Flakzielgeräte 76". 12.4.44
10 It seems likely that the pilot was a man named Rudolf 'Gretchen' Ziegler. Evidence available elsewhere suggests that he conducted more test flights in the early Me 328 prototypes than anyone else—including powered flights. It would appear that the general lack of information available about Ziegler and his work may, anecdotally, be a result of his premature death during the war while testing a pressure cabin. American historian David Myhra conducted a number of postwar interviews with DFS personnel concerning the DFS 228 and DFS 346 high-altitude aircraft and one of his subjects, Meyer, recalled: "In 228/346 a large parachute was placed in the cockpit cabin. The cabin itself was attached to the fuselage centre section by four explosive bolts allowing the cabin to break away from the aircraft in case of an emergency. The 346 was designed to reach 30km but our cockpit design didn't work out as planned. The continuous problem we had was that we couldn't make it tight enough and thus keep it pressurised at altitude. Anyway, our DFS test pilot Ziegler died as a result of the failed testing." The full text is available in part five of Myhra's somewhat oddly named five-part ebook-only Oral History of Germans Taken to the USSR with Their Obsolete DFS 346, self-published in 2013
11 IWM GDC 10/14206 Tätigkeitsbericht der Deutschen Forschungsanstalten und -Institute. Stand September 1942
12 ADRC/T-2 3777/165 Wilhelm Schmidding Werk Bodenbach. Bericht über den Besuch das Herrn Dipl. Ing. Bernd bei der DFS ‚Ernst Udet' in Ainring und Fliegerhorst Hörsching von 2.-4./11.1942
13 USSAFE Office of Asst. Chief of Staff A-2 Technical Intelligence Report No. E-21 Subject: Visit to the Aircraft Construction Institute of the DFS at Prien. 7 July 1945
14 IWM FD4355/45 Vol. 4/764 Messerschmitt an Probü 12.10.42
15 Lieferplan Nr. 222, g.Kdos.Nr. 4863/42 Flugzeug-Programm V-Muster (Messerschmitt AG) 1.11.42
16 Messerschmitt had originally envisioned the Me 328's fuselage being made from welded sheet steel—see Chapters 1 and 2—and had very slowly been constructing a single example throughout 1942. This solitary airframe is identified as the 'Me 328 V02' in Messerschmitt Programm Me 328 B—Bau von 300 Flugzeugen, dated December 15, 1942, and available at IWM FD4925/45. The separate Me 328 V2, without the '0', was a different aircraft—the second DFS-made wooden-skinned prototype. The first three Me 328s were therefore the Me 328 V1, Me 328 V2 and Me 328 V02.
17 ADRC/T-2 3349/474 Messerschmitt Flugbericht Nr. 848/1 Flugzeugführer Baur Me 328 V2 Flug am 5.11.42 in Hörsching.
18 ADRC/MAP 5041/54 Messerschmitt Datenblatt Me 328 B 25.11.42
19 BA-MA RL 36-60 Erprobungskommando 16 Peenemünde-West a./Usedom Br. B. Nr.: 37/42 g.Kdos. 3.12.42
20 In his 1983 book Der Streng Geheime Vogel Me 163, Verlag für Wehrwissenschaften, München
21 The term used by Späte here is 'donnerbock', which translates literally as 'thunder buck' or 'thunder goat' but which, in practice, refers to a highly-tuned, modified and/or rather noisy speed machine—such as a customised motorcycle.
22 ADIK 4081/62 DFS Abteilung Segelflug u. Flugzeugkonstruktion Untersuchungen über Startmöglichkeiten Me 328. „Mistelschlepp" Me 328 auf Do 217 7.12.42
23 NARA T321-59/4807339 St/GL GL/C-Nr. 845/42 g.K. (E/J) St/GL—Befehl Nr. 480 Betrifft: Entwicklungs- und Beschaffungsprogramm „Vulkan" 10. Dez. 1942

C4. JSF TO THE 'STOP' ORDER. DECEMBER 1942 TO SEPTEMBER 1943

1 BA-MA RL 36/62 Messerschmitt Protokoll Me 328 Nr. 4 2.10.42. This document also contains the earliest known

reference to launching the Me 328 from railway lines: "Start with high flight weights. For this purpose, as for the Me 163, a launch car for rail launch is being developed by Rheinmetall-Borsig in collaboration with the Reichsbahn (powder rockets, central guide rail). " For further details of this unusual proposal, see page 104.
2 BA-MA RL 36/62 Messerschmitt Protokoll Me 328 Nr. 5 27.10.42
3 IWM FD4925/45 Messerschmitt Programm Me 328 B—Bau von 300 Flugzeugen 15.12.42
4 ADIK 4003/60 Messerschmitt Projektübergabe Me 328 B 14.12.42
5 ADIK 4004/494 Messerschmitt Me 328 B Leichtes Schnellkampfflugzeug 15.12.42
6 ADRC/T-2 3358/898 DFS Vorläufiges Ergebnisse der Flugerprobung mit Argus-TL-Triebwerken 17.12.42
7 The LS likely standing for Lastensegler or 'cargo glider', a DFS 230 in this case.
8 IWM FD4355/45 Vol. 4/738 Messerschmitt an Herrn Voigt, Herrn Seitz, Probü 18.10.42
9 IWM Milch 18/4029 Stenographischer Bericht über die GL-Besprechung unter Vorsitz von Oberst Vorwald am Sonnabend, dem 16. Januar 1943, 10 Uhr im Reichsluftfahrtministerium
10 Indeed, the post-meeting summary simply recorded: "At the Messerschmitt company, work on the Me 328 and Me 262 jet fighters needs to be pushed forward more quickly". See ADIK 154/470 Bericht Nr. 60 über die Amtschefbesprechung vom 16.1.1943
11 IWM Milch 18/4129 Stenographischer Bericht über die GL-Besprechung unter Vorsitz von General Doerstling am Dienstag, dem 16. Januar 1943, 9 Uhr im Reichsluftfahrtministerium
12 NARA T321-59/807329 Lieferplan Flugzeug-Programm Studie 1015 g.Kdos. Nr. 15384/43 10.2.1943
13 ADIK 154/419 Bericht Nr. 64 über die Amtschefbesprechung vom 11.2.1943
14 NARA T321-54/4800303 Ärztlicher Vorschlag über die Anwendung bemannter Geschosse (nach einem Vortrag vor den Herren Baeumker und Georgii am 8. und 9. Februar 1943). Th. Benzinger 16.11.1943
15 USSAFE Technical Intelligence Report No. E-21 Subject: Visit to the Aircraft Construction Institute of the DFS at Prien 7 July 1945
16 The total number of Me 328s, as of mid-February 1943, was still five: two completed, three still unfinished. These were the now-destroyed DFS-made Me 328 V1; the airworthy DFS-made Me 328 V2; the unfinished DFS-made Me 328 V3; the unfinished DFS-made Me 328 V4 and the unfinished steel-skinned Messerschmitt-made Me 328 V02. These were all (at least nominally, since the V4 was said to have a different cockpit position) of the Me 328 A type.
17 ADRC/MAP 5042/302 DFS Windkanalmessungen am Modell Me 328 von H. Frosch Bericht Nr. 42/6 30. August 1943
18 It is uncertain exactly when the first round took place or for how long—but this was certainly the second of two distinct phases of testing.
19 IWM GDC 3597 (A) Luftfahrtforschungsanstalt Hermann Göring Braunschweig Institut für Aerodynamik Versuche im 2.8m Hochgeschwindigkeitskanal der LFA an Argus-Schubrohren II. Teil. 22.2.1943
20 ADRC/T-2 3595/261 Leistungsvergleich Me 262—Me 328 C. Augsburg, den 3.3.43 Pr/Sz/Ste
21 ADRC/MAP 5042/416 DFS Windkanalmessungen am Modell Me 328 (Fortsetzung I) von H. Frosch Bericht Nr. 42/6a 22. Juni 1943
22 TNA AIR 40/206 BAL des RLM bei Firma Jacobs-Schweyer GmbH, Flugzeugbau, Darmstadt, März 1943
23 IWM GDC 10/5307 aka GDC 3597 (B) Luftfahrtforschungsanstalt Hermann Göring Braunschweig Institut für Aerodynamik Versuche im 2.8m Hochgeschwindigkeitskanal der LFA an Argus-Schubrohren III. Teil. 24.9.1943
24 TNA AIR 40/206 BAL des RLM bei Firma Jacobs-Schweyer GmbH, Flugzeugbau, Darmstadt, April 1943
25 Exactly how this came about and why this decision—despite such seemingly unassailable political backing—was ultimately cancelled is explained in detail, complete with fully referenced archival sources, in Chapter 4 of Messerschmitt Development & Politics by the present author, published by Tempest Books in 2022.
26 ADRC/T-2 2459/469 JSF Bericht über des Tragflügels des Flugzeugmusters Me 328 A, Darmstadt-Flughafen, den 21. Mai 1943
27 ADRC/MAP 5042/289 Messerschmitt AG Büro Darmstadt Gewichte und Schwerpunkt Me 328 B (nach Stand vom 15.5.1943) 26. Mai 1943
28 TNA AIR 40/206 BAL des RLM bei Firma Jacobs-Schweyer GmbH, Flugzeugbau, Darmstadt, Mai 1943
29 ADRC/T-2 2049/692 Messerschmitt Abt. Windkanal WK-Bericht 1-43 Triebwerk Me 328 24.6.1943
30 IWM GDC 10/5307 aka GDC 3597 (B) Luftfahrtforschungsanstalt Hermann Göring Braunschweig Institut für Aerodynamik Versuche im 2.8m Hochgeschwindigkeitskanal der LFA an Argus-Schubrohren III. Teil. 24.9.1943
31 ADRC/MAP 5042/416 DFS Windkanalmessungen am Modell Me 328 (Fortsetzung I) von H. Frosch Bericht Nr. 42/6a 22. Juni 1943
32 TNA AIR 40/206 BAL des RLM bei Firma Jacobs-Schweyer GmbH, Flugzeugbau, Darmstadt, Juni 1943
33 IWM Milch 22/6401 Stenographischer Bericht über die GL-Besprechung am Freitag, dem 9. Juli 1943, 10 Uhr unter Vorsitz des Generalfeldmarschalls Milch im Reichsluftfahrtministerium
34 IWM GDC 10/5365 AVA Drei- und Sechskomponentenmessungen an einem Modell der Me 328 mit Bodenplatte, Bahndamm und Startwagen 16.7.1943
35 AIR 40/2001 ADIK Report No. 14/1946 Tailless Aircraft Development by Lippisch.
36 IWM Milch 23/6831 GL-Besprechung am Dienstag, dem 27 Juli 1943, 19 Uhr, unter Vorsitz des Generalfeldmarschalls Milch im Reichsluftfahrtministerium
37 ADRC/T-2 2602/0273 Büro-Darmstadt Aktenvermert 20.7.43
38 ADRC/T-2 2602/291 JSF 328 B Rumpfmittelstück Juli 1943
39 The original Messerschmitt Me 328 B proposal of December 1942 had specified an overall length of 7.05m—so the type had been stretched by 13cm while undergoing development at JSF.
40 IWM GDC 10/14208 Tätigkeitsbericht der Deutschen Forschungsanstalten und -Institute. Stand 1. August 1943. Deutsche Forschungsanstalt für Segelflug E.V. Flughafen Ainring, Freilassung/Obb., page 190
41 ADRC/MAP 5027/169 Messerschmitt Probü Aktenvermerk Bericht über Besprechung bei Fa. Junkers am 4.8.43 in Dessau; Ausrüstung Me 328 B mit 1 x TL Jumo 004 B (Besprechungen mit den Herren Dr. Franz, Decher und Böttger).
42 ADRC/MAP 5005/123 Messerschmitt 1. Bericht über Standlauf-Versuch mit Me 328 V02 17.8.43
43 TNA AIR 40/206 BAL des RLM bei Firma Jacobs-Schweyer GmbH, Flugzeugbau, Darmstadt, August 1943
44 DMM NL 130 Reitsch, 004a Flugbücher, Bordbuch Bü 181 B-1 PD+PN, W.Nr. 0218
45 ADRC/MAP 5042/302 DFS Windkanalmessungen am Modell Me 328 von H. Frosch Bericht Nr. 42/6 30. August 1943
46 IWM FD4355/45 Vol. 4/426 Messerschmitt an Herrn Dipl.-Ing. Seitz—Probü. Ihre "Stellungnahme der Entwicklungsleitung Me 328 zum Stoppbefehl vom 3.9.43". 29.9.43

C5. 'SELF-SACRIFICE' AIRCRAFT. SEPTEMBER 1943 TO NOVEMBER 1944

1 ADRC/T-2 2008/751 Tätigkeitsbericht der Deutschen Forschungsanstalt für Segelflug "Ernst Udet" Flughafen Ainring, Freilassing/Obb. vom 1. Dezember 1943 bis 31. März 1944
2 TNA AIR 40/206 BAL des RLM bei Firma Jacobs-Schweyer GmbH, Flugzeugbau, Darmstadt, Oktober 1943
3 IWM GDC 10/5307 aka GDC 3597 (B) Luftfahrtforschungsanstalt Hermann Göring Braunschweig Institut für Aerodynamik Versuche im 2.8m Hochgeschwindigkeitskanal der LFA an Argus-Schubrohren III. Teil. 24.9.1943
4 IWM FD4355/45 Vol. 4/426 Messerschmitt an Herrn Dipl.-Ing. Seitz—Probü. Ihre "Stellungnahme der Entwicklungsleitung Me 328 zum Stoppbefehl vom 3.9.43". 29.9.43
5 ADRC/MAP 5042/296 Me 328 C Horizontal- und Steiggeschwindigkeit über Höhe. Darmstadt, den 1.10.43
6 TNA AIR 40/206 BAL des RLM bei Firma Jacobs-Schweyer GmbH, Flugzeugbau, Darmstadt, September 1943
7 TNA AIR 40/206 BAL des RLM bei Firma Jacobs-Schweyer GmbH, Flugzeugbau, Darmstadt, Oktober 1943
8 IWM BIOS Interrogation Report No 187 Ref No AIU/IS/10 7 Oct 46 Main Interest: German Version of the Suicide Weapon (Gp.2) (M.O.S.A.P.)

9 NARA T321-54/4800292 Luftfahrt-Forschungsanstalt München (U. Henschke—H. Peters) Vorschlag zur Aufstellung einer Luftwaffen-Formation zur wirksamen Punktziel-Bekämpfung. Oktober 1943
10 As an aside, despite his incredibly bleak, not to say downright fanatical work in this area during the war, Henschke would later go on to become a pioneer in the use of radiotherapy to treat breast cancer.
11 ADRC/MAP 5042/486 DFS Windkanalmessungen am Modell Me 328 (Abschluss) von H. Frosch 26. Oktober 1943
12 NARA T321-54/4800305 Ministerialdirigent Baeumker Br. B. Nr. 99/43 gKdos. an Georgii 18. November 1943
13 TNA AIR 40/206 BAL des RLM bei Firma Jacobs-Schweyer GmbH, Flugzeugbau, Darmstadt, November 1943
14 TNA AIR 40/206 BAL des RLM bei Firma Jacobs-Schweyer GmbH, Flugzeugbau, Darmstadt, Dezember 1943
15 IWM GDC 10/14210 Tätigkeitsbericht der Deutschen Forschungsanstalt und Institute Stand Dezember 1943
16 ADRC/T-2 2008/751 Tätigkeitsbericht der Deutschen Forschungsanstalt für Segelflug "Ernst Udet" Flughafen Ainring, Freilassing/Obb. vom 1. Dezember 1943 bis 31. März 1944
17 NARA T321-54/4800290 Luftfahrtforschungsanstalt München E.V. Zur Vorlage! Die technischen Ausführungsmöglichkeiten für menschengesteuerte Bomben 12.1.44
18 TNA AIR 40/206 BAL des RLM bei Firma Jacobs-Schweyer GmbH, Flugzeugbau, Darmstadt, Januar 1944
19 IWM BIOS Interrogation Report No 187 Ref No AIU/IS/10 7 Oct 46 Main Interest: German Version of the Suicide Weapon (Gp.2) (M.O.S.A.P.)
20 NARA T321-54/4800370 Deutsche Akademie der Luftfahrtforschung—Der Kanzler. Herrn Generalfeldmarschall Milch als Vizepräsidenten der Akademie vorzulegen 25.2.44
21 ADIK 40/0019 Messerschmitt Büro-Darmstadt Aktenvermerk Me 328 B V1 8677/44 1.3.44
22 TNA AIR 40/206 BAL des RLM bei Firma Jacobs-Schweyer GmbH, Flugzeugbau, Darmstadt, Februar 1944
23 IWM BIOS Interrogation Report No 187 Ref No AIU/IS/10 7 Oct 46 Main Interest: German Version of the Suicide Weapon (Gp.2) (M.O.S.A.P.) and The Sky My Kingdom by Hanna Reitsch, translation by Lawrence Wilson, The Bodley Head, England, 1955
24 Als Hitler's Adjutant 1937-45 by Nicholas von Below, Hase & Koehler Verlag, Mainz, Germany, 1980
25 NARA T321-54/4800363 Abschrift, Geschwaderstab KG 200, Feldpost-Nr. L 02 187, Luftgau-Postamt: Berlin, Br.B.Nr. 38/44 g.Kdos. Technisch—taktische Forderungen für eine bemannte Gleitbombe 1. März 1944
26 NARA T321-54/4800362 Geschwaderstab KG 200, Feldpost-Nr. L 02 187, Luftgau-Postamt: Berlin, Br.B.Nr. 64/44 g.Kdos. 10 März 1944
27 NARA T321-54/4800394 Deutsche Akademie der Luftfahrtforschung der Kanzler Tgb.-Nr. 0033/gKdos (13b) München 2 BS, am 9.3.44
28 NARA T321-54/4800385 Prof. Georgii an Fliegerhaupt.-Ing. Kensche, Prüfstelle der Deutschen Versuchsanstalt für Luftfahrt e.V., Berlin-Adlershof, 16 März, 1944
29 IWM BIOS Interrogation Report No 187 Ref No AIU/IS/10 7 Oct 46 Main Interest: German Version of the Suicide Weapon (Gp.2) (M.O.S.A.P.)
30 NARA T321-54/4800387 Georgii an Herrn Prof. Dr. Ing. H. Schardin, Technische Akademie der Luftwaffe 16 März 1944
31 NARA T321-54/4800388 Lippisch an Herrn Dipl.-Ing. H.G. Snay, Forschungsanstalt Graf Zeppelin 16 März 1944
32 NARA T321-54/4800386 Georgii an Herr Oberst von Lossberg, Reichsluftfahrtministerium 18. März 1944
33 NARA T321-54/4800382 Georgii an Herrn Generalmajor Galland, General der Jagdflieger 18. März 1944
34 NARA T321-54/4800383 Georgii an Herrn Oberst Heigl, Geschwaderstab KG 200, Feldpost-Nr. L 02 187 18. März 1944
35 NARA T321-54/4800384 Georgii an Herrn Direktor H. Jacobs, Firma Schweyer Flugzeugbau, Darmstadt-Flughafen 18. März 1944
36 NARA T321-54/4800345 Georgii an Herr Professor, 23. März 1944
37 NARA T321-54/4800336 Forschungsführung des Reichsministers der Luftfahrt und Oberbefehlshabers der Luftwaffe, AZ: 3921/44 gKdos. 31. März 1944
38 NARA T321-54/4800332 SO-B-Einsatz mit Me 328 B Technische Beurteilung und Vorschläge 31.3.1944
39 TNA AIR 40/206 BAL des RLM bei Firma Jacobs-Schweyer GmbH, Flugzeugbau, Darmstadt, März 1944
40 ADRC/T-2 2008/751 Tätigkeitsbericht der Deutschen Forschungsanstalt für Segelflug "Ernst Udet" Flughafen Ainring, Freilassing/Obb. vom 1. Dezember 1943 bis 31. März 1944
41 IWM BIOS Interrogation Report No 187 Ref No AIU/IS/10 7 Oct 46 Main Interest: German Version of the Suicide Weapon (Gp.2) (M.O.S.A.P.)
42 TNA AIR 40/206 BAL des RLM bei Firma Jacobs-Schweyer GmbH, Flugzeugbau, Darmstadt, Avril 1944
43 NARA T321-54/4800319 Hans Jacobs an Herrn Obering. Kensche, Reichsluftfahrtministerium, Berlin 3 Mai 1944
44 ADIK 40/0256 Jacobs-Schweyer Flugzeugbau GmbH Darmstadt-Flughafen Aktenvermerk 6/16/44 18.5.44
45 IWM Speer FD4971/45-18 GL/C-Pr I Lieferplan Flugzeug-Programm V-Serie 15.5.1944
46 ADRC/T-2 2218/926 Gotha Reisebericht Besucht: Jacobs-Schweyer Flugzeugbau GmbH, Darmstadt Verhandelt wurde mit Herrn Abtlg.-Lt. Lücke (ztw. Herrn Jacobs). Gotha, 5. Juni 1944
47 TNA AIR 40/206 BAL des RLM bei Firma Jacobs-Schweyer GmbH, Flugzeugbau, Darmstadt, Juni 1944
48 ADRC/T-2 2218/926 Gotha Reisebericht Besprechung zwischenden Herren Voigt, Seitz, Behrbohm Mtt / Wegerich GWF in Oberammergau am 20.-22. Juni. Gotha, den 29.6.44
49 ADRC/T-2 2218/926 Gotha Reisebericht Besprechung mit Herrn Seitz, Mtt/Wegerich, GWF in Oberammergau am 21./22.6.44 Betr. Me 328 B V3 bis einsch. V10 (Schulmaschinen) Gotha, den 27.6.44
50 ADRC/T-2 2218/926 Abschrift/Be. Deutsche Forschungsanstalt für Segelflug an die Gothaer Waggonfabrik techn. Büro Flugzeugbau 27.6.44
51 ADRC/T-2 2218/926 Gotha Konstruktionsbesprechung vom 3. Juli 1944 Betrifft: Me 328 B (Schulflugzeuge) Gotha, den 3.7.44
52 ADRC/T-2 2218/926 Gotha Besprechungsnotiz Betr.: Me 328 Gotha, am 14. Juli 1944
53 ADRC/T-2 2218/926 Gotha Reisebericht Besprechung bei Firma Junkers, Techn. Büro, Nordhausen. Betr.: Mistelschlepp Me 328 auf Ju 88 S bezw. Ju 388. Gotha, den 7.9.44
54 ADRC/T-2 2091/189 Gotha Versuchsbericht Nr. 864 (Querruder) Me 328 Belastungsversuche mit dem Querruder 28.9.44
55 ADRC/T-2 2114/26 Gotha Versuchsbericht Nr. 865 (Einstellstück) Me 328 B Belastungsversuche mit dem Einstellstück 5.10.44 and ADRC/T-2 2188/596 Gotha Versuchsbericht Nr. 890 (Landeklappe Me 328 Belastungsversuche mit der Landeklappe 7.10.44
56 ADRC/T-2 2093/104 Gotha Versuchsbericht Nr. 882 328 Belastungsversuche mit dem Führersitz 20.11.44
57 ADRC/T-2 2070/1079 Gotha Versuchsbericht Nr. 884 (Steuerung) 328 Belastungsversuche mit dem Seitenruder 21.11.44
58 USSAFE Technical Intelligence Report No. E-21 Subject: Visit to the Aircraft Construction Institute of the DFS at Prien 7 July 1945

SUMMARY

1 IWM GDC Volkenrode Monograph Organisation, Arbeitsgebiete und Berichte der Forschungsanstalt Graf Zeppelin (FGZ) Stuttgart Ruit by U. Hütter November 1946

APPENDIX II

1 Reitsch appears to be referring to KG 200's technical officer Fliegerstabsingenieur Hans Christian Tilenius. Tilenius had reportedly attended a conference on the suicide mission on April 17 with Oberleutnant Karl-Heinz Lange and while working with Reitsch's group on readying the V-1 for use was simultaneously working with Blohm & Voss to prepare their BV 40 glider for the same purpose. That company was also exasperated by Tilenius's wild ideas—resulting in the BV 40 project being shut down. See *Secret Projects of the Luftwaffe* by Dan Sharp, Tempest Books, 2023, p74-87 for further details.

BIBLIOGRAPHY

Erbert, Hans; Kaiser, Johann B.; Peters, Klaus. *Willy Messerschmitt—Pioneer of Aviation Design.* Schiffer, 1999.

Griehl, Manfred. Der Weg vom Parasitjäger zur Selbstopfermaschine, Flugzeug Nr. 2-5/2001, Flugzeug Publikations, 2001.

Griehl, Manfred. *X-Planes—German Luftwaffe Prototypes 1930-1945.* Frontline Books, 2012.

Lommel, Horst. *Geheimprojekte der DFS Vom Höhenaufklärer bis zum Raumgleiter 1935-1945.* Motorbuch Verlag, 2000.

Lommel, Horst. *Luftfahrt History Heft 7—Messerschmitt Me 328.* LAUTEC Software und Medien, 2004.

Ocker, Peter. *Hans Jacobs—Pionierleben im Flugzeugbau.* Privately published, 2012.

Reitsch, Hanna. *The Sky My Kingdom,* The Bodley Head, 1955.

Sharp, Dan. *Messerschmitt Me 262 Development & Politics.* Tempest, 2022.

Sharp, Dan. *Secret Projects of the Luftwaffe Volume 1: Jet Fighters 1939-1945.* Tempest, 2020.

Späte, Wolfgang. *Der streng geheime Vogel Me 163.* Verlag für Wehrwissenschaften, 1983.

Späte, Wolfgang. *Testpiloten.* Aviatic Verlag, 1993.

Von Below, Nicholas. *Als Hitler's Adjutant 1937-45.* Hase & Koehler Verlag, 1980.

INDEX

Adlershof, 30
Aerodynamische Versuchsanstalt (AVA), 88, 104, 154
Ainring, 10, 32, 33, 35, 41, 48, 77, 85, 117, 148-150, 161
Alpers, Georg-Bernhard, 84
Antz, Hans-Martin, 30
Arado Ar 234, 9, 75, 97, 102, 108
Argus As 014, 10, 18, 153-156
Argus Fernfeuer, 15, 17
Argus Motoren, 17, 18, 32, 36, 41, 42, 51-53, 58-61, 68, 70, 72, 73, 75, 79, 81, 85, 86, 88, 93, 94, 97, 102, 112, 115, 130, 144, 153-156, 161, 162
Aschaffenburg, 139
Augsburg, 30, 33, 39, 53, 73, 76, 85, 93

Baeumker, Adolf, 84, 117, 133, 134, 138, 140-142
Bauaufsichts-Leitung des RLM (BAL), 88, 92, 97, 105, 115, 132, 138-140, 143, 144, 146
Baur, Karl, 41, 43, 71-74, 153
Behrbohm, Hermann, 30, 146
Benzinger, Theodor, 84, 85, 117, 133, 134, 138, 140, 142, 159, 161, 166
Berchtesgaden, 141, 160
Berlin, 13, 30, 78, 85, 142, 148, 162
Betz, Albert, 30, 88, 130, 132
Bley, 132
BMW P 3302, 18
BMW P 3304, 18
Braunschweig, 18, 76, 86
Bücker Bü 181 Bestmann, 117

Caroli, Gerhard, 49
C. Lorenz, 13, 15
Convair F-102 Delta Dagger, 58
Croneiss, Theodor, 30, 39, 40, 53, 68

Darmstadt, 9, 11, 76-78, 85, 92, 132, 139, 142, 155
Deutsche Akademie der Luftfahrtforschung (DAL), 84, 139-142
Deutsche Forschungsanstalt für Segelflug (DFS), 10, 11, 13, 28, 29, 32, 33, 35, 36, 38, 41, 43, 48, 51, 56, 58, 68, 70-78, 81-86, 88, 93, 97, 104, 105, 112, 117, 130, 133, 137-139, 142-144, ,146-150, 152-154, 155, 161
Deutschen Versuchsanstalt für Luftfahrt (DVL), 44, 141
DFS 230, 41, 43, 51, 68, 72, 73, 76, 81
DFS Habicht, 56

Diedrich, Günther, 14, 15, 17, 18
Dittmar, Heini, 29, 30
Doerstling, Egon, 84
Dornier Do 17, 12, 27
Dornier Do 217, 74, 85, 91, 93, 104, 108, 117, 135, 139, 143, 146, 149, 162
Dornier Do P 231, 85

Eisenlohr, Wolfram, 83
Erprobungskommando 16, 73

Fischel, Eduard, 133
Focke-Wulf Ta 153, 85
Focke-Wulf Fw 190, 143, 149, 165, 166
Focke-Wulf Fw 190 D, 85
Focke-Wulf Fw 200, 35, 40, 78, 156
Forschungsanstalt Graf Zeppelin (FGZ), 56, 153
Franz, Anselm, 108, 112, 115
Friebel, Walter, 43, 97, 102
Frydag, Karl, 84

Galland, Adolf, 73, 90, 140, 142, 143
Georgii, Walter, 29, 49, 84, 117, 133, 134, 138, 140-143, 153, 160
Göppingen, 76
Göring, Hermann, 30, 39, 42, 86, 90, 117, 159, 160, 161, 164, 165
Göttingen, 104
Gosslau, Fritz, 15, 17
Gothaer Waggonfabrik (GWF), 143, 146, 147, 149, 153, 162
Gotha Go 145, 18
Graf Hagenburg, 64, 76

Haber, Fritz, 149
Hagemann, 92
Hanke, Karl, 140
Hamburg, 115
Hartwig-Sonneberg, 143
Heigl, Heinz, 140-143, 161, 164-166
Heinkel He 45, 41
Heinkel He 111, 10, 12, 32, 40, 49, 50, 56, 71-74
Heinkel He 177, 35, 40, 43, 83, 135, 143
Heinkel He 280, 75, 84
Heiss, 149
Henschel Flugzeugwerke,
Henschel Hs 293 F, 138

Henschke, Ulrich K., 134-136, 138, 139
Hentzen, Fritz, 30
Himmelheber, Max, 44
Himmler, Heinrich, 117, 159, 161, 164, 165
Hitler, Adolf, 42, 43, 139-141, 158-161, 165
Hoffmann, 102
Hörsching, 49, 70-74, 85, 93, 104, 117, 144, 146, 150, 161, 162
Horten, Reimar, 84
Horten, Walter, 84
Horten Ho 229, 149

Jacobs, Hans, 29, 76, 140, 142-144, 146, 153
Jacobs-Schweyer Flugzeugbau (JSF), 9, 11, 61, 64, 76-78, 85, 88, 90, 92, 105, 115, 130, 132, 133, 138, 140, 142, 147, 153, 155
Jeschonnek, Hans, 39, 42, 43
Junkers Ju 87, 10, 58
Junkers Ju 88, 64, 139, 148, 149
Junkers Ju 188, 143
Junkers Ju 290, 43
Junkers Ju 390, 43

Kahl of Aschaffenburg, 139
Kaiser, 33
Karavodin, Vladimir V., 12
Kensche, Heinz, 141, 142, 144, 148, 149, 161, 162
King, Horace 'Rex', 10, 155
Kittelberger Bregenz, 140, 143, 144, 146, 149, 155
Kleinrath, Kurt, 143
Klöckner, Erich, 48-50, 53, 68, 70-72, 104
Knemeyer, Siegfried, 143
Kokothaki, Rakan, 29, 76, 132
Korten, Günther, 142
Kracht, Felix, 48-50, 70, 85, 142, 150
Küchemann, Dietrich, 88, 130, 132

Lange, Karl-Heinz, 117, 133, 140, 142, 144, 159, 161, 164-166
Lärz, 148
Lechfeld, 9, 78
Lippisch, Alexander, 13, 28, 29, 30, 52, 84, 104, 140, 142, 152
Lucht, Roluf, 39
Luftfahrtforschungsanstalt Hermann Göring (LFA), 86, 104, 130, 153, 154
Luftfahrt-Forschungsanstalt München (LFM), 133, 139
Lusser, Robert, 29, 140, 148, 162

Mannesmannröhren, 115
Marienfeld, Walter, 140, 142, 143
Messerschmitt, Willy, 30, 33, 38, 39, 42, 68, 70, 83, 86, 90, 143, 132, 152
Messerschmitt Bf 109 D, 27, 30, 32
Messerschmitt Bf 109 F, 27, 28, 30, 32
Messerschmitt Bf 109 G, 41, 53, 60, 61, 78
Messerschmitt Me 109 Z, 85, 91
Messerschmitt Bf 110, 10, 32, 33, 40-42, 58, 72
Messerschmitt Enzian, 11
Messerschmitt Me 161, 11
Messerschmitt Me 163, 9, 29, 30, 52, 56, 73, 75, 84, 104, 105, 117, 143, 152, 155
Messerschmitt Me 209, 11, 61, 84, 85, 90, 105, 115
Messerschmitt Me 210, 33, 34, 38-42, 53, 58, 60, 61, 64
Messerschmitt Me 261, 42
Messerschmitt Me 262, 9, 11, 18, 20, 27, 29, 33, 72, 75, 83-88, 90, 105, 115, 132, 152
Messerschmitt Me 264, 9, 35, 40, 42, 43, 46, 64,
Messerschmitt Me 309, 33, 61, 85
Messerschmitt Me 321, 52, 60, 61, 64
Messerschmitt Me 323, 27, 39, 40, 42, 64
Messerschmitt Me 328 Bordflugzeug (parasite), 20, 27, 32, 35, 38, 40, 43, 44, 46, 47, 48, 78, 152
Messerschmitt Me 328 V1, 32, 33, 37, 48, 49, 56, 61, 68, 70-72, 74, 77, 85, 112, 130, 150
Messerschmitt Me 328 V2, 32, 33, 70-73, 83, 85, 92, 93, 104, 105, 108, 112, 117, 130, 133, 139, 144, 150, 153
Messerschmitt Me 328 V02, 37, 53, 61, 71, 72, 77, 85, 112, 114, 115, 130, 150
Messerschmitt Me 328 V3, 32, 85, 130, 138, 139, 144, 150
Messerschmitt Me 328 V4, 70, 72, 85, 130, 144
Messerschmitt Me 328 V5, 71, 85, 130, 144
Messerschmitt Me 328 V6, 70, 71
Messerschmitt Me 328 V7, 70, 71
Messerschmitt Me 328 A, 37, 73, 76, 78, 85, 88, 90, 92, 93, 97, 105, 138, 143, 146, 147, 153, 155
Messerschmitt Me 328 B V1, 77, 88, 90, 92, 93, 97, 105, 115, 117, 130, 132, 138-140, 143, 144, 146, 147, 150
Messerschmitt Me 328 B V2, 105, 130, 132, 138, 139, 140, 144, 150
Messerschmitt Me 328 B V3, 92, 105, 146
Messerschmitt Me 328 B V4, 105
Messerschmitt Me 328 B V5, 105
Messerschmitt Me 328 B V6, 105
Messerschmitt Me 328 B V11, 147
Messerschmitt Me 328 B-0, 143

Messerschmitt Me 328 C, 86-88, 108, 132, 155
Messerschmitt Me 328 SV1, 105
Messerschmitt Me 328 SV2, 105
Messerschmitt Me 328 SV3, 105
Messerschmitt Me 328 T, 132
Messerschmitt Me 329, 39, 40, 52, 53, 64
Messerschmitt Me 364, 46
Messerschmitt Me 410, 39, 58, 64, 84, 135
Messerschmitt P 01-112, 29
Messerschmitt P 05, 30
Messerschmitt P 65, 18
Messerschmitt P 79, 18, 20, 23, 24, 26-30, 32, 34, 37
Messerschmitt P 1095, 115
Messerschmitt P 1111, 11
Messerschmitt P 1112, 11
Milch, Erhard, 39, 40, 42, 52, 53, 68, 75, 83, 84, 90, 97, 102, 139, 140, 142, 143, 159, 160
Munich, 14, 58, 78, 133

Nordhausen, 149

Oberammergau, 11, 146
Oppitz, Kurt, 49, 50

Pasewaldt, Georg, 84, 102
Peenemünde, 30, 105, 112, 150
Peltz, Dietrich, 97, 102, 140
Pendele, Max, 30
Peters, Professor, 134-136, 138, 139, 142
Petersen, Edgar, 39, 83,
Pieler, Heinrich, 92

Regensburg, 30, 33, 39, 61, 64, 76, 115, 117
Reidenbach, Gottfried, 30, 33
Reitsch, Hanna, 9, 11, 117, 133, 139, 140-144, 148, 149, 158-166
Reynst, Francois, 14
Ruden, Paul, 88, 130, 132

Schardin, Hubert, 140, 142
Schelp, Helmut, 13, 15, 17
Schempp-Hirth, 64, 76
Schmidt, Paul, 12, 13, 14, 17, 18, 24, 32, 68
Schmidt SR400, 24
Schmidt SR500, 18, 20, 24
Schmidt SR800, 24
Schmidt SR1000, 24
Schwencke, Dietrich, 140
Seiler, Friedrich, 39, 132
Seitz, Rudolf, 27, 30, 33, 40, 41, 83, 86, 87, 108, 115, 132, 143, 146, 147, 149
Siebel, 84
Skorzeny, Otto, 148
Snay, H G, 142
Sonthofen, 76
Späte, Wolfgang, 48, 72-75, 84
Speer, Albert, 83

Tank, Kurt, 141
Technische Akademie der Luftwaffe, 142
Technische Hochschule Braunschweig, 76

Udet, Ernst, 30, 39
Uhlig, Walter, 108

V-1 (also Fi 103/FZG 76), 68, 75, 148, 150, 160, 162-166
Voigt, Woldemar, 10, 11, 18, 29, 30, 32, 34, 52, 53, 56-61, 64, 65, 68, 70, 72, 75, 76, 83, 132, 146, 152, 153
Von Below, Nicholas, 141, 160
Von Griem, Robert, 140, 142, 166
Von Lossberg, Viktor, 142, 143
Vorwald, Wolfgang, 83, 140, 142, 143

Waldmann, 15, 17
Warschau-Süd, 52, 53, 60, 61, 65, 77, 83, 85
Wegerich, Hans, 146, 147
Wilhelm Schmidding, 70
Willi, 140
Witzell, Karl, 140, 142

Ziegler, Rudolf 'Gretchen', 70, 71, 73, 74, 91, 144, 146
Zobel, Theodor, 86, 88, 97, 130, 153